THE LAW-MAKING PROCESS

LAW IN CONTEXT

Editors: Robert Stevens (Haverford College, Pennsylvania), William Twining (University of Warwick) and Christopher McCrudden (Balliol College, Oxford)

ALREADY PUBLISHED

Accidents, Compensation and the Law (Third Edition), P.S. Atiyah
Company Law and Capitalism (Second Edition), Tom Hadden
Karl Llewellyn and the Realist Movement, William Twining
Cases and Materials on the English Legal System (Third Edition), Michael Zander
Computers and the Law, Colin Tapper
Tribunals and Government, J.A. Farmer
Government and Law, T.C. Hartley and J.A.G. Griffith
Land, Law and Planning, Patrick McAuslan
Landlord and Tenant, Martin Partington
How to do Things with Rules, William Twining and David Miers
Evidence, Proof and Probability, Richard Eggleston
Family Law and Social Policy, John Eekelaar
Consumers and the Law, Ross Cranston
Law and Politics, Robert Stevens
Obscenity, Geoffrey Robertson
Labour Law, Paul Davies and Mark Freedland
Charities, Trusts and Social Welfare, Michael Chesterman

The Law-Making Process

MICHAEL ZANDER

Professor of Law,
London School of Economics

WEIDENFELD AND NICOLSON
London

George Weidenfeld and Nicolson Ltd
91 Clapham High Street, London SW4

ISBN 0 297 77750 5 cased
ISBN 0 297 77751 3 paperback

Printed by Butler & Tanner Ltd
Frome and London

CONTENTS

PREFACE

The chief purpose of this book is to improve the understanding of the law-making process. For many years I have taught the English Legal System course at the London School of Economics and an equivalent course taken by non-law students. Experience has suggested to me that there is a great gap in the existing literature which this book attempts to fill. It is something between a book of cases and materials, on the one hand, and a textbook on the other. It presents a large number of original texts from a variety of sources – cases, official reports, articles, books, speeches and surveys. It also however contains a good deal of the author's own reflections on the subject-matter. The book deals only with the official forms of law-making on a national scale and therefore says nothing about 'private' law-making by lawyers for their clients or by organizations such as trades unions, clubs or companies for their members or shareholders. The book is intended as a companion to the author's *Cases and Materials on the English Legal System* (3rd edn., 1980). There is no overlap between the two books. They are intended to complement each other and together to provide the basic reading required for a university or equivalent course on the legal system. It is hoped that the book will also be of value to anyone concerned to understand how the law-making process actually operates.

Michael Zander

January 1980

CASES EXCERPTED AND CITED

Note: Extracts from cases are indicated by **bold** type.

OFFICIAL PUBLICATIONS EXCERPTED AND CITED

(in chronological order)

BOOKS, PAMPHLETS, MEMORANDA AND ARTICLES EXCERPTED

Abel-Smith, Brian, with Robert Stevens, *In Search of Justice* (Penguin, 1968), pp. 167–73 **201–4**

Angell, E., 'The Amicus Curiae: American Developments of English Institutions', 16 *International and Comparative Law Quarterly*, 1967, p. 1017 **239–40**

Boulton, C. J., 'The Passing of a Public Bill', *The Lawyer*, vol. 7, No. 3, 1964 **18–22**

Braybrooke, E.K., 'Custom as a Source of English Law', 50 *Michigan Law Review*, 1951, pp. 88–5 **256–7**

Butler, R.A., 'The Birth of a Bill', *Parliamentary Affairs*, 1949, p. 210 **2–3**

Cardozo, Benjamin N., *The Nature of the Judicial Process* (Yale University Press, 17th printing 1960), pp. 48–9, 62–3, 111–15, 129, 141, 167–9 **164–5, 200–1**

Cohn, Ernst, 'The German Attorney', *International and Comparative Law Quarterly*, 1960, pp. 586–7 **286**

Coke, *Institutes*, vol. 1, 24b **39**

Cross, Sir Rupert, *Precedent in English Law* (3rd edn, Clarendon Press, 1977), pp. 12–22 **131–7**

Crossman, R.H.S., *Diaries of a Cabinet Minister* (Cape, 1975), vol. 1, pp. 628–9 **28–9**

Dale, Sir William, *Legislative Drafting – a New Approach* (Butterworths, 1977), pp. 331–3 **14–15**

Denning, Lord, 'The Reform of Equity', in C.J. Hamson (ed.), *Law Reform and Law-Making* (BBC, 1953), p. 31 **212**

Devlin, Lord, 'The Process of Law Reform', 63 *Law Society's Gazette*, 1966, pp. 453–62 **300**

Devlin, Lord, 'Judges, Government and Policies', 41 *Modern Law Review*, 1978, pp. 505–11 **207–10**

Devlin, Lord, 'The Judge as Law Maker', *The Judge* (Oxford University Press, 1979), pp. 3, 5, 9, 17 **213–15, 238**

Diamond, Aubrey, 'Codification of the Law of Contract', 31 *Modern Law Review*, 1968, p. 361 **290–6**

Diplock, Lord, 'The Courts as Legislators', Holdsworth Club Lecture, 1965, pp. 5–6 **99–100**

Freeman, M.D.A., 'Standards of Adjudication, Judicial Law-making, and Prospective Overruling', 26 *Current Legal Problems*, 1973, p. 166 **219–24**

Ganz, G., *Public Law*, Winter 1978, pp. 345–6 **270–1**

Griffith, J.A.G., *Parliamentary Scrutiny of Government Bills* (George Allen and Unwin, 1974), pp. 206–7, 231 **26–8**

Griffith, J.A.G., *The Politics of the Judiciary* (Fontana, 1977), pp. 204–5 **206–7**

Hahlo, H.R., 'Here Lies the Common Law', 30 *Modern Law Review*, 1967, p. 241 **287–90**

Hart, Henry and Albert M. Sacks, *The Legal Process* (tentative edn, 1958, mimeographed), pp. 587–8 **181–2**

Hopkins, E.R., 'The Literal Canon and the Golden Rule', 15 *Canadian Bar Review*, 1937, p. 689 **48–9**

Jowitt, Lord, quoted in 25 *Australian Law Journal*, 1951, p. 278 **229–30**

Karlen, Delmar, 'Appeal in England and the United States', 78 *Law Quarterly Review*, 1962, p. 371 **242–3**

Kent, Sir Harold, *In On the Act* (Macmillan, 1979), pp. 43–5 **7–8**

King, A. and Sloman, A., eds., *Westminster and Beyond* (Macmillan, 1973), ch. 12 **22–5**

Lieber, F., *Legal and Political Hermeneutics* (3rd edn, 1880), p. 18 **34–5**

Llewellyn, K.N., *The Bramble Bush* (Oceana edn, 1930), pp. 42–3, 44–5, 47–50, 51–2, 53 **159–64**

Marsh, Norman, 'Law Reform in the United Kingdom: A New Institutional Approach', 13 *William and Mary Law Review*, 1971, p. 263 **272–3, 280–1**

Mason, Alpheus T., *Brandeis* (Viking Press, 1956), pp. 248–51 **173–4**

Moriarty, Michael, 'The policy-making process: how it is seen from the Home Office', in *Penal Policy-Making in England*, ed. Walker, N. (Institute of Criminology, Cambridge, 1977), pp. 132–9 **3–6**

Munday, R.J.C., 'New Dimensions of Precedent', *Journal of the Society of Public Teachers of Law*, 1978, p. 201 **146–52**

Nicol, Andrew, 'Prospective Overruling; A New Device for English Courts', 39 *Modern Law Review*, 1976, p. 542 **234–7**

Radcliffe, Lord, *Not in Feather Beds* (Hamish Hamilton, 1968), pp. 212–216 **179–80, 197–200**

Russell, Sir Charles, 'Behind the Appellate Curtain', Holdsworth Club Lecture, Birmingham University, 1969, pp. 3–8 **170–3**

Sacks, Albert M., *see* Hart, Henry

Samuels, Alec, 'Is it in Force or Isn't It?', *The Magistrate*, November 1979, pp. 173–4 **30–1**

Scarman, Mr Justice, 'A Code of English Law?', Hull University, 1966 **282–5**

ACKNOWLEDGEMENTS

The materials excerpted here are included with the kind permission of those who hold the copyright. A book of this kind would be impossible without their help and I am most indebted to all those who consented to this use of their material. They may be divided into four main groups. There are, first, those who hold copyright over official publications and law reports – the Controller of Her Majesty's Stationery Office, the Incorporated Council of Law Reporting for England and Wales in relation to the *Law Reports* and the *Weekly Law Reports*, and Messrs Butterworths and Co. in regard to the *All England Law Reports*. The second group are the publishers and editors of journals from which extracts have been taken – the *Australian Law Journal*, *Canadian Bar Review*, *Current Legal Problems*, *International and Comparative Law Quarterly*, *Law Quarterly Review*, *Law Society's Gazette*, *Michigan Law Review*, *Modern Law Review*, *New Society*, *New Zealand Law Review*, *Parliamentary Affairs*, *Public Law*, *The Lawyer* and *William and Mary Law Review*. The third group are publishers of extracts in books: Oceana Press, for the extracts from Karl Llewellyn's *Bramble Bush*; the Yale University Press, for extracts from Benjamin Cardozo's *The Nature of the Judicial Process*; the BBC, for extracts from a broadcast on the background to the Criminal Justice Bill which was later published in *Beyond Westminster*, edited by Anthony King and Anne Sloman; the Institute of Criminology, Cambridge, for extracts from a paper by Mr Michael Moriarty published in a Cropwood booklet; Hamish Hamilton Ltd, for extracts from the late Lord Radcliffe's book *Not in Feather Beds*, and Hamish Hamilton and Jonathan Cape Ltd, for an extract from *Diaries of a Cabinet Minister* by the late Richard Crossman. Fourthly there are the individual authors themselves: Professor Brian Abel-Smith, Mr E. Angell, Mr C.J. Boulton, Lord Butler, Mr Mark Carlisle QC, MP, Sir Rupert Cross, Sir William Dale, Mr Edmund Dell MP, Lord Devlin, Professor Aubrey Diamond, Lord Elwyn-Jones, Mr M.D.A. Freeman, Ms G. Ganz, Professor J.A.G.

Griffith, Dr H.R. Hahlo, Professor Delmar Karlen, Sir Harold Kent, Professor Anthony King, Professor Norman Marsh, Mr Michael Moriarty, Dr R.J.C. Munday, Mr Andrew Nicol, Lord Russell of Killowen, Mr Alec Samuels, Lord Scarman, Professor Robert Stevens, Mr D.A.S. Ward and Professor J. Willis. I am extremely grateful to all those listed, and finally to Mrs Soia Llewellyn for permission to use extracts from her late husband's work, *The Bramble Bush*.

1
Legislation

The dominant form of law-making today is legislation. In an average year parliament typically produces between seventy and a hundred statutes running to many hundreds of pages. In addition there are many more thousands of pages of delegated legislation passed under the authority of statutes.

1. The preparation of legislation

The great majority of statutes are introduced by the government of the day. Government bills are drafted by parliamentary counsel to the Treasury acting on the instructions of the government department responsible for the legislation. The Office of Parliamentary Counsel was established in 1869. Its members can be either barristers or solicitors. They number just over 20. Some four of their number are on permanent attachment to the Law Commission (see pp. 275–82 below).

Parliamentary counsel normally work in pairs in close collaboration with the civil servants who instruct them. (By convention the responsible minister rarely sees the Instructions sent from his department to the draftsmen.) Substantial bills may go through many drafts before being published. The work is often done under intense pressure of time. Parliamentary counsel also draft government amendments moved during the passage of legislation and frequently they redraft amendments offered by backbenchers which the government is prepared to accept in principle. Where the government offers support for a bill introduced by a Private Member, it will often be redrafted by parliamentary counsel.

The workload of the small number of lawyers concerned with the drafting of legislation may be judged from the following figures of the number of new pages added to the statute book in the three decades from 1943 to 1972:

1943 to 1952	15,600
1953 to 1962	11,800
1963 to 1972	18,000

(Source: *The Preparation of Legislation*, Report of the Renton Committee, Cmnd. 6053, 1975, p. 35.)

But the stage *before* the Instructions to parliamentary counsel are sent is perhaps even more crucial, since it is then that the policy of the legislation is worked out. Little has been written on this aspect of legislation. One rare contribution on the subject was that of the then Mr R.A. Butler in an article in 1949:

R.A. Butler, 'The Birth of a Bill – the Education Act', *Parliamentary Affairs*, 1949, p. 210

.... when a new Bill is presented to Parliament and is formally read a first time, it already has a history. Bills do not spring like Athene of old, fully fashioned from the head of some ministerial Zeus. They are conceived, they have an embryonic stage, and they are born. For what reasons and in what manner these things take place are proper questions to ask. But they are not simple to answer, for the reasons are manifold and the manner complex.

Some Bills are almost permanent features of the Parliamentary scene, cropping up year after year. The Finance Bill and the Consolidated Fund Bills, for example, are modern legislative symbols of that ancient financial power from which arose the predominance of the House of Commons in the Constitution. The ordinary work of government could not proceed without these measures. It is laid down by the Bill of Rights, 1689, 'That the raising or keeping of a standing army within the kingdom in time of peace unless it be with consent of Parliament is against law', and so every year that consent must be sought in the Army and Air Force (Annual) Bill. The most controversial measures of any session naturally have their origin in the particular doctrines of the political party in power. ... Other major legislation derives from government recognition that the time is ripe for another step forward in that social reform in which we lead the world. Bills of this kind usually command, by their very nature, much wider support, as was so with the Bill which became the Education Act, 1944. Again, all Departments tend to accumulate from experience a list of usually smaller reforms which are desirable but for which it is not easy to find time in crowded Parliamentary sessions. Every year a good number of these 'Departmental' Bills find their way on to the Statute Book, either by themselves or as part of some larger and more comprehensive measure sponsored by the Department concerned....

Every Bill presented to Parliament must be approved by the Cabinet. Where any big piece of legislation is involved the Minister concerned will prepare with the senior officers of his Department a written memorandum which he will then circulate to the Cabinet. If the measure involves considerable expenditure, as most big measures do, the Chancellor of the Exchequer may at the same time circulate a memorandum on these financial implications. The issues involved may then be referred to an *ad hoc* committee which will prepare and circulate a detailed report to the Cabinet. If the Cabinet then approves the main lines of the proposed measure, it will authorize the drafting of the Bill and sometimes the *ad hoc* committee will come before a standing committee of the Cabinet, known as the Home Affairs Committee. Here, with the help of senior officers of the Department concerned who may attend, technical difficulties are thrashed out, legal aspects are discussed with the Law Officers, and the views of other Departments are examined. The minutes of this Committee containing its recommendations are circulated to the Cabinet, by whom the Bill is finally approved.

Little has been published on the inter-relationship between ministers, civil servants and outside interests in this vital earliest stage of legislation. It would be surprising if civil servants were not in many, if not most, cases the main influence.

Very little has been written about the process of preparing legislation from Whitehall's perspective. One rare instance, however, was a paper by a senior Home Office official speaking at a Cambridge conference on penal policy-making in December 1976.

Michael Moriarty, 'The policy-making process: how it is seen from the Home Office', in *Penal Policy-Making in England*, ed. Nigel Walker, Cropwood Conference, Institute of Criminology, Cambridge (1977), pp. 132–9

In general it is unusual for an incoming government to bring with it anything approaching a detailed blueprint of penal policy. This is not really surprising. Although the maintenance of law and order remains a basic task of any government, the methods of performing it are simply not of great political importance in comparison with the major economic and social issues of the day which rightly preoccupy the political parties and other organs of society. Nor is there, among those in the political parties who concern themselves in depth with penal questions, any fundamental difference of approach towards them (though this statement would certainly need some qualification if it were applied to the active rank-and-file members of the parties)....

The absence, usually, of a strong and detailed Party programme on penal matters does not mean that an incoming Home Secretary (or other Home Office Minister) may not have his own well-formed objectives and priorities. A recent example is that Ministerial commitment, since March 1974, to improving bail procedures and developing the parole system. But time and again the Ministerial contribution to penal policy-making, at least as it appears to the observer and participant within the Home Office, lies not in the Minister's bringing in his own fresh policy ideas, but in his operating creatively and with political drive upon ideas, proposals, reports etc. that are, so to speak, already to hand, often within the department but sometimes in the surrounding world of penal thought.

Sources of the Criminal Justice Act 1972

The year 1970 was notable for a sharp rise in the prison population to what was then a peak of 40,000, which gave rise to intensified policy discussions within the Department of ways of developing alternative measures. The Report of the Advisory Council on the Penal System (ACPS) on Non-Custodial Measures (the 'Wootton report')[1] contained a number of relevant proposals, notably a proposal that offenders should carry out community service. The Department instituted an urgent study of the practicalities by a working group with substantial probation service representation. Two other working groups were set up at the same time: one on use of probation resources, the other on residential accommodation for offenders. The main product of the first of these was a proposal to establish experimentally some day training centres, on a model originating in the United States, interest in which had been stimulated by the Howard League for Penal Reform among others. The other group developed ideas for running probation hostels: a substantial adult hostel building programme was established in 1971, following a small-scale experiment promoted by the Department in extending this method of treatment to those over 21. Detailed work on the proposals in the ACPS report on Reparation – the 'Widgery Report'[2] – was also going on.

Thus the Criminal Justice Bill of 1971/2 could be said to be born from a fusion of a Ministerial desire to be active in the criminal justice field, along lines which were identified but not too rigidly pre-determined by them, with a supply of departmental and other raw material that was lying ready or in process of being worked up. Much of the Widgery Report was in tune with a political objective that offenders should recompense their victims. From the Wootton Report the community service proposal appealed partly for its reparatory element, partly because it was a non-custodial penal measure (Ministers were already well aware of the need to try to bring down

1. *Non-custodial and Semi-custodial Penalties* (1970).
2. *Reparation by the Offender* (1971).

the prison population) that would appeal to those who were suspicious of 'softness'. The form in which the community service proposals appeared in the Bill owed something to the specific intention of Ministers that the new measure should be seen as a credible alternative to custodial sentences.

In fact recommendations from the two ACPS reports made up much of the 'core' of the Bill – Part I entitled 'Powers for Dealing with Offenders'. In the form in which it received Royal Assent Part I comprised 24 sections (and one linked Schedule) which related to the main sources of the Bill roughly as follows:

Section	*Subject*	*Origin*
1–6	Compensation	Widgery Report
7–10	Criminal Bankruptcy	–do–
11–14	Suspended prison sentences etc.	Ministerial/ Departmental (s. 12 from Wootton Report)
15–19	Community Service	Wootton Report
20	Day Training Centres	Departmental
21	Breach of Probation	–do–
22	Deferment of Sentence	Wootton Report
23	Forfeiture of Property	–do–
24	"Criminal" driving disqualification	–do–

Not all the sections listed above were in the original 'core': the origin of some of the later starters is illustrative of how penal policy is formed. What became section 14, extending the principle of the First Offenders Act to a wider range of adult offenders, was devised during the preparatory state as a counter-weight to the ending of mandatory suspension of sentence. Other provisions owed their origin, or final form, to the Parliamentary proceedings on the Bill.

However, the bulk of the Bill was devoted to provisions aptly described as Miscellaneous and Administrative Provisions (sections 28 to 62). Some of these supported Part I provisions (e.g. administrative aspects of community service) or were otherwise related to its main themes (e.g. probation hostel provision; legal aid before first prison sentence). Others covered a wide range of topics of varying importance. In source they were hardly less diverse. At least one – increase in penalties for firearms offences – was a 'core provision'; some came from organisations close to the Home Office such as the Justices' Clerks. The provision giving 'cover' for the police to take drunks to a detoxification centre (section 34) had its origin in the report of the Working Party on Habitual Drunken Offenders.[3] Others came from the famous pigeon holes of Whitehall – and these in turn can be sub-divided into, on the one hand, tidying up and, on the other, more substantial though minor changes – for example simplification of parole procedure (section 35).

... In 1970–1 much detailed work was done on community service and criminal bankruptcy in particular, but to a lesser degree on the other major Bill

3. HMSO, 1971.

proposals in working parties run by the Home Office which brought into consultation others whose advice and co-operation were needed. The community service working group included representatives of the probation service, magistracy and voluntary service movement; the criminal bankruptcy group included lawyers of both the Home Office and Lord Chancellor's Office and officials from the Bankruptcy Inspectorate of the (then) Board of Trade.

Beyond this area of activity there was (to move on to a second point) a wider and continuing process of consultation, on particular proposals and on ways of giving effect to them, with many official and non-official interests. A number of Bill proposals affected other Government departments – for instance, Transport and Health and Social Security – in addition to those already mentioned. On any penal policy matter it is necessary to keep the Scottish and Northern Ireland Offices in close touch. The Director of Public Prosecutions was closely involved in the criminal bankruptcy scheme and other Bill matters, at least one of which owed much to his suggestion. Consultation also went on with the police and probation services (the prison service was not greatly affected by the Bill, except as a hopeful beneficiary), the judiciary, magistrates and justices' clerks. The various representative organisations of course play an active part in the consultation process; and the burden on them can be a heavy one, especially as the pace quickens. The task of keeping the consultation process on the move while doing all the other preparatory work also makes considerable demands on the small team of officials working on a Bill.

The object of the consultation process at this stage is primarily to obtain the assessment of practitioners who will have the task of making the provisions of the Bill work. In the case of Bills based on the work of advisory bodies, a wider process of opinion-sounding will already have been carried out by the advisory body, and often there is a further opportunity in the period immediately following publication of a report.

For further reading on the stages leading to the formulation of legislative proposals, see especially W.J. Braithwaite, *Lloyd George's Ambulance Wagon* (1957), a detailed 'inside' account of the preparation of the National Insurance Act 1911 by one of the chief civil servants involved; M.J. Barnett, *The Politics of Legislation: the 1957 Rent Act* (1969); K. Hindell, 'The Genesis of the Race Relations Bill', *Political Quarterly*, 1965, p. 390; and J.J. Richardson, 'The Making of the Restrictive Trade Practices Act, 1956', *Parliamentary Affairs*, 1967, p. 101. See also Sir Noel Hutton, 'Mechanics of Law Reform', 24 *Modern Law Review*, 1961, pp. 18–23.

2. The drafting process

The process of dealing with the instructions to draft a bill is described by Sir Harold Kent, who for many years was a parliamentary draftsman, in his recent autobiography:

Sir Harold Kent, *In on the Act* (1979), pp. 43–5

It starts with the arrival of some sort of instructions from the department responsible for the Bill. In the case of the Gas Undertakings Bill these consisted of two reports of a Departmental Committee with an accompanying letter from Tommy Barnes, the Solicitor to the Board of Trade. He said that the Government broadly accepted the recommendations of the Committee and had authorised the preparation of a Bill; he did not propose to comment on those recommendations in writing but would gladly come over for a talk if that would help.

This was fairly typical of the way a Bill starts, a combination of written material generated inside or outside the department and oral discussions. It was rare in my experience for a formal and comprehensive 'Instructions for a Bill' to be prepared by the department.* Indeed, it was quite common for the draftsman's brief to be entirely the product of oral discussions, and for him to take a hand in the policy-making, especially when a Bill arose suddenly out of a political or economic crisis.

Stainton† liked, if possible, to get a first print of a Bill circulated to the officials concerned before holding his first big conference. Draft Bills were always printed in widely spaced type with wide margins, and were ideal documents on which to make notes and amendments. So Barnes's offer of a talk was not taken up and a first draft was soon sent off to the printer, based largely on my own effort. The Office had a marvellous contract with Eyre & Spottiswoode, the Government printer, whose presses at Drury Lane would work all night in order to deliver our draft Bills first thing in the morning. Stainton ordered twenty copies, twelve for the Board of Trade, six for us, and two spares. That first print contained twenty-six clauses and one Schedule and was twenty-six pages long; a medium-sized Bill of a useful and non-political kind.

The team from the Board of Trade consisted of Tommy Barnes with a clever young barrister called Rupert Sich, who was the latest recruit to his office, and an Assistant Secretary from the Gas division of the department. They were a good team and we discussed the Bill from beginning to end, perhaps for a whole day or more. A few days later the Bill, heavily amended, went off to the printer for a second edition, followed by another conference and another print. During a period of four months, before the Bill was ready for introduction, it went through seven prints, interspersed with conferences, telephone calls and correspondence. This was a shade over the average for a Bill of this kind; it reflected the Staintonian method of non-stop amendment and fair-copying. In the last print there were two more clauses, two more Schedules and eleven more pages than in the first, an increase in bulk of nearly forty-five per cent...:

There is a certain conflict of interest between the draftsman and the department. The former seeks to confine the Bill strictly to matters requiring an alteration of the law. The department is conscious that the Minister would

* Nowadays formal instructions appear to be the norm (ed.).

† Then Kent's superior in the office.

like to make a Parliamentary splash; it also knows that administration is sometimes helped by being able to refer to an Act of Parliament; so it wants to put as much as possible into the Bill. The issue is confused by the fact that even when a new government activity does not need statutory powers, the expenditure involved may, under the rules of the House of Commons, require statutory sanction.

Other occasions of conflict are when the Minister wants a clause to look as attractive politically as possible, and is impatient of the detail needed for precision; or when the department wants its administrative powers drawn widely, or even obscurely, so as to avoid risk of legal challenge, an attitude which hardly pleases a self-respecting draftsman. I remember a clause of mine receiving the dubious compliment of 'nice and vague' from a bureaucrat of seasoned experience.

Ram* was fond of saying that a Bill was hammered out by the operation of the departmental hammer on the anvil of the draftsman's table.... I would call the process a creative partnership in which tensions might arise but a considerable team spirit could be generated. The theory is that the department has the last word on matters of policy, and the draftsman on matters of form or of law, but both parties poach freely on each other's preserves.

There has been some writing on the actual problems faced by the parliamentary draftsman. One example is a paper written by F.A.R. Bennion, himself for many years a draftsman ('Statute law obscurity and the drafting parameters', 5 *British Journal of Law and Society*, 1978, p. 235). In his paper Bennion identified the parameters within which the draftsman had to work:

Legal effectiveness – the draftsman must express the government's intentions in such a way that the statute will have its desired effect.

Procedural legitimacy – the bill must comply with the procedural requirements of each House of Parliament. Parliamentary procedure governs the form of the bill. It decrees, for instance, that a bill have a long title and be divided into clauses. It allows a preamble and schedules but no other type of formulation. It requires amendments to be in a certain form.

Timeliness – the Future Legislation Committee of the cabinet is responsible for the government's timetable of legislation. Usually this is such as to create serious pressure on the draftsman. The pressure of time exists not merely in the period before first publication of a bill but equally after publication for the preparation of amendments.

Certainty – it is usually desired that the text have one construction only. But sometimes it is intended to leave things deliberately some-

* Sir Granville Ram, Senior Parliamentary Counsel (ed.).

what vague – often because those responsible for the bill were themselves unable to agree as to how it should be handled.

Comprehensibility – most statute-users are lawyers or experts, but most politicians are non-lawyers and non-experts. The bill must be comprehensible to both categories.

Acceptability – the language must not excite opposition; the prose style is flat; traditional and often verbose forms are normally preferred. (Bennion described how he incurred considerable criticism when he once used the phrase 'tried his best' instead of the more familiar 'used his best endeavours'.)

Brevity – draftsmen are encouraged to be as brief as possible. In particular they are desired to keep down the number of clauses because MPs have the right to debate each clause if they wish.

Debatability – the bill must be so framed as to allow the main points of policy to be debated. ('If they are buried in confused verbiage, it becomes difficult for Members to perceive what they are and deploy argument.')

Legal compatability – the bill when it becomes law should fit as well as possible with existing law. The language used in one statute should be the same as that used in other statutes to describe the same subject-matter. ('Contrary to most people's beliefs, however, there are no books of precedents in the Parliamentary Counsel's Office in Whitehall. Draftsmen vary in their willingness to spend time hunting for models in earlier legislation. They are discouraged by the knowledge that if they carry out this search it will throw up a variety of examples, not one of which may appear any better than the others.') The draftsman should also indicate in his bill what its effect is on other statutory provisions – by way of repeal or amendment. ('His task is greatly hampered by the chaotic state of the statute book, the lack of arrangement under titles, delays in printing updated official texts, and the absence of computerized search and retrieval systems.')

3. Criticism of the quality of drafting of English statutes

Criticism of the quality of drafting goes back a long way. The Report of the Renton Committee (*The Preparation of Legislation*, 1975, Cmnd. 6053) said that such criticism had been common centuries ago:

2.8 As long ago as the 16th and 17th centuries there were in England many expressions of dissatisfaction with, and projects for reforming, the drafting of statutes and the shape of the statute book. These early critics included

Edward VI ('I would wish that ... the superfluous and tedious statutes were brought into one sum together, and made more plain and short, to the intent that men might better understand them'), Lord Keeper Sir Nicholas Bacon ('a short plan for reducing, ordering, and printing the Statutes of the Realm'), James I ('divers cross and cuffing statutes ... [should] be once maturely reviewed and reconciled; and ... all contrarieties should be scraped out of our books'), and Sir Francis Bacon, when Attorney General ('the reducing of concurrent statutes, heaped one upon another, to one clear and uniform law').

In recent years, however, such criticism has been mounting significantly. (See, for instance, Statute Law Society, 'Statute Law Deficiencies', 1970, and 'Statute Law: the key to clarity', 1972, both published by Sweet and Maxwell.) In May 1973 the government set up a committee under the chairmanship of Sir David Renton whose terms of reference were – 'With a view to achieving greater simplicity, and clarity in statute law to review the form in which Public Bills are drafted, excluding consideration of matters relating to policy formulation and the legislative programme; and to consider any consequential implications for Parliamentary procedure'.

The Report of the Renton Committee on the *Preparation of Legislation* said that it had received evidence from judges, bodies representing the legal and other professions, from non-professional bodies and from prominent laymen, that much statute law lacked simplicity and clarity. The complaints, it said (p. 27), fell into four main categories:

(*a*) *Language*. It was said that the language used was obscure and complex, its meaning elusive and its effect uncertain. The Statute Law Society criticized the language of the statutes as: 'legalistic, often obscure and circumlocutious, requiring a certain type of expertise in order to gauge its meaning. Sentences are long and involved, the grammar is obscure, and archaisms, legally meaningless words and phrases, tortuous language, the preference for the double negative over the single positive, abound'. One type of problem for instance was the piling of one hypothetical provision on another, as in a provision of the National Insurance Act 1946: 'For the purpose of this Part of the Schedule a person over pensionable age, not being an insured person, shall be treated as an employed person if he would be an insured person were he under pensionable age and would be an employed person were he an insured person'.

(*b*) *Over-elaboration*. It was said that the desire for 'certainty' in the application of legislation leads to over-elaboration. The parliamentary draftsman tried to provide for every contingency. The committee said that this was because of concern on the part of the legislature to ensure against the possibility that the legislation will be construed by someone, in some remote circumstances, so as to have a different effect from that envisaged by those preparing the bill in question. As one parliamentary draftsman had put it: 'The object is to secure that in the ultimate resort the judge is driven to adopt the meaning which the draftsman wants him to adopt. If in so doing he can use plain language, so much the better. But this is often easier said than done!' (p. 29).

(*c*) *Structure*. The internal structure of, and sequence of clauses within, individual statutes was considered to be often illogical and unhelpful to the reader:

Each Act has, or should have, an inherent logic, and its provisions should be arranged in an orderly manner according to that underlying logic. But this ideal, it is said, is not always realised. From a logical point of view, the main purpose of a Bill should be made clear early on. This statement of intent, whether it takes the form of the enunciation of general principles or otherwise, is desirable both for the legislators to help them to understand what they are being asked to pass into law, and for the courts to help them to understand the intention of Parliament when they are interpreting the legislation. Statements of intent would also assist those who must obey and advise on the legislation. The intention is now, however, rarely spelt out in the statute itself, although in continental and EEC legislation this is often done in the form of a preamble or in other ways...

Many of the witnesses have said that more attention should be paid to the logical sequence of the provisions of statutes, and that there should be a consistent approach to such questions as what kind of provision should go in the main body of the Act and what in the Schedules, so that people could more easily find their way about them. There is also the criticism that sentences are sometimes too long, and complicated by too many subordinate phrases, and that there should be greater readiness to break up clauses into separate subsections [pp. 30–1].

(*d*) *Arrangement and amendment*. The chronological arrangement of the statutes and the lack of clear connection between various Acts bearing on related subjects were said to cause confusion and made it difficult to ascertain the current state of the law on any given matter. This confusion was increased by the practice of amending an existing Act, not by altering its text (and reprinting it as a new Act) but by passing a new Act which the reader had to apply to the existing Act and work out the meaning for himself:

It is said that among the new statutes which are added to the statute book year by year there are many which are more or less intimately connected with existing statutes and that insufficient assistance is given to the reader in the task of collation which results from the purely chronological arrangement. It becomes increasingly difficult to locate the relevant Acts on any given topic; and, more seriously, once the relevant Acts have been located they may well be found to be distributed among three or four separate volumes, so that reading them together becomes – physically as well as mentally – a formidable task [p. 31].

... But there is another problem. New laws frequently amend existing statutes. Such amendment, however, by no means always takes the form of substituting a fresh and amended text in the statute which is being amended. The 'non-textual' amendment of legislation has been criticised by many of our witnesses, though some of them conceded that its use may be unavoidable. Amendments drafted non-textually have been described as being:

> 'Drafted in a narrative or discursive style producing an inter-woven web of allusion, cross-reference and interpretation which effectively prevents the production of a collection of single Acts each relating to a particular subject, otherwise than by the legislative processes of consolidation and repeal. Often Act is heaped upon Act until the result is chaotic and almost completely unintelligible. Indeed much of the confusion existing in the Statute Book today is directly attributable to referential legislation'.[1]

The other method of amending previous legislation which several witnesses have commended to us is the system of 'textual amendment'. By using this method new statutes which alter the provisions of earlier Acts give effect to such alterations by enacting fresh portions of text which are then added to or substituted for the earlier version.

The committee gave an example of each form of amendment drawn in both cases from the Town and Country Planning Act 1968. Section 149 of the principal Act, the Town and Country Planning Act 1962, was amended *non-textually* by section 37 (3) of the 1968 Act which reads as follows:

For a person to be treated under section 149 (1) or (3) of the principal Act (definitions for purposes of blight notice provisions) as owner-occupier or resident owner-occupier of a hereditament, his occupation thereof at a relevant time or during a relevant period, if not occupation of the whole of the hereditament, must be, or, as the case may be, have been occupation of a substantial part of it.

A corresponding *textual* amendment of section 149 of the principal Act was effected by section 38 of the 1968 Act (with Schedule 4):

1. H.H. Marshall and N.S. Marsh, *Case Law, Codification and Statute Law Revision* (1965).

Section 149
In subsection (1) (*a*), (1) (*b*), (3) (*a*) and (3) (*b*), for the words 'the whole or part' (wherever occurring) there shall be substituted the words 'the whole or a substantial part'.

The non-textual form of amendment was better for MPs in that it was easier to see the effect of the amendment. But it was more difficult for the ordinary user since it not only required reference to earlier legislation but often left considerable doubt as to how the two provisions should be read together (conflated). By contrast, the textual form of amendment enabled the reader to see exactly how the old law had been amended, providing only he had both the old and the new before him. The Committee said it accepted that textual amendments were generally preferable. The needs of MPs could be met by an accompanying memorandum which could show how the amended legislation would look if the proposals being considered for enactment became law (p. 79). (For strong support for textual amendment, see the evidence of F.A.R. Bennion to the Renton Committee in *Renton and the Need for Reform*, published on behalf of the Statute Law Society (1979), pp. 27–60. In his evidence Mr Bennion argued for an even better form of official document which would restate the law after amending legislation, taking into account statutory instruments as well as statutes. The reader would then have everything set out in a connected sequence. The work of organising the material would have been done for him and by lay-out and other visual means it could be made easier to read than is normally the case with statutory materials – see F.A.R. Bennion, 'Statute Law Processing: the Composite Restatement Method', *Solicitors' Journal*, 1980, pp. 71 and 92. Mr Bennion's book *Consumer Credit Control* (1978) is an example of this method of presenting the material.)

The Committee said (para. 6.21) that there was no intention to reflect upon the skill and dedication of the parliamentary draftsman. They had to work under pressure and constraints which made it very difficult for them, with the best will in the world, to produce simple and clear legislation. They were inadequately staffed and were often given gigantic tasks to perform in a race against time. Many statutes were in fact well drafted. 'Nevertheless, after making all due allowance, there remains cause for concern that difficulty is being encountered by the ultimate users of statutes, and this difficulty increases as the statute book continues to grow' (ibid.).

A senior lawyer-civil servant, Sir William Dale, subsequently published a study in which he compared the approach to legislative drafting in France, Germany, Sweden and the United Kingdom. Sir William, a former legal adviser to the Commonwealth Office, concluded that our system was the least satisfactory:

Sir William Dale, *Legislative Drafting – a New Approach* (1977), pp. 331–3

Sir William summarized the features that appeared to make for obscurity or length or both in United Kingdom statutes:

(*a*) long, involved sentences and sections;
(*b*) much detail, little principle;
(*c*) an indirect approach to the subject-matter;
(*d*) subtraction – as in 'Subject to ...', 'Provided that ...';
(*e*) centrifugence – a flight from the centre to definition and interpretation clauses;
(*f*) poor arrangement;
(*g*) schedules – too many and too long;
(*h*) cross-references to other Acts – saving space, but increasing the vexation.

In contrast, lucid and often succinct drafting is to be found in the countries on the European continent, represented in this study by France, Germany and Sweden. The continental lawmakers, influenced by their heritage of codes, think out their laws in terms of principle, or at least of broad intention, and express the principle or intention in the legislation. This is the primary duty of the legislator – to make his general will clear. An orderly unfolding of the concepts and rules follows; and whenever it is necessary to give the meaning of a term, it is done when that term first makes its appearance.

The characteristics of French drafting are clarity of principle, of form and of word, a logical development, economy of expression, and a resultant brevity. The French, as their President has observed, 'like things to be said and done clearly, on the basis of an overall concept'.

In Sweden the laws are drafted in layman's language, often with some generality of expression and even greater brevity. Technical terms are likely to be in the legislative material, the *Proposition*, to which recourse is constantly had. In some laws in the social field the policy is to use general language, set up special courts, and leave them to develop the law in the light of the varying circumstances and changing conditions.

In Germany the practice is to state a principle, and then to fill in the detail with, very often, great thoroughness. There is necessarily some length, but a systematic arrangement. At times one finds thick clusters of sentences. Some contain matter which in the United Kingdom would be put into regulations: German statutes rarely contain a regulation-making power.

Sir William Dale identified one problem as being the lack of any adequate process of revision or review of draft legislation (pp. 334–5):

In France all draft laws are examined and revised as necessary by the Conseil d'Etat; in Sweden many are referred to the Law Council; in Germany there is no similar body, the Ministry of Justice performing an examining and co-ordinating role for all Federal draft laws.

Parliamentary committees then closely scrutinise all draft Bills, in round-the-table discussions attended by ministers and civil servants, and report on the Bills, with draft amendments proposed, to the House. In Germany the scrutiny by the committees of the Bundesrat, the second Chamber, to which the Government *must* under the Constitution first send all its Bills, is particularly efficacious.

4. Proposals for improving the quality of the statute book

Sir William Dale offered a number of possible remedies for the condition of the statute book:

(1) *Changes in drafting technique* – 'We need at least to reduce the verbal impedimenta; to be less fussy over detail, to be more general and concise; and to situate each rule where it belongs, in an orderly and logical development. On this level, the question is largely a matter of style and arrangement. A more profound change is also desirable: a determination to seek the principle, to express it, and to follow up with such detail, illuminating and not obscuring the principle, as the circumstances require' (ibid., p. 335).

(2) *The establishment of a Law Council* to advise the government on draft bills. It would include judges, practising lawyers, academics, lay authors, members of consumer councils, etc. 'Its duty would be to examine [draft bills] from the point of view of coherent and orderly presentation, clarity, conciseness, soundness of legal principle, and suitability for attaining the Government's objective' (p. 336). It would report to the minister responsible. The role of the Law Council would be similar to that played in France by the Conseil d'Etat, which reviews all draft legislation in discussion with an official of the initiating department. If the ministry is not prepared to accept an amendment proposed by the Conseil d'Etat, it states its reasons and the matter is determined by the Council of Ministers. Sir William Dale recognised however that it would not be realistic to expect that the Law Council could match the authority and prestige of the Conseil d'Etat overnight.

(3) *A greater hand in the drafting process to be given to experts in the subject-matter* rather than experts in drafting. Instead of all drafting being done by parliamentary counsel at least some should be done within departments, as was the case in continental countries.

(4) *Improved system for parliamentary examination of legislation.* 'A legislative body is wise to arm itself with the means of criticizing and revising the draft Bills laid before it; and this the continental system of parliamentary working parties provides' (p. 340). The report of such a committee, reflecting discussions with ministers and civil servants and setting out amendments, would be a helpful guide to the House when the bill came to be debated.

The Renton Committee also made many proposals for possible reforms. Most of its proposals related to matters too detailed to consider here (such as the layout of statutes, punctuation, internal cross-referencing, the use of definitions, etc). The Committee thought, however, that consideration should be given to providing a training course for legislative drafting (para. 8.16), and that more draftsmen should be recruited 'as a matter of high priority' (para. 8.22). The use of statements of principle should be encouraged – where detailed guidance was called for in addition, it should be given in schedules (para. 10.13). More use might be made of examples in schedules to show how a bill was intended to work in particular situations (para. 10.07). Long un-paragraphed sentences should be avoided (para. 11.12). Statements of purpose should be used when they are the most convenient method of clarifying the scope and effect of legislation (para. 11.8).

The Committee considered but rejected the idea that there should be some form of prior scrutiny of draft bills. It concluded that 'it must be left to Government departments themselves to decide what advice they should seek before presentation [of legislation] from advisory bodies on the drafting' (para. 18.29, p. 130). Nor was the Committee persuaded that there should be such scrutiny machinery after a bill had been published. ('Having weighed the arguments on both sides, we do not think that there is any practical scope for introducing a new scrutiny stage during the Parliamentary process. This would in our opinion impose strain on a Parliamentary machine which is already under great pressure, and would also add to the labours of the draftsmen who have more than enough to do as it is to keep pace with the legislative programme' (para. 18.33, p. 131).)

The Committee did propose, however, that there should be two new procedures for scrutiny after the completion of the parliamentary process. One would be to tidy up defects in drafting before the Royal Assent by giving the Speaker and the Lord Chancellor, on application of the sponsor of legislation, the power to certify that amendments were of a purely drafting nature. Parliament would then be given the chance of accepting or rejecting them en bloc without debate. Secondly, even after Royal Assent there should be the possibility of redrafting obscure or otherwise badly drafted bills (in whole or part). The method would be to introduce a bill 'to re-enact with formal improvements [section ... of] the [...] Act'. Such bills would be introduced in the House of Lords and would automatically be referred to a Joint Committee of both Houses, which would report either that they were satisfied that the bill contained only formal improvements or that they were not so satisfied. If the Joint Committee reported favourably, the bill would enjoy the expedited parliamentary procedure now available for bills which simply consolidate existing law and add nothing new (pp. 17–18).

In addition, the Renton Committee proposed that there should be continuing review of the condition of the statute book and that this should be undertaken by the Statute Law Committee, which was first established in 1868 and whose members are appointed by the Lord Chancellor who is also its chairman. It now has some two dozen members, including MPs, parliamentary counsel, judges and senior civil servants. The Committee should be required to report, say, every three years and such reports should be laid before parliament. Speaking to the Statute Law Society in April 1978, however, Sir David Renton said that little had been done to implement the recommendations of the Renton Committee. The Committee had recommended that statements of purpose should be included in statutes but 'there have been scarcely any statements of purpose occurring in legislation since we published in May 1975'. The Committee had proposed that there be more explanatory material, but although there had been some improvement, there was still 'a long way to go'. For instance in the Wales Bill there were financial clauses running to eight pages – 'by no means easy to understand'. The explanatory memorandum to the bill endeavoured to explain those eight pages 'in about 15 arid lines on half a page'. That was not good enough because the half page 'tells us nothing about how those new types of clause will work, what the implications are, and exactly what the new machinery will be'.

The Committee had proposed that there be longer intervals between the stages of a bill – to leave some time for reflection. Here the government's record had been deplorable. Between May 1975 and March 1977 no less than 65 bills failed to comply with the suggested intervals – at least two weeks, between publication and second reading, and 14 days between second reading and the start of the committee stage.

But much more important was that the cabinet had decided not to accept the recommendation that the Statute Law Committee keep 'the structure and language of statutes under continuous review'. No explanation had been given for the decision. (See 'Failure to Implement the Renton Report', speech of Sir David Renton, in *Renton and the Need for Reform* (1979), pp. 2–8.)

Further reading: on drafting, see especially Reed Dickerson, *The Fundamentals of Legal Drafting* (1965); G.C. Thornton, *Legislative Drafting* (1970); William Dale, *Legislative Drafting: a New Approach* (1977).

5. Legislative procedure

The sequence of events in the legislative process from first reading to Royal Assent has been described by the Clerk to the House of Commons Select Committee on Procedure, using the Police Bill 1963 by way of illustration.

C.J. Boulton, 'The Passing of a Public Bill', *The Lawyer*, vol. 7, no. 3 (1964)

'POLICE. – Bill to re-enact with modifications certain enactments relating to Police forces in England and Wales, to amend the Police (Scotland) Act 1956, and to make further provision with respect to the Police, *presented by* Mr. Secretary Brooke; supported by Mr. Secretary Noble, Sir Keith Joseph, Mr. Attorney General, Mr. Woodhouse, and Miss Mervyn Pike; read the first time; to be read a second time *To-morrow* and to be printed.'

This extract from the 'Votes and Proceedings of the House of Commons' for 14th November 1963 marks the beginning of the public career of a bill now safely on the Statute Book, whose evolution from a government proposal to part of the law of the land it is proposed to describe. One says 'public' career advisedly, since the order of the House to print a bill marks very often the last lap in its life rather than the first. Virtually all bills are the product of lengthy negotiations with interested parties – whether trade associations, unions, foreign governments, Women's Institutes or rival Departments of State, before ever they reach detailed discussion in Cabinet and the Cabinet itself. The effect of this is frequently to make them, once published, incapable of amendment to any significant extent without disappointing some interest or other, or without loss of face to the government. This fact often provokes the criticism that Parliament is no more than a rubber stamp; but if government on the one hand, and Parliament on the other, are granted their proper functions it is not unreasonable to expect the government to stand by its proposals, while on its part Parliament uses all its rights to debate, to delay, to expose, and to seek explanation and justification. We shall see the methods it has evolved over the centuries to enable it to perform this service for the electorate.

The first 'reading' of the mystical number of three which each bill must have in each House before it can be submitted for the Royal Assent, has long been reduced to a formality, and all that happens in the House is that the Clerk reads the title from a dummy copy, a day is named for the second reading, and an order for printing is made....

The order for second reading 'To-morrow' is a conventional one. Although the bill appeared amongst the orders of the day the next morning, it was well known that the government would not let it be reached until members had had an adequate time to consider the text, and it was, in fact, continued from day to day until 26th November, when the second reading took place. The debate on this question is the occasion for the justification of – and attack upon – the general principles of the bill. Although a bill can be lost at many stages in its career, the second reading is undoubtedly the most important, and the vast majority of bills which get into committee get also on to the statute book. In the case of government bills, the Minister in charge of the department concerned usually opens the debate, and his Parliamentary Secretary replies at the end. Front bench opposition speakers follow the ministerial opening, and precede the winding-up....

Unless a member moves that the bill be sent to a committee of the whole House (or to a Select Committee if a detailed examination with witnesses is required) all bills after second reading (with the exception of certain financial measures) are automatically sent upstairs to a standing committee. These committees consist of from twenty to fifty members and in a session over 450 members are called upon to serve on them. Appointments to standing committees are made by a Select Committee which is charged with having regard to the 'qualifications of those members nominated and to the composition of the House'. The government thus keeps its majority, but the opposition and minority parties are fully represented. The chair is taken by a member selected by the Speaker from a panel of chairmen, who maintains the same standard of impartiality in committee as the Speaker does in the House. The task of the committee is to go through the bill and amend it where desirable, bearing in mind that the general principle of the bill has been approved by the House.

A bill in committee is considered clause by clause and the question that the clause 'stand part of the bill' is put on each one. Before this, however, amendments may be moved – provided that they are relevant, not 'wrecking', and conform to various technical requirements, such as the limitation imposed by any accompanying financial resolution passed by the House. Members of most standing committees are showered with suggestions for amendments from interested bodies – and it is not unknown for them to have ideas of their own. The government's amendments are drafted by the Parliamentary Counsel who prepare their bills; the private member usually seeks the advice of the Public Bill Office. The office, which is staffed by clerks in the service of the House (the counterpart in parliamentary terms of the administrative civil service in government), has charge of a bill throughout its passage; checks that the test is in accordance with the title and otherwise in order; provides the clerk for the standing committee; and supervises the bill through its remaining stages. The committee clerk not only helps members with their amendments, but advises the chairman on their orderliness and assists him in the exercise of his power to select which amendments shall be debated. He then attends the meetings of the committee to keep the minutes and advise the chair and members of the committee without distinction of party on any matter of order that may arise. He keeps the authoritative copy of the bill and enters any amendments as they are made....

Debate in committee is less formal than in the House. Members may speak any number of times on the same question, so that instead of a stylised debate, discussion is often almost conversational in tone....

A bill which has been considered by a committee of the whole House and emerges unamended goes straight on to third reading. Any other bill must have a consideration or 'Report' stage, when further amendments may be moved, or to remove parts added. The government frequently use the report stage to introduce in a form acceptable to them amendments the principle of which they have accepted in committee. The members who have been through the committee stage together very often dominate the debates on report stage. This is partly because many of the points at issue were postponed in the committee at the request of the government, and partly because these members are by now (if they were not before) specialists in the subject, which makes it very difficult for an 'outsider' to break in. The report stage is a useful safeguard, however, against a small committee amending a bill against the wishes of the House, and a necessary opportunity for second thoughts. The Speaker takes account of the time spent on amendments in committee in selecting what is to be discussed, but nevertheless the report stage of the Police Bill occupied over ten hours of the House's time; on one occasion the House sat till after midnight.

There remains third reading, and here, unlike second reading, when a bill may be reviewed in the context of the subject to which it relates, debate must be confined to the contents of the bill. Generally by this stage the battle is recognised to be over, and a few minutes only are spent reviewing the victories and defeats of the campaign, and in paying compliments to the enemy....

But sometimes an opposition feels a duty to harry a bill at every possible opportunity and a division will take place on an amendment (which is more often moved on second reading) to make the question read 'That the Bill be read the third time upon this day six months'. This is the conventional form of rejection: the bill does not resurface after six months if the amendment is carried. This device was adopted to avoid the possibility of reviving a bill in respect of which the question 'That the bill be *now* read the third time' had been defeated—since the word 'now' only applies to the occasion of the vote and does not defeat the bill itself.

Safely read the third time, the bill is endorsed *soit baillé aux Seigneurs* and tied up in a green ribbon together with a message asking the Lords' concurrence. The Clerk of the House proceeds to the 'other place' and hands in the bill at the bar of the House.

Since the House of Lords is not weighed down with as great a press of business as the Commons, and is not to the same extent a political battle-ground, it can afford to exercise less discipline over its members and proceedings than the lower House. Their lordships use their own discretion as to what they will say, and are prepared, for example, to slip in a few amendments on the third reading of a bill, if it will improve it, in a way quite breathtaking to newly ennobled former members of the Commons. Basically, however, the procedure of the two Houses is the same, and the greatest practical difference in the field of legislation is that there are no standing committees in the House of Lords. This means that on a subject of general interest (such as the police) all members are able to put down amendments, and on a highly controversial measure, such as the London Government Bill, this can result in a very protracted committee stage. But there is little tendency to fight battles over again in the Lords, so that the report stage is often a formal tidying-up proceeding. In the case of the Police Bill it lasted fifteen minutes. The third reading provoked no discussion at all. The bill had been read a second time on 21st April, and three days in May were spent on the committee stage. All that remained now was for the Commons to agree to the Lords' amendments.

Under the Parliament Acts 1911 and 1949 disagreement between the two Houses can only delay a bill (if the Commons persist with it) by one month in the case of financial measures, and a year in other cases. In fact, in small matters the two Houses generally give way to each other (their Lordships succeeeded this year in preserving the term 'Admiralty' under the new Defence Ministry arrangements despite a Commons decision to the contrary), and in large matters discretion prevents an open conflict. Occasionally, one House cannot agree with the other's amendments, and it sends a Message to that effect, together with its Reasons. One of the most recent Reasons read 'Because there are too many little owls'. The first House does not then normally insist on its amendment. The Police Bill gave rise to no such conflict; the Lords' amendments were agreed to in ten minutes on 8th June.

Royal Assent to the Police Bill followed on 10th June, when thirty-two Acts were promulgated. At this little ceremony, the Queen is represented by Lords Commissioners, who sit in front of the throne in their scarlet robes and cocked hats. The Speaker of the House of Commons, with the Clerk and such members as have followed him through the lobbies, having been summoned by Black Rod, stand at the bar of the House. The Reading Clerk pronounces the title of each Bill in turn; the Commissioners raise their hats; and the Clerk pronounces *La Reine le veult*. At that moment the Police Bill was dead. Sixty-odd clauses became sixty-odd sections and the Police Act 1964 was born.

If Parliament wishes, it can pass a bill into law on the same day that it is introduced.* It will be seen from the example we have taken, however, that if adequate consideration is to be given to a substantial measure, even though it is not opposed in principle, its passage is not likely to be completed in less than six months. The problems of the managers of the parliamentary time-table can be seen from the fact that in Session 1962–3 sixty public bills received the Royal Assent, and thirty-three others foundered at one stage or another. It is indicative of the control which the government has over parliamentary time, however, that only one government bill fell by the wayside. The real secret of parliament's productivity, though, is its willingness—and ability—to entrust the chair with the discretion to select which amendments shall be debated, and to accept or reject motions to closure debate.

A description of the inter-action between ministers, civil servants, MPs and outside interests in the legislative process emerged from an account of the background to the Criminal Justice Act 1972 in a BBC documentary broadcast on 16 September 1972. The presenter was Professor Anthony King of Essex University, who discussed what happened with the Conservative Minister of State at the Home Office Mr Mark Carlisle, with his opposite number in the Labour Opposition, Sir Elwyn Jones, with one of the senior civil servants involved, Mr Michael Moriarty of the Home Office, and with a backbench MP, Mr Edmund Dell. (By a coincidence the Act in question was also the subject of the extract at p. 3 above from Mr Moriarty's paper.) The transcript is taken from *Westminster and Beyond*, ed. A. King and A. Sloman (1973), chapter 12.

MORIARTY: I'm in charge of the small division which has general responsibility for legislation on the powers of the courts and is also the division that looks after the Advisory Council on the Penal System. So it fell to me and to my staff to report to ministers about the two reports of the Advisory Council on reparation and alternatives to imprisonment, and suggest what might be done about them. And this involved, in fact, putting a memorandum together, collecting the views of various other parts of the Office and, indeed, of other governmental departments that were concerned.

KING: It's not generally realised that civil servants brief their ministers not just behind the scenes but while actual debates are going on on the floor or in committee. Michael Moriarty was present during the second reading debate and I asked him, since he's not allowed to sit next to ministers on the front bench, how he went about communicating with them.

* The second reading of the Commonwealth Immigrants Bill was moved at 4 pm on 27 February 1968 in the House of Commons and the bill passed all stages in the Commons and the Lords on the same day. Notification of the Royal Assent was received in the Lords at 9.45 am on 1 March 1968. The Northern Ireland Bill had its second reading in the House of Commons at 10 pm on 23 February 1972 and the Royal Assent only hours later, on 24 February at 2.11 am (ed.).

MORIARTY: On the whole by rapidly scribbled notes, some of them things that we ourselves realise the minister is going to need from what we hear someone else saying or what we hear him saying, sometimes things that he asks us to produce. The channel of communication is the parliamentary private secretary. These are, on the whole, fairly young MPs, perhaps with a ministerial career before them, who – as it were – learn the trade, and I think you get to know a great deal about what the functions of government ministers are about by understudying in that sort of way.

KING: You do actually sit there, in effect, in the chamber itself? Not technically but in fact?

MORIARTY: That's right, yes. On the right of the Speaker and behind him under the Gallery there is a box, and officials sit there and listen with their papers, scribble their notes, and there's a certain amount of scope for interchange.

KING: Once a Bill's been read a second time – approved in principle that is – it's sent to a committee where amendments can be moved and the various clauses considered in much more detail. In the case of very important pieces of legislation, like the European Communities Bill, the committee may actually consist of the whole House of Commons operating under a somewhat different procedure. But most Bills, including the Criminal Justice Bill, are sent upstairs, as they say, to one of the standing committees. These committees have about two dozen members each and are, in effect, miniature Houses of Commons. The majority party in the whole House also has a majority on the committee and, as in the whole House, there are ministers and Opposition front-bench spokesmen. Standing Committees are not specialised: they consider whatever Bills are sent to them and not just ones on particular topics. But, of course, if an MP is interested in a particular Bill, he can usually see to it that he is included on the appropriate standing committee – or at least he can try.

Everyone agrees that the atmosphere of a standing committee is quite different from that on the floor of the House.

CARLISLE: It's usually considerably more intimate. It's more, I think one can say, constructive. It depends a lot on the Bill. For example, on this Bill the atmosphere throughout was that people were wanting to get down and do a careful revision of the details of the Bill in a constructive manner.

KING: Michael Moriarty describes the contrast in more detail.

MORIARTY: It's a good deal easier and less formal. A committee room is I suppose not much larger than a large school classroom. The MPs, of whom in our case there were about twenty in all, sit at desks facing one another, so to that extent it's a sort of mini-chamber. In place of the Speaker we have a Chairman of the Committee, that is an MP, who is on a low dais. On his left he has the House officials and the *Hansard* people. On the right of the Chairman there is Parliamentary Counsel and then the officials like myself who are there to give advice to the minister on the contents of the Bill.

KING: Let's suppose an MP raises a point and the minister isn't quite sure how he's going to reply: will he in standing committee, actually there and then, turn to you and mutter something to you in order to get some help?

MORIARTY: Yes, because of the geography, which it's slightly difficult to describe. We are, in fact, only a few feet away from the minister, so it's perfectly easy for a minister just to get up from his seat and take a couple of paces so that he can talk quietly to us, or he can even stage whisper from where he's sitting, or he can ask his parliamentary private secretary, sitting just behind him, to turn round and have a word with us. It is all a good deal easier; there's no need for anyone to move to and fro. And, indeed, one occasionally gets a situation where someone from the Opposition or a Government backbencher asks the minister a question and then does a bit of adlibbing while it's perfectly clear that the minister is getting the answer.

KING: One major advantage a minister has in piloting a Bill through the House of Commons is sheer numbers: despite occasional near-embarrassments, he can normally count on having enough votes to get his Bill carried. But he also has another major advantage: the detailed information and advice supplied by civil servants. Part of the job of civil servants working on a Bill is to take all the amendments – on jury service, suspended sentences, and so on – and brief the Minister on them, as Michael Moriarty explained:

MORIARTY: This is the main task of officials during the committee stage. Each morning the Order Paper is brought down from the Parliamentary Section as early as they can, and one then drops everything else and sets to work looking at the amendments, trying to work out exactly what an M.P. is getting at – sometimes, of course, it's quite a job – and this may be because he is approaching something in a confused way or because he's just a lot cleverer than we are on a particular matter. And then one goes through the processes of deciding how far the objective is compatible with the objectives of the Government in the Bill, and how far it's a sensible way of achieving it.

KING: How far is it part of the job of a civil servant to warn a minister of unforeseen consequences of an amendment which he might perhaps be about to accept?

MORIARTY: Oh, I think that is really part of the bread-and-butter of briefing on amendments. Of course, this question, I think, raises in turn the question where the initiative lies, and I suppose this is different on different occasions. In our case, the initiative I think lay with us in the first instance. We would usually tender some briefing and advice on an amendment and, if necessary, Mr Carlisle would discuss these with us, tell us if he saw it differently, and so on. But on the whole he let us get on with working out a brief before telling us what his own thoughts were. But one can certainly see if it worked the other way round: that, if it began with the Minister saying what he thought, it would certainly be the task of the civil servant to say: 'Well, but have you considered A, B, and C?'

KING: Backbenchers and Opposition MPs, however, lack that sort of professional assistance. Where do they get help from? How did Edmund Dell inform himself for purposes of taking part in the Committee proceedings?

DELL: Well, here, of course, I have the great good fortune of having a wife who is very deeply acquainted with this whole area and who was therefore able to draw my attention to all the necessary material on every point on which I wanted to speak. So she was of enormous assistance.

KING: So it was then a question of simply going to the library and reading the stuff up?

DELL: It was a matter of going to the library, reading the stuff up, preparing the speech, and putting the available information before the Minister in the Committee and saying: 'This is information which has obviously not been considered in preparing this Bill.'

KING: And in addition to what an MP can do on his own, there are also organisations willing to help him, as well as to press their views on him. I asked Sir Elwyn Jones where he and his colleagues got their information from.

JONES: Well, you will remember that there were the reports of committees, which were the foundation of the clauses in the Bill, which we were able to call upon. But then in the background there are a large number of bodies, fortunately, in this country – this is one of our strengths as a democracy – like Justice, the British Section of the International Commission of Jurists, like the National Council for Civil Liberties, like the Howard League. There are half a dozen bodies at least who have worked on this sort of problem and whose reports and recommendations are available to us.

The time taken by parliamentary debates

Professor John Griffith has studied the time taken by debates on government bills in three sessions of parliament – 1967–8, 1968–9 and 1970–1. In the first session there were 60 bills which took an average of 23 hours each; in the second, 50 bills averaged 20 hours' debate; in the third, 73 bills averaged 16 hours. These figures cover the aggregate of time devoted to debates in both Houses. (J.A.G. Griffith, *Parliamentary Scrutiny of Government Bills* (1974), pp. 15–16.)

But out of the total of 183 bills no fewer than 74 (40 per cent) were dealt with in less than 5 hours. At the other end of the spectrum, in each of the three sessions there were 7 bills that absorbed over half of the total amount of time. These 21 bills averaged 96 hours of debating time (ibid).

The average distribution of time over the three sessions was:

2nd reading	15%
Committee stage	65%
Report stage	15%
3rd reading	2%
Lords' amendments in Commons	3%
Total	100%

(*Source*: ibid., Table 1.2, p. 17.)

6. The impact on draft bills of the parliamentary process

It is commonly assumed that the process of debate in parliament is not merely the visible manifestation of democracy but a significant part of the business of law-making through legislation. But Professor Griffith's study shows that this is less true than is often supposed, at least if impact is measured by what happens to amendments moved to government bills.

Taking the Committee stage in the House of Commons, one-fifth of amendments were moved by ministers, 10 per cent by government backbenchers and 70 per cent by Opposition Members (Table 3.6, p. 87). The number of amendments agreed to in the three categories was:

Ministers	906 out of 907 (100%)
Government backbenchers	40 out of 436 (9%)
Opposition Members	131 out of 3,074 (4%)

(*Source*: ibid., Table 3.8, p. 93)

Thirty-one of the 40 amendments moved by government backbenchers and agreed to, and 118 of the 131 moved by Opposition Members and agreed to, were agreed without a division. Most were classifiable as drafting, clarificatory or of very minor significance (pp. 93–119).

On Report stage, 56 per cent of amendments were moved by ministers, 6 per cent by government backbenchers and 39 per cent by Opposition Members (Table 4.1, p. 146). The number agreed to in each category was:

Ministers	864 out of 865 (100%)
Government backbenchers	10 out of 89 (11%)
Opposition Members	29 out of 599 (5%)

(*Source*: ibid., Table 4.3, p. 159)

Nine of the ten amendments moved successfully by government backbenchers, and 28 of the 29 moved successfully by Opposition Members, were agreed to without a division (ibid.).

In the entire three sessions there were only 26 substantive matters on which the government was defeated in Committee. On Report the government accepted the defeat in nine of these 26 cases. In the other 17 cases the defeat was reversed (pp. 182–4).

In other words, almost all of the amendments that were moved successfully in the House of Commons were moved by ministers – 94 per cent of those moved successfully in Committee and 96 per cent of those moved successfully on Report. According to Professor Griffith, they are not commonly the result of arguments advanced by Members. 'Usually they reflect later developments in the thinking of civil servants in the department, often reflecting pressures from interest groups' (p. 197). Of the amendments moved by government backbench and Opposition Members that were agreed to 'only a very few can be said to be of any real substance' (p. 202). However there were a larger number of occasions when government amendments were the result of something said by Members. Professor Griffith concluded (pp. 206–7):

> Though the direct impact of the House on Government proposals for legislation was unimpressive, the indirect impact shown by the positive response of Government to points made in committee was certainly deeper. On my estimate there were 365 occasions during these three sessions when Government amendments moved on report were traceable to committee points made by Government backbenchers and Opposition Members. And of these, I have classed one-third (125 in all) as important in varying degrees. This is not an inconsiderable number.
>
> More significant than the counting of amendments is their weight and their effect on bills. Eleven bills, all of importance, were markedly affected by their passage through the House of Commons. In 1967–68 the Medicines Bill, the Race Relations Bill, and the Gaming Bill were changed in several important particulars; the Town and Country Planning Bill was reshaped and improved; and the Civil Aviation Bill emerged as a better and more coherent measure. In 1968–69 the Finance Bill was considerably amended in one important group of provisions, as were the Housing Bill and the Children and Young Persons Bill. In 1970–71, the widest range of amendments was to the Highways Bill while important limited amendments were made to the Finance Bill and to the Immigration Bill.
>
> Against these achievements, must be set the long debates, the hundreds of aborted attempts at amendment, the scores of bills, including some of the greatest importance, which remained effectively unchanged despite the efforts of Opposition Members and, to a lesser extent, of Government backbenchers. But even when Members totally fail to persuade the Government to amend its proposals, other purposes of debate may be fulfilled.
>
> When we added the achievements of non-Ministerial Members in committee to those on report we are left with some sense of great effort making for little result and yet with a sense also that some slipshod thinking by Ministers, civil servants and draftsmen has been removed or clarified and that some bills look much better on third reading than they did on second, and that a few famous victories have been won. Whether this great effort is justified by those improvements is another matter; as is the question of the ways in which the effort might be made more effective.

In the House of Lords the success rate of amendments moved by government backbenchers and Opposition Members was somewhat higher than in the Commons. (Their combined success rate in Committee in the Commons was 6 per cent, compared with 12 per cent in the House of Lords. The success rate on Report was 5 per cent in the Commons, compared with 19 per cent in the Lords.) Professor Griffith said (p. 231):

When all allowance has been made for the dangers of using such statistics, the difference is not only considerable but also confirms the impression given by reading the debates in the Lords: that Ministers in the Lords are more willing to accept amendments than they are in the Commons. Partly this may be because the details of a House of Commons Bill are much more settled and firm by the time it arrives in committee in the Lords so that the effect of amendments can be more clearly seen. But partly it may be because the less contentious, less partisan, atmosphere in the Lords makes amendments moved by those who are not Ministers more likely to be accepted....

A case can always be made out for a second, third or fourth look at any proposal, whether legislative or other. And it is no part of my present task to argue the case for unicameral or bicameral legislatures. What is clear is that, with pressures as they are and with the House of Commons and Government Departments functioning as they do, legislation sometimes leaves the Commons in a state unfit to be let loose on the public. Some kind of reviewing is necessary. And the House of Lords is presently the best reviewing body we have.

The view that parliament provides a somewhat ineffectual form of scrutiny of government ministers was expressed by the late Mr Richard Crossman in his diaries.

R.H.S. Crossman, *The Diaries of a Cabinet Minister* (1975), vol. I, pp. 628–9

I turn finally to the biggest question of all – the relationship of a departmental Minister to Parliament. How effectively does Parliament control him? How careful must he be in his dealings with Parliament? The answer quite simply is that there is no effective parliamentary control. All this time I never felt in any way alarmed by a parliamentary threat, even when we had a majority of only three....

What about legislation? On the Rating Bill and the Local Government Bill there was virtually no parliamentary control. These were specialist Bills and the Opposition got nothing out of them. On the large Rent Bill there was rather more genuine discussion. As a result of Opposition pressure I was able to make a number of improvements in the Bill which I wanted and which I had been told by the Department or the parliamentary draftsmen were quite impossible. Nevertheless, I agree with those who say that the Committee Stage as managed at present is an intolerable waste of time. The Opposition only have a limited number of objections to make and they pour them all out on the early clauses, and then they get tired and give in on the later clauses and schedules which, though they may be very important, are rushed through without any proper attention.

Of course, I was spoilt by having Jim MacColl.* As a result of his presence I never bothered to read any of the Bills I got through. I glanced at them and I read the briefs about them and I also knew the policies from the White Papers and therefore I knew exactly how the briefs and the White Papers corresponded with the clauses of the Bills. But I never bothered to understand the actual clauses, nor did many Members, not even the spokesman for the Opposition. Both sides worked off written briefs to an astonishing extent.

I wonder whether the whole procedure of Standing Committee isn't too formalized today, with Government and Opposition facing each other and debating line by line on amendment. Wouldn't it be possible for the Minister to sit down informally and put the major principles of the Bill for the Committee to discuss? There must be a whole number of Bills on which you ought to be able to get a pooling of minds, which doesn't occur with the Standing Committee procedure in Parliament. I tried to help the Government Members by having a meeting once a week of my own back-benchers to discuss the Bill; it worked very well on the Rent Act but not on the others. I suppose the objection is that you can't do this if the Opposition are really to oppose. But quite frankly, Standing Committee is also intolerable for the Government Members – it is a terrible chore to sit there and listen to the eternal prosying of an Opposition that is usually so badly briefed that it is unable to sustain any long or detailed criticism of a Bill, and even if the Government Members know something about it they have to sit there saying nothing because discussion prolongs the time and the Government's only concern is getting things through as fast as possible.

Question

Could it be reasonably argued that civil servants play as great, and often a greater, role in legislation than MPs and even ministers? If so, is this an inevitable feature of the process, or is it something that should be changed?

But even when a statute has received the Royal Assent it does not necessarily become law. This is because sometimes the statute specifies that it, or parts of it, shall come into force on a date to be fixed by the minister. It is then often a matter of some difficulty to discover

* Joint Parliamentary Secretary, Ministry of Housing and Local Government, 1964–9.

whether any particular part of the Act has or has not come into force. This problem was the burden of a cri de coeur from an academic contributor to *The Magistrate*:

Alec Samuels, 'Is it in force or isn't it?', *The Magistrate*, November 1979, pp. 173–4

Parliament has a nasty habit of passing new laws and then either not bringing them into force, or bringing them into force only after inordinate delay, or bringing them into force piece-meal, often in a sudden and haphazard manner. A new Act may look good on paper, and in political terms, but resources are not made available for implementation, and the thing just lies fatuously and uselessly on the statute book.

The law to be applied in magistrates' courts ought to be simple, straightforward, and readily accessible, and it should be possible easily and immediately to ascertain whether or not it is in force. Although the justices' clerk is probably aware of the true position, the relatively young and inexperienced court clerk in court No. 5 may not be so well informed. This is unfair. The court clerk cannot repeatedly leave his court in order to consult the justices' clerk himself.

The Criminal Law Act 1977 is a good example of how not to do things. The Act was really three Acts contained in one Act, namely conspiracy, squatting, and magistrates' courts procedure. There were five different commencement dates. Statutory instruments brought different bits of the Act into force on different dates. Bits of sections, bits of subsections and bits of paragraphs were brought into force, at different times. There was no progressive or cumulative table of commencement orders. The section providing for the prosecution to disclose statements to the defence before the trial (s. 48) is still not in force, nor is the power to impose a partly suspended sentence (s. 47).

The power to impose a suspended sentence supervision order for a sentence of more than six months is so far applicable only in the Crown Court (Powers of Criminal Courts Act 1973, s. 26, deriving from the Criminal Justice Act 1972), although for two or more imprisonable offences magistrates frequently have the power to sentence to up to twelve months' imprisonment. The Bail Act 1976 took seventeen months to come into operation, because of the complicated rules and forms.

Several parts of the Children and Young Persons Act 1969 have not been brought into force, and it may be that they never will.

The new adoption law (Adoption Act 1976, deriving from the Children Act 1975) is not yet in force, although the freeing for adoption procedure, i.e. freeing the child before the adoption order itself comes to be made, would be very useful. A custodianship order, i.e. to give greater legal powers to foster parents, is still not available to the court (Children Act 1975, Part II). Provisions for legal representation and legal aid for children are only partly in force (Children Act 1975, s. 65). The Domestic Proceedings and Magistrates' Courts Act 1978, providing for completely new law and procedure in domestic cases, is not yet in force, apart from a few minor bits, and the starting date is still unknown.

The annual Administration of Justice Act and similar miscellaneous provisions legislation constantly amend and tinker about with existing statutes, which gradually become a terrible mess, making for terrible difficulties, for example, the Magistrates' Courts Act 1952 and the Guardianship of Minors Acts 1971 and 1973. They are not reprinted or consolidated in one clean copy.

Pleas to parliament

1. Do not pass a new statute unless and until it can be brought into force promptly.
2. Do not put two or more statutes into one statute.
3. Bring the whole of the statute into force at one time.
4. Bring the statute into force on a sensible date, e.g. 2 January or 1 September or 1 October, i.e. following a natural holiday or other break during which the lawyers can study it.
5. Give sufficient advance notice of the commencement date.
6. Draft the statute in such a way that if it really has to be brought into force on different dates this can be simply done, e.g. Part I, Part II, Part III, each part entire and self-contained.
7. If the statute really has to be brought into force in stages, then supply a cumulative table of commencement orders.
8. Remember that the convenience of the users, magistrates, their clerks, advocates, public officials, and ultimately the public at large, is of more importance than the transient convenience of Parliament.

A partial solution to the problem posed by Mr Samuels is to include in the principal Act a schedule of commencement dates, transitional provisions and repeals. This schedule would be amended each time the principal Act was amended, so that the text of the Act with amendments would at all times be up to date – through noting up or reprinting.

7. Delegated legislation

Each year over 2,000 sets of rules and regulations are made by ministers or the Crown in Council or other central rule-making authorities – by comparison with less than a hundred public Acts of parliament. This form of legislation is under the authority of powers delegated by parliament. (The residual power to legislate under royal prerogative is no longer of much importance.) The reason is usually to avoid having too much detail in the main Act and thereby to waste the time of parliamentarians in minutiae. The delegated power to make regulations also enables the responsible minister to respond to new circumstances by amplifying the original rules without troubling parliament with matters of detail that are within principles dealt with in the original legislation. Sometimes, however, parliament leaves to ministers power to issue regulations on matters of principle.

The most sweeping grant of delegated legislative power to the Executive is undoubtedly that in s. 2 (2) of the European Communities Act 1972, which permits Orders in Council and regulations by designated ministers and government departments to be made to give effect to Community instruments and provisions of the Treaties which do not have direct effect (see p. 259 below). The Act provides that such delegated powers are to have the effect of Acts of parliament and can include any provision that could have been included in an Act of parliament except that they may not impose or increase taxation; have retroactive effect; sub-delegate legislative powers; or create new criminal offences punishable with more than two years' imprisonment or fines of over £400.

Most delegated legislation is issued in the form of Statutory Instruments which are available from the Stationery Office. (In 1976 there were 1,962, running to nearly 6,000 pages.) Their drafting is usually left to departments – though in cases of particular importance or difficulty parliamentary counsel will be brought in. The process of outside consultation is usually more fulsome than is the case with legislation proper. The need for secrecy is less, since the principles of the new law have already been laid down and the department is therefore less reluctant to take advice on matters of implementation. In some cases such consultation is even mandatory. Thus procedural regulations for tribunals and inquiries must be submitted in draft to the Council on Tribunals (Tribunals and Inquiries Act 1971, ss. 10, 11).

Parliamentary scrutiny of delegated legislation is usually slight. In many instances the only requirement is that it be laid before parliament. There is no actual procedure for it to be discussed, though any MP who wishes can ask the responsible minister about it or can seek to raise the matter in debate. But more often the enabling Act states that instruments must be laid before parliament and shall become law unless within a period of a few days a resolution is passed to annul it. Occasionally the Act specifies that the instrument will only become law if it is affirmatively approved by resolution of one or both Houses. Since 1973 there has been a Joint Select Committee on Statutory Instruments of both Houses to consider, inter alia, statutory instruments of a general character and those subject to the negative and affirmative resolution procedure. Its function is to review statutory instruments from a technical and not from a policy point of view. Its chairman, to emphasize this point, is a member of the Opposition rather than of the government.

Special procedures regarding scrutiny have been established for European Communities legislation. The question was first considered by the Select Committee on European Community Secondary Legislation of Sessions 1972–3. Its reports (*First Report*, House of Commons, 143, 1972–3; *Second Report*, House of Commons 463–1, 1972–3) led to the setting up of the Select Committee on European Legislation – commonly known as the Scrutiny Committee. The question was further considered by the Select Committee on Procedure of session 1974–5 whose *First Report* (House of Commons, 294, 1974–5) led to the reference of some EEC documents to standing committees.

Consideration of the scrutiny procedures for delegated legislation and Communities Legislation appears in the *First Report from the Select Committee on Procedure*, 1977–8, House of Commons, 588–1, vol. 1, pp. xxix–xlvi.

Judicial scrutiny of ordinary legislation is of course not possible under the constitution. The courts must accept a statute as law. But delegated legislation can be challenged both directly and indirectly before the courts. The subject is a large one and is not dealt with here. (See especially on this topic Stanley de Smith, *Constitutional Law and administrative practice* (3rd edn, 1977), pp. 337–41 and S.A. de Smith, *Judicial Review of Administrative Action* (3rd edn, 1973).

2
Statutory interpretation

1. Interpretation is an inevitable aspect of communication

Statutory interpretation is a particular form of a general problem – the understanding of meaning or, more broadly still, communication. Like M. Jourdain in Molière's *Le Bourgeouis Gentilhomme* who did not know that he was talking prose, most people are probably unaware of the extent to which the use of language necessarily involves interpretation. Even the simplest statement usually relies on an understanding of habits, knowledge, values and purposes shared between the author and the recipient of the communication. The point was made in a homely example a hundred years ago.

Suppose a housekeeper says to a domestic: 'fetch some soup-meat' accompanying the act with giving some money to the latter; he will be unable to execute the order without interpretation, however easy and, consequently, rapid the performance of the process may be. Common sense and good faith tell the domestic, that the housekeeper's meaning was this: 1. He should go immediately, or as soon as his other occupations are finished; or, if he be directed to do so in the evening, that he should go the next day at the usual hour; 2. that the money handed him by the housekeeper is intended to pay for the meat thus ordered, and not as a present to him; 3. that he should buy such meat and of such parts of the animal, as, to his knowledge, has commonly been used in the house he stays at, for making soup; 4. that he buy the best meat he can obtain, for a fair price; 5. that he go to that butcher who usually provides the family, with whom the domestic resides, with meat, or to some convenient stall, and not to any unnecessarily distant place; 6. that he return the rest of the money; 7. that he bring home the meat in good faith, neither adding anything disagreeable nor injurious; 8. that he fetch the meat for the use of the family and not for himself. Suppose, on the other hand, the housekeeper, afraid of being misunderstood, had mentioned these eight specifications, she would not have obtained her object, if it were to exclude all *possibility* of misunderstanding. For, the various specifications would have required new ones. Where would be the end? We are constrained then, always, to leave a considerable part of our meaning to be found out by interpretation, which, in many cases must necessarily cause greater or less obscurity with regard to the exact meaning, which our words were intended to convey. [F. Lieber, *Legal and Political Hermeneutics* (3rd ed., 1880), p. 18.]

Interpretation, in other words, is not something that happens only in cases of doubt or difficulty; it happens whenever anyone tries to understand language used by another person. Usually the process of understanding is instinctive and immediate. It requires no conscious thought and is therefore not even noticed. For the most part we manage in ordinary life without too many difficulties created by misunderstandings. On the other hand, even in family life where the members of the household share broadly common values and common objectives and have a great deal of knowledge about each other's use of language, misunderstandings are far from rare. Interpretation therefore occurs inevitably wherever there is communication; the *problem* of interpretation occurs only when something goes wrong.

It is hardly surprising that in legal affairs there are plenty of ways in which things may go wrong. For one thing, legal documents – whether statutes, contracts, leases, mortgages, wills, bills of exchange – tend to be complex. Their subject-matter is difficult. They use a mixture of ordinary language and technical jargon. They are apt to be long-winded. They are frequently the result of drafting by several hands or at least of consultation with a variety of people. The final draft may reflect a compromise between different points of view. Each of these factors militates against simplicity and clarity of expression.

Secondly, a legal document speaks not only to the present but is usually intended to cope with the future. That indeed is normally its chief function. But the draftsman's capacity to anticipate the future is necessarily limited. Even if he provides for thirteen possible contingencies, he may overlook the possibility of the fourteenth which happens to be the one that actually occurs. The late Professor Lon Fuller of Harvard posed the example of a statute that provides 'It shall be an offence punishable by a fine of five dollars to sleep in any railway station.' Does the offence cover the case of a passenger waiting for a delayed train who was found at 3 am on a station bench, sitting upright but asleep and even snoring? Equally, does it cover the case of the tramp who was stopped on his way into the station carrying a bed-roll and heading for a bench, apparently with a view to settling down for the night? Neither case is adequately dealt with in the statute. No draftsman, however fertile his imagination, can think of everything.

Moreover, space will not permit him to put down everything that he does think of. In order to avoid the danger of misconstruction of the simple request 'fetch some meat for soup', the careful draftsman/communicator would be best advised to specify that he means – from the shop at the bottom of the road; before lunch; at the customary price; meat of the kind normally eaten by the family; that the change be returned etc. In ordinary life, time and patience do not permit such tedious prolixity. Much is left to common sense. But precisely the same is true of legal documents. However pedantic the draftsman, there will be much that he will have to leave to common sense. If everything had to be defined, there would be no end to the document. The draftsman must perforce select what he thinks are the most important matters to be set down. Moreover, there are some things that he cannot foresee simply because later developments are not within the knowledge of anyone at the time. The draftsman who uses the word 'vehicle' in the days of horse-drawn carriages cannot be blamed for any uncertainty as to whether the word applies to motor-cars or aeroplanes.

The third and most important reason for the singular tendency of legal documents to give rise to difficulties is that they commonly reflect attempted solutions to problems affecting different and conflicting interests. A will is the sharing out of property amongst individuals each of whom might prefer to have more than their alloted share; a contract is an agreement between, say, a buyer and a seller who have contrary points of view on the deal; a lease is an allocation of rights and responsibilities between landlord and tenant whose interests diverge at many points. A statute commonly prescribes a new way of dealing with a particular range of problems as between the different groups affected. The problem of drafting language so as to avoid ambiguity and uncertainty is great enough where the relevant parties have broadly the same point of view. It is infinitely greater where they have an incentive to find different meanings in the words used. The English language is richly endowed with words that bear multiple meanings and there is almost no limit to the number of ambiguities that can be found in the ordinary legal document once ingenious and motivated lawyers start picking it over. It is not necessarily a matter of the lawyers being 'bloody-minded'. They may simply be doing their job by looking for ways in which the document can be construed to serve the best interests of their client. Ambiguity here is not the fault of the draftsman nor is it a reflection of the short-comings of the language; it is simply the result of the obvious fact that where people look at a text from different points of view they are apt to find different meanings in the language used.

If problems of interpretation do occur, they may be resolved in a variety of ways. The opposing parties may come to some accommodation of their dispute without ever calling on their lawyers. Or the lawyers may agree on some formula that is acceptable to the clients. But if the disagreement cannot be solved by negotiation and agreement, the only way to secure an authoritative decision is to take it to the courts. This book is concerned with law-making on a national scale and the remainder of this chapter deals with the way in which the courts approach problems of statutory interpretation. But most of what is said here applies as much to the attitude of the courts to the interpretation of instruments drafted by practising lawyers whether they be contracts, leases, mortgages or any other legal document.

2. The three basic rules of statutory interpretation

There are said to be three basic rules of statutory interpretation: the literal rule, the golden rule and the mischief rule.

(a) *The literal rule*

According to the literal rule it is the task of the court to give the words to be construed their plain, ordinary or literal meaning regardless of whether the result is sensible or not. Lord Esher put the proposition succinctly in 1892:

> If the words of an Act are clear, you must follow them, even though they lead to a manifest absurdity. The Court has nothing to do with the question whether the Legislature has committed an absurdity. [*R.* v. *Judge of the City of London Court* [1892] 1 Q.B. 273 at 290.]

In another of the innumerable judicial formulations of the same rule, Lord Bramwell in 1884 similarly rejected the idea that the court should be concerned whether the construction it gives to a statute is absurd:

> I should like to have a good definition of what is such an absurdity that you are to disregard the plain words of an Act of Parliament. It is to be

remembered that what seems absurd to one man does not seem absurd to another.... I think it is infinitely better, although an absurdity or an injustice or other objectionable result may be evolved as the consequence of your construction, to adhere to the words of an Act of Parliament and leave the legislature to set it right than to alter those words according to one's notion of an absurdity. [*Hill* v. *East and West India Dock Co.* (1884) 9 App. Cas. 448 at 464–5.]

(b) *The golden rule*

The so-called 'golden rule' was attributed to Lord Wensleydale by Lord Blackburn in *River Wear Commissioners* v. *Adamson*, in which he said:

I believe that it is not disputed that what Lord Wensleydale used to call the golden rule is right, viz., that we are to take the whole statute together, and construe it all together, giving the words their ordinary signification, unless when so applied they produce an inconsistency, or an absurdity or inconvenience so great as to convince the Court that the intention could not have been to use them in their ordinary signification, and to justify the Court in putting on them some other signification, which, though less proper, is one which the Court thinks the words will bear. [(1877) 2 App. Cas. 743 at 764–5.]

In *Grey* v. *Pearson*, Parke B. said:

I have been long and deeply impressed with the wisdom of the rule now, I believe, universally adopted, at least in the courts of law in Westminster Hall, that in construing wills and indeed, statutes, and all written instruments, the grammatical and ordinary sense of the words is to be adhered to, unless that would lead to some absurdity, or some repugnance or inconsistency with the rest of the instrument, in which case the grammatical and ordinary sense of the words may be modified, so as to avoid the absurdity and inconsistency, but no farther. [(1857) 6 H. L. Cas. 61 at 106.]

According to the golden rule, therefore, the court is supposed to follow the literal approach unless it produces absurdity (and perhaps inconvenience and inconsistency), in which case it should find some other meaning.

(c) *The mischief rule*

The classic statement of the mischief rule is that given by the Barons of the Court of Exchequer in *Heydon's* case (1584) 3 Co. Rep. 7a:

And it was resolved by them, that for the sure and true interpretation of all statutes in general (be they penal or beneficial, restrictive or enlarging of the Common Law), four things are to be discerned and considered:

1st. What was the Common Law before the making of the Act.

2nd. What was the mischief and defect for which the Common Law did not provide.

3rd. What remedy the Parliament hath resolved and appointed to cure the disease of the commonwealth.

And, 4th. The true reason of the remedy; and then the office of all the Judges is always to make such construction as shall suppress the mischief, and advance the remedy and to suppress subtle inventions and evasions for continuance of the mischief, and *pro privato commodo*, and to add force and life to the cure and remedy, according to the true intent of the makers of the Act, *pro bono publico*.

Coke himself later referred to the same approach in his Institutes:

> Equity is a construction made by the judges, that cases out of the letter of a statute, yet being within the same mischief, or cause of the making of the same, shall be within the same remedy that the statute provideth; and the reason hereof is, for that the law-makers could not possibly set down all cases in express terms. [I Inst. 24b.]

3. The three basic rules considered

(a) The dominant rule is the literal rule

There seems to be little dispute that for most of the past hundred years or more the literal rule has been the dominant one. *Maxwell on Interpretation of Statutes* (12th edn, 1969) states that the literal rule was the primary one – the golden and the mischief rules were merely 'other main principles of interpretation'. The literal rule developed in the early nineteenth century. The first sustained judicial support for it appears to have come from the later Lord Tenterden in cases decided in the 1820s. According to one authority,* the golden rule and the literal rule contended for the allegiance of the judges for the next thirty years but by the latter part of the century the literal approach had clearly triumphed. The most rigorous expression of it was Lord Halsbury's statement in *Hilder* v. *Dexter* [1902] A.C. 474 that the draftsman of a statute was the worst person in the world to interpret a statute because he was unconsciously influenced by what he meant rather than by what he had said. He had himself drafted the statute in that case and refused to give judgment on the ground that he might not fully appreciate the literal, objective meaning of the words he had used. One of the chief reasons for this approach was said to be the

* J.A. Corry, 'Administrative Law: Interpretation of Statutes', *University of Toronto Law Journal*, 1935, 286 at 299–300.

length of legislation by comparison with former times. In 1840 Lord Brougham said:

> If we depart from the plain and obvious meaning on account of such views, we in truth do not construe the Act but alter it ... are really making the law and not interpreting it. This becomes peculiarly improper in dealing with a modern statute because the extreme conciseness of ancient statutes was the only ground for the sort of legislative interpretation frequently put upon their words; and the prolixity of modern statutes is still more remarkable than the shortness of the old [*Gwynne* v. *Burnell* (1840) 6 Bing. N.C. 453 at 561.]

A hundred years later Lord Evershed was echoing the same point: 'The length and detail of modern legislation has undoubtedly reinforced the claim of literal construction as the only safe rule.' If the statute was long, this suggested that parliament had expressed its full meaning and that there was no need or scope to imply any additional meanings. Anything omitted was a *casus omissus* which the judge could not supply because that would amount to legislation. But the literal approach was used equally for wills, contracts, and other legal documents, so that the philosophy was by no means based exclusively on the constitutional relationship between courts and parliament nor on the growing length of statutes.

A clear demonstration of the literal approach in operation is the sequence of events in *Magor St Mellons* v. *Newport Corporation*:

Magor and St Mellons v. *Newport Corporation* [1950] 2 All E.R. 1226 (Court of Appeal) and [1951] 2 All E.R. 839 (House of Lords)

The Newport Corporation had expanded its boundaries by taking in large parts of two neighbouring rural districts. The parts taken in were mainly the richer parts whose ratepayers paid the highest rates. The Local Government Act 1933, ss. 151 and 152, provided for reasonable compensation to the two District Councils by the one that had become enriched through the alteration in the boundaries. But the minister made an Order amalgamating the two District Councils into one. The Newport Corporation used this fact to argue that the new council could claim no compensation at all. The statute, it said, provided for compensation only to a surviving council, whereas here the two old councils had been abolished and the claim was therefore invalid.

The trial judge Parker J. and the Court of Appeal (Cohen and Somervell L.JJ.) agreed with the Corporation. Lord Denning, however, dissented. In his view the intention of parliament and of the minister was obvious. The order dissolving the old councils was not their death but their marriage.

LORD DENNING: The burdens which each set of ratepayers had previously borne separately became a combined burden to be borne by them all together. So, also, the rights to which the two councils would have been entitled for each set of ratepayers separately became a combined right to which the combined council was entitled for them all together. This was so obviously the intention of the Minister's order that I have no patience with an ultra-legalistic interpretation which would deprive them of their rights altogether. ... We do not sit here to pull the language of Parliament and of Ministers to pieces and make nonsense of it. That is an easy thing to do, and it is a thing to which lawyers are too often prone. We sit here to find out the intention of Parliament and of Ministers and carry it out, and we do this better by filling in the gaps and making sense of the enactment than by opening it up to destructive analysis.

It may be said that these heroics are out of place, and I agree they are, because I think that Parliament has really made its intention plain enough. The Act which conferred the title to compensation conferred it on each of the district councils, not in its own right, but in right of its ratepayers: (see s. 152 (1) (*b*) of the Act of 1933). The district council was the hand to receive the compensation, but it only received it so that it might give relief to the ratepayers for the increased burden which the change of boundaries cast on them. The amalgamation changed the legal identity of the two district councils, but it did not change the ratepayers at all, nor did it relieve them of their burdens: and there is no reason whatever why the amalgamated council should not claim the compensation due to the ratepayers.

The House of Lords upheld the trial judge and the Court of Appeal. The first judgment was given by Lord Simonds, who said he agreed with the judgment to be given by Lord Morton of Henryton but that he wished to add his reaction to the philosophy expressed by Lord Denning:

LORD SIMONDS: My Lords, the criticism which I venture to make of the judgment of the learned lord justice is not directed at the conclusion that he reached. It is after all a trite saying that on questions of construction different minds may come to different conclusions and I am content to say that I agree with my noble and learned friend. But it is on the approach of the lord justice to what is a question of construction and nothing else that I think it desirable to make some comment for at a time when so large a proportion of the cases that are brought before the courts depend on the construction of modern statutes it would not be right for this House to pass unnoticed the propositions which the learned lord justice lays down for the guidance of himself and, presumably, of others. He said ([1950] 2 All E.R. 1236):

> 'We sit here to find out the intention of Parliament and of Ministers and carry it out, and we do this better by filling in the gaps and making sense of the enactment than by opening it up to destructive analysis.'

The first part of this passage appears to be an echo of what was said in *Heydon's Case* three hundred years ago and so regarded, is not objectionable. But the way in which the learned lord justice summarises the broad rules laid down by SIR EDWARD COKE in that case may well induce grave misconception of the function of the court. The part which is played in the judicial interpretation of a statute by reference to the circumstances of its passing is too well known to need re-statement. It is sufficient to say that the general proposition that it is the duty of the court to find out the intention of Parliament—and not only of Parliament but of Ministers also—cannot by any means be supported. The duty of the court is to interpret the words that the legislature has used. Those words may be ambiguous, but, even if they are, the power and duty of the court to travel outside them on a voyage of discovery are strictly limited: see, for instance, *Assam Railways & Trading Co., Ltd.* v. *Inland Revenue Comrs.* and, particularly, the observations of LORD WRIGHT ([1935] A.C. 445, 458).

The second part of the passage that I have cited from the judgment of the learned lord justice is, no doubt, the logical sequel of the first. The court, having discovered the intention of Parliament and of Ministers too, must proceed to fill in the gaps. What the legislature has not written, the court must write. This proposition which re-states in a new form the view expressed by the lord justice in the earlier case of *Seaford Court Estates, Ltd.* v. *Asher* [1950] A.C. 508 (to which the lord justice himself refers), cannot be supported. It appears to me to be a naked usurpation of the legislative function under the thin disguise of interpretation and it is the less justifiable when it is guesswork with what material the legislature would, if it had discovered the gap, have filled it in. If a gap is disclosed, the remedy lies in an amending Act. For the reasons to be given by my noble and learned friend I am of opinion that this appeal should be dismissed with costs.

Lord Morton said that s. 151 of the 1933 Act made it clear that the only bodies which could claim a financial adjustment were public bodies affected by an alteration of boundaries. The new amalgamated district council was not such a body since it was not in existence when the boundary change took place.

The present case is one in which each of two local authorities loses a wealthy portion of its area and is abolished immediately after the loss occurs. It may be that, if the legislature had contemplated such a state of affairs, some special provisions would have been inserted in the Act of 1933. What these provisions would have been can only be a matter of guesswork. [[1951] 2 All E.R. 839, 845.]

He clearly agreed with Lord Simonds' view of Lord Denning's approach.

LORD MORTON (with whom Lords Simonds and Goddard agreed) said:

In so far as the intention of Parliament or of Ministers is revealed in Acts of Parliament or orders, either by the language used or by necessary implication, the courts should, of course, carry these intentions out, but it is not the function of any judge to fill in what he conceives to be the gaps in an Act of Parliament. If he does so, he is usurping the function of the legislature [at 846].

LORD TUCKER similarly found himself unpersuaded by Lord Denning's approach:

I think it is clear that the situation which has arisen in the present case was never present to the minds of those responsible for the Local Government Act, 1933, and that the language is quite inappropriate to meet it. In these circumstances your Lordships would be acting in a legislative rather than a judicial capacity if the view put forward by DENNING L.J., in his dissenting judgment were to prevail.

But LORD RADCLIFFE, without referring to him or to his approach, nevertheless found a way to reach the same result as Lord Denning:

My Lords, I differ very little from the views expressed by my noble and learned friend, LORD MORTON OF HENRYTON, but that small difference has led me to come to an opposite conclusion as to what should be the fate of this appeal....

He thought that s. 151 of the 1933 Act was not so narrow as to require that the courts give a result which was unjust to the ratepayers of the new amalgamated district council. The sum to which the ratepayers were entitled was not known when the old councils were abolished, but the right to have the sum ascertained was in existence at the moment that the boundary changes were made.

Supposing that it has been the right to an ascertained sum, say £1,000 per annum, there would not have been any dispute that the appellants would have been entitled to receive it. Does it make an essential difference that the sum, though its basis was determined, remained to be ascertained by agreement or arbitration? To me the difference appears as one of form, not of substance.

A similar clash between the strict or literal constructionists and a more liberal school occurred in a will case *Re Rowland*, again featuring Lord Denning as one of the protagonists:

Re Rowland [1963] 1 Ch. 1 (Court of Appeal)

Before going to the Far East a doctor and his wife made identical wills on printed will forms which provided that each left his property to the other, but in the event of the other's death 'preceding or coinciding' with that of the testator, the property was to go to selected alternative relatives. In the case of the husband, his property would in that event go to his brother and nephew. Both husband and wife were aboard a small ship which disappeared in the South Pacific. The circumstances of the disaster were never discovered. The question for the Court of Appeal was whether the property should go to the wife's relations or to those of the husband. The leading judgment for the majority was given by LORD JUSTICE RUSSELL:

What has the testator said? It is in my judgment quite plain that 'coinciding' in the context of 'preceding' means coinciding in point of time; its natural and normal meaning in that context is not coincidence in any other respect, such as type or cause of death, though coincidence in time would normally require coincidence in type or cause. The process of dying may take even an unconscionable time: but the event of death, to which the testator referred, is the matter of a moment, the moment when life is gone for ever. I see no room, therefore, for 'coinciding', in its normal and natural meaning, to involve some broad conception of overlapping or of occurring within a particular period. In my judgment the normal and natural meaning of 'coinciding with' in relation to deaths occurring is the same as 'simultaneous' – namely, as referring to circumstances in which the ordinary man would say that the two deaths were coincident in point of time or simultaneous.

In the light of these considerations did the wife's death on the facts of this case precede the testator's death or coincide in point of time with it? There is certainly no evidence to show that her death preceded his: this is not suggested. Do the facts lead on balance of probabilities to the conclusion that the ordinary man would consider that their deaths coincided in point of time? Or to put, as I think, the same question in different terms, would he, without regard to metaphysical problems of the infinite divisibility of time, consider on the evidence that they died simultaneously? The answer must I think clearly be: No. The evidence is wholly insufficient to warrant the conclusion. ... If the evidence was that the testator and his wife were below decks in their cabin and the vessel plunged abruptly to the bottom of the sea, the view might be taken that their deaths were, metaphysics apart, coincident in point of time. But we simply do not know what happened to them. Counsel for the appellants could not suggest, in the case of either spouse, whether the correct inference was death by drowning, trapped in the ship, or death by drowning, sucked down by the sinking ship after going overboard, or death by shark or similar fish, or by thirst, or by drowning after swimming about or floating for a greater or less period with or without a life-belt. This makes it plain that there is no evidence at all that the deaths were coincident in point of time (in the natural sense of simultaneous) in the mind of the ordinary man.

It was argued that the words 'coinciding with' were not used by this testator in what I have described as their natural meaning. The suggestion is that this testator (in his particular armchair) meant something wider – something which during the hearing was described as 'on the same occasion and by the same cause'. It was pointed out that the wills of the spouses were made at a time when they knew they were going in 1956 to employment in the Pacific which would involve such perils or risks as may be inherent in (inter alia) travel between islands and atolls in small ships. Therefore, it was said, this testator should be considered as having had in mind just this kind of episode, and accordingly this phrase in this will should be construed as embracing this event. This appears to me to be a wholly erroneous approach to the problem of construction. One may hazard the guess that if he could now be asked to whom in the events which happened he would wish his property to go, he would say that he would wish it to go to his selected alternates. That would not mean, however, that he has expressed that wish by his will: his answer would be consistent with his having selected language which failed to appreciate all the possible circumstances which would make that outcome desirable. It is an unsound approach to the construction of the will to ask oneself what the testator, if he had thought of an event not covered by the natural and normal meaning of his language, would have wished had he directed his mind to the event. The question is what events does his language cover? To ask more is to desert the source from which his intention is to be gathered, his will as proved.

Moreover, what is really meant by the suggestion that 'coinciding with' should be taken as meaning 'on the same occasion and by the same cause'? Presumably 'on the same occasion' is intended to contain a time element and to indicate deaths roughly about the same time. But how roughly? This seems quite uncertain. In any event it is implicit in this proposition that the alternative beneficiaries would have taken even if the evidence had demonstrated clearly that the wife survived the testator, and by survival had become entitled to his estate under the first part of the will. The suggested construction would thus involve a divesting of a vested interest, a process which is generally recognised as one which requires a clear expression of intention. I cannot for my part see that the testator's language can be stretched to produce such a result.

In the last analysis the appellants really are asking the court to hold (a) that the testator was intending to cover any situation in which it was uncertain whether his wife had survived him – a private solution to the problem which s. 184 of the Law of Property Act, 1925,* was designed to solve: and also,

* The effect of s. 184 is explained below in the dissenting judgment of Lord Denning (ed.).

I think, (b) that he was intending to cover any situation in which the wife survived him by so short a time that the disposition in her favour would be of no use to her. The testator's language, however, is not such as reveals either of these intentions. As I have indicated, the key to his expressed intention is the context of the words 'preceding or', which demonstrate that 'coinciding with' means 'coinciding in point of time with'. This cannot be equated with 'if we shall die together' in the sense in which people are referred to as commorientes. For these reasons I am clearly of the opinion that the testator's language does not fit the facts of the case, so far as they are known. To hold otherwise would not in my judgment be to construe the will at all: it would be the result of inserting in the will a phrase which the testator never used by guessing at what a man in his position would have wished had he directed his mind and pen to the facts as they now confront us. There is no jurisdiction in this court to achieve a sensible result by such means.

LORD JUSTICE HARMAN agreed:

It is for those claiming under the gift over to prove their case that the deaths of the testator and his wife were coincident. This word in the context in which it appears can in my judgment only be a reference to the time and not the occasion of death. In other words, 'coincident' is equivalent to 'simultaneous'. That was the only event which the testator on the language he used could have contemplated. He had already made the gift to his wife if she survived him and to the defendants if she did not. Can these deaths on the evidence be held to have been simultaneous. ... I am satisfied that it cannot. Not enough is known. It is not even known at what date, within a week, the ship went down, nor is the whereabouts of either the testator or his wife at that time certain. One or other of them may easily have survived the going down of the ship and the event is too uncertain to infer a simultaneous death, as was possible for COHEN J., in the case of two persons killed in close proximity to each other by the same bomb.

If this meaning of the word be out of the question, it is argued that 'coincident' is a little looser and can mean in this will 'at about the same time and as a result of the same catastrophe'. This in my opinion is an impossible view. The will has provided for both possibilities of survivorship and there is no warrant for introducing a reference to something other than time, namely, the same catastrophe. I am, therefore, of the same opinion as the learned judge and would dismiss this appeal.

But LORD DENNING M.R. dissented:

The question now is: what is to happen to the estate of Dr Rowland? It has been sworn at £2,798 2s. 6d. Is it to go to his brother and his nephew? Or is it to go to his wife's niece? This all depends on whether her death 'coincided with' his death. If it did, then under his will his property goes to his own relatives. If her death did not 'coincide with' his, then under s. 184 of the Law of Property Act, 1925, she, being younger than her husband, is deemed to have survived him, and his property will go under his will to his wife, and thence under her will to her niece. So the critical question is: What does the word 'coincide' mean in this will? And this seems to me to raise a point of some importance in the interpretation of wills.

One way of approach, which was much favoured in the nineteenth century, is to ask simply: what is the ordinary and grammatical meaning of the word 'coincide' as used in the English language? On that approach, the answer, it is said, is plain: it means 'coincident in point of time', and that means, so it is said, the same as 'simultaneous' or 'at the same point of time'. So, instead of interpreting the word 'coincide', you turn to interpreting the word 'simultaneous'. At that point you run into a difficulty, because, strictly speaking, no two people ever die at exactly the same point of time; or, at any rate, you can never prove that they do. LORD SIMONDS said in *Hickman* v. *Peacey* (1) that 'proof of simultaneous death is impossible'. If, therefore, the word 'coincide' is given its ordinary and grammatical meaning, it would lead to an absurdity, for it would mean that the testator was providing in his will for an impossible event.

In order to avoid that absurdity, you must do, it is said, what COHEN J. did in *Re Pringle, Baker* v. *Matheson* (2), you must interpret the word 'coincide' to mean death in such circumstances that the ordinary man would infer that death was simultaneous. So the argument proceeds to ask: when would an ordinary man say death was simultaneous?, and the answer is given: he would say so when two people are both blown to pieces at the same moment, such as by a bomb falling on the room in which they are sitting, or by an aircraft in which they are travelling exploding in mid-air. In short, where there is instantaneous death at the same instant of time. Thus a little latitude is allowed to the word 'coincide'. It covers death so close together that there is no measurable period of time between them. But no further latitude is allowed. According to this argument, if the deaths are separated by any measurable interval, even by so much as a few seconds, they do not 'coincide'....

I must confess that, if ever there were an absurdity, I should have thought we have one here ... It seems to me that the fallacy in that argument is that it starts from the wrong place. It proceeds on the assumption that, in construing a will, 'It is not what the testator meant, but what is the meaning of his words' that matters. That may have been the nineteenth century view; but I believe it to be wrong and to have been the cause of many mistakes. I have myself known a judge to say: 'I believe this to be contrary to the true intention of the testator, but nevertheless it is the result of the words he has used'. When a judge goes so far as to say that, the chances are that he has misconstrued the will. For in point of principle the whole object of construing a will is to find out the testator's intentions, so as to see that his property is disposed of in the way he wished. True it is that you must discover his intention from the words that he has used; but you must put on his words the meaning which they bore to him. If his words are capable of more than one meaning, or of a wide meaning and a narrow meaning, as they often are, then you must put on them the meaning which he intended them to

1. [1945] 2 All E.R. at 235; [1945] A.C. at 345.
2. [1946] 1 All E.R. at 93; [1946] Ch. at 131.

convey, and not the meaning which a philologist would put on them. In order to discover the meaning which he intended, you will not get much help from a dictionary. It is very unlikely that he used a dictionary, and even less likely that he used the same one as you. What you should do is to place yourself as far as possible in his position, taking note of the facts and circumstances known to him at the time, and then say what he meant by his words. ... I decline, therefore, to ask myself: what do the words mean to a grammarian? I prefer to ask: what did Dr Rowland and his wife mean by the word 'coincide' in their wills? When they came to make their wills it is not difficult to piece together the thoughts that ran through their minds. The doctor might well say: 'We are going off for three years to these far-off places and in case anything happens to either of us we ought to make our wills. If I die before you, I would like everything to go to you, but if you die before me, I should like it to go to my brother and his boy.' She might reply: 'Yes, but what if we both die together. After all, one of those little ships might run on the rocks or something and we might both be drowned: or we might both be killed in an aeroplane crash'. 'To meet that', he would say, 'I will put in that if your death coincides with mine, it is to go to my brother and his boy just the same'. He would use the words 'coinciding with', not in the narrow meaning of 'simultaneous', but in the wider meaning of which they are equally capable, especially in this context, as denoting death on the same occasion by the same cause. It would not cross Dr Rowland's mind that anyone would think of such niceties as counsel for the first defendant has presented to us. I decline to introduce such fine points into the construction of this will. I would hold that Dr Rowland, when he made his will, intended by these words 'coinciding with' to cover he and his wife dying together in just such a calamity as in fact happened: and that we should give his words the meaning which he plainly intended they should bear. I would allow the appeal accordingly.

Question

Consider the strengths and weaknesses of the approach of the judges for the majority and of Lord Denning's dissenting views in both the previous cases.

The virtues of the literal approach were outlined in an article in the *Canadian Bar Review* in 1937:

E.R. Hopkins, 'The Literal Canon and the Golden Rule', 15 *Canadian Bar Review*, 1937, p. 689

Literal interpretation means nothing if plain words may be qualified according to common sense and justice as conceived judicially. If the absurdity clause were given free rein, the judicial inquiry would be 'what ought the Act to mean', rather than 'what does the Act mean': the former process has been variously impugned as 'juristic chemistry', 'spurious interpretation', and 'evasion'.

Then, should the literal canon be dislodged from, or relegated to the position of a presumption in a modern theory of interpretation? . . . It is submitted that the formal approach is within its province most consonant with the judicial function. In our constitutional theory, the function of innovation rests primarily with legislative bodies. It is true that the final word in law-making must rest with the courts and that the exercise of any conscious mental process involves an element of discretion: yet, if the assignment of legislative power to parliament is to be otherwise than fictional, the process of interpretation must be divorced so far as may be from that of legislation. What must be sought for by the courts are criteria of meaning as objectivized and impersonal as can be found, so that the initial discretion inherent in legislation will be impaired as little as possible by a supervening discretion in interpretation. From this point of approach, the present attitude of the courts toward the literal canon, namely, that words are to be assigned their plain literal meaning in their context, merits more sympathy than it is currently accorded. Recognizing the defects of any theory of statutory construction and without finding in literalness the quality of eternal verity, the judges have proceeded on the basis that the literal canon is founded on truths approximately accurate and criteria sufficiently objectivized for a workaday world and a busy court. The patent meaning is treated as the surest guide to the latent meaning of the statute, and the field of discretion which trenches upon the field of legislation while not eliminated is at any rate reduced to a minimum. If individual hardship, or a socially undesirable result, follows, legislative machinery provides the appropriate corrective, and if, as has been suggested, the literal canon has sometimes been inexpertly applied, it must be remembered that to indict a workman is not necessarily to criticize his tools. While it will undoubtedly be necessary where the statutory meaning is obscure to make extensive and important demands upon judicial discretion, hope may be expressed that an improved draftmanship and a more studious regard to the boundaries of literal theory may result in at once an extension of the province and an improvement in the process of formal construction.

But the literal rule has also been subjected to severe criticism:

(1) The most fundamental objection to the rule is that it is based on a false premise, namely that words have plain, ordinary meanings apart from their context. Professor H.L.A. Hart of Oxford has argued that a word has a core meaning 'or standard instance in which no doubts are felt about its application' even though at the edges there is a margin of uncertainty.[1] But Professor Lon Fuller has contested this by urging that meaning attaches not to individual words but to sentences and paragraphs, and that 'surely a paragraph does not have a "standard instance" that remains constant whatever the context

1. H. Hart, 'Positivism and the Separation of Law and Morals', 71 *Harvard Law Review*, 1958, 593 at p. 607.

in which it appears'.[2] If a statute seem to have a core meaning 'this is because we can see that, however one might formulate the precise objective of the statute, *this* case would still come within it'.[3]

(2) Those who apply the literal approach often talk of using the 'dictionary meaning' of the words in question, but dictionaries normally provide a number of alternative meanings.

(3) The plain-meaning approach cannot be used for general words, which are obviously capable of bearing several meanings.

(4) Not infrequently the courts say that the meaning of the words is 'plain' but then disagree as to their interpretation.[4]

(5) The plain-meaning theory may be acceptable outside the court room, since it could be true that a high proportion of statutory materials and other legal documents can in fact be interpreted without recourse to any mischief or golden rule. But in the court room there are by definition two parties, usually represented by counsel, arguing over the meaning of the relevant passage. It makes little sense to dispose of the issue between them by reference to the plain meaning when there are two meanings in issue.

The most common retort from those who favour the literal approach is that, in spite of some problems, it promotes the certainty which is one of the chief objectives of any legal system. But does it?

If all judges *always* followed the policy of literalism, it may be that there would be some gain in certainty. But in practice they do not. Even the most diehard advocates of the literal approach sometimes lapse into some alternative method. One commentator has written[5] '[T]he doctrine of literalness can never be applied successfully to general words. For they always include something more than the scope and object of the statute require and so it leads to ridiculous results'. Judges were torn between a feeling of obligation to adhere to the doctrine and a feeling of revolt against what they regarded as an absurdity and injustice. So if literalness seemed too ridiculous or threatened things which the judge regarded as fundamental, he exerted himself to escape its conclusions. Even those judges who in-

2. L. Fuller, 'Positivism and Fidelity to Law – a Reply to Professor Hart', 71 *Harvard Law Review*, 1958, 630 at p. 663.

3. Ibid.

4. See, for instance, *London and N.E. Railway Co.* v. *Berriman* [1946] A.C. 278. In *Ellerman Lines* v. *Murray* [1931] A.C. 126 all the judges agreed that the meaning was 'plain' but there were at least three different views as to what the plain meaning was.

5. J.A. Corry, 'Administrative Law: Interpretation of Statutes', *University of Toronto Law Journal*, 1935, 286 at pp. 301–3.

sisted strongly upon the principle of literal adherence to the words, deserted it in such circumstances. 'Lord Tenterden, who fathered the doctrine, sometimes found that literal meanings could not have been intended.[6] And Lord Bramwell, who affirmed the doctrine with his usual vigour and challenged anyone to show him an absurdity so great as to entitle him to depart from the plain meaning, had some interesting lapses.[7] . . . Lord Halsbury stated the doctrine of literalness as uncompromisingly as anyone. But in a case before the House of Lords in 1890 he deserted it and appealed to the "equity of the statute".'[8]

The result of the inevitable inconsistency as to the application of the literal approach is that it loses much of its claim to be the basis of greater certainty. Lord Justices Russell and Harman in *Re Rowland* may justify their decision on the ground that it will assist in the future by reducing litigation if lawyers can predict that the court will adopt the literal approach. But a lawyer advising Dr Rowland's brother and nephew is bound to tell them that there is at least some chance of persuading the court to take a reasonable line. The testator plainly intended to leave his property to the brother and nephew if he and his wife died in the same accident. (Lord Justice Russell himself recognised this when he said 'One may hazard the guess that if he could now be asked to whom in the events which happened he would wish his property to go, he would say that he would wish it go to his selected alternates. That would not mean, however, that he had expressed that wish by his will' ([1963] 1 Ch. 1, 17). The chance of succeeding in such a case is good enough to justify litigation. A lawyer would properly tell the client that there are many judges who insist on applying the literal approach but that equally there are others who prefer a more liberal approach and even the literalists can sometimes be persuaded to adopt a more relaxed approach. It is only if judges uniformly applied the literal approach that the lawyer would have to advise that the chances of success were negligible.

If the literal approach does not therefore reduce litigation, does it promote better and more precise draftsmanship? There can be no doubt that the draftsman in the *Rowland* case used the word 'coinciding' inappropriately. Had he thought more carefully about the problem he might have used a phrase such as 'if we die in or as the result

6. *Margate Pier Co.* v. *Hannam* (1819) 3 B. & Ald. 266; *Edwards* v. *Dick* (1821) 4 B. & Ald. 212; *Bennett* v. *Daniel* (1830) 10 B. & C. 500.

7. E.g., *Twycross* v. *Grant* (1877) 46 L.J.C.P. 636; *Ex parte Walton* (1881) 17 Ch.D. 746; *Hill* v. *East and West India Dock Co.* (1884) 9 App. Cas. 448.

8. *Cox* v. *Hakes* (1890) 15 App. Cas. 506.

of the same accident' or, better still, he might have said, 'if my wife does not survive me by thirty days'. Will draftsmen be frightened into using language more accurately by dreadful warnings such as the *Rowland* case? To imagine that this is likely to be the result of such decisions strains credulity. First, it has to be assumed that the potential draftsmen even become aware of the Court of Appeal's ruling in the *Rowland* case. Most legal drafting is done by solicitors who are extremely busy and have little time to pore over the law reports. Some will notice the case; many will not. Some drafting, especially of wills, is done by laymen. It is obvious that they are highly unlikely to come to hear of the decision. If the case concerns a statutory provision, it is more likely that at least some of the small number of parliamentary draftsmen will see the report and note its significance.

But even assuming that the draftsman sees the decision, what difference will it make in practice to the quality of his work in his office? He does not need the Court of Appeal to tell him that he has to take care in drafting to select the right formula and the appropriate words. It is part of the nature of the activity. He has had it dinned into him ever since he came to the office as an articled clerk, pupil barrister or other junior. It is impossible to draft the simplest document without being all too conscious of the problem of finding the right phrase to express one's meaning. If he reads of the fate of some unfortunate draftsman's phrase in a report such as the *Rowland* case, it is improbable that he will do his work better that day as a result. He is already doing his work as well as he can according to his lights. There are far more effective pressures on him to draft well than the remote possibility that his labours will one day fall foul of the High Court or Court of Appeal. His superiors and colleagues in the office will be reading his work and making suggestions in any event. (As has been seen, parliamentary draftsmen work in pairs in order to improve the quality of their work.) The probable benefits of the literal approach in terms of improved draftsmanship are at best therefore highly speculative. When set against the manifest disadvantage of deciding an actual case in a sense contrary to what the judges believe to be the reasonable result for those parties, they appear unimpressive.

The literalist approach makes too little allowance for the natural ambiguities of language, for the frailties of even the most skilled of draftsmen and for the impossibility of foreseeing future events. In its 1969 report *The Interpretation of Statutes*, the Law Commission said:

To place undue emphasis on the literal meaning of the words of a provision is to assume an unattainable perfection in draftsmanship; it presupposes that the draftsmen can always choose words to describe the situations intended to be covered by the provision which will leave no room for a difference of opinion as to their meaning. Such an approach ignores the limitations of language, which is not infrequently demonstrated even at the level of the House of Lords when Law Lords differ as to the so-called 'plain meaning' of words [para. 30.]

The literal approach is based on a narrow concentration on the actual words used, to the exclusion of the surrounding circumstances that might explain what the words were actually intended to mean. It is very closely connected with the traditional common law rule that excludes evidence as to the meaning of written documents. Llewellyn Davies wrote of this:

A very marked feature of the common law rules for the construction of written instruments has been the rigidity with which they excluded all extrinsic evidence, and their insistence that the meaning of a document must be ascertained from its words as they stood. This attitude may well have originated in what Pollock and Maitland call the 'mystical awe' with which the early Common Law regarded the written instrument, and there can be no doubt but that the particular solemnity attributed to the instrument under seal has exercised a great influence on the attitude of the courts towards the written law.*

It is a characteristic of some primitive legal systems that they attach excessive weight to the importance of words so that, for instance, the plaintiff who makes a slip in stating his claim is nonsuited. The literal approach to language by lawyers may be a form of this tradition. The draftsman is in effect punished for failing to do his job properly (except that it is his client, or in the case of statutes, the wider community, that bears the cost). The punitive or disciplinarian school of judicial interpretation remains a powerful element in the operation of the English legal system. ('If the draftsman has not got it right, let him try again and do better next time.')

At first sight the literal approach to statutory interpretation could be said to be based on a sense of the court's deference to the sovereignty of parliament. ('It is not for the court to put words into parliament's mouth – we are simply the humble servants who will faithfully implement parliament's will providing only that we are told clearly what parliament desires.') But this humble posture is misleading. It

* D.J. Llewellyn Davies, 'The Interpretation of Statutes in the Light of their Policy', 35 *Columbia Law Revoiew*, 1935, 519 at p. 522.

conceals an ancient tradition amongst the judges that the common law is a superior form of creation to statutes. The judges have for instance often applied the presumption that parliament does not intend to alter the common law unless it plainly states its intention to do so. (According to *Maxwell* 'few principles of statutory interpretation are applied as frequently'.†) The literal approach is part of the same philosophy. ('We cannot be expected to move unless we are given clear marching orders. If we do not consider the marching orders to be clear enough we will refuse to budge and the fault will be parliament's not ours.') This is hardly the attitude of the interpreter that is likely to produce the best results.

A final criticism of the literal approach to interpretation is that it is defeatist and lazy. The judge gives up the attempt to understand the document at the first attempt. Instead of struggling to discover what it means, he simply adopts the most straightforward interpretation of the words in question—without regard to whether this interpretation makes sense in the particular context. It is not that the literal approach necessarily gives the wrong result but rather that the result is purely accidental. It is the intellectual equivalent of deciding the case by tossing a coin. The literal *interpretation* in a particular case may in fact be the best and wisest of the various alternatives, but the literal *approach* is always wrong because it amounts to an abdication of responsibility by the judge. Instead of decisions being based on reason and principle, the literalist bases his decision on one meaning arbitrarily preferred. The limitations of this approach may be seen in a case decided a hundred years ago.

Whiteley v. *Chappell* (1868–9) 4 L.R.Q.B. 147

A statute made it an offence for anyone in an election of guardians of the poor 'wilfully, fraudulently and with intent to affect the result of such election ... to personate any person entitled to vote at such election'. The defendant was charged with personating someone who was deceased. The full text of the judgments delivered in the case is as follows:

LUSH J.: I do not think we can, without straining them, bring the case within the words of the enactment. The legislature has not used words wide

† *Maxwell on the Interpretation of Statutes* (12th edn, 1969), p. 116.

enough to make the personation of a dead person an offence. The words 'a person entitled to vote' can only mean, without a forced construction, a person who is entitled to vote at the time at which the personation takes place; in the present case, therefore, I feel bound to say the offence has not been committed. In the cases of *Rex* v. *Martin*, and *Rex* v. *Cramp* (Russ. & Ry. 324, 327) the judges gave no reasons for their decision; they probably held that 'supposed to be entitled' meant supposed by the person personating.

HANNEN J.: I regret that we are obliged to come to the conclusion that the offence charged was not proved; but it would be wrong to strain words to meet the justice of the present case, because it might make a precedent, and lead to dangerous consequences in other cases.

HAYES J. concurred.

If the court applied the literal approach, its refusal to discuss the problem was perfectly correct. It gave no attention to the question whether the statute was designed to protect the integrity of the election by preventing voting in the name of *anyone* else or whether it was aimed rather at the protection of the votes of living voters. In another statute it had been made an offence to personate 'a person entitled or supposed to be entitled to any prize money'. In *Rex* v. *Martin* and *Rex* v. *Crump*, cited by Lush J., the court had held that 'supposed to be entitled' could include the case where the personation was of someone known to be dead. Counsel for the prosecution argued that these cases were in point and that they reflected the policy of trying to stop personation by anyone. 'The gist of the offence', he argued, 'is the fraudulently voting under another's name; the mischief is the same, whether the supposed voter be alive or dead.' Counsel for the defence, on the other hand, drew the court's attention to the Parliamentary Registration Act, s. 83 of which made it an offence to personate 'any person whose name appears on the register of voters, whether such person be he alive or dead'. Under the statute being considered by the court there was no express reference to the dead voter – 'the person must be entitled, that is could have voted himself'.

But the court did not do counsel the courtesy of paying any attention to their arguments. The judges looked at the words of the statute and nothing else. A dead person plainly was not entitled to vote. Ergo, the prosecution failed. Similarly, in the *Rowland* case, according to the dictionary or the plain meaning, 'coinciding' means two things occurring at the same moment. There being no evidence that Dr and Mrs Rowland died at the same moment, the will was inoperative and the property passed under the provisions of the Law of Property Act. The approach is mechanical, divorced both from the realities of the use of language and from the expectation and aspirations of the human beings concerned and, in that sense, it is irresponsible.

(b) What of the golden rule?

If the literal rule is unacceptable, is the golden rule any better? The answer must be that it is not – for the golden rule is based on the literal rule. It tells the judge to follow the literal approach unless that results in absurdity, in which case he should find some other solution. Admittedly, the golden rule does at least have the saving grace that it may protect the court from egregious foolishness. But it does so only in the rare case where the judge is prepared to hold that the result is so absurd or unreasonable as virtually to require that he find some other construction. It is better to have such a rule than not to have it, but it provides an answer to very few cases. Most statutory interpretation problems that come before the courts do not present such easy answers. There is usually a difficult choice to be made between two fairly plausible arguments. (If the matter were clear-cut, one would assume that the lawyers would so advise their clients and the case would normally not reach the court.) The golden rule therefore only rescues the court in a tiny number of instances.

Moreover, there is no way of predicting what will strike a court as an absurdity sufficiently clear to justify this exceptional response. The point was made by John Willis in a famous article:

> What is an 'absurdity'? When is the result of a particular interpretation so 'absurd' that a court will feel justified in departing from a 'plain meaning'? There is the difficulty. 'Absurdity' is a concept no less vague and indefinite than 'plain meaning': you cannot reconcile the cases upon it.* It is infinitely more a matter of personal opinion and infinitely more susceptible to the influence of personal prejudice. The result is that in ultimate analysis the 'golden rule' does allow a court to make quite openly exceptions which are based not on the social policy behind the Act, not even on the total effect of the words used by the legislature, but purely on the social and political views of the men who happen to be sitting on the case....
>
> What use do the courts make of the 'golden rule' today? Again the answer is the same—they use it as a device to achieve a desired result, in this case

* Contrast *Vacher* v. *London Society of Compositors* [1913] A.C. 107, 117, 118 and *Washington* v. *Grand Trunk Railway*, 28 S.C.R. 184, where the court refused to find an absurdity, with *Ex parte Walton*, 17 Ch.D. 746 and The *Ruahepu* [1927] P. 47, where the court did find an absurdity. See also *The Altrincham Electric Supply Co. Ltd* v. *Sale U.D.C.* (1936) 154 L.T.R. 379, in which the arbitrator, the trial judge and a majority of the House of Lords applied the literal interpretation, and the Court of Appeal and a minority of the House of Lords applied the mischief rule.

as a very last resort and only after all less blatant methods have failed. In those rare cases where the words in question are (a) narrow and precise, and (b) too 'plain' to be judicially held not plain, and yet to hold them applicable would shock the court's sense of justice, the court will, if it wishes to depart from their plain meaning, declare that to apply them literally to the facts of this case would result in an 'absurdity' of which the legislature could not be held guilty, and, invoking the 'golden rule', will work out an implied exception. [John Willis, 'Statute Interpretation in a Nutshell', 16 *Canadian Bar Review*, 1938, pp. 13–14.]

One serious objection to the golden rule is therefore that it is erratic. One can never know whether a particular conclusion will be so offensive to the particular judge to qualify as an absurdity and, if so, whether the court will feel moved to apply the golden rather than the literal rule. There are plenty of decisions in which the courts have preferred to follow the literal approach notwithstanding the fact that it led to absurdity. But a further and equally strong objection is that the rule is silent as to how the court should proceed if it does find an unacceptable absurdity. It must find an answer to the problem, but the rule gives the court no guidance as to how it should set about the task. The golden rule is therefore little more than an unpredictable safety-valve to permit the courts to escape from some of the more unpalatable effects of the literal rule. It cannot be regarded as a sound basis for judicial decision-making.

(c) Is the mischief rule any better?

The mischief rule is a very great improvement on the other two, in that it at least encourages the court to have regard to the context in which the doubtful words appear. It is therefore entirely different from the literal and the golden rules which direct attention instead purely at the words themselves. Language cannot be properly understood without some knowledge of the context. ('Teach the children a game' is not likely to be intended to include strip poker.) It is therefore obviously sensible to permit and even encourage the court to go beyond the narrow confines of the disputed phrase itself. The mischief rule is designed to get the court to consider why the Act was passed and then to apply that knowledge in giving the words under consideration whatever meaning will best accord with the social purpose of the legislation.

But a crucial issue is where the court may look to discover 'the mischief'. As Lord Diplock explained in *Black Clawson* [1975] A.C. 591

at 638, when the mischief rule was first propounded, the judges were not supposed to look further than the statute itself:

LORD DIPLOCK: Statutes in the sixteenth century and for long thereafter in addition to the enacting words contained lengthy preambles reciting the particular mischief or defect in the common law that the enacting words were designed to remedy. So, when it was laid down, the 'mischief' rule did not require the court to travel beyond the actual words of the statute itself to identify 'the mischief and defect for which the common law did not provide', for this would have been stated in the preamble. It was a rule of construction of the actual words appearing in the statute and nothing else. In construing modern statutes which contain no preambles to serve as aids to the construction of enacting words the 'mischief' rule must be used with caution to justify any reference to extraneous documents for this purpose.

The right to inquire into the background to, and reasons for, legislation is therefore restricted. What then is permitted?

4. Understanding the context – Statutes and judicial decisions

(a) The court can read the whole statute

There is no doubt, first of all, that a court may read the whole of the statute that has produced the problem. It may also read both *the long and the short title*. Until well into the nineteenth century, the long title could not be considered in construing a statute – on the ground that it was not regarded as part of the statute. But the modern view, which emerged during the nineteenth century, is that the title of the statute may be consulted for the purpose of ascertaining its meaning.*

It may also read *the preamble*. Old statutes commonly had lengthy preambles setting out the purposes of the legislation; today they are rare. But the House of Lords ruled decisively in 1957 that the courts could have regard to the preamble when construing a statute. The case was *Attorney General* v. *Prince Ernest Augustus of Hanover* [1957] A.C. 436, in which the courts had to consider an application by the Prince to be recognised as a British subject under a statute which granted British nationality to 'all persons lineally descended from the Electoress Sophia of Hanover'. Lord Normand said (at 467, 468):

When there is a preamble it is generally in its recitals that the mischief to be remedied and the scope of the Act are described. It is therefore clearly

* For examples see, for instance *Fisher* v. *Raven* [1964] A.C. 210; *Brown* v. *Brown* [1967] P. 105 at p. 110; *Haines* v. *Herbert* [1963] 1 W.L.R. 1401 at 1404.

permissible to have recourse to it as an aid to construing the enacting provisions. ... The courts are concerned with the practical business of deciding a *lis*, and when plaintiff puts forward one construction of an enactment and the defendant another, it is the court's business in any case of some difficulty, after informing itself of what I have called the legal and factual context including the preamble, to consider in the light of this knowledge whether the enacting words admit of both the rival constructions put forward. If they admit of only one construction, that construction will receive effect even if it is inconsistent with the preamble, but if the enacting words are capable of either of the constructions offered by the parties, the construction which fits the preamble may be preferred.

In *Prince Ernest's* case it was found that the enacting words were clear and they could not therefore be affected by contrary indications in a rather vague preamble.

Marginal notes printed at the side of sections in an Act which purport to summarise their effect have sometimes been used as an aid to construction. But the weight of the authorities is to the effect that they are not part of the statute and should not be considered, for they are 'inserted not by Parliament nor under the authority of Parliament but by irresponsible persons' (*Re Woking Urban Council (Basingstoke Canal) Act 1911* [1914] 1 Ch. 300 per Phillimore L.J. at 322).

The *headings* prefixed to sections or sets of sections in some statutes are regarded as preambles to those sections. They may explain ambiguous words. But clear words in the statute cannot be affected by contrary indications in the heading (*R.* v. *Surrey (N.E. Area) Assessment Committee* [1948] 1 K.B. 29 at 32, 33).

Schedules to a statute are treated as fully part of the statute and may be used in construing the Act.

By one of the more bizarre rules of statutory interpretation, punctuation is supposed to be disregarded in the construction of statutes since there was normally no punctuation in ancient statutes. Before 1850 there was no punctuation and there was no authority for the printers to insert any thereafter. In a modern tax case Lord Reid said 'even if punctuation in more modern Acts can be looked at (which is very doubtful), I do not think that one can have any regard to punctuation in older Acts' (*I.R.C.* v. *Hinchy* [1960] A.C. 748 at 765). The effect of this principle is that existing punctuation in a statute can be ignored or, if the court chooses, it can re-punctuate the words in a way different from that in the text.

An Act is to be read as a whole, so the court can and indeed should read all of a statute in order to understand any particular part of it.

So, in *Gibson* v. *Ryan* [1968] 1 Q.B. 250 the question for the court was whether an inflatable rubber dinghy and a fish basket found on the appellant were within the meaning of the word 'instrument' in s. 7 (1) of the Salmon and Freshwater Fisheries Protection (Scotland) Act 1951. The Divisional Court said they were not. Diplock L.J. referred to s. 10 of the Act which drew a distinction between instruments on the one hand, boats on the other hand and baskets on the third hand.

But sometimes the court may find that a word used in one part of a statute is not to be given the same meaning as the same word in a different part of the same statute. Everything depends on the particular context.

(b) The court can read earlier statutes

Sometimes, by tracing the history of a particular phrase back through earlier Acts one can throw light on its meaning. If the language changes between one statute and another, inferences can be drawn from the fact; alternatively, sometimes understanding of meaning can be based on a similarity of language in the present Act and some earlier statute when the historical position was different. In *Armah* v. *Government of Ghana* [1968] A.C. 192 the court had to interpret s. 5 of the Fugitive Offenders Act 1891 which required that evidence should raise 'a strong or probable presumption that the fugitive committed the offence'. Lord Reid showed that nineteenth-century Acts drew a distinction between two kinds of evidence – that which raised a strong presumption of guilt and that which simply gave reason to inquire into guilt. The distinction, he said, must have been known to those who framed the 1891 Act and indicated that the disputed words must refer to the first kind of evidence. It was therefore not sufficient for the magistrate to be satisfied that there was enough evidence against the fugitive on which a jury might properly convict.

A phrase used in one Act can be construed by reference to the same or a similar phrase used in earlier Acts – at least if the Acts deal with the same subject-matter. But the qualification about the similarity of the subject-matter is not always made. The Betting and Gaming Act 1960, for instance, required an applicant for a betting shop to insert a notice 'in a newspaper circulating in the authority's area'. It was held that an advertisement in *Sporting Life* was sufficient and that the Act did not require an advertisement either in a local paper or in a national paper circulating in the area. The court drew a distinction between the 1960 Act and s. 12 of the Highways Act 1959 which specifically referred to 'a local newspaper circulating in the area' (*R.* v. *Westminster Betting Licensing Committee, ex p. Peabody Donation Fund* [1963] 2 Q.B. 750).

The last case cited is an example of the court inferring that the draftsman of one piece of legislation is aware of the use of similar phrases in earlier Acts and that a difference in wording between one Act and another is conscious and intentional. This theory, based on the omniscience of parliamentary draftsmen, is often carried to improbable lengths. It may be that the draftsman of say, the latest Rent Act will be aware of the use of language in previous Rent Acts – though given the extreme length and complexity of such legislation even that may be assuming a good deal too much. But it is hardly reasonable to assume that the draftsman has in mind the language used in a mass of other prior statutes which have no direct connection with the one he is presently engaged in drafting.

An example of the court being influenced by the assumption that parliament must be deemed to have been aware of earlier legislation and non-usage regarding the meaning of the words 'immoral conduct' was *Crook* v. *Edmondson.* Consider whether the majority's view in this regard was reasonable?

Crook v. *Edmondson* [1966] 1 All E.R. 833 (Divisional Court, Q.B.D.)

E., a male, was charged with persistently soliciting for immoral purposes through 'kerb-crawling' in a public place contrary to s. 32 of the Sexual Offences Act 1956. The Act was a consolidation measure. Its preamble said it was to 'consolidate . . . the statute law of England and Wales relating to sexual crimes, to the abduction, procuration and prostitution of women and to kindred offences'. The statute repealed, inter alia, the Vagrancy Act 1898, s. 1 (1) of which made it an offence for a male person persistently to solicit or importune for immoral purposes in any public place. The justices dismissed the case on the ground that although the conduct of the accused was immoral it was not within the meaning of 'immoral purposes' in the 1956 Act. The prosecution appealed. The Divisional Court was divided.

WINN L.J.: In my judgment the words 'immoral purposes' in their ordinary meaning connote in a wide and general sense all purposes involving conduct which has the property of being wrong rather than right in the judgment of the majority of contemporary fellow citizens. In that sense, as the justices appreciated, the words are, at least arguably, apt to cover the conduct alleged against the respondent in the present case.

However I am convinced at least of this. That Parliament cannot be supposed to have used those words in their general sense, as comprising all wrong conduct, in a statute relating solely to sexual offences; soliciting persons to commit non-sexual crime is dealt with by the law relating to accessories before the fact or specifically by statute, e.g., in respect of mutiny, breach of security or Post Office offences. It seems to me to follow that the 'immoral purposes' here in question must be immoral in respect of sexual conduct. If, then, some limitation is properly to be put on the words the problem is to define their meaning in less general terms. There is a presumption in construing a consolidating statute that it is not intended to alter the law enacted by any statute which it repeals and a further, perhaps less persuasive, presumption that words or phrases which have obtained, at the time when any enactment is passed, an accepted meaning by force of decisions or usage of courts or even of the public, have been used by Parliament to convey the like meaning and effect. The court has not been informed by affirmative evidence, nor were the justices, that in 1898 sexual intercourse or intimacy between a man and a female prostitute was 'immoral', in the sense of the definition which I have adopted (scilicet without reference to any matrimonial implication). What is known, by concession of counsel for the appellant, is that there is no reported case in which any court so treated, or it seems was invited so to treat, such conduct. Parliament must be taken, I think, to have been aware of what may be perhaps termed 'this non-usage', extending over a period of over fifty years before 1956, no less than of the usage which had by then become general of relying on the Act of 1898 in charging males with inviting homosexual intimacies whether or not for reward. If s. 32 of the Act of 1956 is to be given the meaning contended for by the prosecution it effected a marked change not shown to be intended by any other provision of the Act of 1956. In their context in the Act of 1898 the words 'solicits ... for immoral purposes' may well, it seems to me, have been intended to relate not merely to soliciting for homosexual intimacies but also to the soliciting of customers for prostitutes, sometimes called 'pimping', as well as conceivably, to persuasion of girls to become prostitutes. In my judgment such a context and the context of subject-matter of trading in or exploiting prostitution even more plainly displayed by s. 22 to s. 31 and s. 33 to s. 36 of the Sexual Offences Act, 1956, must, apart altogether from any considerations derived from the history and application of the relevant legislation and practice, produce a controlling effect on the construction of s. 32 of the Act of 1956. A possible view of that effect might be that it is equivalent to expanding the phrase in the section into: such immoral purposes as are referred to in this part of the Act of 1956. That was the view of the justices and I concur in it solely for the purposes of the present appeal and to the extent which they require: I am not prepared, however, to attempt any definition of the section. It is enough to say that in my view the conduct alleged was not an offence under the section.

It is noteworthy, I think, as the justices thought, when considering how special is the s. 32 offence, that the penalty is six months' imprisonment on summary trial, or on an indictment two years; that any person may arrest, without a warrant, any person found committing it; that a person accused under the section has no right to claim to be tried on indictment under s. 25 of the Magistrates' Courts Act, 1952; that women cannot be charged with the offence. For the reasons which I have endeavoured to state, whilst I recognise that the prosecution had in this case the good motive of protecting virtuous women from annoyance, I think that they have sought to put on the relevant words a meaning which is not only new but unwarranted. I would dismiss this appeal.*

LORD PARKER C.J.: I have had the advantage of reading the judgment which has just been delivered by WINN L.J.; I entirely agree and have nothing to add.

SACHS J., read the following judgment: The essence of the case for the prosecution was that the respondent spoke in succession to two known common prostitutes in a street which they frequent in order to solicit for prostitution: there was no evidence of the respondent having approached anyone other than a common prostitute. It is thus an inference that can and probably should be drawn that at the material time each woman was herself soliciting — offering herself for payment. On giving the matter further consideration it now seems to me that there arose a serious issue whether the prosecution had on those facts established a prima facie case that the respondent had solicited or importuned anyone. Do the words 'solicit or importune' when properly construed apply to a man who has done no more than approach a common prostitute who has in fact already offered herself to him for money?

This issue, however, was one which was not canvassed before this court, ... nor was it part of the question raised for the consideration of this court, i.e.,

> 'The question for the opinion of the High Court is whether the persistent importuning by a man of a woman for the purpose of having sexual intercourse with him, is an offence under s. 32 of the Sexual Offences Act, 1956.'

It would in these circumstances not be proper for me to express an opinion on this issue, although had it been raised it might have enabled a decision to be reached in this case without having to deal with the above question.

On that question itself I have the considerable misfortune to differ, with natural diffidence, from the views of the majority of this court. I agree that 'immoral purposes' in s. 32 of the Act of 1956 must relate to sexual purposes. I also consider (in agreement, I think, with what has been said by WINN L.J.), that one cannot insert the words 'another man' after the word 'importune' (so as to make it read 'solicit or importune another man for immoral purposes') either in s. 32 of the Act of 1956 or in the earlier Vagrancy Act, 1898. I am, however, unable to agree that in s. 32 one can in effect substitute for the broad words 'immoral purposes' some such words as 'purposes which by

* In the debates on the Street Offences Act 1959 however the Lord Chancellor said that s. 32 of the 1956 Sexual Offences Act covered pestering of women by men and that there was therefore no need for an amendment to cover such solicitation (House of Lords, *Hansard*, vol. 216, col. 806.).

other provisions of this Act are declared to be offences': and a fortiori would be unable to agree to such a substitution in the Act of 1898. As in other matters which touch the field of public morals (cf. per the speeches of VISCOUNT SIMONDS, LORD MORRIS OF BORTH-Y-GEST and LORD HODSON in *Shaw* v. *Director of Public Prosecutions* [1962] A.C. 220, 268, 292, 293), it seems to my mind appropriate that the decision as to what is an 'immoral purpose'' should be the responsibility of the jury of the day or of whoever is entrusted with that decision in lieu of a jury. I would, incidentally, be averse to that decision being fettered by the result of any preliminary inquiry either what were the prevalent sexual vices at the end of the last century or what were then the prevalent views on some aspect of sexual immorality. If on the basis just expressed it were found that the now unfortunately prevalent conduct known as kerb crawling (i.e. a man from a slowly driven car importuning ordinary young women to accompany him for sexual intercourse) fell within the ambit of s. 32, that would not seem to me inherently wrong. Accordingly, I would have preferred to reserve the position as to what is the answer to the exact question posed in the Case Stated: whilst on the particular facts of this case not regretting the failure of this prosecution as proposed by my lords.

But *Farrell* v. *Alexander* [1977] A.C. 59, shows that the assumption that the draftsman knew of the existing statutory precedents or even case law should not *necessarily* be made. The House of Lords was interpreting the meaning of the words 'any person' in the Rent Act 1968, a consolidation measure. In 1972 the Court of Appeal had held that the words in that context meant 'the landlord' and did not include tenants, agents and other middlemen. In its 1972 decision the Court of Appeal had placed emphasis on the fact that in 1921 the Court of Appeal had construed the words 'any person' in a similar provision of an earlier Act in such a way as to limit its meaning to landlords. In 1949 and 1965 there had been further legislation on the same topic and parliament had used the same phrase. It was contended that this showed that parliament intended the phrase to mean only landlords. Lord Wilberforce disagreed:

LORD WILBERFORCE (at 74): My Lords, I have never been attracted by the doctrine of parliamentary endorsement of decided cases: it seems to me to be based upon a theory of legislative formation which is possibly fictional. But if there are cases in which this doctrine may be applied, and I must respect the opinions of those judges who have so held, any case must be a clear one. ... This case is certainly not such a case. It really cannot be said if our reasoning is to have any contact with reality that the draftsman of the Act of 1949 (a) must have had in mind a decision of 1921 [*Remmington* v. *Larchin* [1921] 3 K.B. 404], whose reported headnote opens with the words 'that section 8 (1) was reasonably capable of two constructions' and all of the judgments in which underlined the ambiguity and obscurity of the enactment, (b) decided to perpetuate this ambiguity while removing one of the grounds of the decision, (c) should have committed Parliament to the continued existence of a lacuna or loophole which had no merits to commend it.

To impute such a process of thought to the architect of the new section and to those who voted it into existence really strains credibility.

LORD SIMON OF GLAISDALE likewise thought the doctrine was sometimes carried too far:

It is a fact that a parliamentary draftsman (like any draftsman) does acquaint himself thoroughly with the existing law (statutory and judge-made) before starting to draft. Any draftsman of a rent restriction Act after 1921 may be presumed (nor is it an idle presumption) to have had *Remmington* v. *Larchin* in mind. When, then, he used language which had been interpreted in *Remmington* v. *Larchin* he presumptively used it in the sense in which it had there been interpreted. If therefore the object of statutory interpretation were to ascertain what Parliament meant to say, the *Barras* doctrine would indeed be potent and primary. But the object of statutory interpretation is rather to ascertain the meaning of what Parliament has said. On this approach the previous judicial interpretation is merely one of the facts within the knowledge of the draftsman in the light of which he will draft.... If Parliament wishes to endorse the previous interpretation it can do so in terms.... The sovereignty of Parliament is fundamental constitutional law; but courts of law have their own constitutional duties, important amongst which is to declare the meaning of a statutory enactment. To pre-empt a court of construction from performing independently its own constitutional duty of examining the validity of a previous interpretation, the intention of Parliament to endorse the previous judicial decision would have to be expressed or clearly implied. Mere repetition of language which has been the subject of previous judicial interpretation is entirely neutral in this respect – or at most implies merely the truism that the language has been the subject of judicial interpretation, for whatever (and it may be much or little) that is worth [at 90–1.]

In this particular case the House of Lords decided to extend the meaning of 'any person' to include a wider range of persons and it was therefore seeking for ways around the argument that parliament must have been assumed to have meant the same by the phrase as in the cases decided in 1949 and 1965 and 1968. The 1968 Act was a consolidation Act and three of the Lords (Lords Wilberforce, Simon and Edmund-Davies) said that if the words of a consolidation measure were clear there was no need to refer to the legislative antecedents. Again this is a way for a court to disembarrass itself of the awkward fact that the legislative history suggests a different answer to the problem than the one it had in mind. Given the difference of judicial opinion over the meaning of the words 'any person', it was somewhat disingenuous to argue that they were so clear as not to require elucidation, inter alia, from the previous legislation on the subject.

5. Understanding the context – evidence beyond statutes and judicial decisions

In the *Attorney General* v. *Prince Ernest Augustus* [1957] A.C. 436 Lord Simonds, normally a strict constructionist, stated that in interpreting a statute 'I conceive it to be my right and duty to examine every word of a statute in its context, and I use 'context' in its widest sense, which I have already indicated as including not only other enacting provisions of the same statute, but its preamble, the existing state of the law, other statutes in pari materia, and the mischief which I can by those *and other legitimate means*, discern the statute was intended to remedy' (at 461, emphasis supplied).

By his phrase 'and other legitimate means' Lord Simonds suggested that the search for the context might properly go beyond the statute itself, other statutes and the precedents. In 1938 John Willis, in his article 'Statute Interpretation in a Nutshell', argued that the mischief rule was 'without doubt unworkable' because of the narrow way in which the courts interpreted the nature of the materials that might be consulted: 'You cannot interpret an Act in the light of its policy without knowing what that policy is: that you cannot discover without referring to all the events which led up to the legislation: but a well-settled rule of law forbids reference to any matters extrinsic to the written words of the Act as printed'. (*Canadian Bar Review*, 1938, p. 15.) But since that time there has been some development of the law.

(a) General historical background

The courts have always been willing to hear counsel state what he understands the general historical setting of legislation to have been, where this is relevant. Counsel may certainly cite earlier cases for this purpose and may also probably refer to legal textbooks. Often the court will refer to such surrounding circumstances in the course of its judgment. But this is not to say that the court would welcome citation by counsel of historical works by learned non-lawyer authors. If this were attempted by counsel, it would be likely to be resisted by the court.

(b) Government publications

There are two categories of official publication. One is the report of a committee – Royal Commission, departmental committee, Law Commission, etc. – which precedes and leads to the statute in question. The second is any other form of material. The rule in regard to the latter is supposed to be clear – the courts may not look at any such document either for the purposes of understanding the mischief or of construing the words in question. The courts are not, for instance, permitted to look at the explanatory memorandum attached to all bills before parliament. (See *Escoigne Properties Ltd* v. *I.R.C.* [1958] A.C. 549). In *Katikiro of Buganda* v. *Attorney General* [1961] 1 W.L.R. 119, a White Paper containing the recommendations of a constitutional conference held in Uganda was held inadmissible as an aid to the construction of the Buganda Agreement, 1955 (Order in Council, 1955).

There are three House of Lords decisions on the use that may be made of official reports that are followed by legislation.

In *Eastman Photographic Materials Co. Ltd* v. *Comptroller General of Patents* [1898] A.C. 571, Lord Halsbury reacted favourably to the suggestion that the court should consider the report of a Royal Commission which had led up to the passing of the Act under consideration: 'I think no more accurate source of information as to what the evil or defect which the act of Parliament now under consideration was intended to remedy could be imagined than the Report of that Commission' (at p. 575). But in 1935 in *Assam Rly Co. Ltd* v. *Inland Revenue Cmnr* [1935] A.C. 445 the House again had to decide whether to consider a Royal Commission report which had led to the enactment of a taxing provision. Counsel for one party argued that the report should be received as evidence of the intention of the legislature in passing the relevant section. The House of Lords rejected this contention, LORD WRIGHT saying (at 458):

> But on principle no such evidence for the purpose of showing the intention, that is the purpose or object, of an Act is admissible; the intention of the legislature must be ascertained from the words of the statute with such extraneous assistance as is legitimate. ... It is clear that the language of a Minister of the Crown in proposing in Parliament a measure which eventually becomes law is inadmissible and the Report of Commissioners is even more removed from value as evidence of intention, because it does not follow that their recommendations were accepted.

He distinguished the dictum of Lord Halsbury in the *Eastman Photographic* case on the basis that the Royal commission had been admitted there simply as 'extraneous matter to show what were the surrounding circumstances with reference to which the words were used' (at 459).

But the locus classicus on the admissibility of official reports that precede legislation is now the *Black-Clawson* case.* The Law Lords divided as to whether such reports could be consulted in the construction of the disputed words under consideration. Two (Lords Reid and Wilberforce) thought that they could not, even where the legislation corresponded exactly with the draft bill in the report; two (Lords Dilhorne and Simon of Glaisdale) disagreed. Lord Diplock thought they could be used to understand the context, including the construction of an ambiguous phrase, so as to give effect to parliament's aim. But all five held that the reports were admissible for the purpose of understanding the mischief with which the legislation was intended to deal. The relevant extracts from all five judgments are set out below. They are set out at length not so much to state the law as for their intrinsic interest on the general problem of the search for the context.

LORD REID (at 613–14): It has always been said to be important to consider the 'mischief' which the Act was apparently intended to remedy. The word 'mischief' is traditional. I would expand it in this way. In addition to reading the Act you look at the facts presumed to be known to Parliament when the Bill which became the Act in question was before it, and you consider whether there is disclosed some unsatisfactory state of affairs which Parliament can properly be supposed to have intended to remedy by the Act. There is a presumption which can be stated in various ways. One is that in the absence of any clear indication to the contrary Parliament can be presumed not to have altered the common law further than was necessary to remedy the 'mischief'. Of course it may and quite often does go further. But the principle is that if the enactment is ambiguous, that meaning which relates the scope of the Act to the mischief should be taken rather than a different or wider meaning which the contemporary situation did not call for. The mischief which this Act was intended to remedy may have been common knowledge 40 years ago. I do not think that it is today. But it so happens that a committee including many eminent and highly skilled members made a full investigation of the matter and reported some months before the Act was passed: Foreign Judgments (Reciprocal Enforcement) Committee 1932 (Cmd. 4213).

I think that we can take this report as accurately stating the 'mischief' and the law as it was then understood to be, and therefore we are fully entitled to look at those parts of the report which deal with those matters.

* *Black-Clawson International Ltd* v. *Papierwerke Waldhof-Aschaffenburg A.G.* [1975] A.C. 591.

But the report contains a great deal more than that. It contains recommendations, a draft Bill and other instruments intended to embody those recommendations, and comments on what the committee thought the Bill achieved. The draft Bill corresponds in all material respects with the Act so it is clear that Parliament adopted the recommendations of the committee. But nevertheless I do not think that we are entitled to take any of this into account in construing the Act.

Construction of the provisions of an Act is for the court and for no one else. This may seem technical but it is good sense. Occasionally we can find clear evidence of what was intended; more often any such evidence, if there is any, is vague and uncertain. If we are to take into account evidence of Parliament's intention the first thing we must do is to reverse our present practice with regard to consulting Hansard. I have more than once drawn attention to the practical difficulties that would involve, but the difficulty goes deeper. The questions which give rise to debate are rarely those which later have to be decided by the courts. One might take the views of the promoters of a Bill as an indication of the intention of Parliament but any view the promoters may have had about questions which later come before the court will not often appear in Hansard and often those questions have never occurred to the promoters. At best we might get material from which a more or less dubious inference might be drawn as to what the promoters intended or would have intended if they had thought about the matter, and it would, I think, generally be dangerous to attach weight to what some other members of either House may have said. The difficulties in assessing any references there might have been in Parliament to the question before the court are such that, in my view, our best course is to adhere to present practice.

If we are to refrain from considering expressions of intention in Parliament it appears to me that a fortiori we should disregard expressions of intention by committees or royal commissions which reported before the Bill was introduced. I may add that we did in fact examine the whole of this report—it would have been difficult to avoid that—but I am left in some doubt as to how the committee would have answered some of the questions which we have now to answer, because I do not think that they were ever considered by the committee.

LORD WILBERFORCE (at 629–30): My Lords, we are entitled, in my opinion, to approach the interpretation of this subsection, and of the Act of 1933 as a whole, from the background of the law as it stood, or was thought to stand, in 1933 and of the legislative intention. As to these matters the report to which my noble and learned friend, Lord Reid, has referred is of assistance. He has set out in his opinion the basis upon which the courts may consult such documents. I agree with his reasoning and I only desire to add an observation of my own on one point. In my opinion it is not proper or desirable to make use of such a document as a committee or commission report, or for that matter of anything reported as said in Parliament, or any official notes on clauses, for a direct statement of what a proposed enactment is to mean or of what the committee or commission thought it means – on this point I am in agreement with my noble and learned friend Lord Diplock. To be concrete, in a case where a committee prepared a draft Bill and accompanies that by a clause by clause commentary, it ought not to be permissible, even if the proposed Bill is enacted without variation, to take the meaning of the Bill from the commentary. There are, to my mind, two kinds of reason for this. The first is the practical one, that if this process were allowed the courts would merely have to interpret, as in argument we were invited to interpret, two documents instead of one – the Bill and the commentary on it, in particular annex V, paragraph 13. The second is one of constitutional principle. Legislation in England is passed by Parliament, and put in the form of written words. This legislation is given legal effect upon subjects by virtue of judicial decision, and it is the function of the courts to say what the application of the words used to particular cases or individuals is to be. This power which has been devolved upon the judges from the earliest times is an essential part of the constitutional process by which subjects are brought under the rule of law – as distinct from the rule of the King or the rule of Parliament; and it would be a degradation of that process if the courts were to be merely a reflecting mirror of what some other interpretation agency might say. The saying that it is the function of the courts to ascertain the will or intention of Parliament is often enough repeated, so often indeed as to have become an incantation. If too often or unreflectingly stated, it leads to neglect of the important element of judicial construction; an element not confined to a mechanical analysis of today's words, but, if this task is to be properly done, related to such matters as intelligibility to the citizen, constitutional propriety, considerations of history, comity of nations, reasonable and non-retroactive effect and, no doubt, in some contexts, to social needs.

LORD DIPLOCK (at 637–8): I do not understand any of your Lordships go so far as to suggest that a court is entitled to put a strained construction on the words in s. 8 in order to give them the effect the committee thought they had, if this would involve departing from their plain and natural meaning. It is for the court and no one else to decide what words in a statute mean. What the committee thought they meant is, in itself irrelevant. Oral evidence by members of the committee as to their opinion of what the section meant would plainly be inadmissible. It does not become admissible by being reduced to writing.

What is suggested is that recourse may be had to the report as an aid to construction in order to ascertain, first, what the existing law was understood to be upon the subject matter of the Act; and, secondly, what was the mischief for which Parliament intended to provide a remedy by the Act.

As regards the first of these purposes for which recourse may be had to the report, the Act deals with a technical subject matter – the treatment to be accorded by courts in the United Kingdom to judgments of foreign courts. The expressions used in it are terms of legal art which were in current use in English and Scots law at the time the Act was passed. In order to understand their meaning the court must inform itself as to what the existing law was upon this technical subject matter. In order to do this it may have recourse to decided cases, to legal textbooks or other writings of recognised authorities, among whom would rank the members of the committee. Their report contains a summary of the existing law, as they understood it. As such it is part of the material to which the court may have recourse for the purpose of ascertaining what was the existing law upon the subject matter of the Act. There is, however, no real doubt as to what it was....

The acceptance of the rule of law as a constitutional principle requires that a citizen, before committing himself to any course of action, should be able to know in advance what are the legal consequences that will flow from it. Where those consequences are regulated by a statute the source of that knowledge is what the statute says. In construing it the court must give effect to what the words of the statute would be reasonably understood to mean by those whose conduct it regulates. That any or all of the individual members of the two Houses of the Parliament that passed it may have thought the words bore a different meaning cannot affect the matter. Parliament, under our constitution, is sovereign only in respect of what it expresses by the words used in the legislation it has passed.

This is not to say that where those words are not clear and unambiguous in themselves but are fairly susceptible of more than one meaning, the court, for the purpose of resolving – though not of inventing – an ambiguity, may not pay regard to authoritative statements that were matters of public knowledge at the time the Act was passed, as to what were regarded as deficiencies in that branch of the existing law with which the Act deals. Where such statements are made in official reports commissioned by government, laid before Parliament and published, they clearly fall within this category and may be used to resolve the ambiguity in favour of a meaning which will result in correcting those deficiencies in preference to some alternative meaning that will leave the deficiencies uncorrected. The justification of this use of such reports as an aid to the construction of the words used in the statute is that knowledge of their contents may be taken to be shared by those whose conduct the statute regulates and would influence their understanding of the meaning of ambiguous enacting words.

LORD DILHORNE (at 622–3): The task confronting a court when construing a statute is to determine what was Parliament's intention. In a perfect world the language employed in the Act would not be capable of more than one interpretation but due in part to the lack of precision of the English language, often more than one interpretation is possible. Then, to enable Parliament's intention to be determined, as I understand the position, one may have regard to what was the law at the time of the enactment and to what was the mischief at which it was directed.

That one can look at such reports to discern the mischief is now, I think, established but there is a difference of opinion as to what may be looked at in such reports. Can one have regard to the recommendations of the committee or commission? Where a draft Bill is attached to the report, as is now frequently the case, and was the case in this instance, can one refer to the terms of the draft Bill when they have been enacted without material alteration by Parliament? Can one refer to the notes on the clauses of the draft Bill appended to it by the committee, and in the present case to the terms of the draft conventions prepared by the committee and attached to their report? Is it legitimate to make use of such parts of a report as an aid to the construction of the Act?

In my opinion it is. The reason why one is entitled to consider what was the mischief at which the Act was aimed is surely that that will throw a revealing light on the object and purpose of the Act, that is to say the intention of Parliament; what more accurate source of information both as to the law at the time and as to the evil or defect which the Act was intended to remedy can be imagined than the report of such a committee or, for that matter, the reports of the Law Commission?

The contrary view seems to impose on judges the task of being selective in their reading of such reports. What part may they look at and what not? Have they to stop reading when they come to a recommendation? Have they to ignore the fact, if it be the fact, that the draft Bill was enacted without alteration? To ignore what the committee intended the draft Bill to do and what the committee thought it would do? I think not.

I think so to hold would be to draw a very artificial line which serves no useful purpose. What weight is to be given to a committee's recommendation is another matter. That may depend on the particular circumstances. If the report of the committee merely contains recommendations, while I think that regard can be had to them, little weight may be attached to them as it may not follow that Parliament had accepted them. Parliament may have decided to go further or not so far. But where, as here, a draft Bill is attached to the report, then one can compare its provisions with those of the Act and if there is no difference or no material difference in their language, then surely it is legitimate to conclude, as Greene M.R. did in *Shenton* v. *Tyler* [1939] Ch. 620, that Parliament had accepted the recommendation of the committee and had intended to implement it. In such a case that recommendation becomes as it did in *Eastman Photographic Materials Co. Ltd.* v. *Comptroller-General of Patents, Designs, and Trade Marks* [1898] A.C. 571 the most accurate source of information as to the intention of Parliament....

It does not follow that if one can have regard to the whole of a committee's report, one ought also to be able to refer to Hansard to see what the Minister in charge of a Bill has said it was intended to do. In the course of the passage of a Bill through both Houses there may be many statements by Ministers, and what is said by a Minister in introducing a Bill in one House is no sure guide as to the intention of the enactment, for changes of intention may occur during its passage. But when a Bill is drafted by such a committee as that in this case and enacted without alteration, then, I repeat, in my opinion it is legitimate to have regard to the whole of the committee's report, including the terms of the draft Bill attached to it, to the committee's notes on its clauses and to the draft conventions annexed to the report, for they constitute a most valuable guide to the intention of Parliament.

LORD SIMON OF GLAISDALE (at 646–7, 649, 651–2): A public report to Parliament is an important part of the matrix of a statute founded on it. Where Parliament is legislating in the light of a public report I can see no reason why a court of construction should deny itself any part of that light and insist on groping for a meaning in darkness or half-light. I conclude therefore that such a report should be available to the court of construction, so that the latter can put itself in the shoes of the draftsman and place itself on the parliamentary benches – in much the same way as a court of construction puts itself (as the saying goes) in the armchair of a testator. The object is the same in each case – namely, to ascertain the meaning of the words used, that meaning only being ascertainable if the court is in possession of the knowledge possessed by the promulgator of the instrument. ...

The most difficult question in this appeal, to my mind, arises out of the modern practice of annexation to a report to Parliament of a draft Bill with a commentary on it. Is such a commentary available to a court construing the ensuing statute? ...

My conclusion is that, regardless of the draft Bill and the commentary thereon, the Greer report is available as an aid to construction. ... It is, thus, strictly, unnecessary to decide whether the commentary on the draft Bill is also available as an aid to construction. But the technique of a draft Bill with commentary is so common nowadays in reports to Parliament as to excuse, I hope, some expatiation on the matter. The argument against recourse to such a commentary is that if what Parliament or parliamentarians (or, indeed, any promulgators of a written instrument) think is the meaning of what is said is irrelevant, so must be the opinion of any draftsman, including the draftsman of a Bill annexed to a report to Parliament. But I confess that I find this less than conclusive. In essence, drafting, enactment and interpretation are integral parts of the process of translating the volition of the electorate into rules which will bind themselves. ... The commentary on a draft Bill in a report to Parliament is not merely an expression of opinion – even if it were only that, it would be an expression of expert opinion, and I can see no more reason for excluding it than any other relevant matter of expert opinion. But actually it is more: that experts publicly expressed the view that a certain draft would have such-and-such an effect is one of the facts within the shared knowledge of Parliament and the citizenry. To refuse to consider such a commentary, when Parliament has legislated on the basis and faith of it, is for the interpreter to fail to put himself in the real position of the promulgator of the instrument before essaying its interpretation. It is refusing to follow what is perhaps the most important clue to meaning. It is perversely neglecting the reality, while chasing shadows. As Aneurin Bevan said: 'Why read the crystal when you can read the book?' Here the book is already open: it is merely a matter of reading on. Certainly, a court of construction cannot be precluded from saying that what the committee thought as to the meaning of its draft was incorrect. But that is one thing: to dismiss, out of hand and for all purposes, an authoritative opinion in the light of which Parliament has legislated is quite another.

So, as at present advised, I think that your Lordships would have been entitled, if necessary, to consider the commentary of the Greer committee on the draft Bill.

Questions

1. Lord Reid stated that because it was not possible to consult parliamentary debates, *a fortiori* the courts should not look at reports of committees and royal commissions. Do you agree that this follows *a fortiori*?

2. Lord Wilberforce rejected the notion of looking at committee reports to construe the words of the statute on the ground, inter alia, that it would require the courts to interpret two documents instead of one. Is this a convincing reason – particularly in view of the fact that Lord Wilberforce accepted that the courts could look at the reports for the purpose of understanding the mischief?

3. Lord Wilberforce's second main reason was the fear that if courts could look at reports to construe statutes the constitutional role of courts as interpreters of statutes would somehow be degraded. He had in mind especially, he said, the fact that interpretation required not only analysis of words but concern for 'intelligibility to the citizen, constitutional propriety, considerations of history, comity of nations, reasonable and non-retroactive effect and, no doubt, in some contexts, to social needs' (at 629–30). Do you think this is a good reason for not considering reports of committees on questions of construction?

4. Lord Diplock said that neither the written nor the oral evidence of the committee would make its view as to what the words in a statute meant admissible. He also said however that the courts may refer to the report of a committee to resolve an ambiguity of construction – because knowledge of the contents of a published report that has been laid before parliament may be taken to be shared by those whose conduct the statute regulates. Are these two statements reconcilable? (In the later case of *Davis* v. *Johnson* [1979] A.C. 264 at 329–30 Lord Diplock made it clear that his view was the same as that of Lords Reid and Wilberforce.)

5. Lords Reid and Wilberforce thought that the reports of official committees were admissible for the purpose of understanding the mischief but not for the purpose of construing the actual words of the statute. How can judges read a document for one purpose but exclude it from their minds for another? (See also pp. 77–82 below.)

(c) Parliamentary debates

The rule as to the admissibility of parliamentary debates is tolerably clear. Until recently it was agreed that no reference could legitimately be made by a court to anything said in the course of parliamentary debates. The rule was, however, brought into issue by Lord Denning in the course of the Court of Appeal's decision in *Davis* v. *Johnson*, where he confessed that he had been aided in reaching his view by what had been said in parliament:

Davis v. *Johnson* [1979] A.C. 264 (Court of Appeal)

The case concerned the provisions of the Domestic Violence and Matrimonial Proceedings Act 1976 and in particular whether the Act provided protection for cohabitees as well as wives.

LORD DENNING M.R. (at 276–7): Some may say, and indeed have said, that judges should not pay any attention to what is said in Parliament. They should grope about in the dark for the meaning of an Act without switching on the light. I do not accede to this view. In some cases Parliament is assured in the most explicit terms what the effect of a statute will be. It is on that footing that members assent to the clause being agreed to. It is on that understanding that an amendment is not pressed. In such cases I think the court should be able to look at the proceedings. And, as I read the observations of Lord Simon of Glaisdale in *Dockers' Labour Club and Institute Ltd* v. *Race Relations Board*[1] he thought so too. I would give an instance. In the debate on the Race Relations Act 1968 there was, I believe, a ministerial assurance given in Parliament about its application to clubs; and I have a feeling that some of their Lordships looked at it privately and were influenced by it: see *Charter* v. *Race Relations Board*.[2] I could wish that, in those club cases, we had been referred to it. It might have saved us from the error which the House afterwards held we had fallen into. And it is obvious that there is nothing to prevent a judge looking at these debates himself privately and getting some guidance from them. Although it may shock the purists, I may as well confess that I have sometimes done it. I have done it in this very case. It has thrown a flood of light on the position. The statements made in committee disposed completely of counsel for the respondent's argument before us.

The House of Lords [1979] A.C. 317 did not however look kindly on Lord Denning's approach. All five Lords said expressly that he was wrong. Lord Kilbrandon and Lord Salmon did not elaborate but the other three added some reasons and further thoughts:

LORD DILHORNE (at 337): There is one other matter to which I must refer. It is a well and long established rule that counsel cannot refer to Hansard as an aid to the construction of a statute. What is said by a Minister or by a member sponsoring a Bill is not a legitimate aid to the interpretation of an Act. As Lord Reid said in *Beswick* v. *Beswick* [[1968] A.C. 58 at 73–4]

> 'In construing any Act of Parliament we are seeking the intention of Parliament, and it is quite true that we must deduce that intention from the words of the Act ... For purely practical reasons we do not permit debates in either House to be cited: it would add greatly to the time and expense involved in preparing cases involving the construction of a statute if counsel were expected to read all the debates in Hansard, and it would often be impracticable for counsel to get access to at least the older reports

1. [1974] 3 All ER 592 at 600, 601; [1976] AC 285 at 299.
2. [1973] 1 All ER 512 at 526, 527; [1973] AC 868 at 899–901.

of debates in select committees of the House of Commons; moreover, in a very large proportion of cases such a search, even if practicable, would throw no light on the question before the court...'

If it was permissible to refer to Hansard, in every case concerning the construction of a statute counsel might regard it as necessary to search through the Hansards of all the proceedings in each House to see if in the course of them anything relevant to the construction had been said. If it was thought that a particular Hansard had anything relevant in it and the attention of the court was drawn to it, the court might also think it desirable to look at the other Hansards. The result might be that attention was devoted to the interpretation of ministerial and other statements in Parliament at the expense of consideration of the language in which Parliament had thought to express its intention. While, of course, anyone can look at Hansard, I venture to think that it would be improper for a judge to do so before arriving at his decision and before this case I have never known that done. It cannot be right that a judicial decision should be affected by matter which a judge has seen but to which counsel could not refer and on which counsel had no opportunity to comment.

LORD SCARMAN (at 349–50): There are two good reasons why the courts should refuse to have regard to what is said in Parliament or by Ministers as aids to the interpretations of a statute. First, such material is an unreliable guide to the meaning of what is enacted. It promotes confusion, not clarity. The cut and thrust of debate and the pressures of executive responsibility, essential features of open and responsible government, are not always conducive to a clear and unbiased explanation of the meaning of statutory language. And the volume of parliamentary and ministerial utterances can confuse by its very size. Secondly, counsel are not permitted to refer to Hansard in argument. So long as this rule is maintained by Parliament (it is not the creation of the judges), it must be wrong for the judge to make any judicial use of proceedings in Parliament for the purpose of interpreting statutes.

LORD DIPLOCK (at 329) drew a distinction between consulting parliamentary debates and continental courts or the European Court of Justice looking at *travaux préparatoires*:

I have had the advantage of reading what my noble and learned friends, Viscount Dilhorne and Lord Scarman, have to say about the use of Hansard as an aid to the construction of a statute. I agree with them entirely and would add a word of warning against drawing too facile an analogy between proceedings in the Parliament of the United Kingdom and those travaux préparatoires which may be looked at by the courts of some of our fellow member states of the European Economic Community to resolve doubts as to the interpretation of national legislation or by the European Court of Justice, and consequently by English courts themselves, to resolve doubts as to the interpretation of community legislation. Community legislation, viz regulations and directives, are required by the EEC Treaty to state reasons on which they are based, and when submitted to the EEC Council in the form of a proposal by the EEC Commission the practice is for them to be accompanied by an explanatory memorandum by the Commission expanding the reasons which appear in more summary form in the draft regulation or directive itself. The explanatory memoranda are published in the Official Journal together with the proposed regulations or directives to which they relate. These are true travaux préparatoires: they are of a very different character from what is said in the passion or lethargy of Parliamentary debate; yet a survey of the judgments of the European Court of Justice will show how rarely that court refers even to these explanatory memoranda for the purpose of interpreting community legislation.

There is of course nothing to stop a judge from 'cheating' by looking at the debates in the library, as Lord Denning indicated in *Davis* v. *Johnson* he had sometimes done. Evidence of 'cheating' may appear somewhat obliquely. In a Privy Council case in 1932, for instance, the judgment contains a passage taken virtually verbatim from the speech of Lord Carrington in the House of Lords on the British North America Act 1867. There is no reference to the source of the passage in the judgment but it is clear that parliamentary records were in fact consulted – see *In re The Regulation and Control of Aeronautics in Canada* [1932] A.C. 54. Occasionally the gist of parliamentary debates may be brought to the judges' attention by the more respectable route of reading to the court the analysis of legislative history in a textbook (see *Bradford City Council* v. *Lord Commissioners* (1978) unreported – referred to by Lord Denning in *The Discipline of Law* (1979), p. 10). Lord Denning has more recently discovered a new approach to this problem by stating, tongue in cheek, 'As to the statute, we are not allowed to read Hansard; but you can. You can find it if you turn up the debate' – and he gives the Hansard reference in a footnote (*R.* v. *IRC, ex parte Rossminster Ltd* [1979] 3 All E.R. 385 at 399).

6. Views of the Law Commission

The English and Scottish Law Commissioners (see p. 275 below) produced a major report on the problem in 1969 (*The Interpretation of Statutes*). It found that 'there is a tendency in our systems, less evident in some recent decisions of the courts but still perceptible, to over-emphasise the literal meaning of a provision (i.e. the meaning in the light of its immediate and obvious context at the expense of the meaning to be derived from other possible contexts; the latter include the "mischief" or general legislative purpose . . . which underlie the provision' (para. 80). The mischief rule stated in *Heydon's* case it thought was preferable to either the literal or the golden rule. The literal rule placed undue emphasis on the narrow meaning of words without regard to their context. The golden rule provided no way of testing the existence of absurdity, inconsistency or inconvenience, or to measure their quality or extent. But although the mischief rule was a better approach, it reflected a 'very different constitutional balance between the Executive, Parliament and the public than would now be acceptable'. Particularly under its fourth head, it did not make clear how the judge should balance his sense of the desirable remedy against the language used in the statute. Also *Heydon's* case was somewhat outdated in assuming that statute was subsidiary or supplemental to the common law, 'whereas in modern conditions many statutes mark a fresh point of departure rather than a mere addition to, and qualification of, common law principles'. (p. 20, para. 33.) Also 'if a court has inadequate means of discovering the policy behind a statute, a mere exhortation to consider that policy may not be very effective' (paras. 32–2).

The Law Commissions said that in their view the 'ultimate function of a court in the interpretative process' was 'to decide the meaning of the provision, taking into account, among other matters, the light which the actual language used, and the broader aspects of legislative policy arrived at by the golden and mischief rules, throw on that meaning' (para. 29).

In relation to the statute itself, it made only two main suggestions (paras. 41–5): (1) *punctuation* should be taken into account in interpreting statutory provisions; and (2) *marginal notes and headings* should both be available as aids to construction.

The Commissions however made more proposals regarding materials outside the statute itself:

(1) The courts should be able to refer to the *reports of official committees* for the purpose of understanding not only the mischief but also 'the nature and scope of the remedy provided':

It, is, of course, true that the specific recommendations of, for example, an official committee preceding the introduction of legislation may not have been accepted in whole or in part in the first place by the sponsors of the legislation or subsequently by parliament. If the resulting act makes clear which recommendations have been accepted and which rejected no problem arises. A practical difficulty may, however, occur where the meaning of a provision in an act varies according to whether it is, or is not, read in the context of a recommendation of an earlier committee which was before, but not necessarily accepted by, parliament. But it is also true, although less likely, that parliament may not have accepted in its entirety a committee's assessment of the mischief to be dealt with by legislation; yet the report of a committee could under existing law be considered in ascertaining the mischief. We think that any rigid distinction between the admissibility of material in ascertaining the mischief and in ascertaining the remedy provided is unjustified. It should be borne in mind that a court would not be bound to imply from the presence of a recommended remedy in, for example, a committee report that parliament accepted the remedy. Furthermore, if a court were entitled to look not only at a committee report but also at a White Paper, published after the appearance of the committee report but before or in connection with the Bill to which it related, the White Paper might inform the court as to the extent to which the recommendations had at that stage been accepted by the Government. The court of course would still have to determine whether any recommendations so accepted were in fact embodied in the resulting Act. [para. 52.]

(2) The courts should continue not to be allowed to consult *parliamentary debates* (para. 61). The Commissions gave a number of reasons. One was the unreliability of the debates as a source of guidance. It had been said that the process of legislation was not 'an intellectual exercise in the pursuit of truth but an essay in persuasion or perhaps almost seduction,' and that, in these circumstances, 'to appeal from the carefully pondered terms of the statute to the hurly-burly of Parliamentary debate is to appeal from Philip sober to Philip drunk'.* On the other hand, in many countries such materials were admissible and the courts learned to discriminate between the value of different kinds of material. The leading speeches of ministers, for instance, were regarded as more weighty than other speeches. Legislative debates tended to be regarded as less helpful than reports of legislative committees. But in our system there was no system for producing such committee reports. Another serious problem was the availability of parliamentary debates to practitioners.

In the setting of our own system we recognise that many legal practitioners, notably solicitors in places where library facilities are not conveniently available, may find it difficult to refer to the volumes of Hansard, and in particular to those volumes, not to be found in many libraries, which contain the reports of Parliamentary Standing Committees. We do not wish however to exaggerate this difficulty, as, if the legislative history of statutes was admissible, it is probable that the burden on the lawyer and other users of statutes would be lightened by the inclusion in text-books of the significant extracts from the legislative history of the statutes with which they deal. [para. 60.]

* J.A. Corry, 'The Use of Legislative History in the Interpretation of Statutes', 32 *Canadian Bar Review*, 1954, 624 at 631–2.

In reaching its conclusion the Commissions said they had been much influenced especially by three considerations:

(*a*) the difficulty arising from the nature of our Parliamentary process of isolating information which will assist the courts in interpreting statutes; (*b*) the consequent difficulty of providing such information as could be given in a reasonably convenient and readily accessible form; and (*c*) the possibility that in some cases the function of legislative material in the interpretative process could be better performed by specially prepared explanatory material available to Parliament when a Bill is introduced and modified, if necessary, to take account of amendments during its passage through Parliament. [para. 61.]

The Commissions did not even recommend that the court should be able to look at the amendments moved during the debates. One reason was that it would be difficult to extend this to amendments proposed but not made and that it would also have to consider statements in the debates as to the reasons underlying the rejection or withdrawal of an amendment. Moreover the value to be derived from such information would be outweighed by the burden on users of statutes of getting and studying copies of amendments (para. 62).

(3) The Commissions recommended the use of a *new type of explanatory memorandum* to assist the courts in the search for the context in which statutory provisions should be read. It would be a mixture of three existing documents:

(a) the preamble that used to be a feature of statutes;

(b) the explanatory memorandum attached to a bill, published for the benefit principally of members of the two Houses, giving a brief summary of its provisions;

(c) Notes on Clauses prepared by civil servants as a detailed brief to the minister responsible for piloting the legislation through each House.

The Law Commissions' proposed new explanatory memorandum would be drafted by the promoters of the bill and the bill to which it related would specifically authorise its use as an aid to interpretation. Ideally the document would be amended as the bill itself was amended and would receive ultimate parliamentary approval. Its status would be like that of a preamble under present law and practice. If this took up too much parliamentary time, an alternative would be to give the power to amend and approve to officials. Or officials might be required to submit it for parliamentary approval on Third Reading or perhaps by laying it before the House like an

Order in Council. But the document would not bind the courts:

> [E]ven if the explanatory statement were amended during the course of the Bill's passage and given some measure of Parliamentary approval, it would be no more binding on the courts than much other contextual material (e.g., other provisions of the statute, earlier legislation dealing with the same subject matter and non-statutory material dealing with the mischief) of which under the existing law the courts are entitled to take account. It might however give assistance to the courts in making more explicit the contextual assumptions which at present have to be gleaned sometimes with great difficulty from a number of sources of varying reliability. No interpretative device can relieve the courts of their ultimate responsibility for considering the different contexts in which the words of a provision might be read, and in making a choice between the different meanings which emerge from that consideration. The existence of an explanatory statement would not prevent a court from regarding the meaning of the words in an enacting provision in the light of other relevant contexts as so compelling that it must be preferred to a meaning suggested by the statement. As we have already pointed out, even Continental courts, which have a much wider freedom than our courts to consider contextual material outside the statute itself, are not bound by that material. [Para. 70.]

In order to test the viability of the idea, it might be used first for selected topics – for instance bills implementing Law Commission reports. The usefulness of an explanatory memorandum might be especially great for the kind of codification measures that the Law Commissions were to bring forward (see pp. 282 below):

> The degree of particularity in which the applications of these principles to specific situations are stated in the code may vary, but, even where detailed application is lacking, a court is expected to discover in the code the principles from which the answer to a particular problem can be worked out. In such a situation we think that an explanatory and illustrative commentary on the code could provide authoritative, but not compelling guidance on the interpretation of the code, which would be particularly valuable in the early years of the operation of the code.

But ten years after the Law Commissions' report on statutory interpretation it seemed that it had had little impact. The proposals regarding the admissibility of official reports as a means to aid in the construction of statutes had been rejected by the House of Lords in the *Black–Clawson* case (above, p. 68) – though there is evidence in the report of the case that the law lords actually looked at the Law Commission's report.* The only instance in which there appears to have been any attempt to implement the proposal that the Act

* See p. 69 above, per Lord Reid.

itself permit reference to some other report for guidance, was the case of the Animals Bill in 1969 – the year of the Law Commission's report.

When first introduced, the Animals Bill provided in clause 11 (2) that 'in ascertaining the meaning of any provisions of this Act, regard may be had to the Report of the Law Commission on Civil Liability for Animals (Law Commission No. 13)'. But the bill did not reach the statute book. The 1970 General Election intervened and when the measure was reintroduced by the incoming Conservative Government one of the amendments that had been made to the Labour Government's bill was the dropping of clause 11 (2).

Nor has there been any experiment with the proposal for an explanatory memorandum. The objection to the proposal seems to be based principally on concern for the parliamentary time that it would take to vet the document; and the fear that it would simply add to the burden of the courts without greatly assisting them – would the explanatory memorandum itself require an explanatory memorandum? Perhaps most potent still is simple conservatism.

The Renton Committee did not think that explanatory materials prepared for the benefit of legislators should be admissible for the purposes of judicial interpretation. To do so, it thought, would risk having a 'split level statute' of which only the primary stage would have been debated in parliament (*The Preparation of Legislation*, 1975, Cmnd. 6053, para. 19.24).

In February 1980 Lord Scarman introduced a bill to give effect to the Law Commission's 1969 Report. It would have permitted courts in interpreting statutes to consult any relevant report of a Royal Commission, committee or other body, made to or laid before parliament, or any document declared by the Act to be relevant. The bill also specified that among the principles to be applied in the interpretation of Acts was that a construction 'which would promote the general legislative purpose underlying the provision in question is to be preferred to a construction which would not'. However, the law lords gave the bill a frosty reception and it was withdrawn (House of Lords, *Hansard*, vol. 405, cols. 276–306, 13 February 1980).

7. Presumptions and subordinate principles of interpretation as an aid to construction

There are a number of presumptions that have been applied by the courts to assist in the construction of statutes. They are set out at length with a wealth of examples in *Maxwell*. It is not necessary here to do more than to give a brief mention of the best known:

(1) Penal statutes should be construed strictly in favour of the citizen.

(2) It is to be presumed that a statutory provision was not intended to change the common law.

(3) It is presumed that municipal law is to be interpreted to be in conformity with international law.

(4) Normally, statutes creating criminal offences require a blameworthy state of mind (*mens rea*) in the defendant.

(5) It is presumed that parliament did not intend to oust the jurisdiction of the courts.

(6) It is presumed that a statute does not have retrospective effect.

(7) Words take meaning from the context: *Noscitur a sociis*. (Thus in the Refreshment Houses Act 1860 dealing with houses 'for public refreshment, resort and entertainment', the last word was held not to cover theatrical or musical entertainment but to refer rather to refreshment rooms and the reception and accommodation of the public – *Muir* v. *Keay* (1875) L.R. 10 Q.B. 594 at 597–8). *Expressio unius exclusio alterius* – the express mention of one member of a class by implication excludes other members of the same class. (The word 'land' would normally include mines but a reference to 'lands, houses and coalmines' may mean that no mines are included in the word 'land'.) *Ejusdem generis* – general words at the end of a list of more particular words take their meaning from the foregoing list. (So the statement in the Sunday Observance Act 1677 that 'no tradesman, artificer, workman, labourer or other person whatsoever' shall work on a Sunday was held not to apply to a coach proprietor, farmer, barber or estate agent. The words 'other person whatsoever' were held to be confined to persons in similar occupations to those more specifically defined in the list.)

8. Are the rules, principles, presumptions and other guides to interpretation binding on the courts?

The main principles of statutory interpretation – the literal rule, the golden rule and the mischief rule – are all called rules, but this is plainly a misnomer. They are not rules in any ordinary sense of the word since they all point to different solutions to the same problem. Nor is there any indication, either in the so-called rules or elsewhere, as to which to apply in any given situation. Each of them may be applied but need not be. The same is true of every one of the principles, presumptions or other guides to interpretation that fill the 350 or so pages of *Maxwell on The Interpretation of Statutes*. In other words for most problems of interpretation there is nothing in that book (nor in any other book) which tells one how to solve the difficulty that has arisen. For every proposition, there is one or more counter-principle. Each side in litigation will always find support in the authorities for whatever principle of interpretation it wishes to advance. The rules and principles of interpretation therefore do little or nothing to solve problems. They simply justify solutions usually reached on other grounds.

Professors Hart and Sacks give a helpful example. The bear trainer who comes to the station with his bear sees a notice 'No dogs allowed on the trains'. By applying the maxim *expressio unius exclusio alterius*, he would claim to be entitled to board the train with the bear. (The express mention of dogs not being allowed may be used to argue that other animals, including bears, are allowed.) The competing argument is that if dogs are not allowed on, *a fortiori*, or by analogy, bears are not either. The solution to the problem does not depend on the deployment of maxims but on some notion as to what the rule is intended to achieve and the application of whatever interpretation best suits this objective.* It is the judge and not the rule or principle that determines the outcome. The principles may suggest an answer but there will usually be a counter-principle to suggest the opposite result. Justice Frankfurter of the United States Supreme Court said of statutory interpretation 'Though my business throughout most of my professional life has been with statutes, I come to you empty-handed. I bring no answers. I suspect the answers to the problems of an art are in its exercise'.† Sir Carleton Allen summarized his lengthy discussion of the problems of statutory interpretation with the words 'we are driven in the end to the unsatisfying conclusion that the whole matter ultimately turns on impalpable and indefinable elements of judicial spirit or attitude'.‡

* H. Hart and A. Sacks, *The Legal Process* (1958, unpublished), p. 1409.

† *The Record of the Association of the Bar of the City of New York*, 1947, 213 at 216–17.

‡ C.K. Allen, *Law in the Making* (7th ed., 1964), pp. 526, 529.

9. Would legislation to state the rules of statutory interpretation help?

In most countries there is some form of Interpretation Act for the assistance of draftsmen, defining common terms or stating that, for instance, the male shall include the female unless the context indicates otherwise. But some countries have gone beyond guidance on such minor matters to attempt to guide the judges on the main problems of interpretation. Thus for instance the New Zealand Interpretation Act 1888 provided 'Every Act, and every provision or enactment thereof, shall be deemed remedial, whether its immediate purport is to direct the doing of anything Parliament deems to be for the public good, or to prevent or punish the doing of anything it deems contrary to the public good, and shall accordingly receive such fair, large, and liberal construction and interpretation as will best ensure the attainment of the object of the Act and of such provision or enactment according to its true intent, meaning, and spirit.' (The provision is now to be found in the Acts Interpretation Act 1924, s. 5 (j)). Obviously the purpose behind the provision was to deter the judges from applying a narrow, literal approach to interpretation. It was a modern restatement of the mischief rule in *Heydon's* case – cast in mandatory form. The provision has been part of the law of New Zealand for some ninety years. How has it worked? The answer was given by Mr Denzil Ward who for twenty-four years had been a parliamentary draftsman in New Zealand. The Act, he said, had been invoked occasionally but for every case in which it had been applied there were many others in which it had been ignored. The courts in fact had continued to apply the 'heterogeneous collection of canons of construction developed by the English courts over a period of several hundred years':

D.A.S. Ward, 'A Criticism of the Interpretation of Statutes in the New Zealand Courts', *New Zealand Law Journal*, 1963, p. 293

Sometimes it is difficult to discover just which approach has been favoured by the court. Usually no reason is given for preferring one approach to any other. The most that can be said is that some judges at some periods have been fairly consistent in using the approach that they prefer.

Thus we occasionally find a court applying the 'mischief rule' laid down in *Heydon's* case ...

Sometimes it is clear that the court, by its concentration on the actual words it is construing, is applying the 'literal rule' which in the nineteenth century dominated the judicial approach to a spate of legislation in general terms.

Sometimes ... it applies one of the presumptions (such as the presumption that a statute is not intended to alter the common law or the presumption of *mens rea*) which developed mainly during the eighteenth century when the courts regarded themselves more as standing between parliament and the people than as interpreters of authoritative texts. Alternatively a presumption may be brought into play to reinforce one of the other rules.

There are other cases where a court applies one of the maxims (such as the '*ejusdem generis* rule') which are really no more than condensed statements of the ordinary use of English; or decides the case on any one of a number of subsidiary and technical 'rules' secreted in the judgments of the past.

These 'rules' and presumptions and maxims are inconsistent, and often flatly contradict each other, but they are treated in the textbooks and in judgments as having equal validity today, regardless of the differing social, political, and constitutional conditions in which they arose. The 'literal rule' cannot be reconciled with the 'mischief rule'. Many of the presumptions have become unreal in these days when legislation invades so many aspects of life with its administrative machinery for the Welfare State, its taxes, its controls, and its innumerable minor offences. Some of them cannot be reconciled with the statement in s. 5 (j) that every enactment shall be deemed remedial.

The result is chaos. It is impossible to predict what approach any court will make to any case. The field of statutory interpretation has become a judicial jungle. It is only fair to say that the jungle has been inherited; but our courts have been so busy cultivating the trees that they have lost sight of the pathway provided by parliament in the Acts Interpretation Act.

It is obvious from this account that a statutory enactment of the mischief rule has not been successful in New Zealand. It is predictable that the result would be much the same if it were tried in the United Kingdom. The Law Commissions in their 1969 report on statutory interpretation were surely right in offering the possible explanation of the New Zealand history that 'exhortations to the courts to adopt "large and liberal" interpretations beg the question as to what is the real intention of the legislature, which may require in the circumstances either a broad or a narrow construction of language' (para. 33). But the Law Commissions did nevertheless propose that it should be provided by statute that among the principles to be applied in the interpretation of statutes was that 'a construction which would promote the general legislative purpose underlying the provision in question is to be preferred to a construction which would not'. The Renton Committee supported this proposal (see *The Preparation of Legislation*, 1975, Cmnd. 6053, para. 19.28). But the House of Lords did not support the idea – see p. 82 above.

10. What is the court's proper function in interpreting a statute?

(a) To seek out the intention of parliament?

There are innumerable statements in judicial decisions that the chief duty of a court faced with a problem of statutory interpretation is to discover the intention of parliament. But this approach has also been severely criticized. Thus it has been pointed out* that it is a fiction to speak of the intent of the legislature, which is an abstraction that can have no intention. In most cases only a few people drafted the statute, only a few spoke in the debates, many voted against it and many more had little notion of what they were voting about when they voted in favour. Whose intention represents that of the legislature? Frequently it is manifest that the draftsmen did not anticipate the problem that has occurred or, in other cases, that the statute did not provide any clear solution. For these reasons the concept of legislative intention is today widely discredited.

But these points can be met.† An amorphous group can have an intention even though it cannot be linked to any particular individuals. Those who voted against it obviously did not share the intent – but under the ordinary principles of democracy the majority prevails and the minority can for this purpose be disregarded. Those who voted without fully understanding the subject are deemed to have accepted the intention that emerges from the document. Those who were actively involved in formulating and promoting the statute could be said to be those who had a subjective intent which may or may not have been reflected in the ultimate language of the document. Matters that were not anticipated could still be said to be covered by the legislative intent in the sense that the statute may show how such problems should be solved. The authors of the statute may not have foreseen the particular problem, but they may nevertheless have had an intention which covers the situation that occurs – through reasoned elaboration of their text or by way of analogy.

Of course, the fact that there is some generalized intent implicit in a statute does not mean that there will have been something

* See, for instance, M. Radin, 'Statutory Interpretation', 43 *Harvard Law Review*, 1930, p. 863; Douglas Payne, 'The Intention of the Legislature in the Interpretation of Statutes', *Current Legal Problems*, 1956, p. 96.

† This discussion is based largely on Reed Dickerson, *The Interpretation and Application of Statutes* (1975), pp. 67–86. This seems to the writer to be the best book on the subject of statutory interpretation presently available.

approaching a specific intent in regard to the problem under consideration. If the concept of intention is required to mean detailed answers to the problem in hand, it must be conceded that in many cases no such intention can be said to have existed. But if the concept of intention is defined in a broader and more realistic way, it does have genuine application to the situation. Certainly in the layman's sense the legislators had an intention and the layman's common-sense approach seems sufficiently close to the real situation to make the word 'intention' not as inappropriate as has often been suggested.

Those who have objected to the phrase 'legislative intention' have tended to prefer the seemingly more objective phrase 'legislative purpose'. This phrase, it is argued, avoids most of the difficulties associated with the word 'intention'. It has already been argued that some of these objections have been exaggerated, but perhaps the more telling argument is that, on analysis, 'legislative purpose' is really only a different way of stating the same concept as 'legislative intent'. Both are ways of stating that the function of the interpreter is to give the words, to the best of his ability, a meaning that reflects the objectives of those responsible for the statute, insofar as this has been expressed in the language used.

(b) To give effect to what parliament has said, rather than what it meant to say ?

The school of thought which insists on focusing prime attention on the words used regardless of context has a fundamental point of great importance. If the words and meaning of the statute *are* clear, then the fact that there is strong evidence to suggest that some other meaning was intended cannot prevail. The intellectual integrity of the process demands that there be some limitation to the process of 'interpretation'.Humpty Dumpty was wrong in suggesting that you can make words mean whatever you want. The point may be made by reference to the will in the *Rowland* case (p. 44, above). If the evidence had shown that Dr Rowland survived his wife by, say, forty-eight hours by clinging onto a raft which eventually sank, it would be straining the meaning of words to have held that their deaths coincided. On the other hand, if it had appeared that they died within half an hour of each other – he in New York, she in Melbourne – it would surely have been within the legitimate elaboration of the word 'coinciding' in the context to have held that it covered the event. In both cases it would have been obvious that the testator would have wished his property to go to his own relatives rather than to his wife's, but in the one case it would have been reasonable and in the other case unreasonable to have given effect to his intention.

The literalists are therefore not wrong to focus attention on the text. Their error is rather to focus exclusive attention on the text, and to deny the importance of seeing and comprehending at least some of the context. Clearly there must be some limit to the amount of context that the court has the time and the inclination to consider. But to apply the literal approach is unnecessarily to put on blinkers.

(c) Should interpretation reflect changing times?

It is a familiar principle of statutory interpretation that 'the words of an Act will generally be understood in the sense they bore when it was passed'.* The statute should be construed, it has been said, 'as if we had read it the day after it was passed'.† But it is a familiar fact, notwithstanding this principle, that interpretation does change with the times. Albie Sachs and Joan Hoff Wilson, for instance, have shown how in the nineteenth century the courts in both England and America consistently interpreted the statutory words 'any person' in such a way as to deprive women of the right to participate in public life – by voting, being elected to office or becoming a member of a profession. Finally, in 1929 the Privy Council in an appeal from Canada (*Edwards* v. *Attorney General, Canada* [1930] A.C. 124) held that women were persons. ('The exclusion of women from all public offices is a relic of days more barbarous than ours ...') Lord Sankey swept away nearly fifty years of judicial history with the brief statement 'The word "person" may include members of both sexes, and to those who ask why the word should include females, the obvious answer is why not. In these circumstances the burden is upon those who deny that the word includes women to make out their case' (at p. 138). What had changed was not the statutory formula but the approach of the judges. The climate of the times had altered and what was unthinkable in the latter part of the nineteenth century had become tolerable and indeed unexceptionable in the late 1920s. (See generally Albie Sachs and Joan Hoff Wilson, *Sexism and the Law*, 1978, Martin Robertson, pp. 4–66.)

An equally clear if less dramatic example was the change between 1876 and 1928 in judicial attitudes to the problem of liability without

* *Maxwell on Interpretation of Statutes* (12th edn., 1969), p. 85.
† *Sharpe* v. *Wakefield* (1888) 22 Q.B.D. 239.

fault. In 1876 the House of Lords decided *River Wear Commissioners* v. *Adamson* (1876) 1 Q.B.D. 546 (Ct of App.); (1877) 2 App. Cas. 742 (H. of L.). Under the Harbour Clauses Act 1847, the owner of every vessel 'shall be answerable to the undertakers [the harbour authority] for any damage done by such vessel or by any person employed about the same to the harbour dock ...' A ship which had been abandoned was blown by a gale into a harbour and crashed into the dock causing considerable damage. In spite of the clear words of the statute, both the Court of Appeal and the House of Lords (though for different reasons) held that the shipowner was not liable. The notion of liability without fault was clearly so offensive to the judges that they found that parliament could not have intended such a result. Almost fifty years later in 1928 the House of Lords took the exactly opposite view of the same section on similar facts. (*The Mostyn* [1927] P. 25.) What had changed was the judges' attitude to allocation of losses in the light of insurance – Lord Haldane actually referred to the fact. It is inevitable and proper that the courts should reflect changing attitudes in their approach to statutes. But if the process of pouring contemporary attitudes into old statutes is carried too far, the judges will be exceeding their proper role. Here again they must find the right balance between adherence to precedent and continuity on the one hand, and a necessary flexibility and creativity on the other.

Two cases that illustrate the way the courts have dealt with the problem of trying to reconcile statutory words with changing times are *Adedigba* and *Re Bravda*, both decided by the Court of Appeal in February 1968 and both of which required interpretation of statutory provisions that were more than a hundred years old and that had been interpreted judicially on many occasions.

R. v. *Bow Road Domestic Proceedings Court, Ex parte Adedigba* [1968] 2 All E.R. 89 (Court of Appeal)

An unmarried Nigerian woman applied for maintenance against the putative father of her two children both of whom were born abroad. The court considered the effect of *R.* v. *Blane* (1849) 13 Q.B. 769, which had held that no maintenance could be awarded under the statute to a woman whose children were born abroad and which had been applied many times.

LORD DENNING M.R. (at 92): None of those cases is binding on this court: and I think that the time has come when we should say that *R.* v. *Blane* in 1849 was wrongly decided and also the two cases which followed it. It seems plain to me that if the mother and father are both here and the child is here, the words of the statute are satisfied. I can see no possible reason for denying the court's jurisdiction to order maintenance; and every reason for giving them jurisdiction. The father ought to be made to pay for the child ...

I know that since *R.* v. *Blane* the statutory provisions have been re-enacted in virtually the same words; but that does not trouble me. I venture to quote some words that I used in *Royal Crown Derby Porcelain Co., Ltd.* v. *Russell* [1949] 2 K.B. 417, 429]:

> 'I do not believe that whenever Parliament re-enacts a provision of a statute it thereby gives statutory authority to every erroneous interpretation which has been put on it. The true view is that the court will be slow to overrule a previous decision on the interpretation of a statute when it has long been acted on, and it will be more than usually slow to do so when Parliament has, since the decision, re-enacted the statute in the same terms, but if a decision is, in fact, shown to be erroneous, there is no rule of law which prevents it being overruled.'

Nor am I troubled by the fact that *R.* v. *Blane* has stood for 118 years. It is not a property or commercial case. It has not formed the basis of titles or commercial dealings. It is the sort of precedent which we can and should overrule when it is seen to be wrong. Only yesterday in *Conway* v. *Rimmer* [1968] 1 All E.R. 874 LORD MORRIS OF BORTH-Y-GEST used words appropriate to the situation:

> 'Though precedent is an indispensable foundation on which to decide what is the law, there may be times when a departure from precedent is in the interests of justice and the proper development of the law.'

If we were to affirm today *R.* v. *Blane* as being the law of this land, the only consequence would be a reference to the Law Commission; then a report by them; and eventually a Bill before Parliament. It would be quite a long time before the law could be set right. Even then the law would only be set right for future cases. Nothing could be done to set right this present case. The mother here would not get maintenance for the child which she needs now. So I would overrule *R.* v. *Blane* now. In the days of 1849 the question may not have been of any particular social significance; but now there are many illegitimate children here in England who were born abroad. It is only right and just that the mothers of those children should be able to take out proceedings against the fathers, and that the fathers should be ordered to pay reasonable maintenance for their own children. Otherwise what is the position? The children will be left to the care of the State. The national assistance fund will have to pay—the father will get out of his just responsibilities. That would be a most undesirable state of affairs.

SALMON L.J. (at 94): It is only if one goes back to the Statute of Elizabeth in 1576 that there is any warrant for the view that Parliament was legislating only for illegitimate children born in this country. The aphorism that time marches on and the law marches with it was just as valid in 1849 when *R.* v. *Blane* was decided as it is today, but its validity was then perhaps not so generally recognised. In 1849 time had indeed marched on since the reign of Elizabeth, and today it has marched on still further. There is no reason to suppose that Parliament intended then or now that the law should be the same as it was in 1576.

It is said that however wrong the decision in *R.* v. *Blane* may have been, it was made 118 years ago. Moreover, it has been followed ever since, as it had to be followed, by the courts on which it was binding; and accordingly the principle of stare decisis should apply. Certainly we do not readily interfere with the decisions which have stood for 118 years, or, indeed, for any lengthy period of time. This is particularly true of decisions in fields in which it might be said that the community has arranged its affairs in accordance with what has been regarded as the law for many years past. It is, for example, very true of decisions relating to the law of contract; but even in that field, the courts reverse a very old decision when they are completely satisfied that it was wrong. For example, recently this court* overruled *The Parana*† which had stood for nearly ninety years and had been generally accepted as stating the law relating to the measure of damage for breach of contract for the carriage of goods by sea; and the House of Lords‡ upheld the decision of this court.

In the present case none of these considerations underlying the principle of stare decisis apply. I do not suppose that the incidence of illegitimate children being conceived and born abroad has been affected in the slightest by the decision in *R.* v. *Blane*. I think it unlikely that any woman in Nigeria, or indeed anywhere else, would forbear to conceive and give birth to an illegitimate child abroad because she might contemplate that if she and the child came to this country with the putative father, she would not, according to the law as laid down in *R.* v. *Blane*, ever have a chance of recovering any sum from him by way of maintenance for the child. Nor do I think that putative fathers have arranged their affairs on the basis that *R.* v. *Blane* was correctly decided; and if they had, I should have no qualms about upsetting it.

The only matter which has given me any pause is that there has been a great deal of legislation concerning this subject in the last 118 years, and Parliament has never taken the opportunity of correcting *R.* v. *Blane*. The father has contended that since Parliament has not corrected *R.* v. *Blane* it must be taken to have approved and endorsed the decision. It is quite true that it is a principle of construction that the courts may presume that when there has been a decision on the meaning of a statute, and the statute is re-enacted in much the same terms, it was the intention of Parliament to endorse the decision; but this is merely a rule of construction for the guidance of the courts. It is not a presumption which the courts are bound to make (see *Royal Crown Derby Porcelain Co., Ltd.* v. *Russell*, [1949] 2 K.B. 417). It is always possible

* *The Heron* [1966] 2 Q.B. 695.
† (1877) 2 P.D. 118.
‡ [1967] 3 All E.R. 686.

that Parliament, however vigilant, may overlook a decision. I think that *R.* v. *Blane* has been overlooked by the legislature. I am certainly not satisfied that it was the intention of Parliament to endorse it. Indeed, if that decision had been considered by Parliament at any time when the intervening legislation was passed, I have little doubt but that it would have been corrected for it manifestly works gross injustice.

[Lord Justice Edmund Davies delivered a concurring judgment.]

In the second case the court was again unanimous but its decision went the other way. (Lord Justice Salmon was a member of the court on both occasions.)

In the Estate of Bravda [1968] 2 All E.R. 217 (Court of Appeal)

A testator made a will on one side of a piece of notepaper. Evidence showed that two independent witnesses signed first but that his two daughters, who were the chief beneficiaries under the will then signed above them 'to make it stronger'. The gift to the daughters was challenged on the ground that under s. 15 of the Wills Act 1837 a beneficiary who signed the will as attesting witnesses could not take a gift. (The Wills Act s. 15 stated that 'if any person shall attest the execution of any will ... to whom ... any beneficial devise ... shall be given, such device ... shall so far only as concerns such person ... be utterly null and void'.) All three judges refused to adjust the traditional interpretation of s. 15:

WILLMER L.J. (at 221): The suggestion was made that s. 15 of the Wills Act, 1837, was never intended to apply in a case where there was already a valid execution by two unimpeachable witnesses. It has been suggested that the object of the section was merely to ensure that a will would not fail altogether if one or both of the two witnesses required were named as beneficiaries, as had been the case earlier. In other words, what is said is that the object of the section was merely to ensure that both those witnesses would be 'credible' witnesses. That result was achieved by requiring that they should forgo any benefits they would otherwise derive, but that the will would be left unimpaired. That is a point which does not appear to have been argued in the court below. It is not, of course, raised in the notice of appeal. There has been no cross-notice on behalf of the plaintiffs; and I do not think, in those circumstances, that the point is strictly open in this court. If it were open, I should merely say that, in my judgment, it is a point of no substance, for two reasons. One is that I think the words of the section are much too plain to admit of this rather tortuous construction. Secondly, I think that, after 130 years, it is now much too late to endeavour to put this entirely new construction on the well-known words of this section.

RUSSELL L.L. (at 224): It was debated in argument (the point originating from the Bench) whether s. 15 could be construed so as not to destroy a benefit given to an attesting witness if, without that witness, there were not less than two other witnesses to whom no benefit was given. This suggestion was made by analogy from the old law. A will of realty, for example, before the Wills Act 1752, required three credible witnesses for validity, a beneficiary not being a credible witness; but, as I understand it, provided there were three credible witnesses, the will was valid and a fourth witness, being a beneficiary, could take his benefit. The Act of 1752 first introduced the system found in s. 15 of the Wills Act 1837, by which all witnesses were in effect made credible by avoiding any benefit given. I would have thought it a very reasonable system of law that benefits to witnesses are not avoided if there are two independent witnesses; but the other view has been generally accepted in the authorities for a very long time indeed, and the language of s. 15 of the Act of 1837 is, I think, too forthright to be overcome by the analogy suggested. I have not myself looked at the language of the Act of 1752.

I would welcome a change in the law in this regard. I would expect most people to regard the outcome of this case as monstrously unfair to the testator and to his daughters. I do myself; but every time a beneficiary is an attesting witness, s. 15 of the Wills Act 1837 deprives him of his benefit and defeats the testator's intention. This is considered necessary to ensure reliable unbiased witnesses of due execution; but why it was thought necessary to interfere in cases where there are the requisite number of unbiased witnesses, I cannot imagine. I regretfully agree that the appeal succeeds.

SALMON L.J. (at 224): With very great regret, I also agree that this appeal succeeds. I was at an early stage struck by the force of the argument on the part of the defendant. I confess that I tried very hard to find some way round it—some ground on which in conscience I could find in favour of the plaintiffs; but I have failed. The words of s. 15 of the Wills Act 1837, are too plain, and the evidence filed on behalf of the plaintiffs is wholly inadequate. Section 15 makes it clear that, if any person attests the execution of any will to whom or to whose wife or husband any benefit is given under the will, then that part of the will which gives the benefit shall be null and void, but such person shall be a competent witness to prove the validity or invalidity of the will.

That statutory provision makes it impossible for the intentions of the testator to be carried out in the case of a beneficiary signing the will as a witness. That is the very object of the statutory provision. So, when the court is faced with the kind of problem which arises in this case, it is not open to the beneficiary to urge that the intention of the testator must not be defeated. Parliament has clearly laid down that, when the testator intends to benefit a person who signs the will as a witness, the testator's intention shall be defeated. I wholly agree with RUSSELL L.J., for the reasons which he gives, that it is high time that this provision of the Wills Act, 1837, should be amended, so that, when there are two independent credible witnesses, the mere fact that a beneficiary has also signed as a witness should not operate (as it now does) to defeat the intention of the testator.

Question

Why was the court prepared to move in *Adedigba* but not in *Re Blane*? One of the chief reasons given for the decision in *Adedigba* was that no one could reasonably be said to have arranged his affairs in reliance on the decision in *R.* v. *Blane*. But would the reasonable expectations of testators have been upset if the court had interpreted s. 15 of the 1837 Wills Act in such a way as to discount the signatures of beneficiaries if there were already two independent witnesses? (Cf. *Beswick* v. *Beswick* [1966] Ch. 538 (C.A.), [1968] A.C. 58 (H.L.) in which the Court of Appeal gave a statutory provision a startling interpretation in order to reform the law but the House of Lords reversed the decision on this point.)

Note

In this particular instance parliament intervened with remarkable speed to correct the defect in the law revealed by *Re Bravda*. The Court of Appeal's decision was handed down on 2 February 1968. On 14 February a private member's bill was introduced to deal with the problem. It was reintroduced under a new title (the Wills Bill) on 21 February. It received the Royal Assent in May only three months after the Court of Appeal had asked for legislative action.

(d) Will membership of the Common Market change the principles of statutory interpretation?

There are dicta in some recent cases suggesting that adherence to the EEC Treaty (on which see further, p. 259 below) may in the long run have an impact on the approach of English courts to questions of statutory interpretation. Lord Denning, here as in so much else, has been the leader. In *Bulmer* v. *Bollinger* he described the differences between the English and the European approach to statutory interpretation:

H.P. Bulmer Ltd. v. *J. Bollinger S.A.*
[1974] 1 Ch. 401 at 425 (Court of Appeal)

Action was brought over use of the word 'champagne' in champagne cider and champagne perry. There was a request for the case to be transferred to the European Court for a ruling as to whether such use infringed Community regulations. The court refused to make a reference and this point was then appealed. In the course of refusing the appeal, Lord Denning spoke of the nature of Community Law.

LORD DENNING M.R.:

10. *The principles of interpretation*

It is apparent that in very many cases the English courts will interpret the Treaty themselves. They will not refer the question to the European Court at Luxembourg. What then are the principles of interpretation to be applied? Beyond doubt the English courts must follow the same principles as the European Court. Otherwise there would be differences between the countries of the nine. That would never do. All the courts of all nine countries should interpret the Treaty in the same way. They should all apply the same principles. It is enjoined on the English courts by section 3 of the European Communities Act 1972, which I have read.

What a task is thus set before us! The Treaty is quite unlike any of the enactments to which we have become accustomed. The draftsmen of our statutes have striven to express themselves with the utmost exactness. They have tried to foresee all possible circumstances that may arise and to provide for them. They have sacrificed style and simplicity. They have forgone brevity. They have become long and involved. In consequence, the judges have followed suit. They interpret a statute as applying only to the circumstances covered by the very words. They give them a literal interpretation. If the words of the statute do not cover a new situation – which was not foreseen – the judges hold that they have no power to fill the gap. To do so would be a "naked usurpation of the legislative function": see *Magor and St Mellons Rural District Council* v. *Newport Corporation* [1952] A.C. 189, 191. The gap must remain open until Parliament finds time to fill it.

How different is this Treaty! It lays down general principles. It expresses its aims and purposes. All in sentences of moderate length and commendable style. But it lacks precision. It uses words and phrases without defining what they mean. An English lawyer would look for an interpretation clause, but he would look in vain. There is none. All the way through the Treaty there are gaps and lacunae. These have to be filled in by the judges, or by Regulations or directives. It is the European way. That appears from the decision of the Hamburg court in *In re Tax on Imported Lemons* [1968] C.M.L.R. 1.

Likewise the Regulations and directives. They are enacted by the Council sitting in Brussels for everyone to obey. They are quite unlike our statutory instruments. They have to give the reasons on which they are based: article 190. So they start off with pages of preambles, 'whereas' and 'whereas' and 'whereas'. These show the purpose and intent of the Regulations and directives. Then follow the provisions which are to be obeyed. Here again words and phrases are used without defining their import. ... In case of difficulty, recourse is had to the preambles. These are useful to show the purpose and intent behind it all. But much is left to the judges. The enactments give only an outline plan. The details are to be filled in by the judges.

Seeing these differences, what are the English courts to do when they are faced with a problem of interpretation? They must follow the European pattern. No longer must they examine the words in meticulous detail. No longer must they argue about the precise grammatical sense. They must look to the purpose or intent. To quote the words of the European court in the *Da Costa* case [1963] C.M.L.R. 224, 237, they must deduce "from the wording and the spirit of the Treaty the meaning of the community rules." They must not confine themselves to the English text. They must consider, if need be, all the authentic texts, of which there are now six: see *Sociale Verzekeringsbank* v. *Van der Vecht* [1968] C.M.L.R. 151. They must divine the spirit of the Treaty and gain inspiration from it. If they find a gap, they must fill it as best they can. They must do what the framers of the instrument would have done if they had thought about it. So we must do the same. Those are the principles, as I understand it, on which the European Court acts.

Lord Denning returned to the theme in 1977:

Buchanan and Co. Ltd v. *Babco Forwarding and Shipping* (*UK*) *Ltd*
[1977] 2 W.L.R. 107
(Court of Appeal)

Defendants agreed to carry 1,000 cases of the plaintiffs' whisky to Iran. The contract was subject to the terms and conditions of the Convention on the Contract for the International Carriage of Goods by Road, set out in the Schedule to the Carriage of Goods by Road Act 1965. The whisky was stolen from the defendants. The plaintiffs had to pay the excise duty and claimed this sum from the defendants. Judgment was given for the plaintiffs and the Court of Appeal dismissed the appeal. In the course of giving judgment, attention was given to the interpretation of an international convention scheduled to a UK statute:

LORD DENNING: This article 23, paragraph 4, is an agreed clause in an international convention. As such it should be given the same interpretation in all the countries who were parties to the convention. It would be absurd that the courts of England should interpret it differently from the courts of France, or Holland, or Germany. Compensation for loss should be assessed on the same basis, no matter in which country the claim is brought. We must, therefore, put on one side our traditional rules of interpretation. We have for years tended to stick too closely to the letter – to the literal interpretation of the words. We ought, in interpreting this convention, to adopt the European method. I tried to describe it in *H.P. Bulmer Ltd.* v. *J. Bollinger S.A.* [1974] Ch. 401, 425–426. Some of us recently spent a couple of days in Luxembourg discussing it with the members of the European Court, and our colleagues in the other countries of the nine.

We had a valuable paper on it by the President of the court (Judge H. Kutscher) which is well worth studying: 'Methods of interpretation as seen by a judge at the Court of Justice, Luxembourg 1976.' They adopt a method which they call in English by strange words – at any rate they were strange to me – the 'schematic and teleological' method of interpretation. It is not really so alarming as it sounds. All it means is that the judges do not go by the literal meaning of the words or by the grammatical structure of the sentence. They go by the design or purpose which lies behind it. When they come upon a situation which is to their minds within the spirit – but not the letter – of the legislation, they solve the problem by looking at the design and purpose of the legislature – at the effect which it was sought to achieve. They then interpret the legislation so as to produce the desired effect. This means that they fill in gaps, quite unashamedly, without hesitation. They ask simply: what is the sensible way of dealing with this situation so as to give effect to the presumed purpose of the legislation? They lay down the law accordingly. If you study the decisions of the European Court, you will see that they do it every day. To our eyes – shortsighted by tradition – it is legislation, pure and simple. But, to their eyes, it is fulfilling the true role of the courts. They are giving effect to what the legislature intended, or may be presumed to have intended. I see nothing wrong in this. Quite the contrary. It is a method of interpretation which I advocated long ago in *Seaford Court Estates Ltd.* v. *Asher* [1949] 2 K.B. 481, 498–499. It did not gain acceptance at that time. It was condemned by Lord Simonds in the House of Lords in *Magor and St. Mellons Rural District Council* v. *Newport Corporation* [1952] A.C. 189, 191, as a 'naked usurpation of the legislative power'. But the time has now come when we should think again. In interpreting the Treaty of Rome (which is part of our law) we must certainly adopt the new approach. Just as in Rome you should do as Rome does. So in the European Community, you should do as the European Court does.

LORD JUSTICE ROSKILL agreed: I would like to support what Lord Denning M.R. has said and what Lawton L.J. will say regarding the need to alter the traditional English method of approach to questions of construction of statutes such as the Act of 1965 which give effect on a matter of municipal law to international conventions. Some such conventions are drafted in languages other than English. The English language though used may in other cases not be the predominant language of the convention, or in yet other cases may at the most be only of equal force with one or more other European languages. Now that this country has joined the European Community our courts are likely to be increasingly concerned with the interpretation of legislation of one kind or another of which English is not the original or the dominant language. Such legislation is likely also to fall for interpretation in the courts of other members of the community. It would be disastrous if our courts were to adopt constructions of such legislation different from those of other courts whose method of approach is different and far less narrow than ours merely because of over-rigid adherence to traditional – some might call them chauvinist – English methods. Conflict would arise between courts in different jurisdictions within the European Community with the untoward consequences to which Lord Denning M.R. and Lawton L.J. refer and if it became known that if a party sued in one country one result would follow, but if in another country another – a state of affairs which has arisen in other branches of the law between, for example, this country and the United States – what is sometimes known as forum-shopping would be encouraged, whereas within the community it should be discouraged. I think in the future our courts should be far more ready, in cases where international conventions, especially those affecting the members of the European Community, are under judicial consideration, to assimilate their approach to questions of the construction of our legislation giving effect to those conventions to that which the courts of other members of the community are likely to adopt. The doctrine once proclaimed in the phrase 'Athanasius contra mundum' caused much trouble many centuries ago. That attitude of mind has no place in our courts in the latter part of the 20th century.

If the methods of English judges facing international and especially European materials are to change, it would be surprising if, gradually, this did not have some impact on their methods in dealing with ordinary English cases.

(e) What is the proper limit to the creative function of the interpreter?

There are few today who deny that the interpreter of legislation exercises some creative role. In recent years this has even become conventional wisdom amongst the judges themselves. In 1965, for instance, Lord Diplock told his audience at Birmingham University:

Lord Diplock, 'The Courts as Legislators', Holdsworth Club Lecture, 1965, pp. 5–6

... there are also cases – many more than one would expect – where there is room for dispute as to what the rule of conduct really is. This is so as much with rules laid down by Act of Parliament as with those which have evolved at common law. ...

... [E]very revenue appeal that comes before the court – generally after any dispute of fact there may have been has already been decided by the Commissioners – involves a dispute as to whether a particular kind of gain is taxable, whether a particular kind of document attracts stamp duty. Whenever the Court decides that kind of dispute it legislates about taxation. It makes a law taxing all gains of the same kind or all documents of the same kind. Do not let us deceive ourselves with the legal fiction that the court is only ascertaining and giving effect to what Parliament meant. Anyone who has decided tax appeals knows that most of them concern transactions which Members of Parliament and the draftsman of the Act had not anticipated, about which they had never thought at all. Some of the transactions are of a kind which had never taken place before the Act was passed: they were devised as a result of it. The court may describe what it is doing in tax appeals as interpretation. So did the priestess of the Delphic oracle. But whoever has final authority to explain what Parliament meant by the words that it used makes law as much as if the explanation it has given were contained in a new Act of Parliament. It will need a new Act of Parliament to reverse it.

(See, to similar effect, Lord Radcliffe, p. 197 below; Justice Cardozo, p. 200 below; Lord Devlin, pp. 207, 213 below; Lord Edmund-Davies, p. 232 below; Lord Pearson, p. 232 below.)

But how can one describe the extent of judicial creativity in statutory interpretation? One helpful image is that used by Reed Dickerson in his major book *The Interpretation and Application of Statutes* (1975). Dickerson uses the simile of the restorer of an ancient vase. Everything depends on how much of the original vase is available to him. Sometimes he is simply making a substitute for a small piece missing from the body of the vase. 'Here he is guided by the adjacent contours, and, if he is skilful, the result blends well enough to attract little or no attention. ... His job is harder if the vase has been decorated, but the difficulty is small if the decoration follows a discernible pattern' (p. 26). In this activity there is some creativity but it is of the lowest order. It still falls within the general heading of 'ascertainment of meaning' in the sense of discovering something that is in a real sense latent in the material.

But the position is plainly very different if the craftsman has only a single piece and the decoration is free and non-recurring. Here by imaginative speculation he must attempt to produce something 'in the general style' of the original without being able to pretend that his effort will necessarily approximate to it very closely. Here the element of creativity is very considerable. The greater the range of choice open to the judge, the greater his law-making as opposed to his law-finding function. If the statute is a Bill of Rights with broad, open-textured provisions, the scope for judicial legislation will be vast compared with the opportunities offered by the tight provisions of, say, an income tax Act. There is, however, no general way that the proper limit of the creative function of judges in statutory interpretation can usefully be defined. The judge should be open and sensitive to the subtleties and complexity of language, to the fallibility of draftsmen and to the variety of interests that may be reflected in legal documents. On the other hand he must respect the limits of language and not place on the disputed words a meaning they will not fairly bear. The judges must not threaten to compete with the legislature, but they should recognize that intelligent interpretation necessarily involves a creative function.

On statutory interpretation generally, see especially: Reed Dickerson, *The Interpretation and Application of Statutes* (1975); Rupert Cross, *Statutory Interpretation* (1976); *Maxwell on the Interpretation of Statutes* (12th edn, 1969); Felix Frankfurter, 'Some Reflections on the Reading of Statutes', 47 *Columbia Law Review*, 1947, p. 527.

3
Binding precedent – the doctrine of *stare decisis*

It is difficult to conceive of a legal system in which precedent plays no part at all. One of the fundamental characteristics of law is the objective that like cases should be treated alike. It is therefore natural that other things being equal one court should follow the decision of another where the facts appear to be similar. But in the common law systems precedents have a greater potency than simply as models for imitation. The rules *require* that in certain circumstances a decision be followed whether the second court approves of the precedent or not. Thus in *Re Schweppes Ltd's Agreement* [1965] 1 All E.R. 195 the Court of Appeal, with Willmer L.J. dissenting, ordered discovery of documents in a case involving restrictive trade practices. On the same day the same three judges gave judgment in a second case involving the same point – *Re Automatic Telephone and Electric Co. Ltd's Agreement* [1965] 1 All E.R. 206. Judgment in the second case was delivered by Lord Justice Willmer who simply said: 'If the matter were res integra, I should have been disposed to dismiss the appeal in this case for the same reasons as those which I gave in my judgment in the previous case. It seems to me, however, that I am now bound by the decision of the majority in the previous case. In these circumstances, I have no alternative but to concur in saying that the appeal in the present case should be allowed.' The second decision was therefore unanimous. The example illustrates not only the impact of binding precedent but also the fact that under the English system the effect is instantaneous. In civil law countries based on Roman law, by contrast, precedents may be followed and commonly are, but there is no rule requiring that they be followed.

The doctrine of binding precedent is called *stare decisis* (more precisely *stare rationibus decidendis*, keep to the decisions of past cases). It must be distinguished from the very different doctrine of *res judicata*. *Res judicata* signifies that the parties to a litigated dispute cannot reopen it after the normal period for an appeal has lapsed or after they have exhausted their right to appeal. There is an exception in criminal cases, permitting the later reopening of a case *on the facts* if it appears that there may have been a miscarriage of justice. But, subject to that, the parties are bound by the result of the case once it is finally concluded. *Stare decisis* is a doctrine that affects not the parties but everyone else – it concerns the impact of the decision for the future on others in the community and especially on later courts.

The first essential ingredient of the doctrine of binding precedent is a hierarchy of courts and rules that indicate the inter-relationship of the different courts.

1. The hierarchy of courts and the doctrine of binding precedent

(a) The House of Lords

The decisions of the House of Lords are binding on all lower courts. For virtually all this century they were also binding on the House of Lords itself. The House of Lords ruled in *London Tramways* v. *London County Council* [1898] A.C. 375* that it was bound by its own decisions. In fact this rule was virtually settled nearly forty years earlier in *Beamish* v. *Beamish* (1861) 9 H.L.C. 274, but the *London Tramways* case finally decided the matter. LORD HALSBURY delivered the only speech, of which the crucial passage (at 380) was perhaps:

Of course I do not deny that cases of individual hardship may arise, and there may be a current of opinion in the profession that such and such a judgment was erroneous; but what is that occasional interference with what is perhaps abstract justice, as compared with the inconvenience – the disastrous inconvenience – of having each question subject to being re-argued and the dealings of mankind rendered doubtful by reason of different decisions, so that in truth and in fact there would be no real final court of appeal. My lords, 'interest rei publicae' is that there should be 'finis litium' sometime and there can be no 'finis litium' if it were possible to suggest in each case

* Professor Rupert Cross has rightly pointed out that the appellant was London Tramways *not*, as stated in the law report, the different company London Street Tramways – see Cross, *Precedent in English Law* (3rd edn, 1977), p. 107, n. 4.

that it might be reargued because it is 'not an ordinary case' whatever that may mean.

In the decades that followed, the doctrine that the House of Lords was bound by its own decisions seemed solidly established even though it was criticised from time to time – see especially Lord Wright's famous article 'Precedent', *Cambridge Law Journal*, 1944, p. 118. On 26 July 1966 however, Lord Gardiner, the Lord Chancellor, read a statement on behalf of himself and all the other Lords of Appeal in Ordinary announcing that the House of Lords would in future regard itself as free to depart from its own previous decisions:

Practice statement (Judicial Precedent) [1966] 1 W.L.R. 1234

Their Lordships regard the use of precedent as an indispensable foundation upon which to decide what is the law and its application to individual cases. It provides at least some degree of certainty upon which individuals can rely in the conduct of their affairs, as well as a basis for orderly development of legal rules.

Their Lordships nevertheless recognise that too rigid adherence to precedent may lead to injustice in a particular case and also unduly restrict the proper development of the law. They propose therefore to modify their present practice and, while treating former decisions of this House as normally binding, to depart from a previous decision when it appears right to do so.

In this connection they will bear in mind the danger of disturbing retrospectively the basis on which contracts, settlements of property and fiscal arrangements have been entered into and also the especial need for certainty as to the criminal law.

This announcement is not intended to affect the use of precedent elsewhere than in this House.

The above is the statement that appears in the law reports. However it was issued to the press with the following additional explanatory note:

Since the House of Lords decided the English case of *London Street Tramways* (sic) v. *London County Council* in 1898, the House have considered themselves bound to follow their own decisions, except where a decision has been given per incuriam in disregard of a statutory provision or another decision binding on them.

The statement made is one of great importance, although it should not be supposed that there will frequently be cases in which the House thinks it right not to follow their own precedent. An example of a case in which the House might think it right to depart from a precedent is where they consider that the earlier decision was influenced by the existence of conditions which no longer prevail, and that in modern conditions the law ought to be different.

One consequence of this change is of major importance. The relaxation of the rule of judicial precedent will enable the House of Lords to pay greater attention to judicial decisions reached in the superior courts of the Commonwealth, where they differ from earlier decisions of the House of Lords. That could be of great help in the development of our own law. The superior courts of many other countries are not rigidly bound by their own decisions and the change in the practice of the House of Lords will bring us more into line with them.

The House of Lords' Practice Statement was hailed as an event of great consequence, but in the first decade and more that has passed since 1966 it has become apparent that the new freedom to depart from previous decisions will be used extremely sparingly. The point came up in *Jones* v. *Secretary of State for Social Services* [1972] 1 A.C. 944 which was heard specially by seven Lords. The case required interpretation of a statutory provision regarding injury benefit in the light of the House of Lords' own prior decision in *Re Dowling* [1967] 1 A.C. 725. Four Lords (Wilberforce, Dilhorne, Diplock and Simon) were clear that the House's 1967 decision in *Dowling* was wrong and, of these, three thought that it should be departed from under the 1966 Practice Statement but one (Lord Simon) thought it should not. The other three Lords (Reid, Morris and Pearson) thought the *Dowling* decision was right but they also addressed themselves to the question of what they would have thought if they had shared the view that *Dowling* was wrong. They all took the view that they would not have been prepared to depart from it. All the Lords seemed to be agreed that the mere finding that an earlier decision is wrong would not in itself be enough to justify the House from departing from the decision. More was required. The following statements give some clues as to the kind of circumstances in which the House might consider it appropriate to depart from one of its own prior decisions:

LORD REID (at 966): I would not seek to categorise cases in which it [the Practice Statement] should or cases in which it should not be used. As time passes experience will provide some guide. But I would venture the opinion that the typical case for reconsidering an old decision is where some broad issue is involved, and that it should only be in rare cases that we should reconsider questions of construction of statutes or other documents. ... Holding these views. I am firmly of opinion that *Dowling's* case ought not to be reconsidered. No broad issue of justice or public policy is involved nor is any question of legal principle. The issue is simply the proper construction of complicated provisions in a statute.

LORD WILBERFORCE (at 995): On a question of construction of an Act of Parliament, as to which this House has the last word until Parliament itself intervenes, there are strong objections against a change of course by this House. Unless the cases, first and subsequent, wholly coincide, there may be a doubt which decision of the House ... prevails, and litigants may be encouraged in future disputes ... to take the chance of an appeal here, in the hope of procuring a departure.

LORD PEARSON (at 996): ... in my opinion the decision in *Dowling's Case* ought to be followed for several reasons. First, there is the principle of stare decisis. A decision of this House has had the distinctive advantage of being final both in the sense that it put an end to the litigation between the parties and in the sense that it established the principle embodied in the ratio decidendi. Consequently it provided a firm foundation on which commercial, financial and fiscal arrangements could be based.* Also it marked a definite step in the development of the law, irreversible except by Act of Parliament. This distinctive advantage of finality should not be thrown away by too ready use of the recently declared liberty to depart from previous decisions. [Lord Pearson also drew attention to the fact that the decision in *Dowling*, counting the judges at all three levels, had only been by six to five. A majority of six to five was not very strong but it showed that the view that prevailed was a tenable view.] That seems to me to be a sufficient reason for not overruling the decision in *Dowling's* case. If a tenable view taken by a majority in the first appeal could be overruled by a majority preferring another tenable view in a second appeal, then the original tenable view could be restored by a majority preferring it in a third appeal. Finality of decision would be utterly lost.

LORD DIPLOCK (at 1014–15): It [*Dowling's* case] is a recent decision, but I see no greater reason for perpetuating recent error than for leaving ancient error uncorrected. [The decision could be reversed by Parliament but] it would be unrealistic to suppose that this could be done quickly. [In the meanwhile harmful practical consequences would follow for victims of accidents so that Lord Diplock would have overruled *Dowling's* case notwithstanding that it was] a decision on the construction of a statute which after some delay could be put right by Parliamentary action.

LORD SIMON OF GLAISDALE (at 1023–6): I am clearly of the opinion that it would be wrong now to seek to depart from that decision [in *Dowling*] for the following reasons: (1) The declaration of 26 July 1966 itself implies that the power to depart from a previous decision of your Lordships House is one to be most sparingly exercised. (2) A variation of view on a matter of statutory construction ... would I should have thought, rarely provide a suitable occasion.... (3) Your Lordships will, I apprehend, be reluctant to encourage frequent litigants like the Secretary of State for Social Services in this type of case or the Commissioners of Inland Revenue in revenue cases to reopen arguments once concluded against them ... (4) On the instant issue there is obviously much to be said for each side ... (5) ... despite dire prophecy the decision in *Dowling's* case has not rendered the statutory scheme unwork-

* It is not apparent how commercial, financial or fiscal arrangements could be based on the decision in *Dowling*, which ruled that a decision by statutory authorities that an injury arose from an accident was final (ed).

able ... (6) If *Dowling's* case really causes inconvenience, it seems to me that the remedy lies far more appropriately with the legislature than in your Lordships' House sitting judicially. Parliament has facilities for advice (both from the executive and from industry) as to all possible repercussions, which your Lordships do not have.... (9) I am left uncertain what would be the effect of overruling *Dowling's* case on decisions thereafter come to on the basis that it was correctly decided. Before departing from a previous decision your Lordships, I surmise, would require to be positively satisfied that such a course would not involve unacceptably the re-opening of issues long concluded or the risk of individual hardship in cases intermediately decided.

The same broadly negative view about the chances of getting the House of Lords to change its mind was given in *Fitzleet Estates* v. *Cherry* [1977] 1 W.L.R. 1345. There have, however, been at least a few cases in which the House of Lords has gone back on its own previous decisions. In *Miliangos* [1976] A.C. 443 it changed the rule that a damages award in an English court had to be expressed in sterling. The decision (which is considered further below, p. 111) was based largely on the changed position of sterling in the modern world. In *Herrington* v. *British Railways Board* [1972] A.C. 877 the House softened its 1929 ruling that an occupier owed virtually no duty of care to a trespasser even when he was a child. The reason appears to have been a change in the climate of opinion as to the acceptable distribution of risks between occupiers and those injured on their premises. (Lord Pearson, for instance, said that the previous decision's 'formulation of the duty of occupier to trespasser is plainly inadaquate for modern conditions' (at 930). Lord Diplock said he explained the decision as reflecting 'the general development of legal concepts since 1929 as to the source of one man's duty to take steps for the duty of another' (at 935).) In a third case the House of Lords in the *Johanna Oldendorff* [1974] A.C. 479 departed from its own prior decision in *The Aello* [1961] A.C. 135 as to when a ship became 'an arrived ship'.

Questions

1. What appear to be the grounds on which the House of Lords will and will not reconsider one of its own previous decisions?

2. Is there any reason why the House should be less ready to reconsider a decision involving a point of statutory construction than a common law point?

3. Should the fact that the earlier decision is a relatively recent one be influential?

4. If the House of Lords departs from its earlier decision, could it later return to it? In other words is the effect of departing from its decision the same as over-ruling it?

5. Would one expect any final appeal court to reconsider its own decisions readily?

(b) The Court of Appeal, Civil Division

There are two main issues to be explored. One is the relationship between the Court of Appeal and the House of Lords, and the other is the relationship of the Court of Appeal towards its own previous decisions.

(i) *Is the Court of Appeal necessarily bound by the decisions of the House of Lords?*

Until recently there had never been any doubt about the fact that the Court of Appeal was bound by the decisions of the House of Lords. But in *Broome* v. *Cassell* [1971] 2 Q.B. 354 the Court of Appeal had the temerity to hold (unanimously) that the House of Lords had been wrong in its view in *Rookes* v. *Barnard* [1964] A.C. 1129, at 1221–31, per Lord Devlin, on the circumstances in which exemplary damages could be awarded. In *Rookes* v. *Barnard* Lord Devlin, with the unanimous approval of his brethren, had laid down that exemplary damages could only be awarded in three types of circumstances. The trial judge in *Cassell* v. *Broome* regarded himself as bound by this ruling. But the Court of Appeal (Lord Denning M.R., Salmon and Phillimore L.JJ.) held that the House of Lords' decision on this was not binding because it ignored two other House of Lords cases, *Hulton* v. *Jones* decided in 1910 and *Ley* v. *Hamilton* decided in 1935. They therefore invoked the doctrine that the House of Lords in *Rookes* v. *Barnard* had acted *per incuriam*. The suggestion was not well received. When the case went on appeal to the House of Lords, Lord Hailsham delivered a magisterial rebuke to Lord Denning and his colleagues.

> I am driven to the conclusion that when the Court of Appeal described the decision in *Rookes* v. *Barnard* as decided 'per incuriam' or 'unworkable' they really only meant that they did not agree with it. But, in my view, even if this were not so, it is not open to the Court of Appeal to give gratuitous advice to judges of first instance to ignore decisions of the House of Lords in this way. ... The fact is, and I hope it will never be necessary to say so again, that, in the hierarchical system of courts which exists in this country, it is necessary for each lower tier, including the Court of Appeal, to accept loyally the decisions of the higher tiers [[1972] A.C. 1027 at 1054].

Lords Reid, Wilberforce, Diplock and Kilbrandon all agreed with Lord Hailsham that it was not open to the Court of Appeal to advise judges to ignore decisions of the House of Lords on the ground that they were decided per incuriam, or were unworkable.

Nevertheless the issue came up again only two years later. In *Schorsch Meier G.m.b.h.* v. *Henning* [1975] 1 Q.B. 416 the Court of Appeal held by two to one (Lord Denning and Foster J., Lawton L.J. dissenting) that judgment in an English court could be given in a currency other than sterling notwithstanding a clear decision to the contrary by the House of Lords in 1961 in the *Havana Railways* case. Lord Denning based his view on the maxim *cessante ratione cessat ipsa lex* (when the reason for the rule goes the rule lapses):

LORD DENNING (at 424–5): Why have we in England insisted on a judgment in sterling and nothing else? It is, I think, because of our faith in sterling. It was a stable currency which had no equal. Things are different now. Sterling floats in the wind. It changes like a weathercock with every gust that blows. So do other currencies. This change compels us to think again about our rules. I ask myself: Why do we say that an English court can only pronounce judgment in sterling? Lord Reid thought that it was 'primarily procedural': see the *Havana* case [1961] A.C. 1007, 1052. I think so too. It arises from the form in which we used to give judgment for money. From time immemorial the courts of common law used to give judgment in these words: 'It is adjudged that the plaintiff *do recover* against the defendant £X' in sterling. On getting such a judgment the plaintiff could at once issue out a writ of execution for £X. If it was not in sterling, the sheriff would not be able to execute it. It was therefore essential that the judgment should be for a sum of money in sterling: for otherwise it could not be enforced.

There was no other judgment available to a plaintiff who wanted payment. It was no good his going to a Chancery Court. He could not ask the Lord Chancellor or the Master of the Rolls for an order for specific performance. He could not ask for an order that the defendant do pay the sum due in the foreign currency. For the Chancery Court would never make an order for specific performance of a contract to pay money. They would not make it for a sterling debt....

Those reasons for the rule have now ceased to exist. In the first place, the form of judgment has been altered. In 1966 the common law words 'do recover' were dropped. They were replaced by a simple order that the defendant 'do' the specified act. A judgment for money now simply says that: 'It is [this day] adjudged that the defendant do pay the plaintiff' the sum specified: see the notes to R.S.C., Ord. 42, r. 1 and the appendices [in the *Supreme Court Practice*, vol. II]. That form can be used quite appropriately for a sum in foreign currency as for a sum in sterling. It is perfectly legitimate to order the defendant to pay the German debt in Deutschmarks. He can satisfy the judgment by paying the Deutschmarks: or, if he prefers, he can satisfy it by paying the equivalent sum in sterling, that is, the equivalent at the time of payment.

In the second place, it is now open to a court to order specific performance of a contract to pay money. In *Beswick* v. *Beswick* [1966] Ch. 538; [1968] A.C. 58, this court and the House of Lords held that specific performance could be ordered of a contract to pay money, not only to the other party, but also to a third party. Since that decision, I am of opinion that an English court has power, not only to order specific performance of a contract to pay in sterling, but also of a contract to pay in dollars or Deutschmarks or any other currency.

Seeing that the reasons no longer exist, we are at liberty to discard the rule itself. Cessante ratione legis cessat ipsa lex. The rule has no support amongst the juridical writers. It has been criticised by many. Dicey [*Dicey & Morris*, *The Conflict of Laws*, 9th ed. (1973), p. 883] says:

> 'Such an encroachment of the law of procedure upon substantive rights is difficult to justify from the point of view of justice, convenience or logic.'

Only last year we refused to apply the rule to arbitrations. We held that English arbitrators have jurisdiction to make their awards in a foreign currency, when that currency is the currency of the contract: see *Jugoslavenska Oceanska Plovidba* v. *Castle Investment Co. Inc.* [1974] Q.B. 292. The time has now come when we should say that when the currency of a contract is a foreign currency – that is to say, when the money of account and the money of payment is a foreign currency – the English courts have power to give judgment in that foreign currency:

FOSTER J. simply said he agreed with the judgment of Lord Denning and with his reasons. But LORD JUSTICE LAWTON did not agree. He was, he said, a timorous member of the court. 'I stand in awe of the House of Lords'. He regarded himself bound by the *Havana Railways* decision. It was disturbing to find that a rule which did injustice to a foreign trader was based, as he thought it was, on archaic legalistic nonsense. 'It is however my duty to apply the law, not to reform it' (at 430).

The case did not go to the House of Lords, but the issue did, only a year later, in *Miliangos* v. *George Frank (Textiles) Ltd* [1976] A.C. 443 which, as has already been seen, raised precisely the same problem. In *Miliangos* the trial judge Bristow J. had to choose between the 1961 House of Lords decision in the *Havana Railways* case that judgment could only be given in sterling and the Court of Appeal's decision in *Schorsch Meier* holding that this was no longer the case. He chose the House of Lords' decision on the ground that it was still binding on him – parliament had not altered it nor had the House of Lords itself. It represented the view of the law held in this country for some 350 years – [1975] 1 Q.B. 487 at 492. On appeal to the Court of Appeal, Lord Denning, Stephenson and Geoffrey Lane L.JJ. held unanimously that they were bound by the Court of Appeal's decision in *Schorsch Meier* [1975] 1 Q.B. 416. But the House of Lords held that the Court of Appeal had been wrong – though it agreed with the Court of Appeal that the rule regarding the currency of judgments should be changed.

Miliangos v. *George Frank (Textiles) Ltd*
[1976] A.C. 443

LORD SIMON OF GLAISDALE (at 472): Since the Court of Appeal is absolutely bound by a decision of the House of Lords and (at least on its civil side) by a previous decision of the Court of Appeal itself, it would be surprising if the meaning and application of the maxim 'cessante ratione' were really that accepted by the majority of the Court of Appeal in *Schorsch Meier* and again by the learned Master of the Rolls in the instant case. For as such it would enable any court in the land to disclaim any authority of any higher court on the ground that the reason which had led to such higher court's formulation of the rule of law was no longer relevant. A rule rooted in history could be reversed because history is the bunk of the past. Indeed, taken literally, there is no ground for limiting 'lex' to judge-made law. Coke, apparently the originator of the tag (Co.Litt. 70b), was quite prepared to say that a statute which conflicted with reason could be declared invalid by the courts (*Dr Bonham's Case* (1610) 8 C.Rep. 107a, 118a).... It would be easy to compile a bulky anthology of authoritative citations to show that those courts of law which are bound by the rule of precedent are not free to disregard an established rule of law because they conceive that another of their own devising might be more reasonable....

To sum up on this part of the case: (1) the maxim in the form 'cessante ratione cesset ipsa lex' reflects one of the considerations which your Lordships will weigh in deciding whether to overrule, by virtue of the 1966 declaration, a previous decision of your Lordships' House; (2) in relation to courts bound by the rule of precedent the maxim 'cessante ratione cessat ipsa lex,' in its literal and widest sense, is misleading and erroneous; (3) specifically, courts which are bound by the rule of precedent are not free to disregard an otherwise binding precedent on the ground that the reason which led to the formulation of the rule embodied in such precedent seems to the court to have lost cogency; (4) the maxim in reality reflects the process of legal reasoning whereby a previous authority is judicially distinguished or an exception is made to a principal legal rule; (5) an otherwise binding precedent or rule may, on proper analysis, be held to have been impliedly overruled by a subsequent decision of a higher court or impliedly abrogated by an Act of Parliament; but this doctrine is not accurately reflected by citation of the maxim 'cessante ratione cessat ipsa lex.'

Lord Simon dissented on the question whether the rule should now be changed; Lords Wilberforce and Fraser expressly agreed with Lord

Simon on the maxim *cessante ratione*. Lord Cross went even further and thought that although normally the Court of Appeal was bound to follow its previous decisions, it should not have done so in *Miliangos* – since the Court of Appeal's decision in *Schorsch Meier* was wrong in departing from the *Havana* decision of the House of Lords:

LORD CROSS (at pp. 495–6): It will be apparent from what I have said that I do not view the decision of this House in the *Havana* case with any enthusiasm. Indeed, to speak bluntly, I think it was wrong on both points. But as Lord Reid said in *Reg* v. *Knuller (Publishing, Printing and Promotions) Ltd.* [1973] A.C. 435, 455, the fact that we no longer regard previous decisions of this House as absolutely binding does not mean that whenever we think that a previous decision was wrong we should reverse it. In the general interest of certainty in the law we must be sure that there is some very good reason before we so act. In the *Schorsch Meier* case [1975] Q.B. 416, 425, Lord Denning M.R., with the concurrence of Foster J., took it on himself to say that the decision in the *Havana* case that our courts cannot give judgment for payment of a sum of foreign currency – though right in 1961 – ought not to be followed in 1974 because the 'reasons for the rule have now ceased to exist'. I agree with my noble and learned friend, Lord Wilberforce, that the Master of the Rolls was not entitled to take such a course. It is not for any inferior court – be it a county court or a division of the Court of Appeal presided over by Lord Denning – to review decisions of this House. Such a review can only be undertaken by this House itself under the declaration of 1966. Moreover, although one cannot but feel sympathy for Stephenson and Geoffrey Lane L.JJ. in the embarrassing position in which they found themselves, I think that it was wrong for the Court of Appeal in this case to follow the *Schorsch Meier* decision. It is no doubt true that that decision was not given 'per incuriam' but I do not think that Lord Greene M.R., when he said in *Young* v. *Bristol Aeroplane Co. Ltd.* [1944] K.B. 718, 729 that the '*only*' exceptions to the rule that the Court of Appeal is bound to follow previous decisions of its own were those which he set out, can fairly be blamed for not foreseeing that one of his successors might deal with a decision of the House of Lords in the way in which Lord Denning dealt with the *Havana* case.

It remains to be seen whether the Court of Appeal will now accept the very strong indications from the House of Lords, first in *Broome* v. *Cassell* and then in *Miliangos*, that the Court of Appeal *is* absolutely bound by the decisions of the House of Lords – whatever it may think of them. In his autobiographical book *The Discipline of Law*, 1979 Butterworths, Lord Denning has made it clear (p. 308) that he does not regard the Court of Appeal's *lèse-majesté* in *Schorsch Meier* as having been necessarily wrong:

If in the *Schorsch Gmbh* v. *Henning* case we had held ourselves bound by the *Havana* case, we would have given judgment in sterling. In that event, in the *Miliangos* case the Swiss firm [the plaintiffs] would automatically have taken judgment in sterling also. ... The Swiss firm would not have appealed. The House of Lords would never have had the opportunity of overruling the *Havana* case. The law would still have been that an English court could only give judgment in sterling. That would have been a disaster for our trade with countries overseas.

Questions

1. Is a court ever justified in knowingly breaking the rules of precedent in order to precipitate an appeal so as to get a more authoritative ruling on the matter?

2. Do you think the House of Lords is right to insist that the Court of Appeal should loyally follow its decisions, no matter what?

(ii) *The Court of Appeal and its own decisions*

The classic modern statement of the rule of *stare decisis* for the Court of Appeal (Civil Division) is that in *Young* v. *Bristol Aeroplane Co. Ltd*:

Young v. *Bristol Aeroplane Company Ltd*
[1944] K.B. 718 (Court of Appeal)

Plaintiff claimed damages for injuries at work. The defendant argued that his claim was bad since according to a Court of Appeal decision, *Perkins* v. *Hugh Stevenson & Sons, Ltd* [1940] 1 K.B. 56, a claim for common law damages was barred where the injured workman had received compensation under the Workmen's Compensation Acts. The plaintiff appealed.

LORD GREENE M.R. in the course of giving judgment for a full court of six judges said (at 723, 725):

The question thus raised as to the jurisdiction of this court to refuse to follow decisions of its own was obviously one of great general importance and directions were given for the appeal to be argued before the full court. It is surprising that so fundamental a matter should at this date still remain in doubt. To anyone unacquainted with the rare cases in which it has been suggested or asserted that this court is not bound to follow its own decisions or those of a court of co-ordinate jurisdiction the question would, we think, appear to be beyond controversy. Cases in which this court has expressed its regret at finding itself bound by previous decisions of its own and has stated in the clearest terms that the only remedy of the unsuccessful party is to appeal to the House of Lords are within the recollection of all of us and numerous examples are to be found in the reports. When in such cases the matter has been carried to the House of Lords it has never, so far as we know, been suggested by the House that this view was wrong and that this court could itself have done justice by declining to follow a previous decision of its own which it considered to be erroneous. On the contrary, the House has, so far as we are aware, invariably assumed and in many cases expressly stated that this court was bound by its own previous decision to act as it did.

... The Court of Appeal is a creature of statute and its powers are statutory. It is one court though it usually sits in two or three divisions. Each division has co-ordinate jurisdiction, but the full court has no greater powers or jurisdiction than any division of the court. Its jurisdiction is mainly appellate, but it has some original jurisdiction. ... Neither in the statute itself nor (save in two cases mentioned hereafter) in decided cases is there any suggestion that the powers of the Court of Appeal sitting with six or nine or more members are greater than those which it possesses when sitting as a division with three members. In this respect, although we are unable to agree with certain views expressed by Greer L.J. ([1]) as will presently appear, we think that he was right in saying that what can be done by a full court can equally well be done by a division of the court. The corollary of this is, we think, clearly true, namely, that what cannot be done by a division of the court cannot be done by the full court....

On a careful examination of the whole matter we have come to the clear conclusion that this court is bound to follow previous decisions of its own as well as those of courts of co-ordinate jurisdiction. The only exceptions to this rule (two of them apparent only) are those already mentioned which for convenience we here summarize: (1) The court is entitled and bound to decide which of two conflicting decisions of its own it will follow. (2) The court is bound to refuse to follow a decision of its own which, though not expressly overruled, cannot, in its opinion, stand with a decision of the House of Lords. (3) The court is not bound to follow a decision of its own if it is satisfied that the decision was given per incuriam.

Two main issues have arisen since the decision in *Young's* case in 1944. One is whether the House of Lords' Practice Statement in July 1966 could in any way be invoked by the Court of Appeal to release it from the rule that it was generally bound by its own decisions and, secondly, if not, what is the extent of the exceptions to the rule in *Young's* case.

Is the Court of Appeal bound to follow Young v. *Bristol Aeroplane?*

Since 1966 Lord Denning has led a campaign to establish the principle that the House of Lords' Practice Statement should apply to the Court of Appeal as well. (In view of this campaign, there was some irony in the categorical assertion by Lord Denning in *Miliangos* (p. 111, above) that the Court of Appeal had to follow its own decision in *Schorsch Meier* because it was bound to do so). The culmination of this campaign came in *Davis* v. *Johnson*:

1. *In re Shoesmith* [1938] 2 K.B. 637, 644.

Davis v. *Johnson* [1979] A.C. 264

The appellant and the respondent were cohabiting as man and wife in a council flat. The respondent was the father of the applicant's daughter. After much violence the applicant fled to a refuge for battered women. She applied under the Domestic Violence and Matrimonial Proceedings Act 1976 for an injunction to restrain him from using violence and ordering him to vacate the flat. At the hearing the respondent argued that the Court of Appeal was bound to follow its own two previous and very recent decisions given on the interpretation of the 1976 Act – which had ruled that a person with a proprietary interest in property could not be excluded by an injunction granted under the 1976 Act. The case was heard by five judges. Three (Lord Denning, Sir George Baker P., and Shaw L.J.) held that the Court of Appeal was free to depart from its previous decisions. Two (Goff and Cumming–Bruce L.JJ.) disagreed:

LORD DENNING M.R. (at 278–83):

Departure from previous decisions

I turn to the second important point: can we depart from those two cases? Although convinced that they are wrong, are we at liberty to depart from them? What is the correct practice for this court to follow?

On principle, it seems to me that, whilst this court should regard itself as normally bound by a previous decision of the court, nevertheless it should be at liberty to depart from it if it is convinced that the previous decision was wrong. What is the argument to the contrary? It is said that, if an error has been made, this court has no option but to continue the error and leave it to be corrected by the House of Lords. The answer is this: the House of Lords may never have an opportunity to correct the error; and thus it may be perpetuated indefinitely, perhaps for ever. That often happened in the old days when there was no legal aid. A poor person had to accept the decision of this court because he had not the means to take it to the House of Lords. It took 60 years before the erroneous decision in *Carlisle and Cumberland Banking Co* v. *Bragg*[1] was overruled by the House of Lords in *Gallie* v. *Lee* ([1971] A.C. 1004). Even today a person of moderate means may be outside the legal aid scheme, and not be able to take his case higher, especially with the risk of failure attaching to it. That looked as if it would have been the fate of Mrs Farrell when the case was decided in this court[2], but she afterwards did manage to collect enough money together, and by means of it to get the decision of this court reversed by the House of Lords. Apart from monetary considerations, there have been many instances where cases have been settled pending an appeal to the House of Lords; or, for one reason or another, not taken there, especially with claims against insurance

1. [1911] 1 KB 489.
2. *Farrell* v. *Alexander* [1976] QB 345 at 359.

companies or big employers. When such a body has obtained a decision of this court in its favour, it will buy off an appeal to the House of Lords by paying ample compensation to the appellant. By so doing, it will have a legal precedent on its side which it can use with effect in later cases. I fancy that such may have happened in cases following *Oliver* v. *Ashman*. By such means an erroneous decision on a point of law can again be perpetuated forever. Even if all those objections are put on one side and there is an appeal to the House of Lords, it usually takes 12 months or more for the House to reach its decision. What then is the position of the lower courts meanwhile? They are in a dilemma. Either they have to apply the erroneous decision of the Court of Appeal, or they have to adjourn all fresh cases to await the decision of the House of Lords. That has often happened. So justice is delayed, and often denied, by the lapse of time before the error is corrected. The present case is a crying instance. If it took the ordinary course of appeals to the House, it would take some months before it was decided. Meanwhile many women would be denied the protection which Parliament intended they should have. They would be subjected to violence without redress; because the county court judges would have to say to them: 'We are sorry but the Court of Appeal says we have no jurisdiction to help you.' We were told that, in this very case, because of the urgency, the House might take special measures to hear it before Christmas. But, even so, I doubt whether they would be able to give their decision until well on in the New Year. In order to avoid all the delay, and the injustice consequent on it, it seems to me that this court, being convinced that the two previous decisions were wrong, should have the power to correct them and give these women the protection which Parliament intended they should have. It was suggested that, if we did this, the county court judges would be in a dilemma. They would not know whether to follow the two previous decisions or the later decision of this court. There would be no such dilemma. They should follow this later decision. Such a position always arises whenever the House of Lords corrects an error made by a previous decision. The lower courts, of course, follow the latest decision. The general rule is that, where there are conflicting decisions of courts of co-ordinate jurisdiction, the later decision is to be preferred, if it is reached after full consideration of the earlier decision: see *Minister of Pensions* v. *Higham* ([1948] 2 K.B. 153, 155).

So much for principle. But what about our precedents? What about *Young* v. *Bristol Aeroplane Co Ltd*?

The position before 1944

I will first state the position as it was before the year 1944. The Court of Appeal in its present form was established in 1873. It was then the final court of appeal. Appeals to the House of Lords were abolished by that Act and only restored a year or two later. The Court of Appeal inherited the jurisdiction of the previous courts of appeal such as the Court of Exchequer Chamber and the Court of Appeal in Chancery. Those earlier courts had always had power to reconsider and renew the law as laid down in previous decisions; and, if that law was found to be wrong, to correct it; but without disturbing the actual decision. I take this from the statements of eminent judges of those days who knew the position. In particular in 1852 Lord St Leonards L.C. in *Bright* v. *Hutton, Hutton* v. *Bright*[3] said in the House of Lords:

> '... you are not bound by any rule of law which you may lay down, if upon a subsequent occasion, you should find reason to differ from that rule; that is, that this House, *like every Court of Justice*, possesses an inherent power to correct an error into which it may have fallen.' ...

Young v. *Bristol Aeroplane Co Ltd*[4]

The change came about in 1944. In *Young* v. *Bristol Aeroplane Co Ltd* the court overruled the practice of a century. Lord Greene MR[5], sitting with a court of five, laid down that this court is bound to follow its previous decision as well as those of co-ordinate jurisdiction, subject to only three exceptions: (i) where there are two conflicting decisions, (ii) where a previous decision cannot stand with a decision of the House of Lords, (iii) if a previous decision was given per incuriam.

It is to be noticed that the court laid down that proposition as a rule of law. That was quite the contrary of what Brett M.R. had declared in *The Vera Cruz (No 2)*[6] in 1884. He said it arose only as a matter of judicial comity. Events have proved that in this respect that Brett M.R. was right and Lord Greene M.R. was wrong. I say this because the House of Lords in 1898 had held itself bound by its own previous decisions as a rule of law: see *London Street Tramways Co. Ltd* v. *London County Council*[7]. But yet in 1966 it discarded that rule. In a statement it was said[8]:

> 'Their Lordships nevertheless recognise that too rigid adherence to precedent may lead to injustice in a particular case and also unduly restrict the proper development of the law. They propose, therefore, to modify their present practice, and while treating former decisions of this House as normally binding, to depart from a previous decision when it appears right to do so.'

That shows conclusively that a rule as to precedent (which any court lays down for itself) is not a rule of law at all. It is simply a practice or usage laid down by the court itself for its own guidance; and, as such, the successors of that court can alter that practice or amend it or set up other guidelines, just as the House of Lords did in 1966. Even as the judges in *Young* v. *Bristol Aeroplane Co. Ltd* thought fit to discard the practice of a century and declare a new practice or usage, so we in 1977 can discard the guidelines of 1944 and set up new guidelines of our own or revert to the old practice laid down by Brett M.R. Nothing said in the House of Lords, before or since, can stop us from doing so. Anything said about it there must needs be obiter dicta. This was emphasised by Salmon L.J. in this court in *Gallie* v. *Lee*[9]:

> 'The point about the authority of this court has never been decided by the House of Lords. In the nature of things it is not a point that could

3. (1852) 3 H.L. Cas. 341 at 388.
4. [1944] K.B. 718.
5. [1944] K.B. 718 at 729, 730.
6. (1884) 9 P.D. 96 at 98.
7. [1898] A.C. 375.
8. [1966] 1 W.L.R. 1234.
9. [1969] 2 Ch. 17 at 49.

ever come before the House for decision. Nor does it depend on any statutory or common law rule. This practice of ours apparently rests solely on a concept of judicial comity laid down many years ago and automatically followed ever since. ... Surely today judicial comity would be amply satisfied if we were to adopt the same principle in relation to our own decisions as the House of Lords has recently laid down for itself by pronouncement of the whole House.'

The new guidelines

So I suggest that we are entitled to lay down new guidelines. To my mind, this court should apply similar guidelines to those adopted by the House of Lords in 1966. Whenever it appears to this court that a previous decision was wrong, we should be at liberty to depart from it if we think it right to do so. Normally, in nearly every case of course, we would adhere to it. But in an exceptional case we are at liberty to depart from it.

Alternatively, in my opinion, we should extend the exceptions in *Young* v. *Bristol Aeroplane Co. Ltd*[10] when it appears to be a proper case to do so. I realise that this comes virtually to the same thing, but such new exceptions have been created since *Young* v. *Bristol Aeroplane Co. Ltd*. For instance, this court can depart from a previous decision of its own when sitting on a criminal cause or matter: see the recent cases of *R.* v. *Gould*[11] and *R* v. *Newsome*, *R* v. *Brown*[12]. Likewise by analogy it can depart from a previous decision in regard to contempt of court. Similarly in the numerous cases when this court is sitting as a court of last resort. There are many statutes which make this court the final court of appeal. In every jurisdiction throughout the world a court of last resort has, and always has had, jurisdiction to correct the errors of a previous decision: see *Webster* v. *Ashton-under-Lyne Overseers*, *Hadfield's Case*[13]. In the recent case of *Tiverton Estates Ltd* v. *Wearwell Ltd*[14], we extended the exceptions by holding that we could depart from a previous decision where there were conflicting principles as distinct from conflicting decisions, of this court: likewise we extended the notion of per incuriam in *Industrial Properties (Barton Hill) Ltd* v. *Associated Electrical Industries Ltd*[15]. In the more recent cases of *Re K (wardship: care and control)*[16]; and *Re S (BD)* v. *S (DI) (infants: care and con-* *(minors) (wardship: care and control)*[16]; and *Re S (BD)* v. *S (DI) (infants: care and control)*[17], this court in its jurisdiction over children did not follow the earlier statute are plain, then it is not open to any decision of any court to contradict the statute; because the statute is the final authority on what the law is. No court can depart from the plain words of a statute. On this ground may be rested the decisions in *W and J B Eastwood Ltd* v. *Herrod (Valuation Officer)*[19]; and *Hanning* v. *Maitland (No 2)*[20], where this court departed from previous interpretations of a statute. In *Schorsch Meier GmbH* v. *Hennin*[21], we introduced

10. [1944] K.B. 718.
11. [1968] 2 Q.B. 65.
12. [1970] 2 Q.B. 711.
13. (1873) L.R. 8 C.P. 306.
14. [1975] Ch. 146.
15. [1977] Q.B. 580.
16. [1977] Fam. 179.
17. [1977] Fam. 109.
18. [1962] 1 W.L.R. 886.
19. [1968] 2 Q.B. 923.
20. [1970] 1 Q.B. 580.
21. [1975] Q.B. 416 at 425.

another exception on the principle 'cessante ratione legis cessat ipsa lex'. This step of ours was criticised by the House of Lords in *Milliangos* v. *George Frank (Textiles) Ltd*[22]; but I venture to suggest that, unless we had done so, the House of Lords would never have had the opportunity to reform the law. Every court would have held that judgments could only be given in sterling. No one would have taken the point to the House of Lords, believing that it was covered by *Re United Railways of the Havana and Regla Warehouses*[23]. In this present case the applicant, Miss Davis, was at first refused legal aid for an appeal, because the point was covered by the two previous decisions. She was only granted it afterwards when it was realised by the legal aid committee that this court of five had been specially convened to reconsider and review those decisions. So, except for this action of ours, the law would have been regarded as settled by *B* v. *B* and *Cantliff* v. *Jenkins*; and the House of Lords would not have had the opportunity of pronouncing on it. So instead of rebuking us, the House of Lords should be grateful to us for giving them the opportunity of considering these decisions.

The truth is that the list of exceptions from *Young* v. *Bristol Aeroplane Co. Ltd* is now getting so large that they are in process of eating up the rule itself; and we would do well simply to follow the same practice as the House of Lords.

SIR GEORGE BAKER P. agreed, but he put his principle rather differently (at 290–1):

I have listened with care to counsel for the applicant's careful argument that *Young's* case does not bind this court. I cannot agree with that, but I am prepared to accept that there should be, and must be, a further carefully limited exception which is in part founded on an extension of, or gloss on, the second exception in *Young's* case that the court is bound to refuse to follow a decision of its own which though not expressly overruled cannot in its opinion stand with a decision of the House of Lords.

I would attempt to define the exception thus: 'The court is not bound to follow a previous decision of its own if satisfied that that decision was clearly wrong and cannot stand in the face of the will and intention of Parliament expressed in simple language in a recent Act passed to remedy a serious mischief or abuse, and further adherence to the previous decision must lead to injustice in the particular case and unduly restrict proper development of the law with injustice to others.' My reasons, briefly, are (1) the practice statement in the House of Lords which recognises the danger of injustice, (2) that there is a conflict between a statutory provision and a decision which has completely misinterpreted the recent statute and failed to understand its purpose, (3) and to me the most compelling, by his judicial oath a judge binds himself to do 'right to all manner of people after the laws and usages of this Realm'. Here, by refusing the injunction, I would be doing a great wrong to the applicant, her child, and many others by following a decision which I firmly believe is not the law. The statute is the law, the final authority.

22. [1976] A.C. 443.

23. [1961] A.C. 1001.

It is said that the proper course for this court is to be bound by the precedent of *B* v. *B*, whatever we may think of it, give leave to appeal and grant an injunction until the hearing which can be expedited. If one learns anything in the Family Division it is that the unexpected always happens in family affairs. There is no certainty that this case will ever reach the House of Lords. The respondent may end his tenancy. The applicant may decide to go and stay elsewhere. There are many possibilities which could lead to the withdrawal of legal aid which is not normally given in order that an important point of law may be decided where the decision will not benefit the immediate parties.

For the rest, I agree with the judgment of Lord Denning M.R.

SHAW L.J. put his exception to *Young's* case even more narrowly (at 308):

For my part I venture to think that if in 1944 a sutuation like the present had been in contemplation a further exception might have found a place in the judgment in *Young* v. *Bristol Aeroplane Co. Ltd.* It would be in some such terms as that the principle of stare decisis should be relaxed where its application would have the effect of depriving actual and potential victims of violence of a vital protection which an Act of Parliament was plainly designed to afford to them, especially where, as in the context of domestic violence, that deprivation must inevitably give rise to an irremediable detriment to such victims and create in regard to them an injustice irreversible by a later decision of the House of Lords.

Neither of the other two judges, however, would go along with the majority:

GOFF L.J. (at 292): In my judgment, with the greatest respect to those who think otherwise, this court when exercising its civil jurisdiction is bound by the general rule in *Young's* case, save possibly where it is the final court of appeal, and further the class of exceptions is closed. My reasons for this conclusion are the necessity for preserving certainty in our law, which has great value in enabling persons to obtain definite advice on which they can order their affairs, the care which should always be taken to see that hard cases do not make bad law and the oft repeated occasions on which *Young's* case has been approved on the highest authority....

CUMMING-BRUCE L.J. (at 311) agreed: It seems to me that in any system of law the undoubted public advantages of certainty in civil proceedings must be purchased at the price of the risk of injustice in difficult individual situations. I would think that the present practice holds the balance just about right. The temptation to depart from it would be much less seductive if there could be readier access to the House of Lords. The highest tribunal is within the reach of those whose modest means enable them to qualify for legal aid, and of the extremely rich. Its doors are closed, for practical purposes, to everyone else. The injustice which today is liable to flow from the fact that unsatisfactory old cases are so seldom capable of review in the House of Lords would be mitigated or removed if Parliament decided to give this court and the

House of Lords power to order that costs in the House of Lords should be paid by the Exchequer in those cases in which this court or the House of Lords on an application for leave to appeal certified that an appeal to the House of Lords was desirable in order to enable that House to review a decision regarded as mistaken but binding on the Court of Appeal. The expense to the public and any resulting inconvenience would be infinitely less than that which would flow from a relaxation of the present practice in respect of stare decisis as declared in *Young's* case. I consider that we are bound to act in accordance with the practice as stated in *Young's* case and the *Morelle Ltd* case[24]. This is because I consider that the constitutional functions of their Lordships sitting in their judicial capacity include the function of declaring with authority the extent to which the Court of Appeal is bound by its previous decisions, and the function of defining with authority the exceptional situations in which it is open to this court to depart from a previous decision. So I hold that this court is bound by the declaration made by Viscount Dilhorne, Lord Simon of Glaisdale and Lord Russell of Killowen in *Farrell* v. *Alexander*[25], that this court is bound by precedent exactly as stated by Scarman L.J.[26] in his judgment in the Court of Appeal in that case affirming the declaration made by Lord Hailsham of St Marylebone L.C. in *Cassell & Co. Ltd* v. *Broome*[27], a declaration again which commanded the express assent of a majority of their Lordships' House.

The House of Lords [1979] A.C. 317 rejected the view of the majority and admonished the Court of Appeal to abide by its own previous decisions save to the extent allowed by *Young's* case:

LORD DIPLOCK (at 326, 328): In an appellate court of last resort a balance must be struck between the need on the one side for the legal certainty resulting from the binding effect of previous decisions and on the other side the avoidance of undue restriction on the proper development of the law. In the case of an intermediate appellate court, however, the second desideratum can be taken care of by appeal to a superior appellate court, if reasonable means of access to it are available; while the risk to the first desideratum, legal certainty, if the court is not bound by its own previous decisions grows ever greater with increasing membership and the number of three-judge divisions in which it sits, as the arithmetic which I have earlier mentioned shows. So the balance does not lie in the same place as in the case of a court of last resort. That is why Lord Gardiner L.C.'s announcement about the future attitude towards precedent of the House of Lords in its judicial capacity concluded with the words: 'This announcement is not intended to affect the use of precedent elsewhere than in this House.'... In my opinion, this House should take this occasion to re-affirm expressly, unequivocably and unanimously that the rule laid down in the *Bristol Aeroplane* case as to stare decisis is still binding on the Court of Appeal.

LORD SALMON (at 344): I am afraid that I disagree with Lord Denning M.R. when he says that the Court of Appeal is not absolutely bound by its

24. [1955] 2 Q.B. 379.
25. [1977] A.C. 59.
26. [1976] Q.B. 345 at 371.
27. [1972] A.C. 1027 at 1055.

own decisions and may depart from them just as your Lordships may depart from yours. As my noble and learned friend, Lord Diplock, has pointed out, the announcement made in 1966 by Lord Gardiner L.C. about the future attitudes of this House towards precedent ended with the words: 'This announcement is not intended to affect the use of precedents elsewhere than in this House.' I would also point out that that announcement was made with the unanimous approval of all the Law Lords, and that, by contrast, the overwhelming majority of the present Lords Justices have expressed the view that the principle of stare decisis still prevails and should continue to prevail in the Court of Appeal. I do not understand how, in these circumstances, it is even arguable that it does not. I sympathise with the views expressed on this topic by Lord Denning M.R., but until such time, if ever, as all his colleagues in the Court of Appeal agree with those views, stare decisis must still hold the field. I think that this may be no bad thing. There are now as many as 17 Lords Justices in the Court of Appeal, and I fear that if stare decisis disappears from that court there is a real risk that there might be a plethora of conflicting decisions which would create a state of irremediable confusion and uncertainty in the law. This would do far more harm than the occasional unjust result which stare decisis sometimes produces but which can be remedied by an appeal to your Lordships' House. I recognise, as Cumming-Bruce L.J. points out, that only those who qualify for legal aid or the very rich can afford to bring such an appeal. This difficulty could however be surmounted if when the Court of Appeal gave leave to appeal from a decision it has felt bound to make by an authority with which it disagreed, it had a power conferred on it by Parliament to order the appellants and/or the respondents' costs of the appeal to be paid out of public funds. This would be a very rare occurrence and the consequent expenditure of public funds would be minimal.

Lord Dilhorne (at 336), Lord Kilbrandon (at 340) and Lord Scarman (at 349) all expressly agreed. There can therefore be no doubt that in the view of the House of Lords the Court of Appeal is bound by its own decisions – subject to the exceptions admitted in *Young's* case. Lord Denning, writing in *The Discipline of Law* (1979), p. 300, described the House of Lords' decision as a 'crushing rebuff'. 'My arguments were rejected by the House of Lords. So my plea failed.' But he remained unrepentant:

I am consoled to find that there are many intermediate Courts of Appeal in the Commonwealth which adopt the course which I have advocated. So this has made my dissent worthwhile. There are the Courts of Appeal in New South Wales, Victoria, South Australia and New Zealand. In particular, in *Bennett* v. *Orange City Council* [1967] 1 N.S.W. 502 Wallace P. said: 'Giving full credit to the desirability of certainty in the law (which occasionally appears to be a pious aspiration) I consider than even an intermediate Court of Appeal may, on special occasions and in the absence of higher authority on the subject in hand, play its part in the development of the law and in ensuring that it keeps pace with modern conditions and modern thought, and accordingly, in an appropriate case, I do not think that an earlier decision of the Court (including this Court) should be allowed to stand when justice seems to require otherwise.'

Lord Denning said that these words from New Zealand prompted the question whether the Court of Appeal should always simply cut short parties who wished to reargue points already settled by the Court of Appeal? Should they apply the leap-frog procedure under the Administration of Justice Act 1969, s. 12, for sending cases direct to the House of Lords? In either case the House of Lords would then not have the benefit of the views of the Court of Appeal.

Questions

1. Do you prefer the view of the House of Lords or of Lord Denning as to whether the Court of Appeal should be bound to follow its own prior decisions?

2. Is the Court of Appeal bound to follow the views on this matter expressed by the House of Lords? (See, on this, further p. 158 below.)

If Young's case is binding on the Court of Appeal, what is the extent of the exceptions?

Lord Greene in *Young's* case (p. 114, above) stated three exceptions to the general rule that the Court of Appeal was bound by its own decisions:

Prior conflicting decisions: The first was where there were two conflicting prior decisions and it had to decide between them. This could happen in two possible ways. One is where the two conflicting decisions were both reached before *Young's* case in 1944 established that the Court was bound by its own decisions. The second possibility is that the Court discovers a conflict where previously it had thought that none existed. This happened in a series of cases relating to annulment of marriage. In *Casey* v. *Casey* [1949] P. 420 the Court of Appeal held that English courts had no jurisdiction to hear a petition for nullity when the marriage was voidable and the only links with this country were that the marriage was celebrated in England and the petitioner resided in England. In *Ramsay Fairfax* v. *Ramsay Fairfax* [1956] P. 115 this case was distinguished by the Court of Appeal, which held that English courts did have jurisdiction to annul a marriage wherever it had been celebrated and whether or not it was voidable, provided both parties were resident in England. In *Ross-Smith* v. *Ross-Smith* [1961] P. 39 the Court of Appeal treated the two cases as irreconcilable and chose to follow the former. Presumably once the Court of Appeal has decided which of two conflicting decisions to follow, the other is then regarded as overruled and the Court cannot therefore in a fourth case later change its mind and return to the discarded decision.

Inconsistent House of Lords' decision: the second exception was where a Court of Appeal decision, though not expressly overruled, could not stand with a decision of the House of Lords. Where the House of Lords' decision is subsequent to that of the Court of Appeal this exception creates no problem. This is simply a case of implied overruling. But does the doctrine also cover the case of inconsistency with a *prior* decision of the House of Lords? This would happen where the Court of Appeal held that one of its decisions had been wrongly decided because it had ignored a then-existing House of Lords' decision. This is precisely what did happen in *Fitzsimmons* v. *The Ford Motor Co. Ltd* [1946] 1 All E.R. 429 where the Court of Appeal refused to follow two earlier decisions of its own because they were inconsistent with a previous decision of the House of Lords. This was in spite of the fact that in both cases the Court of Appeal had actually discussed the House of Lords decision.

In *Miliangos* (p. 111 above) two Law Lords disagreed as to whether the Court of Appeal could disregard one of its own decisions because it conflicted with a prior decision of the House of Lords. It will be recalled that the Court of Appeal in *Schorsch Meier* (p. 109 above) had refused to follow the earlier House of Lords' decision in the *Havana Railways* case. Lord Denning in *Miliangos* said that Lord Greene's second exception did not permit it to reopen the question. It had simply to follow its own decision in *Schorsch Meier* since the House of Lords' decision had been prior to and not after *Schorsch Meier* ([1975] Q.B. at 502). Lord Simon in the House of Lords agreed ([1976] A.C. at 479); whilst Lord Cross thought, to the contrary, that the Court of Appeal in *Miliangos* should have followed the *Havana Railways* case and not its own erroneous decision in *Schorsch Meier* ([1976] A.C. at 496). The point remains to be settled.

Per incuriam: The third and most difficult exception is where the earlier decision was given per incuriam. In *Miliangos* [1975] Q.B. 487

(at 503) LORD DENNING gave some guidance as to the meaning of the phrase 'per incuriam':

Another exception is where a previous decision has been given per incuriam. 'Such cases,' said Lord Greene M.R. in *Young* v. *Bristol Aeroplane Co. Ltd.* [1944] K.B. 718, 729 – 'would obviously be of the rarest occurrence and must be dealt with in accordance with their special facts.' So it has been held that a decision is not given per incuriam because the argument was not 'fully or carefully formulated': see *Morelle Ltd.* v. *Wakeling* [1955] 2 Q.B. 379, 399, or was 'only weakly or inexpertly put forward': *Joscelyne* v. *Nissen* [1970] 2 Q.B. 86, 99; nor that the reasoning was faulty: *Barrington* v. *Lee* [1972] 1 Q.B. 326, 345 by Stephenson L.J. To these I would add that a case is not decided per incuriam because counsel have not cited all the relevant authorities or referred to this or that rule of court or statutory provision. The court does its own researches itself and consults authorities; and these may never receive mention in the judgments. Likewise a case is not decided per incuriam because it is argued on one side only and the other side does not appear. The duty of counsel, in those circumstances, as we all know, is to put the case on both sides to the best of his ability: and the court itself always examines it with the utmost care, to protect the interests of the one who is not represented. That was done in the *Schorsch Meier* case itself.

The cases in which we have interfered are limited. One outstanding case recently is *Tiverton Estates Ltd.* v. *Wearwell Ltd.* [1975] Ch. 146, where this court in effect overruled *Law* v. *Jones* [1974] Ch. 112, on the ground that a material line of authority was not before the court and that the point called for immediate remedy.

But the leading statement of the principle of per incuriam is by Lord Evershed in *Morelle* v. *Wakeling:*

Morelle v. *Wakeling* [1955] 2 Q.B. 379
(Court of Appeal)

The Court of Appeal had to decide whether to follow its own previous decision given the same year. It was contended that the previous decision was given per incuriam, in that the arguments were brief (counsel for one side having only been instructed the afternoon before the hearing) and the law was highly specialized.

The Court of Appeal sat with five judges. LORD EVERSHED M.R. gave the judgment of the Court (at 406):

As a general rule the only cases in which decisions should be held to have been given per incuriam are those of decisions given in ignorance or forgetfulness of some inconsistent statutory provision or of some authority binding on the court concerned: so that in such cases some part of the decision or some step in the reasoning on which it is based is found, on that account, to be demonstrably wrong. This definition is not necessarily exhaustive, but cases not strictly within it which can properly be held to have been decided per incuriam must, in our judgment, consistently with the stare decisis rule which is an essential feature of our law, be, in the language of Lord Greene M.R., of the rarest occurrence. In the present case it is not shown that any statutory provision or binding authority was overlooked, and while not excluding the possibility that in rare and exceptional cases a decision may properly be held to have been per incuriam on other grounds, we cannot regard this as such a case. As we have already said, it is, in our judgment, impossible to fasten upon any part of the decision under consideration or upon any step in the reasoning upon which the judgments were based and to say of it: 'Here was a manifest slip or error'. In our judgment, acceptance of the Attorney-General's argument would necessarily involve the proposition that it is open to this court to disregard an earlier decision of its own or of a court of co-ordinate jurisdiction (at least in any case of significance or complexity) whenever it is made to appear that the court had not upon the earlier occasion had the benefit of the best argument that the researches and industry of counsel could provide. Such a proposition would, as it seems to us, open the way to numerous and costly attempts to re-open questions now held to be authoritatively decided. Although as was pointed out in *Young* v. *Bristol Aeroplane Co. Ltd.*, a 'full court' of five judges of the Court of Appeal has no greater jurisdiction or higher authority than a normal division of the court consisting of three judges, we cannot help thinking that, if the Attorney-General's argument were accepted, there would be a strong tendency in cases of public interest and importance, to invite a 'full court' in effect to usurp the function of the House of Lords and to reverse a previous decision of the Court of Appeal. Such a result would plainly be inconsistent with the maintenance of the principle of stare decisis in our courts.

Other exceptions to stare decisis in the Court of Appeal

Although only three exceptions where mentioned in *Young's* case and although the House of Lords in *Miliangos* urged the Court of Appeal to follow its own decisions unless one of the three exceptions mentioned in *Young* applied, a considerable number of other exceptions appear in fact to have been created. Lord Denning set out a long list in the section of his judgment in *Davis* v. *Johnson* headed 'The new guidelines' (p. 118 above). He could have added two more. In *Boys* v. *Chaplin* [1968] 2 Q.B. 1, all three members of the Court of Appeal held that three judges in the Court of Appeal are not bound by an earlier decision of two judges on an interlocutory appeal – i.e. an appeal on a preliminary point. In *Worcester Works Finance Ltd* v. *Cooden Engineering Co. Ltd* [1972] 1 Q.B. at 217 Lord Denning himself said that 'although decisions of the Privy Council are not binding on this Court, nevertheless when the Privy Council disapproves of a previous decision of this Court or casts doubt upon it, we are at liberty to depart from the previous decision'. There are other examples of the Court of Appeal preferring a later decision of the Privy Council to its own prior decision – see, for instance, *Doughty* v. *Turner Manufacturing Co. Ltd* [1964] 1 Q.B. 518 in which the Court of Appeal followed the Privy Council's decision in the *Wagon Mound No. 1* [1961] A.C. 388 rather than its own decision in *Re Polemis* [1921] 3 K.B. 560. Therefore even if the Court of Appeal is generally bound to follow its own decisions, the total list of recognized exceptions is a long one.

(c) The Court of Appeal, Criminal Division

The Court of Appeal (Criminal Division) is the successor of the Court of Criminal Appeal which was set up in 1907 and which existed until it became one of the divisions of the Court of Appeal in 1966. The Court of Criminal Appeal had in turn been the successor of the old Court for Crown Cases Reserved.

In principle, in all three stages of its existence – as Court for Crown Cases Reserved, Court of Criminal Appeal and Court of Appeal (Criminal Division)—the basic rule has been that stare decisis applied. But it has always been true that the doctrine has not been rigidly enforced and there are not a few examples where the court has refused to follow an earlier decision. (See, for instance, *Ring* (1892) 61 L.J.M.C. 116; *Power* [1919] 1 K.B. 572; *Norman* [1924] 2 K.B. 315; and *Newsome and Browne* [1970] 2 Q.B. 711.) The greater flexibility on the criminal side was formally recognised in *R.* v. *Taylor* in 1950:

R. v. *Taylor* [1950] 2 K.B. 368 (Court of Criminal Appeal)

The appellant had pleaded guilty to a charge of bigamy. He had been advised to do so because the facts of the case were virtually identical to those of *R.* v. *Treanor*, a previous decision of the Court of Criminal Appeal. Judgment was given by LORD GODDARD C.J. on behalf of himself and the other six members of the court:

I desire to say a word about the reconsideration of a case by this court. The Court of Appeal in civil matters usually considers itself bound by its own decisions or by decisions of a court of co-ordinate jurisdiction. For instance, it considers itself bound by its own decisions and by those of the Exchequer Chamber; and, as is well known, the House of Lords also always considers itself bound by its own decisions.* In civil matters this is essential in order to preserve the rule of stare decisis.

This court, however, has to deal with questions involving the liberty of the subject, and if it finds, on reconsideration, that, in the opinion of a full court assembled for that purpose, the law has been either misapplied or misunderstood in a decision which it has previously given, and that, on the strength of that decision, an accused person has been sentenced and imprisoned it is the bounden duty of the court to reconsider the earlier decision with a view to seeing whether that person had been properly convicted. The exceptions which apply in civil cases ought not to be the only ones applied in such a case as the present, and in this particular instance the full court of seven judges is unanimously of opinion that the decision in *Rex* v. *Treanor* was wrong.

But the true scope of *Taylor* is unclear. In *Newland* (1953) 37 Cr. App. Rep. 154, 167, for instance, Lord Goddard doubted the wisdom of the Court of Criminal Appeal's decision in the 1933 case of *Manley*. But instead of indicating that the Court would decline to follow it, he hoped instead that *Manley* might some day be considered by the House of Lords.

(d) Divisional Courts

The leading authority on whether a Divisional Court is bound by its own decisions is that of *Police Authority for Huddersfield* v. *Watson*, in which Lord Goddard C.J. made it clear that the rule was the same as that applied in *Young* v. *Bristol Aeroplane Co. Ltd* to the Court of Appeal (Civil Division):

Police Authority for Huddersfield v. *Watson*
[1947] 1 K.B. 842 (Divisional Court, Q.B.D.)

The Divisional Court had to consider whether it was bound by its own prior decision in *Garvin* v. *Police Authority for City of London* [1944] K.B. 358.

LORD GODDARD C.J. (at 846–8): Mr Streatfield has argued that it is open to us to depart from *Garvin's* case if we think it was wrongly decided. As we have not heard his full argument, I prefer only to say this: Nothing that I have heard in this case, as far as the argument has gone, satisfies me that *Garvin's* case was wrongly decided; but whether it was rightly decided or not I am clearly of opinion that we ought to follow it. This court is made a final court of appeal in these matters, and I can imagine nothing more disastrous than that where the court has given a decision upon the construction or appli-

* This was of course before the House of Lords' Practice Statement of July 1966.

cation of this Act another court should give a decision contrary to the decision already given, because there then would be two conflicting cases. You might get a court consisting perhaps of different judges choosing one of those decisions, and another court choosing the other decision, and there would be no finality in the matter at all. For myself, I think we ought to hold that we are bound by this decision. [Lord Goddard referred to the rule laid down in *Young* v. *Bristol Aeroplane Co. Ltd* for the guidance of the Court of Appeal.]

If that is the rule which is applicable in the Court of Appeal – it is to be remembered that Court of Appeal judgments are reviewable in the House of Lords, at any rate by leave – and the Master of the Rolls pointed out in the course of his judgment that in some cases Court of Appeal judgments are final, as in bankruptcy, and in others are reviewable by the House of Lords, and yet he draws no distinction—and if, therefore, in a court most of whose decisions are reviewable, although it may be only by leave, in the House of Lords, those decisions are binding on the court, how much more important is it that this court, which is a final court, should follow its own decisions and consider that it ought to give full force and effect to them. Otherwise, as I have said, a great deal of uncertainty would be introduced into the law.

I know that in the writings of various eminent people the doctrine of stare decisis has been canvassed from time to time. In my opinion, if one thing is certain it is that stare decisis is part of the law of England, and in a system of law such as ours, where the common law, and equity largely, are based on decisions, it seems to me it would be very unfortunate if a court of final appeal has given a decision and has laid down a definite principle and it cannot be said the court has been misled in any way by not being referred to authorities, statutory or judicial, which bear on the question, that it should then be said that that decision was not to be a binding authority.

[Atkinson and Lewis JJ. agreed.]

This means that the exceptions recognised in *Young's* case are equally accepted as exceptions in the Divisional Court – see e.g. *Nicholas* v. *Penny* [1950] 2 K.B. 466.

A Divisional Court exercising civil jurisdiction is bound by the decisions not only of the House of Lords but also of the Court of Appeal, Civil Division – see *Read* v. *Joannon* (1890) 25 Q.B.D. 300 at 302–3. Equally a Divisional Court exercising criminal jurisdiction was bound by decisions of the Court of Criminal Appeal and is now bound by its successor, the Court of Appeal (Criminal Division) – see *Ruse* v. *Read* [1949] 1 K.B. 377 at 384. See also *Carr* v. *Mercantile Products Ltd* [1949] 2 K.B. 601 at 605 per Goddard C.J. holding that a Divisional Court exercising criminal jurisdiction was bound by a decision of the civil Court of Appeal. In *R.* v. *Northumberland Compensation Appeal Tribunal* [1951] 1 K.B. 711 the Divisional Court, per Goddard C.J., refused to follow one of its own decisions on the ground that it was inconsistent with an earlier decision of the House of Lords. But this was implicity disapproved of by the House of Lords in *Cassell* v. *Broome* [1972] A.C. 1004, when the Lords held that the Court of Appeal had been wrong to treat one of the House of Lords' earlier decisions (*Rookes* v. *Barnard*) as mistaken. By the same token, presumably the Divisional Court should follow its own decisions rather than an earlier decision of the House of Lords, even if it concludes that the earlier House of Lords' decision is inconsistent with its own later decision.

(e) Trial courts

The decisions of trial courts are not binding on that court. Thus the decisions of the High Court are not binding on any High Court judge, and the decisions of the county court and of magistrates' courts are not binding on those courts. But magistrates' courts and county courts are bound by the decisions of the High Court and of all the appellate courts.

The High Court is bound by the decisions of higher courts, but a problem arises where these conflict. Should the High Court judge, for instance, follow the Court of Appeal or an inconsistent House of Lords' decision? As has been seen (p. 110 above), this dilemma faced Bristow J. in *Miliangos* v. *George Frank (Textiles) Ltd* [1975] 1 Q.B. 487 and he chose to follow the House of Lords' decision in *Havana Railways* (holding that damages had to be awarded in sterling), rather than the Court of Appeal's decision in *Schorsch Meier* (holding that this ancient rule had lapsed). But when the case went to the House of Lords, one of the Law Lords criticised the trial judge:

LORD SIMON OF GLAISDALE (at 477, 478): Greatly as I sympathise with Bristow J. in his predicament, I feel bound to say, with all respect, that I think he was wrong.... It is the duty of a subordinate court to give credence and effect to the decision of the immediately higher court, notwithstanding that it may appear to conflict with the decision of a still higher court. The decision of the still higher court must be assumed to have been correctly distinguished (or otherwise interpreted) in the decision of the immediately higher court. For example, in the instant case, in my respectful opinion, Bristow J. should have assumed that the Court of Appeal in *Schorsch Meier* had correctly interpreted and applied the maxim "cessante ratione ..." and had in consequence correctly held that it was not bound to apply the *Havana* decision [1961] A.C. 1007 to the facts judicially ascertained in *Schorsch Meier*. Any other course is not only an invitation to legal chaos but in effect involves a subordinate court sitting in judgment on a decision of its superior court. That is contrary to law. Moreover, in this respect, as so often, the law is a distillation of practical experience, even though all knowledge of the experience may be lost. Here, however, the experience is recoverable. If a subordinate court fails to abide loyally by the judgment of its superior court, the decision of the subordinate court is likely to be appealed to the superior court, which is in turn likely to vindicate its previous decision.

LORDS WILBERFORCE and CROSS both said simply that no one except the House of Lords could review decisions of the House of Lords. They did not however express any views on whether a trial judge faced with the dilemma of Bristow J. should do as he did.

Precedents that are not binding

The decisions of lower courts are never binding. Thus the House of Lords cannot be bound by a decision of the Court of Appeal nor the Court of Appeal by a decision of the High Court. The decisions of the Judicial Committee of the Privy Council are not binding on any of the courts in the United Kingdom.

A non-binding precedent may of course be of very great persuasive power. The precise extent of its persuasive power will depend on all the circumstances. Precedents, as will be seen, are minutely weighed and measured for their proper impact and effect. But a precedent that does not bind the court considering it cannot by some mysterious process create law that is in some way binding. If a decision is not binding on the court it means that the court is ultimately free to accept or to reject the rule for which the case stands. The nature of this process will be explored in the next chapter.

2. A comparison with some other countries

The English doctrine of precedent is unlike that followed in civil law countries and is not even identical to that operating in other common law jurisdictions. Professor Sir Rupert Cross, in his book *Precedent in English Law*, has described some of the differences between our system and others:

Rupert Cross, *Precedent in English Law*
(3rd ed. 1977), pp. 12–22

COMPARISON WITH FRANCE[1]

Although there are important differences between them, the French legal system may be taken as typical of those of western Europe for the purposes of the present discussion.

1. For precedent in International Law see *Trendtex Trading Corporation* v. *Central Bank of Nigeria*, [1977] 1 All E.R. 881.

From the standpoint of strict legal theory, French law is not based on case-law (*la jurisprudence*) at all. The Civil and Penal Codes are theoretically complete in the sense that they (and other statutory provisions) are supposed to cover every situation with which the ordinary courts are concerned. It can still be argued that, strictly speaking, case-law is not a source of law in France because a judge is not obliged to consider it when coming to a decision. Art. 5 of the Civil Code forbids his laying down general rules when stating a decision, and it would be possible for a French appellate court to set aside a ruling founded exclusively on a past decision on the ground that the ruling lacked an adequate legal basis.[2] None the less, there is a substantial body of case-law dealing with the construction of the Codes and the solution of problems on which they are in fact silent. Moreover, there is no code governing the *droit administratif* of the Conseil d'Etat, which is not numbered among the ordinary courts, and it is mainly based on case-law.

From the practical point of view one of the most significant differences between English and French case-law lies in the fact that the French judge does not regard himself as absolutely bound by the decision of any court in a single previous instance. He endeavours to ascertain the trend of recent decisions on a particular point. To quote a distinguished French legal writer: 'The practice of the courts does not become a source of law until it is definitely fixed by the repetition of precedents which are in agreement on a single point.'[3]

Three of the principal reasons for the difference between the French and English approaches to the doctrine of precedent are that the need for certainty in the law was formerly felt more keenly by the English judge than most of the judges on the Continent, the highly centralized nature of the hierarchy of the English courts, and the difference in the position of the judges in the two countries.

The need for certainty

The first point has been stressed by Dr Goodhart. The continental judge has no doubt always wanted the law to be certain as much as the English judge, but he has felt the need less keenly because of the background of rules provided first by Roman law and codified custom, and later by the codes of the Napoleonic era. These resulted in a large measure of certainty in European law. Roman law was never 'received' in England, and we have never had a code in the sense of a written statement of the entirety of the law. 'English justice, if it were not to remain fluid and unstable, required a strong cement. This was found in the common-law doctrine of precedent with its essential and peculiar emphasis on rigidity and certainty.'[4]

2. David and De Vrees, *The French Legal System*, p. 115.

3. Lambert, 'Case-method in Canada', 39 Yale L.J. 1 at p. 14. A helpful account of the operation of precedent in France together with examples of the judgments of French courts is given by Lawson, 'Negligence in Civil Law', pp. 231–5. See also O. Kahn-Freund, C. Lévy and B. Rudden, *A Source-book of French Law*, pp. 98–140. In Spain it seems that two decisions of the Supreme Court constitute a 'doctrina' binding on inferior courts, though the Supreme Court may later alter the 'doctrina' (Neville Brown, 'The Sources of Spanish Law', 5 Int. Comp. L.Q. 367, (1956)).

4. 'Precedent in English and Continental Law', 50 L.Q.R. 40 at p. 62 (1934).

The hierarchy of the courts

The French judicial system is based on the division of the country into districts. So far as civil cases are concerned, each district has a court of first instance and a court of appeal. The district courts of first instance are not bound by their own previous decisions or those of any other district court of first instance, nor are such courts of first instance bound by the previous decisions of their own appellate courts or that of any other district. The district appellate courts are not bound by their own past decisions or those of any other district court of appeal. There is a right of appeal on points of law from the district appellate court to the *Cour de Cassation* in Paris. In theory, this body is not bound by any previous decision of its own, and the district courts are not bound to follow an individual decision of the *Cour de Cassation* in a previous case. So far as the actual litigation under consideration by the *Cour de Cassation* is concerned, that court may remit it for re-hearing by an appellate court of a district near to that from which the appeal came. If the case should be brought before the *Cour de Cassation* again, it is only since 1967 that the Court has had power finally to dispose of the case instead of remitting it to yet another district court of appeal with a binding direction concerning the manner in which it was to be decided.

The more serious criminal cases are tried by a district assize court from which there is no appeal apart from the possibility of an application to the *Cour de Cassation* on a question of law which may result in an order for a new trial.

With a system of courts as decentralized as that which has just been sketched, it would have been difficult for France to have evolved a doctrine of precedent as rigid in every respect as our own. Even if the *Cour de Cassation* had come to treat itself and the district courts as absolutely bound by each of its past decisions, there would almost inevitably have been considerable flexibility at the level of the district courts of appeal. It would have been too much to expect anything approximating to the uniformity of decision demanded of the English judges. French law owes its uniformity to the various codes in which it is declared and to *la doctrine* – the opinions of jurists – rather than to *la jurisprudence*.

The different position of the judges

The French judge occupies a very different position from that of his English counterpart. In the first place, there are fewer judges of our superior courts than there are members of the French judiciary. Secondly, the French judiciary is not, like ours, recruited from the Bar but from the civil service, and thirdly, many French judges are relatively young and inexperienced men. They go into the Ministry of Justice with the intention of taking up a judicial career and become junior judges in small district courts after what is little more than a period of training. The result is that the judiciary tends to be considered as less important in France than in England, and, although it is difficult to assess the significance of these matters, it is generally, and probably rightly, assumed that they help to explain the greater regard which is paid to case-law in this country than that which is paid to it on the Continent. Still more important is the fact that the judges have been the architects of English law.

'The common law is a monument to the judicial activity of the common law judge. He, not the legislator or the scholar, created the common law. He still enjoys the prestige of that accomplishment.'[5]

Further reasons for the difference

Allowance must also be made for the difference in the structure of the judgments of English and French courts and for the vast number of cases decided by the *Cour de Cassation.* A rule that a single precedent should be binding would be unlikely to develop when it was difficult to discover a precise *ratio decidendi* and it is not always easy to extract a precise *ratio* from a French judgment. A rule that one single decision of an appellate court should suffice to constitute a binding precedent is hardly likely to develop in a jurisdiction in which there are numerous appeals. The House of Lords only hears some 30 appeals from the English courts each year, but some 10,000 cases are dealt with annually by the different chambers of the *Cour de Cassation.*

Notwithstanding the great theoretical difference between the English and French approaches to case-law, and the total absence of rules of precedent in France, the two systems have more in common than might be supposed. In the first place, French judges and writers pay the greatest respect to the past decisions of the *Cour de Cassation.*

Secondly, the manner in which the English judges interpret the *ratio decidendi* of a case tends to assimilate their attitude towards a legal problem to that of their French counterparts. . . . It would be wrong to say that, in deciding case D, an English High Court judge of first instance considers cases A and B, decided by the Court of Appeal, together with case C, decided by another High Court judge of first instance, in order to see whether the law has become 'definitely fixed by the repetition of precedents which are in agreement on a single point'. However, his attitude towards the *ratio decidendi* of Case A might be profoundly affected by the observations of the judges in cases B and C. English case-law is not the same as *la jurisprudence*, but it is a mistake to suppose that our judges permanently inhabit a wilderness of single instances.

CONTRAST WITH U.S.A.

Although the North American practice of giving judgment in the form of elaborate discussions of previous cases is more like the English than the continental, the United States Supreme Court and the appellate courts in the different states do not regard themselves as absolutely bound by their past decisions. There are many instances, some American lawyers would say too many, in which the Supreme Court has overruled a previous decision.

Thanks to the change of practice in the House of Lords, the English rules of precedent may come to approximate more closely to the North American, but two reasons why the North American rules should remain more lax suggest themselves. These are the number of separate State jurisdictions in the former country and the comparative frequency with which the North American courts have to deal with momentous constitutional issues.

5. Von Mehren, *The Civil Law System*, 839.

Numerous jurisdictions

A multiplicity of jurisdictions produces a multiplicity of law reports which has, in its turn, influenced the teaching of law and led to the production of 'restatements' on various topics. The 'case method' of instruction which, in one form or another, prevails in most North American law schools, aims at finding the best solution of a problem on the footing of examples from many jurisdictions, and few schools confine their instruction to the law of any one State. The restatements are concise formulations and illustrations of legal principles based on the case-law of the entire United States and, from time to time, model codes and sets of uniform rules relating to various branches of the law are produced in a form fit for immediate adoption by the legislature. Judges who have been trained by the case method and who are familiar with the restatement and kindred documents will tend to concentrate on recent trends after the fashion of the French courts.

Constitutional issues

When a court is construing a written constitution the terms of that document are the governing factor and the case-law on the meaning of those terms is only a secondary consideration. This point was put very clearly by Frankfurter J. when he was giving judgment in the Supreme Court. He said:

> The ultimate touchstone of constitutionality is the Constitution itself, and not what we do about it.[6]

A further reason why North American courts in general, and the United States' Supreme Court in particular, should not apply our rule of the absolute binding effect of a single decision to constitutional matters is provided by the momentous nature of the issues involved in such cases. To quote Lord Wright:

> It seems clear that, generally speaking, a rigid method of precedent is inappropriate to the construction of a constitution which has to be applied to changing conditions of national life and public policy. An application of words which might be reasonable and just at some time, might be wrong and mischievous at another time.[7]

When the difficulty of amending the Constitution of the United States is borne in mind, it is scarcely surprising that the Supreme Court has become less and less rigorous in its adherence to the principle of *stare decisis*.

CONTRAST WITH SCOTLAND

The following remarks made by a Scottish court as recently as 1950 certainly suggest that the Scottish doctrine of precedent is less strict than our own.

6. *Graves* v. *New York*, 306 U.S. 466 at p. 491 (1939). The importance of the fact that the United States' Supreme Court is frequently concerned with constitutional problems is stressed by Goodhart in 'Case Law in England and America' in *Essays in Jurisprudence and the Common Law*. See also Goodhart, 'Some American Interpretations of Law', in *Modern Theories of Law*, p. 1.

7. 'Precedents', 8 C.L.J. 118 at p. 135.

> If it is manifest that the *ratio decidendi* upon which a previous decision has rested has been superseded and invalidated by subsequent legislation or from other like cause, that *ratio decidendi* ceases to be binding.[8]

No doubt it would be quite incorrect to represent the English judiciary as a body which pays no attention to the maxim *cessante ratione cessat lex ipsa*, but the House of Lords considers that it should be treated as a ground for creating an exception to a binding rule when that is possible, not as a ground for disregarding it. The maxim also indicates a fact to be taken into account by an English court when deciding whether to overrule a case which it has power to overrule.[9]

CONTRAST WITH PARTS OF THE COMMONWEALTH

The Judicial Committee of the Privy Council used to be the final court of appeal for all Commonwealth countries outside the United Kingdom. The Judicial Committee has never considered itself to be absolutely bound by its own previous decisions on any appeal. The form in which the decisions are expressed is often said to militate against the adoption of a rigid rule of precedent, for the judgment of the Committee consists of advice tendered to the Sovereign together with the reasons upon which such advice is based....

The Judicial Committee is, however, strongly disposed to adhere to its previous decisions.[10] The decisions of the Privy Council are only of strong persuasive authority in the English courts.

The right of appeal to the Privy Council has been abolished in some Commonwealth countries, including Canada, and, so far as appeals from the High Court [the highest court in Australia] are concerned, Australia.[11] In the days when there was still an appeal to the Privy Council, the Supreme Court of Canada regarded itself as bound by its own past decisions although there was a saving clause relating to 'exceptional circumstances'.[12] Since the abolition of the right of appeal to the Privy Council, the Supreme Court of Canada has claimed the power of declining to follow its own past decisions as it is the successor to the final appellate jurisdiction of the Privy Council which is not bound by its own past decisions.[13]

The High Court of Australia does not regard itself as absolutely bound by its own past decisions.[14] As long ago as 1879 it was said to be of the utmost importance that in all parts of the Empire where English law prevails, the interpretation of that law by the courts should be as nearly as possible the

8. *Beith's Trustees* v. *Beith* [1950] S.C. 66 at p. 70; see also *Douglas-Hamilton* v. *Duke and Duchess of Hamilton's ante-nuptial marriage contract trustees*, [1961] S.L.T. 305 at p. 309.

9. *George Frank (Textiles) Ltd.* v. *Miliangos*, [1971] A.C. 443 at pp. 472–6.

10. *Fatuma Binti Mohamed Bin Salim and Another* v. *Mohamed Bin Salim*, [1952] A.C. 1.

11. An appeal to the Privy Council still lies from the appellate courts of the Australian states. The High Court is the supreme federal court in Australia.

12. *Stewart* v. *Bank of Montreal* (1909), 41 S.C.R. 522 at p. 535. See '*Stare Decisis* in the Supreme Court of Canada', by Andrew Joanes, 36 *Canadian Bar Review* 174 (1958).

13. *Re Farm Products, Marketing Act* (1957), 7 D.L.R. (2nd) 257 at p. 271.

14. *A G. for N.S.W.* v. *Perpetual Trustees Co.* (1952), 85 C.L.R. 189.

same.[15] It is for this reason that, in the absence of some special local consideration to justify a deviation, the Australian and Canadian courts would be loath to differ from decisions of the House of Lords, but there does not appear to be any question of the decisions of the House being binding in either country. The High Court of Australia in fact stated that a leading decision on the English criminal law (since largely overruled by an English statute) was to be treated as no authority in Australia,[16] and the Judicial Committee of the Privy Council has held in a civil case that the Australian High Court was right not to follow a decision of the House of Lords on exemplary damages.[17]

For further reading on precedent see especially: Rupert Cross, *Precedent in English Law* (3rd edn, 1977); C.K. Allen, *Law in the Making* (7th edn, 1964); Julius Stone, *Legal Systems and Lawyers' Reasonings* (1964), Chapters 6, 7 and 8; A.L. Goodhart, 'Precedent in English and Continental Law', 50 *Law Quarterly Review*, 1934, p. 40; and on the history of the doctrine, see T. Ellis Lewis, 'The History of Judicial Precedent', *Law Quarterly Review*, vol. 46 (1930), pp. 207, 341; vol. 47 (1931), p. 411; vol. 48 (1932), p. 230. See also T.B. Smith, *The Doctrines of Judicial Precedent in Scots Law* (1952).

15. *Trimble* v. *Hill*, 5 App. Cas. 342 at p. 345.
16. *Parker* v. *R.*, [1963] A.L.R. 524.
17. *Australian Consolidated Press, Ltd.* v. *Uren*, [1967] 2 All E.R. 523.

4
Law reporting

One of the essential elements in a system based on precedent is some tolerably efficient method for making the precedents available to those wishing to discover the law. An unreported decision is technically of precisely the same authority as one that is reported, but decisions that are unreported are more or less inaccessible to all but scholars.* It is through law reporting that the common law is available to the profession and anyone else wishing to know the law. Law reporting in England goes back to the earliest days of the system but even today it has not yet become fully official nor is it organised in what one might think was a systematic way.

1. The history of law reporting

There have been three distinct periods in the history of law reporting. The first, dating from 1282 to 1537, was the period of the Year Books. They are not law reports in the full modern sense, since they appear to have been designed more as guides to pleadings and procedure for advocates than as accounts of the decisions of the courts. They were written originally in Norman French and later in law French – a mixture of Norman French, English and Latin. In modern times they have been published in two editions – the Rolls Series (R.S.) and the Selden Society Series (S.S.) They are mainly of historical and antiquarian interest. Practitioners virtually never have occasion to consult or cite the Year Books.

*Unreported Court of Appeal decisions are however now briefly summarized in *Current Law*.

The second period was that from 1537 to 1865. When the Year Books ceased around 1537, private sets of reports started to appear. They began to include summaries of counsel's argument and of the judges' decisions. The citation of reports in court became more common as the reports improved in quality. Some were excellent – the best is probably Coke, whose reports were published between 1600 and 1658. Coke was also a judge, as was Dyer (Chief Justice of the Common Pleas) and Saunders (Chief Justice of the King's Bench). But contemporaneous reports were rare until the end of the eighteenth century. The private reports are now collected in one great series – the English Reports. These are occasionally, cited in the courts.

The third period is that dating from 1865, when the profession was responsible for establishing the Incorporated Council of Law Reporting for England and Wales. The Council produces a series called The Law Reports and although they are not an official publication, they are regarded as the most authorititative reports. (Any law report to be regarded as worthy of the name must be prepared by a barrister – solicitors have no standing in this field of legal work). The reporter must have been present in court when the judgment was delivered. In addition to The Law Reports there are of course a great variety of other series – the Weekly Law Reports, the All England Law Reports, Lloyd's List Reports, Criminal Appeal Reports etc.

An official committee inquired into the whole system of law reporting in 1940. Its report is of value partly for the historical background it presented of the system:

Report of the Law Reporting Committee (HMSO, 1940)

4. It is a commonplace to lawyers at least that the law of this country consists substantially of legislative enactments and judicial decisions. The former are made known to the public in the most solemn form, printed at the public expense and preserved under conditions which ensure that they shall be permanently and authentically recorded. With the latter it always has been and still is far otherwise. Yet the importance of accurate and permanent reports of judicial decisions is and always has been obvious. We need not discuss at what stage in our legal history the theory of the binding force of precedent first appeared. In its present form it would have received little favour from the judges of the 14th and 15th centuries but already it was plain, as the pages of the Year Books testify, that uniformity and certainty of the law, the essentials of its just administration, cannot be attained without some measure of judicial consistency. As late as the latter half of the 18th century, on the one hand Blackstone wrote 'For it is an established rule to abide by former precedents, where the same points come again in litigation; as well to keep

the scale of justice even and steady, and not liable to waver with every new judge's opinion; as also because the law in that case being solemnly declared and determined, what before was uncertain, and perhaps indifferent, is now become a permanent rule, which it is not in the breast of any subsequent judge to alter or vary from, according to his private sentiments: he being sworn to determine, not according to his own private judgments, but according to the known laws and customs of the land; not delegated to pronounce a new law, but to maintain and expound the old one'.[1] On the other hand Lord Mansfield took a more elastic view of the relation of precedent to principle. 'The law of England', he said, 'would be a strange science indeed if it were decided upon precedents only. Precedents serve to illustrate principles, and to give them a fixed certainty. But the law of England, which is exclusive of positive law, enacted by statute, depends upon principles; and these principles run through all the cases according as the particular circumstances of each have been found to fall within the one or other of them'.[2] To-day, whatever the reasons may be, the theory of the binding force of precedents is firmly established, if not unreservedly, at least only with some such reservation as that a decision need not be followed if it appears to have been given *per incuriam* e.g. by reason of a relevant statute not having been called to the attention of the court.

6. ... It may seem strange but it is true that except for a brief interlude in the reign of King James I the State has taken no part in, and made no financial contribution to, the publication of law reports.... Apart from this single instance of State aid or interference the task of law reporting has been, as it still is, left wholly to private enterprise. Nor do we find any record of supervision by the State of an enterprise so vitally affecting the common welfare except that by a Statute of Charles II in 1662 (14 Car. II C. 33, S. 2) it was enacted that 'All Books concerned the Common Lawes of this Realm shall be printed by the special allowance of the Lord Chancellor or Lord Keeper of the Great Seal of England for the time being the Lords Cheife Justices and Lord Cheife Baron for the time being or one or more of them or by theire or one or more of theire appointments'....

It was left, as we have said, to private enterprise to preserve in law reports that part of our law which consists of judicial decisions. How was this task performed? It is at this stage necessary to recall that at an early date in our legal history the right was established to cite as an authority before any tribunal a law report which had annexed to it the name of a barrister. It is probable that this right arose from a still earlier privilege of a member of the Bar as *amicus curiæ* to inform the court of a relevant decision of which he was aware. It was his right and perhaps his duty to give oral evidence of the law by stating that such and such a decision had been given. Thence followed the right to cite his written report of decisions which he personally vouched as a member of the Bar. Nor must it be forgotten that if it was the privilege of a barrister to write reports that might be cited to the courts, it

1. 1 Comm. 69.
2. *Jones* v. *Randall* (1774) Cowper 37, 39.

was his privilege alone except so far as His Majesty's Judges from time to time might for the public benefit and perhaps their private profit devote a part of their leisure to the compilation of reports.

Here then was a field for private enterprise, for profit and for abuse. In earlier times, as now, the barrister must rely both on reason and authority, and if he must choose between them, would choose the latter. To the law-reporter the opportunity was given and he took advantage of it. It has been calculated that in the period between 1535 (when the Year Books ceased) and 1765 (when Burrow's Reports began to appear) more than one hundred persons were responsible for volumes of reports. Great names are among them – Dyer, Plowden, Coke, Saunders – and their reports have at all times been of high authority. But there are many others to whom perhaps a higher degree of authority is likely to-day to be given than was by their contemporaries. Some indeed were of such ill repute that, rule or no rule, privilege or no privilege, the judges would not listen to quotations from them. Of them Sir Harbottle Grimson wrote in 1657: 'A multitude of flying reports (whose authors are as uncertain as the times when taken ...) have of late surreptitiously crept forth ... we have been entertained with barren and unwanted products; which not only tend to the depraving the first grounds and reason of our students at the common law, and the young practitioners thereof, who by such false lights are misled; but also to the contempt of our common law itself, and of divers our former grave and learned justices and professors thereof; whose honoured and revered names have, in some of the said books, been abused and invocated to patronise the indigested crudities of these plagiaries.'

The last third of the eighteenth century saw an improvement which the first half of the nineteenth century maintained. Douglas, who in the Preface to his Report showed the high purpose that he meant to serve, Burrows with his introduction of headnote and scientific division of his report, Durnford and East with their Term Reports, which for the first time aimed at a timely and regular publication – these and other reporters at least set a standard which had not been reached in earlier times. Moreover, at some date which we cannot discover, but which the late Sir Frederick Pollock put as at least later than 1782, the Judges or some of them were willing to revise reports of their judgment or even to supply written copies of them to the reporter, and a custom grew up whereby as a matter of professional etiquette some one reporter in each Court was supposed to have a monopoly of this assistance from the Judge. This reporter was thus in a sense 'authorised' and his reports were known as 'authorised' or 'regular' reports as distinguished from other reports, which were 'irregular' or 'unauthorised'. This did not, however, prevent all reports, whether regular or irregular, from being cited if they satisfied the single condition of being vouched by the name of a barrister. And so the flood of reports did not subside but, on the contrary, was increased by a new kind of publication which, anonymous in title and originally disclaiming any intention of competing with the regular reports, became in due course a serious rival and by its merits and in particular by its speedier publication commanded a larger sale than any of the regular reports. Such was the Law Journal first published in 1822 as a weekly and in 1830 as a monthly series. It was natural that its immediate success should provoke competition and it was in due course followed by the Jurist, established in 1837, the Law Times in 1843, the Weekly Reporter, established in 1852 and united in 1858 with the already established Solicitor's Journal....

7. This was the condition of affairs when in 1863 certain members of the Bar inspired and led by the late W.T.S. Daniel, Q.C., commenced the agitation which led to the establishment of the series of reports known to us all as 'The Law Reports'.... The objective which Mr. Daniel had from the outset was to establish a series of Reports under the control of the profession. It was still to be private enterprise in the sense that it received no State aid and was subject to no State interference. But it was not to be profit-making except so far as was necessary to render it self-supporting. No other purpose was to be served than to produce the best possible reports at the lowest possible price for the benefit of the profession and of the public at large. Inaugurated with such aims and under such auspices such a series, it was confidently hoped, would drive all competitors from the field and thus there would be established a single series of reports, accurate and scientific, reporting all cases that ought to be reported and none that ought not to be reported.

11. In the face of no little difficulty Mr. Daniel and his friends carried the day. A council representative of the profession was established consisting of two *ex officio* members, the Attorney-General and the Solicitor-General for the time being, eight barristers, two of whom were chosen by each of the four Inns of Court, two serjeants chosen by Serjeants' Inn and two solicitors chosen by the Incorporated Law Society. This council, whose constitution remains substantially unchanged except that Serjeants' Inn has ceased to exist and therefore is not represented, was in 1870 incorporated under the Companies' Acts with the title "The Incorporated Council of Law Reporting for England and Wales." Its first object as stated in its Memorandum of Association was "the preparation and publication in a convenient form, at a moderate price, and under gratuitous professional control of Reports of Judicial Decisions of the Superior & Appellate Courts of England."

12. With the issue of the "Law Reports" the old authorised Reports disappeared except that Best and Smith and Beavan and a few others for a very short time continued their publications. In 1867 the Jurist, one of the Reports, also ceased. The other Reports, the Law Journal, the Law Times, the Weekly Reporter and Solicitors' Journal, continued and still continue, the last-named series under the name of the Solicitors' Journal, and to them there have been added two more publications, the "Times Law Reports" first published in 1884 and the "All England Reports" first published in 1936.

2. Criticisms of the present system

The report then referred to a number of criticisms made of the system – cost, repetition of the same case in different sets of reports and the problem of tracing cases.

14(e) The next criticism is of a far-reaching and very different character. Its substance really is not so much that the Reports are numerous, as that, being numerous, they are what they are. The 'Law Reports' are recognised as accurate: against them the criticism is made that they are incomplete in that they omit to report cases which ought to be reported, not merely cases of a special character which are properly relegated to special Reports, but cases in which light is thrown upon general legal principles or the construction of Acts of Parliament. Against other general Reports it is said that, while they may to some extent make good the deficiencies of the Law Reports by reporting cases not reported there, yet their accuracy is not beyond challenge and it is a grave matter if, as has more than once happened in recent years, the profession and the public are misled by an inaccurate Report. In our opinion it is impossible to emphasise too strongly the seriousness of this criticism. Further it is said that even the number of Reports does not ensure safety, but on the contrary decisions of importance may be unreported and at some future date be disinterred from their grave in forgotten shorthand notes. The complaint is echoed of an old editor of a text-book well known in its day, 'Watkins' Principles of Conveyancing': 'Is the law of England to depend upon the private notes of an individual and to which an individual only can have access? ... Is a paper evidencing the law of England to be buttoned up in the side pocket of a judge or to serve for a mouse to sit upon in the dusty corner of a private library? If the Law of England is to be deduced from adjudged cases, let the reports of those adjudged cases be certain, known and authenticated.'

(*f*) Finally, the criticism is heard that far too many cases are reported. It is said that the hearing of suits is protracted and the time of the Court wasted by the citation of authorities of doubtful relevance, and that, if counsel is not darkened, at least first principles are apt to be obscured by the introduction of exceptions and refinements which had better be forgotten.

The Committee considered but rejected the idea that there should be any form of monopoly for a single official set of reports:

To such a proposal or anything like it we are unanimously opposed. It ignores, as we think, the fundamental fact that the law of England is what it is not because it has been so reported but because it has been so decided. Thus, as we have said before in this report, it is the privilege, if not the duty, of a member of the Bar to inform the court, whether as counsel engaged in the case or as *amicus curiæ*, of a relevant decision whether it has been reported or not. So it is the duty of a Judge to follow the decision of a competent court whether reported or not: it may well be that there has not been time to report it. The very basis of the rule of precedent is the need for certainty and uniformity – suppose that a decision has been given on a question of (say) banking or insurance law or some other topic of professional interest which is likely to be quickly disseminated amongst a large circle of interested persons, and suppose that it be reported by a barrister in a Journal, whether devoted exclusively to law reports or not, is a judge to approach that question of law unaware of the previous decision, unless it has been reported in the Law Reports or other official Reports? Is a lawyer to advise his client 'This is the law according to Mr. Justice A, but his decision has not been reported in the Law Reports: if then your case comes, not before him, but before Mr. Justice B, the latter may come to a different decision, for he may not be told what Mr. Justice A has decided?' And what of a text-book writer? Is he to ignore decisions except those reported in the Law Reports? It appears to us that it is only necessary to ask these questions to show that a monopoly of citation would run counter to the spirit in which English law has been administered these many centuries.

Nor would it be right if some reporters were specially licensed – to put a check on the multiplicity of reports:

In our view such proposals are fundamentally wrong. They strike, as we think, at the base of a principle which is one of the pillars of freedom, that the administration of justice must be public. The decision of the court must be open for publication, discussion and criticism. It is not consistent with this principle that a licence to report should be given to one man and withheld from another. If a case is once reported, then, as we have already pointed out, it is proper that it should be cited in order that the law may be interpreted and administered in the same way for all men. Nor can a Judge by any means deny the right to publish as law that which he has decided to be law. Technical competence of the reporter there ought to be, and it exists to some extent in the requirement that a report should be vouched by a barrister-at-law; but that is a very different thing from monopolistic reporting....

19. We repeat, and it cannot be said too often, that the first essential of a Report is accuracy. In that lies its value as a precedent. In this respect the Law Reports maintain a remarkably high standard and they are assisted by the fact that the judges themselves read and approve the reports of their decisions before they are published. We have been told that the same privilege is sometimes given to the Reports of Patents, etc., cases, and to the Law Journal Reports, but to no other Reports. For this reason it has been generally but not universally the custom in the courts to demand that, if a case is reported in the Law Reports, it should be cited from those Reports and no other. We venture to hope that this practice may except in very special circumstances be rigidly enforced. We were indeed told that by some persons other reports were preferred for the very reason that it was supposed that they contained judgments as actually delivered and not as the judges, on second thoughts, would like to have delivered them. We need perhaps say no more about this point of view than that it appears to us a somewhat unscientific way of regarding an exposition of law.

The Committee considered whether it should recommend that a shorthand writer take down the exact text of every judgment, that this should be sent to the judge for correction and that a copy should be filed with the office of the Records of the Court. This would avoid the occasional instance of faulty reporting. It would also ensure a full record of all decisions. The Committee said the proposal would obviously cost money and it would impose an additional burden on the judges. It thought on the whole that most decisions that ought to be reported, were. ('What remains is less likely to be a treasure house than a rubbish heap in which a jewel will rarely, if ever, be discovered', p. 20). On the whole it did not think there was a need to record all judgments.

A strong dissenting report from Professor A.L. Goodhart dealt with the fact that large numbers of reports were uncorrected by the judges and many more were not reported at all. An unreported decision was nevertheless authoritative law.

He dealt in turn with the three problems mentioned by the Committee. The cost of having each judgment recorded he thought would not be great. The burden on the judges revising them would equally, he thought, not be serious. Nor need it add greatly to delays in getting publication. The advantage would be to reduce inaccurate reports. Judges would be able to delete phrases which did not accord with their considered opinions. He hoped that shorthand writers would be attached to each court and that judgments would be placed after revision in an official library.

This proposal was however not implemented. The only reports that are lodged officially anywhere are those of the Court of Appeal, Civil Division. From 1951 the Lord Chancellor's Department required that they all be placed in the Bar Library in the Royal Courts of Justice in the Strand. Access to the Bar Library was open principally to barristers and, with permission, to solicitors and others. Since 1978 these reports have all been moved to the Supreme Court Library in the Royal Courts to which lawyers and members of the public alike have free access. Case-name and subject indexes are maintained on a cumulative basis. Unreported judgments of the House of Lords are kept in the Record Office of the House of Lords, where they can be consulted by the public. But there is no subject index and there is therefore no way of tracing a decision on a particular point unless one happens to know its name beforehand.

Judgments of no other courts are officially filed anywhere. However there are shorthand writers who attend the proceedings of all the courts save county courts and magistrates' courts. They take down the evidence, legal arguments and judgments in civil cases or the judge's summing-up in Crown Courts. If anyone wants to have copies of the judge's summing-up or his judgment, they can order it from the shorthand writers. In some courts, especially in London, the process of taking down the proceedings is done by tape-recording equipment – but the work of transcription is still mostly done by the shorthand writers.

What finds its way into the pages of the law reports is, however, to an extent a matter of happenstance. It has been estimated that only about a quarter of the decisions of the Civil Division of the Court of Appeal appear in the officially sanctioned *Weekly Law Reports*. About 70 per cent of those of the House of Lords and the Privy Council appear and about 10 per cent of those of the Court of Appeal, Criminal Division. The body of case law as reflected in the *Weekly Law Reports* grows at the rate of three volumes per year.

The question whether it is satisfactory to leave the decision as to the reporting of cases to the decisions of law reporters was addressed by Dr Olive Stone, then of the London School of Economics:

Olive Stone, 'Knowing the Law', 24 *Modern Law Review*, 1961, 475 at pp. 476–77

Even if proper reports or transcripts were available of all cases, it seems very doubtful if the final decision on whether a case is reportable should lie with an editor responsible to no one but those who employ him. Surely this is pre-eminently a decision to be taken by a committee, which should have the fullest information about all cases decided, and should not be drawn exclusively from practising members of the Bar. Solicitors, law teachers and magistrates should obviously be represented, and in the field of family law (which suffers greatly from meagre reporting), there is also a case for representation of the social services to counterbalance the excessive stress on the types of litigation most profitable to the legal profession.

A more recent evaluation of some of the problems in the field of law reporting was published in 1978:

R.J.C. Munday, 'New Dimensions of Precedent', *Journal of the Society of Public Teachers of Law*, 1978, p. 201

Three recent developments in the field of precedent have added considerably to the volume of authorities upon which the legal profession has a tendency to draw....

A New Generation of Law Reports

Complaints concerning the bulk of English case-law are perennial. No-one recently has troubled to calculate just how many reported cases our system possesses. But in 1951 it was estimated that in common law and equity there existed more than 312,000 reported decisions. Such statistics on their own mean little. However, the clear trend today is for an increasing number of cases to be reported, either in complete or abbreviated form, in an expanding range of law reports....

In themselves, new series of law reports may be quite innocuous, if not desirable additions to the lawyer's armoury. Even if they do add appreciably to the volume of reported cases, there exist digests which compile and list all the decided authorities and these are perfectly capable of coping with any fresh additions. The bulk of case-law is tolerated by the common lawyer as an occupational hazard. Our rules of practice of course conspire to this result in as much as counsel are under a duty to the court to cite all relevant authorities, and an authority is probably still taken to mean an account of a case, whether written or oral, attested to by a member of the Bar present at the decision. The existence of a published report of a case does at least ensure that there is a permanent and reliable record of the judgment. However, the proliferation of series of reports raises a number of serious practical problems which were diagnosed by the Law Reporting Committee in 1940: namely, those of expense and accommodation, not to mention needless duplication, the difficulty of tracing authorities, the danger of textual variants and inaccuracies, and the fact that important cases can still be overlooked.

But problems of another kind are also posed by the type of case currently reported in some of the new volumes. Several series now devote their pages to judgments of tribunals. One point of practice which Devlin, L.J. in 1962 insisted that tribunals at large observe was that they should not consider themselves bound by an over-rigid doctrine of precedent nor should they pursue consistency at the expense of the merits of individual cases.[1] Although it is possible to exaggerate the effect of this prohibition, it is permitted to wonder whether the reams of tribunal reports accumulating on the shelves may not encourage abandonment of a practice, considered by some to constitute one of the great procedural differences between courts and tribunals. There must be a danger, wherever lawyers are in the offing, that available legal materials will come to be used in an orthodox, lawyer-like manner. Such decisions are already from time to time being cited as authorities before the law courts. It is conceivable that this mounting body of reported tribunal law will contribute to a more rigid adherence to a system of precedent similar to that which binds English courts. Such a development might not be viewed kindly by those who would hold flexibility to be one of the great virtues of the tribunal.

Citation of Overseas Authorities

... English judges with increasing frequency, are prepared to have recourse to overseas authorities in order to lend support to their judgments, either

1. *Merchandise Transport Ltd* v. *B.T.C.* [1962] 2 Q.B. 173, 193.

where the English law may be in doubt or where a new judicial approach is being advocated ... and sometimes, one suspects, simply for the pleasure of citing them. In 1962 Megarry V.-C. already detected that citation of overseas authorities was beginning to find favour with the English Bench and felt that it was to be encouraged: '(l)et authors and editors be more industrious, let the Bar be more comprehensive, and let the Bench be more uniformly receptive: all three contributions must be made,' he declared.[2] These exhortations to greater endeavour have elicited a stern rebuke from certain quarters, but are clearly being heeded by a substantial portion of the judiciary. The practice has revealed itself to be capable of abuse...

The question of the rôle of the courts in matters of law reform is much to the forefront of legal minds at present. The balance between what is coming to be termed 'judicial activism' and 'strict constructionism' is delicate to maintain,[3] particularly in light of the greater freedom permitted to the House of Lords following its Practice Statement of 1966.[4] The position of the Court of Appeal in this process is vexed and the members of that Court are sometimes openly divided on how they perceive their function. As *Farrell* v. *Alexander* shows,[5] the Master of the Rolls felt that in order to spare parties unnecessary expense and to do justice in that particular case the Court of Appeal should be free to depart from binding rules which it now felt to be wrong. Scarman L.J., in contrast, took a broader view of the Court's responsibilities and expressed serious reservations:

> '... I have immense sympathy with the approach of Lord Denning M.R. I decline to accept his lead only because I think it damaging to the law in the long term – though it would undoubtedly do justice in the present case. To some it will appear that justice is being denied by a timid, conservative adherence to judicial precedent. They would be wrong. Consistency is necessary to certainty – one of the great objectives of law. The Court of Appeal – at the very centre of our legal system – is responsible for its stability, its consistency, and its predictability.... The task of law reform, which calls for wide ranging techniques of consultation and discussion that cannot be compressed into the forensic medium, is for others.'[6]

Although the extent to which the courts should be entitled to take the initiative in reforming the law is a highly contentious issue today, suffice it to say that the tempo of judicial lawmaking is quickening perceptibly[7] and one

2. *Lawyer and Litigant in England* (1962), p. 163.

3. The expression 'judicial activism' gained some currency in England through the publication of Jaffe, *English and American Judges as Lawmakers* (1969). See Lord Edmund-Davies, 'Judicial Activism' [1975] *Current Legal Problems 1*.

4. [1966] 1 W.L.R. 1234.

5. [1976] Q.B. 345.

6. *Ibid.* at p. 371. See also *Ulster-Swift Ltd. and Pigs Marketing Board (Northern Ireland)* v. *Taunton Meat Haulage Ltd. and Fransen Transport NV* [1977] 1 Lloyd's Rep. 346, 351, *per* Megaw L.J.

7. Diplock, *The Courts as Legislators*, 1965 (Holdsworth Club Presidential Address); Hailsham, *The Problems of a Lord Chancellor*, 1972 (Holdsworth Club Presidential Address).

strong fillip to such law reform is provided by the lessons we can derive from overseas jurisdictions.

Whilst recognising the desirability of the legal mind remaining receptive to other countries' solutions to legal problems, a number of observations deserve to be made on this developing interchange of ideas. The question of how far the court is entitled to go in modifying accepted doctrines of English law in light of them and the broader and more delicate problem of demarcating the respective bounds of Parliament's and the judiciary's preserves have already been adverted to. Scarman L.J.'s reservations in *Farrell* v. *Alexander* are not simply the technical quibbles of a narrow-minded magistrate. On the contrary, they accurately reflect the *malaise* within the profession over the uncertainty which is coming to infect our law. These problems are far from resolving themselves at present and our increasing willingness to examine and adopt overseas solutions contributes further to the dilemma.

But on a more practical plane, recurrent references to overseas case-law – as also references to what one might term the new generation of law reports – inevitably puts pressure on libraries, both professional and scholastic, to subscribe to the series of reports in question. Whilst encouraging the profession to avail themselves of foreign materials, Megarry V.-C. also urged that the Law Courts equip themselves with sets of Commonwealth law reports. Apart from the financial difficulties facing many libraries, the very problem of finding shelf-space to accommodate such acquisitions provides a source of anxiety. In addition, given libraries equipped with the volumes in question, the new receptivity to overseas solutions, in particular, can contribute substantially to the time spent by lawyers and students in researching any given problem. These factors ineluctably figure amongst the penalties which must be paid for the open-mindedness which is coming to possess the profession. But, if used intelligently and with a proper sense of discretion, the comparative lawyer can but approve the developing willingness on the part of the Bench to look with favour upon overseas jurisdictions' solutions to problems akin to our own.

Unreported Cases

Before turning to consider broader questions of policy affecting our methods of law reporting, it remains to examine one further development in the realm of precedent: namely, the rise to prominence of the unreported case. That the citation of unreported cases is on the increase scarcely requires a statistical proof. Such a trend was to be expected from the moment that the Bar Library made available all transcripts in civil cases delivered in the Court of Appeal. In the absence of an indexing system the new facilities were little used at first. But the more recent practice of the English edition of *Current Law*, which produces monthly lists of all such unreported cases along with brief summaries of their contents, and the *New Law Journal*, which periodically notes select unreported Court of Appeal decisions, has doubtless centributed to the popularity of such transcripts as a source of authorities, merely by rendering them more readily accessible. . .

Although, as has been indicated already, there is no novelty in the citation of unreported cases, it is becoming increasingly widespread and we are fast approaching the point where serious thought must needs be given to a practice which gives rise to a number of significant problems. Not the least disturbing is that the unreported case renders the practitioner's search after precedent considerably more arduous. Given the quickening geographical fragmentation of the Bar, even Court of Appeal transcripts are not immediately available to barristers practising in the provinces. Similarly, academics and law students will often be in no position to study the unreported judgments referred to by judges. This all serves to add to the inaccessibility of the law not only to the layman – who has presumably grown accustomed to such a state of affairs – but, paradoxically, even to the lawyer.[8]

The solutions considered

As most lawyers would recognise that citation of unreported cases poses a problem, it remains to examine some of the possible solutions. Predictably, a wide range of views are entertained on the subject. Considered by some as the apotheosis of legal scholarship, others would see the availability of transcripts of judgments as no more than a prudent safeguard against important decisions going unreported. Others again would reject them as a needless extravagance for a system already swamped with reported authorities. The only point of general consensus is dissatisfaction with the present state of affairs.

(*i*) *The Report of the Law Reporting Committee.* The first body to pay serious attention to the state of English law reporting in this century was the Law Reporting Committee which was set up in 1939 by the Lord Chancellor, under the chairmanship of Simonds J., to report and advise on the problems posed by the increasing number of law reports. Its report was published in March 1940. Apart from Professor Goodhart's vigorous dissent, the conclusions of the Committee were singularly temperate and the report was soon forgotten, as there were other and more pressing matters engaging attention in 1940. The problems posed by a multiplicity of law reports – expense, storage, repetition, tracing of authorities, important cases being overlooked and too many cases being reported – were all considered, but the general view that no large measure of reform was either necessary or possible.... *In medio stat virtus*. Maintenance of the *status quo* remains a possible stance. However, conditions have altered materially since 1940 and the volume of cases, both reported and unreported, to which reference may and is now being made has risen sharply. One would not expect such a committee sitting today to report with such obvious equanimity.

(*ii*) *Prohibitions on citation.* A second position which may commend itself is to prohibit the citation of unreported cases altogether.... Although, as it were, disposing of the problem at a stroke, this solution at the same time presents a number of disadvantages. Firstly, it entails abandonment of the traditional rule of practice that it is the privilege, if not the duty, of the

8. 'Such is the ingratitude of man that the resultant headaches for practitioners, teachers and reporters have led some to sigh again for the old days when the obscurity surrounding the unreported was usually impenetrable': Megarry, *Miscellany-at-Law* (1955), p. 303.

advocate to inform the court of all relevant authorities, whether reported or not, of which he has cognisance. To draw the line at cases which are reported may bring practical benefits, but smacks of the arbitrary, given the mild idiosyncracies of our system of law reporting. In any event, certain transcripts were made available in 1951 and it has become standard practice to make reference to them as and when need arises. Therefore, stern resistance to such an initiative might be expected. But far more telling is the consideration that such a broad prohibition would confer an even greater law-making monopoly – if one may put it so indelicately – upon the editors of the law reports. If, as is generally agreed, the basic difficulty is that the profession at times felt itself at the mercy of the law reporters who exercise the discretion whether or not to report any given case, citation of unreported authorities at least permits repair of the occasional inadvertent omission. Banning the citation of unreported cases is liable to encourage law reports, which take their responsibilities very seriously, to report even larger numbers of cases, which in the context of our general argument is to defeat the very purpose behind introducing such a prohibition in the first place.

(*iii*) *Computers.* Distasteful though it may sound to the majority of lawyers, it is conceivable that the computer offers a further alternative. Given that it were possible to devise adequate programmes and equipment, all judgments delivered in the High Court, the Court of Appeal and the House of Lords might be stored in one vast electronic memory whence they could be retrieved at will. In a way that is a variant on an American theme and can be viewed as broadly analogous to the activities pursued since the 1880's by the West Publishing Company's National Reporter System which offers complete coverage of decisions in American jurisdictions. When it is perceived that this system already comprises about 5000 volumes and well over 5 million closely-printed double-columned pages, the idea of introducing published reporting on such a scale in this country swiftly loses its charm. But even in computerised form, such an approach to law reporting has little to commend it. It proceeds upon the specious assumption that all judgments are worthy of preservation and citation, which is manifestly not the case. If anything, it would tend to encourage the trends adverted to earlier – namely, the obsessive citation of case-law as an end in itself and the unintelligent search after exact precedent. Whatever other uses the computer may have in the legal context, as a means of storing and disgorging all judgments delivered on any given theme its introduction would be totally undesirable.*

(*iv*) *Professor Goodhart's suggestions.* The most cogently argued reforms have been those recommended by Professor Goodhart in his dissentient report for the Law Reporting Committee. He considered that in order to reduce the possibility of important cases being omitted from the reports through inadvertence, to avoid textual variants and to ensure that some reliable record of High Court judgments be retained, a shorthand note of all judgments should be made and a transcript prepared. This transcript would then be sent to the judge to be corrected and subsequently returned by the judge and filed at a Central Office at the Law Courts. There would thus be extant a corrected

* See, however, p. 152 below.

copy of every judgment delivered in the High Court which law reporters, in particular, could consult. Professor Goodhart repudiated the suggestion that such a scheme would be too expensive or that it would involve undue waste of time and effort for the judges. Such an arrangement, he argued, would bring us into alignment with most Commonwealth jurisdictions which retain copies of their High Court judgments. It would also reduce the risk of vital cases being overlooked by the reports and would ensure that there existed a single authoritative text of any given judgment, rather than a number of sometimes significant textual variants, as at present. If anything, the arguments in favour of such a scheme, which found favour with Sir William Holdsworth, are stronger today than ever they were in 1940 when the recommendation was made. However, this modest proposal, which would not lead to an inevitable increase in the volume of reported case-law, has largely been ignored.

IV

To the outsider it must appear paradoxical that a legal system which traditionally relies upon its reported precedent to as great an extent as our own should have paid such casual regard to its methods of law reporting. The common lawyer in the past has tended to accept the vagaries of his system unreflectingly. But with the deluge of case-law being reported today and the widening scope of authorities to which persistent reference is being made, a more critical stance may be expected of him and it is permitted to wonder whether the day is not far off when intervention of some kind becomes inevitable. The lawyer is torn by two competing sentiments. On the one hand, counsel's right to cite all relevant authorities is an established privilege which he associates with common law method and upon which he is by upbringing reluctant to impose trammels. On the other hand, the volume of reported precedent is beginning to reach disturbing proportions and, even though the ancients may not have taken our precise meaning, exhortations to the profession to make wider and concerted use of foreign materials and the availability of transcripts is but to heap Pelion upon Ossa.

3. Computer retrieval systems

Contrary to the view expressed by Mr Munday, the development of computer aids to law-report retrieval is now a definite reality in England and possibly in other parts of the UK as well. In 1979 a report was published by a sub-committee of the Society for Computers and Law on the feasibility of a link-up with the American system Lexis which had for five years or more already offered a computer retrieval service to American law firms. (Copies of the report 'A National Law Library – the Way Ahead', are available from the Society for Computers and Law, 11 High Street, Milton, near Abingdon, Oxon. For a summary of the report see *New Law Journal*, 22 February 1979, p. 203.)

The report recommended that Lexis would not be suitable for the British market because of its cost, but Butterworths decided nevertheless to go ahead with this system – see *New Law Journal*, 24 May 1979, p. 507. It began operations in 1980, offering access to all cases reported in the main series of reports back to 1945 together with all American materials. It was beginning the huge task of putting all statutes and statutory instruments onto the data bank and to extend its case reports. The cost was approximately £1,000 a year for the terminal, plus about £1 a minute or £60 an hour for use. At about the same time in 1980 Eurolex, a competitor, began providing a computer retrieval service. At the outset the Eurolex service had a data base limited to five years' worth of Weekly Law Reports and Times Law Reports (going back from 1980), and Common Market Law Reports, European Court Reports, European Human Rights Reports, European Commercial cases and the European Law Digest. It was planning to expand its UK cases and to include all statutes.* The cost would be lower than that of the Lexis system. The terminal could be one used for other services (the Lexis terminal is 'dedicated', i.e. can only be used for that system). Also the hourly charge for actual use would be an average of some £40, as against £60 for Lexis. On the other hand, the data base for Lexis was initially greater.

For details of the launch of a National Law Library to promote study and use of computer retrieval systems, see *Guardian Gazette*, 30 January 1980, p. 1.

* In March 1980 Eurolex was still negotiating to get permission to use Weekly Law Reports and to use the already existing statutes in force on tape owned by the Stationery Office. It was hopeful of getting permission.

5
How precedent works

Precedents are the raw material from which lawyers and judges distil rules of law. Anyone wishing to state the law on a matter not governed by statute – whether he be a judge, a practitioner, an academic or a student – must look at the decided cases. But how does he use the raw material?

The first principle is that anything relevant may be grist to the mill. If there is a clear decision of the House of Lords which is precisely in point, one need usually search no further. If in that case all five Law Lords agreed that the rule of law is X, then for all practical purposes one may assume that it is X. One may still argue that Y would be a better rule and, if one is advising a client prepared to litigate all the way up to the House of Lords, one may consider with him the practical prospects of persuading the Lords to change the rule. But, subject to that rather remote possibility, lawyers are likely to agree that the rule on that point is X.

At the opposite extreme, search for relevant precedents may reveal nothing more than a decision on the point by a county court judge reported briefly only in the *Solicitors' Journal*, and a remark to the same effect made in the course of giving judgment on a related point in a decision of the High Court of Australia. Anyone wishing to propound the rule in England would be likely to say that there was virtually no authority on the matter. He would cite the county court decision and the remark of the Australian court and would then speculate as to whether the rule on which they appeared to agree would be likely to commend itself to a court somewhat higher in the hierarchy than the county court. Little confidence could be placed in the precedents as giving authoritative guidance as to the prevailing role, but for what they are worth they are the best available. In other words, even the slenderest of authorities are some evidence of the law.

Usually, the relevant precedents will be a mixed bag of decisions of different levels of court, different degrees of relevance to the facts under consideration, coming from different periods and, often, appearing to state conflicting rules. The lawyer's task then is to organize the available material in the most coherent fashion depending on his purpose. A lawyer advising a client will start with the bias that he wishes, if possible, to provide advice that the client will find constructive and encouraging. He will therefore seek to marshall the material in such a way as to enable him to tell the client that he can do what he wishes to do – subject however to the important caveat that he will not want to lose the client through incompetence. The better he is as a lawyer the more likely it is that he will draw his client's attention to the weaknesses and doubts about his analysis of the state of the law.

If he is preparing a legal argument to be presented on behalf of his client in court, he will try to present the precedents in the most attractive form with as few concessions to his opponent as possible. It is a rule of professional etiquette that counsel must cite to a court all the relevant precedents whether they help his client's case or not. But this is only common sense. Far better to draw the court's attention to an awkward precedent and so have the first opportunity of dealing with it oneself – by showing that it can be explained away – than to have it produced as a trump card by one's opponent.

If the person in question is a scholar writing a book, he will present his material as objectively as he can. But he too may have a bias in the sense that he favours one approach to the problem under consideration rather than another, and may be seeking to persuade the reader that his approach is justified by the state of the authorities. In the case of the practitioner who is paid to represent the interests of a client, everyone understands and forgives a little stretching of the argument to favour the client's point of view. If the authorities do not quite go all the way for his client, he is permitted to push them to their utmost limits and then a little further in the hope of persuading the court to adopt his argument. Providing the arguments are not far-fetched, the lawyer's reputation will not suffer from such imaginative exegesis of the precedents. The case of the scholar, however, is different. When presenting an analysis of what the law is, he is expected to remain severely within the limits of straightforward analysis. As will be seen, this may still offer a good deal of scope but it will not normally give as much licence for 'interpretation' as is available to the practitioner.

The case of the judge is different again. In a sense his position is somewhere between that of the practitioner and of the scholar. He will normally have heard argument from opposing counsel each seeking to persuade the judge to adopt his view of the precedents and to reject that offered by his learned friend. Having made up his mind as to which argument he prefers he will present it in his judgment as representing the law. He will wish to be 'right' in the sense of not being the subject of a successful appeal by the disappointed loser. Judges, until they become members of the highest court, are accustomed to the minor irritation of being told by a superior court that their view of the law was wrong. It is simply an occupational hazard. (They may still on occasion harbour the distinct feeling that it was the appeal court rather than themselves that got the law wrong but such feelings are normally veiled in decent silence. Only Lord Denning permits himself the luxury of sometimes informing the world that he prefers his own solution to the problem to that offered by his 'superiors' in the House of Lords.) But, however, case-hardened or thick-skinned he may be, a judge would normally prefer to be upheld than reversed on appeal and he will therefore have some concern for the likely opinion of other judges when formulating his decision. He will also wish if possible to avoid merited criticism from writers in the professional and scholarly journals. The more unpredictable his decision, the more likely that he will be subjected to waspish attack by some indignant academic expert. Also his sense of the dignity of his office will tend to incline the judge to construct his decision in such a way as to conform with professional expectations.

On the other hand, a judge is not a machine. Some attention will be given later in this book to the vexed question of whether judges do, or should, allow their personal views to obtrude into their decision-making, but it is obvious that where two arguments are presented by counsel there will frequently be enough merit in both to make a decision either way a practicable possibility. If one side is so weak as to make its success highly improbable, the client will normally accept the advice of his lawyers and withdraw or settle the dispute. Litigated cases whether they raise issues of law or of fact almost by definition can often be decided respectably either way. Much may then depend on the particular way the judge sees the question. His view of the precedents may be affected by some feeling about the respective merits of the two parties before him or by some sense that the law on the point 'ought to be' *X* rather than *Y*. In a marginal case such impressions can have an effect.

In fact, the person most likely to bring a dispassionate and 'objective' approach to the process of reading the precedents may be the law student. He has no client; the facts of the problem with which he is dealing are usually stated in so arid a way as to denude it of emotional impact; and he will probably lack the self-confidence to have any strong opinion as to what the law on the point ought to be. He will be likely to come to the question of what the law on that point is with the belief that there is a 'right' answer which he wants to discover. The judge, the practitioner and the scholar all know that there are no right answers – there are only better or worse answers, answers that are more or less likely to find acceptance in the courts or in the eyes of the client, the profession or the community. There are answers that will solve the particular problem and stand the test of time, and others that will not. But whatever the particular vantage point or perspective of the person concerned, the raw material with which he is dealing will be the same precedents and the methods he uses will be the same professional techniques.

1. Professional techniques for using precedents

(a) Ratio, dictum or obiter dictum

The first thing a lawyer wants to know when inspecting a precedent is whether the proposition of law in which he is interested forms the *ratio decidendi* of the case, or whether it is only something said which is *dictum* or *obiter dictum*.

The ratio (pronounced rayshio) of a case is its central core of meaning, its sharpest cutting edge. It is the ratio and only the ratio that is capable of being binding. Whether it *is* binding will depend on the position in the hierarchy of the court that decided the case and of the court that is now considering it. Thus, as has been seen, the ratio of a decision of the House of Lords binds all lower courts; the ratio of a High Court decision binds only the county courts; the ratio of a county court decision binds no one; the ratio of a Court of Appeal case binds the Court of Appeal and all lower courts but does not bind the House of Lords.

If the proposition of law does not form part of the ratio it is by definition either dictum or obiter dictum. (Dicta or judicial dicta is the term used when they relate to a matter in issue in the case; obiter dicta are dicta that are more peripheral. Obiter dictum is however also commonly used to cover both meanings.)

Dicta may be of very great persuasive weight but they cannot under any circumstances be binding on anyone. The most carefully considered and deliberate statement of law by all five Law Lords which is dictum cannot bind even the lowliest judge in the land. Technically he is free to go his own way. In practice, of course, weighty obiter pronouncements from higher courts are likely to be followed and will certainly be given the greatest attention, but in strictest theory they are not binding. (For an example of a weighty dictum, see p. 188 below in the discussion of *Hedley Byrne*.) This is the reason that technically the Court of Appeal is not bound by statements in the House of Lords that the Court of Appeal should follow its own decisions. Such a statement cannot form part of the ratio of the House of Lords decision since a case in the House of Lords does not require a decision as to the handling of precedents by the Court of Appeal and therefore anything said on the subject is necessarily obiter (see pp. 117–18 above).

Being bound therefore is a function of three different elements – the precedent must have been pronounced by a court that stands in the hierarchy in a position to bind the present court, the proposition of law must have formed the ratio of that decision and, thirdly, it must be relevant to the facts of the present case. (The issue of relevance is considered below.) An obiter dictum does not qualify, since it fails to meet the second test.

But, other things being equal, a statement of law that is the ratio of the case even if it is not binding ranks higher than the same statement of law that is only an obiter dictum. Thus if the House of Lords, for instance, is evaluating a proposition of law emanating from the Court of Appeal, it will regard it as weightier if it proves to be the ratio of the case than if it turns out to have been said obiter. So the distinction between ratio and obiter dicta is of importance whether or not the case is capable of being binding in the particular situation.

There have been many definitions of the ratio decidendi. My own is – a proposition of law which decides the case, in the light or in the context of the material facts. If there appear to be more than one proposition of law which decide the case, it has more than one ratio and both are binding – see *Jacobs* v. *L.C.C.* [1950] A.C. at 369. Any statement of law, however carefully considered, which was not the basis of the decision is obiter.

The crucial problem in ascertaining the ratio of a case is usually to determine how widely or narrowly the principle of law should be stated. Another way of putting this is, at what level of abstraction should the facts be stated? The law report will state a mass of facts, some of which will be properly part of the ratio and others of which will be ignored. The judge in the concluding part of his judgment may indicate what he conceives the ratio to be – but normally judges do not do this explicitly. They know that, in any event whatever they say, later courts have the right to interpret and re-interpret the ratio of their case. The ratio of each case must take into account the facts of that particular case and then generalise from those facts as far as the statement of the court and the circumstances indicate is desirable.

Thus the case may have concerned an action brought by a blind purchaser of a defective car. The fact that the purchaser was blind would not be part of the ratio of the case unless the fact of blindness was relevant to the rule of law. This would only be the case if the rule formulated by the court depended in some way on the purchaser's capacity to inspect the car visually. The rule might then be different for a purchaser who was blind. But if the defect in the car would have been equally obvious to or equally hidden from a sighted and a blind purchaser, then the rule for both situations would be framed without reference to the fact of blindness. Equally, the fact of blindness would not be part of the ratio if the rule were framed without regard to the purchaser's ability or otherwise to inspect the car. The greater the number of facts in the ratio, the narrower its scope; conversely, the fewer, or the higher the level of abstraction, the broader the reach of the ratio – the more fact situations it covers.

Karl Llewellyn's famous book *The Bramble Bush* based on lectures first given at Columbia Law School has a passage which helps to elucidate the meaning of the ratio decidendi:

K.N. Llewellyn, *The Bramble Bush*
(1930, Oceana edition 1975), pp. 42, 43

... 3) The court can decide the particular dispute only according to a general rule which covers a whole class of like disputes. Our legal theory does not admit of single decisions standing on their own.... But how wide, or how narrow, is the general rule in this particular case?... That is a troublesome matter. The practice of our case-law, however, is I think fairly stated thus: it pays to be suspicious of general rules which look too wide; it pays to go slow in feeling *certain* that a wide rule has been laid down at all, or that, if seemingly laid down, it will be followed. For there is a fourth accepted canon:

4) *Everything, everything, everything, big or small, a judge may say in an opinion, is to be read with primary reference to the particular dispute, the particular question before him.* You are not to think that the words mean what they might if they stood alone. You are to have your eye on the case in hand, and to learn how to interpret all that has been said *merely* as a reason for deciding *that* case *that* way.

... I do believe, gentlemen, that here we have as fine a deposit of slow-growing wisdom as ever has been laid down through the centuries by the unthinking social sea. Here, hardened into institutions, carved out and given line by rationale. What is this wisdom? Look to your own discussion, look to any argument. You know where you would go. You reach, at random if hurried, more carefully if not, for a foundation, for a major premise. But never for itself. Its interest lies in leading to the conclusion you are headed for. You shape its words, its content, to an end decreed. More, with your mind upon your object you use words, you bring in illustrations, you deploy and advance and concentrate again. When you have done, you have said much you did not mean. You did not mean, that is, *except* in reference to your point. You have brought generalization after generalization up, and discharged it at your goal; all, in the heat of argument, were over-stated. None would you stand to, if your opponent should urge them to *another* issue.

So with the judge. Nay, more so with the judge. He is not merely human, as are you. He is, as well, a lawyer; which you, yet, are not. A lawyer, and as such skilled in manipulating the resources of persuasion at his hand. A lawyer, and as such prone without thought to twist analogies, and rules, and instances, to his conclusion. A lawyer, and as such peculiarly prone to disregard the implications which do not bear directly on his case.

More, as a practiced campaigner in the art of exposition, he has learned that one must prepare the way for argument. You set the mood, the tone, you lay the intellectual foundation – all with the case in mind, with the conclusion – all, because those who hear you also have the case in mind, without the niggling criticism which may later follow. You wind up, as a baseball pitcher will wind up – and as in the pitcher's case, the wind-up often is superfluous. As in the pitcher's case, it has been known to be intentionally misleading.

With this it should be clear, then, why our canons thunder. Why we create a class of dicta, of unnecessary words, which later readers, their minds now on quite other cases, can mark off as not quite essential to the argument. Why we create a class of *obiter dicta*, the wilder flailings of the pitcher's arms, the wilder motions of his gum-ruminant jaws. Why we set about, as our job, to crack the kernel from the nut, to find the true rule the case in fact decides: the *rule of the case*.

Now for a while I am going to risk confusion for the sake of talking simply. I am going to treat as the rule of the case the *ratio decidendi*, the rule *the court tells you* is the rule of the case, the ground, as the phrase goes, upon which the court itself has rested its decision. For there is where you must begin, and such refinements as are needed may come after.

The court, I will assume, has talked for five pages, only one of which portrayed the facts assumed. The rest has been discussion. And judgment has been given for the party who won below: judgment affirmed. We seek the rule. . . .

Perhaps in this, as in judging how far to trust a broadly stated rule, we may find guidance in the facts the court assumes. Surely this much is certain: the actual dispute before the court is limited as straitly by the facts as by the form which the procedural issue has assumed. What is not in the facts cannot be present for decision. Rules which proceed an inch beyond the facts must be suspect.

But how far does that help us out? What are *the* facts? The plaintiff's name is Atkinson and the defendant's Walpole. The defendant, despite his name, is an Italian by extraction, but the plaintiff's ancestors came over with the Pilgrims. The defendant has a schnautzer-dog named Walter, red hair, and $30,000 worth of life insurance. All these are facts. The case, however, does not deal with life insurance. It is about an auto accident. The defendant's auto was a Buick painted pale magenta. He is married. His wife was in the back seat, an irritable, somewhat faded blonde. She was attempting back-seat driving when the accident occurred. He had turned around to make objection. In the process the car swerved and hit the plaintiff. The sun was shining; there was a rather lovely dappled sky low to the West. The time was late October on a Tuesday. The road was smooth, concrete. It had been put in by the McCarthy Road Work Company. How many of these facts are important to the decision? How many of these facts are, as we say, legally relevant? Is it relevant that the road was in the country or the city; that is was concrete or tarmac or of dirt; that it was a private or a public way? Is it relevant that the defendant was driving a Buick, or a motor car, or a vehicle? Is it important that he looked around as the car swerved? Is it crucial? Would it have been the same if he had been drunk, or had swerved for fun, to see how close he could run by the plaintiff, but had missed his guess?

Is it not obvious that as soon as you pick up this statement of the facts to find its legal bearings you must discard some as of no interest whatsoever, discard others as dramatic but as legal nothings? And is it not clear, further, that when you pick up the facts which are left and which do seem relevant, you suddenly cease to deal with them in the concrete and deal with them instead in *categories* which you, for one reason or another, deem significant? It is not the road between Pottsville and Arlington; it is 'a highway'. It is not a particular pale magenta Buick eight, by number 732507, but 'a motor car', and perhaps even 'a vehicle'. It is not a turning around to look at Adorée Walpole, but a lapse from the supposedly proper procedure of careful drivers, with which you are concerned. Each concrete fact of the case arranges itself, I say, as the *representative* of a much wider abstract *category* of facts, and it is not in itself but as a member of the category that you attribute significance to it. But what is to tell you whether to make your category 'Buicks' or 'motor cars' or vehicles'? What is to tell you to make your category 'road' or 'public highway'? The court may tell you. But the precise point that you have up for study is how far it is safe to trust what the court says. The precise issue which you are attempting to solve is whether the court's language can be taken as it stands, or must be amplified, or must be whittled down.

This brings us at last to the case system. For the truth of the matter is a truth so obvious and trite that it is somewhat regularly overlooked by students. *That no case can have a meaning by itself!* Standing alone it gives you no guidance. It can give you no guidance as to how far it carries, as to how much of its language will hold water later. What counts, what gives you leads, what gives you sureness, *that is the background of the other cases* in relation to which you must read the one. They color the language, the technical terms used in the opinion. But above all they give you the wherewithal to find which of the facts are significant, and in what aspect they are significant, and how far the rules laid down are to be trusted.

Here, I say, is the foundation of the case system. For what, in a case class, do we do? We have set before you, at either the editor's selection or our own, a *series* of opinions which in some manner are related. They may or may not be exactly alike in their outcome. They are always supposedly somewhat similar on their legally relevant facts. Indeed, it is *the aspects in which their facts are similar* which give you your first guidance as to what *classes* of fact will be found legally relevant, that is, will be found *to operate alike*, or to operate *at all*, upon the court. On the other hand, the states of fact are rarely, if ever, quite alike. And one of the most striking problems before you is: when you find two cases side by side which show a difference in result, then to determine *what* difference in their facts, or *what* difference in the procedural set-up, has produced that difference in result.

This, then, is the case system game, the game of matching cases. We proceed by a rough application of the logical method of comparison and difference.

And here there are three things that need saying. The first is that by this matching of facts and issues in the different cases we get, to come back to where we started, some indication of when the court in a given case has over-generalized; of when, on the other hand, it has meant all the ratio decidendi that it said. 'The Supreme Court of the United States,' remarks the sage Professor T.R. Powell, 'are by no means such fools as they talk, or as the people are who think them so.' We go into the matter expecting a certain amount of inconsistency in the broader language of the cases. We go into the matter set in advance to find distinctions by means of which we can reconcile and harmonize the outcomes of the cases, even though the rules that the courts seem to lay down in their deciding may be inconsistent. We are prepared to whittle down the categories of the facts, to limit the rule of one case to its new whittled narrow category, to limit the rule of the other to its new other narrow category – and thus to make two cases stand together. The first case involves a man who makes an offer and gets in his revocation before his offer is accepted. The court decides that he cannot be sued upon his promise, and says that no contract can be made unless the minds of both parties are at one at once. The second case involves a man who has made a similar offer and has mailed a revocation, but to whom a letter of acceptance has been sent before his revocation was received. The court holds that he can be sued upon his promise, and says that his offer was being repeated every moment from the time that it arrived until the letter of acceptance was duly mailed. Here are two rules which are a little difficult to put together, and to square with sense, and which are, too, a little hard to square with the two holdings in the cases. We set to work to seek a way out which will do justice to the holdings. We arrive perhaps at this, that it is not necessary for the two minds to be at one at once, if the person who has received an offer thinks, and thinks reasonably, as he takes the last step of acceptance, that the offeror is standing by the offer. And to test the rule laid down in either case, as also to test our tentative formulation which we have built to cover both, we do two things. First and easiest is to play variations on the facts, making the case gradually more and more extreme until we find the place beyond which it does not seem sense to go. Suppose, for example, our man does think the offeror still stands to his offer, and thinks it reasonably, on all his information; but yet a revocation has arrived, which his own clerk has failed to bring to his attention? We may find the stopping-place much sooner that we had expected, and thus be forced to recast and narrow the generalization we have made, or to recast it even on wholly different lines. The second and more difficult way of testing is to go to the books and find further cases in which variations on the facts occur, and in which the importance of such variations has been put to the proof. The first way is the intuitional correction of hypothesis; the second way is the experimental test of whether an hypothesis is sound. Both are needed. The first to save time. The second, to make sure.... Not the least important feature in the cases you are comparing will be their dates. For you must assume that the law, like any other human institution, has undergone, still undergoes development, clarification, change, as time goes on, as experience accumulates, as conditions vary. The earlier cases in a series, therefore, while they *may* stand unchanged today, are yet more likely to be forerunners, to be indications of the first gropings with a problem, rather than to present its final solution even in the state from which they come. That holds particularly for cases prior to 1800. It holds in many fields of law for cases of much more recent date. But in any event you will be concerned to place the case in time as well as in space, if putting it together with the others makes for difficulty.

The third thing that needs saying as you set to matching cases, is that on your materials, often indeed on all the materials that there are, a perfect working out of comparison and difference cannot be had. In the first case you have facts *a* and *b* and *c*, procedural set-up *m*, and outcome *x*. In the second case you have, *if* you are lucky, procedural set-up *m* again, but this time with facts *a* and *b* and *d*, and outcome *y*. How, now, are you to know with any certainty whether the changed result is due in the second instance to the absence of fact *c* or to the presence of the new fact *d*? The court may tell you. But I repeat: your object is to *test* the telling of the court. You turn to your third case. Here once more is the outcome *x*, and the facts are *b* and *c* and *e*; but fact *a* is missing, and the procedural set-up this time is not *m* but *n*. This strengthens somewhat your suspicion that fact *c* is the lad who works the changed result. But an experimentum crucis still is lacking. Cases in life are not made to our hand. A scientific *approach* to prediction we may have, and we may use it as far as our materials will permit. An exact science *in result* we have not now. Carry this in your minds: a scientific approach, no more. Onto the green, with luck, your science takes you. But when it comes to putting you will work by art and hunch. ...

But if you arrive at the conclusion that a given court did not mean all it said in the express ratio decidendi it laid down, that the case must really be confined to facts narrower than the court itself assumed to be its measure, then you are ready for the distinction that I hinted at earlier in this lecture, the distinction betwen the ratio decidendi, the court's own version of the rule of the case, and the *true* rule of the case, to wit, what *it will be made to stand for by another later court*. For one of the vital elements of our doctrine of precedent is this: that any later court can always reexamine a prior case, and under the principle that the court could decide only what was before it, and that the older case must now be read with that in view, can arrive at the conclusion that the dispute before the earlier court was much narrower than that court thought it was, called therefore for the application of a much narrower rule. Indeed, the argument goes further. It goes on to state that no broader rule *could* have been laid down ex-cathedra, because to do that would have transcended the powers of the earlier court.

You have seen further that out of the matching of a number of related cases it is your job to formulate a rule that covers them all in harmony, if that can be done, and to test your formulation against possible variants on the facts. Finally, to test it, if there is time, against what writers on the subject have to say, and against other cases.

The ratio is therefore something that can be ascertained tentatively as soon as the case has been decided. The law reporter in preparing his account of the case will attempt a formulation of the ratio which he will state in his headnote. He will base this partly on the facts of the case, partly on what the judge has said in his judgment and partly on his sense of the proper limits of the doctrine formulated in the case. Thereafter the ratio may be widened in later cases (by reducing the facts stated in it or thus raising the level of abstraction), or, conversely, it may be narrowed by the opposite process. The ratio is therefore not a fixed entity but a formula that is capable of adjustment according to the force of later developments.

The process has been described in another classic American book:

Benjamin N. Cardozo, *The Nature of the Judicial Process* (1921), pp. 48–9

The implications of a decision may in the beginning be equivocal. New cases by commentary and exposition extract the essence. At last there emerges a rule or principle which becomes a datum, a point of departure, from which new lines will be run, from which new courses will be measured. Sometimes the rule or principle is found to have been formulated too narrowly or too broadly and has to be reframed. Sometimes it is accepted as a postulate of later reasoning, its origins are forgotten, it becomes a new stock of descent, its issue unite with other strains, and persisting permeate the law. You may call the process one of analogy or of logic or of philosophy as you please. Its essence in any event is the derivation of a consequence from a rule or a principle or a precedent which, accepted as a datum, contains implicitly within itself the germ of the conclusion. In all this, I do not use the word philosophy in any strict or formal sense. The method tapers down from the syllogism at one end to mere analogy at the other. Sometimes the extension of a precedent goes to the limit of its logic. Sometimes it does not go so far. Sometimes by a process of analogy it is carried even farther. That is a tool which no system of jurisprudence has been able to discard. A rule which has worked well in one field, or which, in any event, is there whether its workings have been revealed or not, is carried over into another. Instances of such a process I group under the same heading as those where the nexus of logic is closer and more binding. At bottom and in their underlying motives, they are phases of the same method. They are inspired by the same yearning for consistency, for certainty, for uniformity of plan and structure. They have their roots in the constant striving of the mind for a larger and more inclusive unity, in which differences will be reconciled, and abnormalities will vanish.

The process is illustrated in the Appendix to this chapter, through an account of the development of the action in tort for negligent misstatements.

Questions

1. Who formulates the ratio of a case?

2. How does one discover the right level of abstraction at which to state the ratio?

3. What determines whether a proposition of law is ratio or obiter? Can it move from one category to the other?

(b) Is the precedent distinguishable?

Having assigned the statement of law to one or other of the two categories of ratio or dictum, the lawyer will wish to determine its relevance to the facts in issue. If one side can marshall a precedent that is binding and in point, that will conclude the debate. The only way for the opponent to avoid losing the case is by showing that the case is *distinguishable*. The process of distinguishing is important, however, not simply as the only means of avoiding a threatening precedent that is binding but equally as a means of avoiding one that is merely of persuasive authority. Very commonly the lawyers on one side of an argument will produce one or more precedents that they claim are in point and which their opponents claim are distinguishable, whilst in turn their opponents rely on a different line of authorities which the first side maintain have no relevance. Distinguishing between factual situations and applying the appropriate rule of law is one of the lawyer's and judge's most crucial functions. It is the business of drawing lines, or seeing how far to take a particular rule and of expanding or contracting the scope of rules to meet new circumstances. The question is always the same – are there any material differences between the facts of the present case and the facts of the precedents to warrant the rule being different?

Sometimes the court distinguishes the indistinguishable – as the only way to escape from the clutches of an unwelcome precedent which would otherwise be binding. This process brings the law into disrepute, for it abuses the integrity of the process and cheapens the intellectual tools of the trade. This cannot be said however of the two cases that follow because, although they give opposite answers to virtually identical facts, they were decided by the same judges on the same day:

Whitton v. *Garner* [1965] 1 All E.R. 70
(Divisional Court, Q.B.D.)

BRABIN J., delivered the first judgment at the invitation of LORD PARKER C.J.: This is an appeal by way of Case Stated from a decision by the justices for the county of Lancaster sitting at Bolton. They heard a summons under the Affiliation Proceedings Act, 1957, by the respondent, who maintained that the appellant was the putative father of her child. The respondent is, and at all material times was, a married woman, and the point that arises is whether a married woman can be a single woman within the meaning of s. 1 of the Affiliation Proceedings Act, 1957 [which provided for claims for maintenance to be made by a single woman against the putative father of her child]. That is a matter which has been decided many times in the affirmative. In this particular case, at the time when the summons was taken out the respondent was living in the same house as her husband. She gave evidence before the justices, and the justices found as a fact on that evidence, that for four years she had occupied a separate bedroom in the house in which both parties lived and that she and her husband had lived separate and apart during the whole of that time. The respondent gave further evidence, and a finding of fact was made by the justices in respect of it, that the child had been registered by the respondent's husband as his child, but that such registration was made without the respondent's consent, approval or knowledge.

It is submitted on behalf of the appellant that the justices could not come to the finding that the respondent was a single woman within the meaning of s. 1, because she and her husband were both living in the same house. It is urged further that there is a rule of law that the magistrates cannot, in such circumstances, act on the evidence of the respondent complainant unless that part of her evidence is corroborated. I know of no such rule of law. The rule of law in respect of corroboration is by statute laid down in s. 4 (2) of the Act of 1957. There is no rule of law specifically relating to s. 1 of the Act. Clearly, when a husband and wife are living in the same house, it is much more difficult for a wife in those circumstances to establish that she is a single woman within the meaning of s. 1 of the Act of 1957. This matter was dealt with by this court in *Watson* v. *Tuckwell* (1947) 63 T.L.R. at p. 635, when LORD GODDARD C.J., said:

'I agree that if a husband and wife are found living under the same roof, it is prima facie evidence that the parties are living together; but it is no more than prima facie evidence. It is evidence that can be rebutted, and if the justices are satisfied that it has been rebutted they are justified in finding that there was a de facto separation. It is clearly a question of fact, and, in my opinion, there is evidence upon which they could find that fact.'

Applying that direction to this particular appeal, the evidence of the respondent that she lived separate and apart from her husband over this period of four years and that, during that time, there had been no access to her by her husband, was evidence which the justices could accept or reject. The justices accepted that evidence, and it appears from the Case Stated that, on these material matters in the respondent's evidence, no cross-examination was addressed to the respondent in respect of them. The prima facie presumption that exists when husband and wife are living in the same house was rebutted in this case to the satisfaction of the justices and, in my judgment, the justices were right in holding that, on the evidence called before them, the respondent was a single woman within the meaning of s. 1 of the Act of 1957. I, therefore, consider that this appeal should be dismissed.

ASHWORTH J.: I agree.

LORD PARKER C.J.: I also agree.

Giltrow v. *Day* [1965] 1 All E.R. 73
(Divisional Court, Q.B.D.)

Case Stated.

This was a Case Stated by justices of the county of Middlesex Quarter Sessions in respect of their adjudication on an appeal sitting at The Guildhall, Westminster, London, on Mar. 20, 1964. On that day the respondent, Ivor Day, appeared before the justices of the county of Middlesex Quarter Sessions as appellant against an order made by the magistrates' court sitting at Ealing on Feb. 6, 1964, whereby the respondent was adjudged to be the putative father of a male child born to the appellant, Maureen Margaret Giltrow, on May 8, 1963, and the magistrates' court ordered that he pay to the appellant the weekly sum of £1 5s. towards the maintenance of the child until he reach the age of sixteen years. The general grounds of the appeal were stated to be that the order was made against the weight of evidence in that the respondent, on the evidence, could not have been held to be the putative father of the child, and that the order was wrong in law in that the appellant was not a single woman within the meaning of the Affiliation Proceedings Act, 1957. At the hearing of the appeal the first ground was not proceeded with, and the appeal was heard only on the preliminary issue of law before the justices, who allowed the appeal.

BRABIN J. The justices who heard this appeal have carefully set out the facts as they find them in the Case as stated. It is quite clear from their findings that the appellant and her husband had ceased to have sexual intercourse together or to occupy the same bedroom since August, 1961, and that, from that date, the appellant had not visited her husband's bedroom. The husband

and wife lived together in a flat, and the flat was occupied by reason of an arrangement by which the appellant supplied services in respect of, no doubt, the main building. There were two children of the marriage, one who slept with the father and one who slept with the mother, and, when the mother became pregnant, the child who slept with her then moved into the husband's bedroom. The finances of the household were provided by the husband, as they had always been, and the appellant bought the food and cooked the meal which the husband ate daily in the house. The husband always prepared his own breakfast, and his mid-day meal was eaten away from home. These arrangements existed before, and were continued after, the parties occupied separate bedrooms. There is no doubt that the appellant and her husband were not living in amity; they each went their separate ways. The one manifestation of that after August, 1961, when the marriage in the normal circumstances might be said to have broken down, was that the appellant ceased to do the mending of the husband's clothes or to clean his bedroom, but a cleaner was provided who did the latter. There was further evidence as found by the justices that, on one occasion and one only at Christmas, 1963, when the appellant was entertaining some friends, the husband unexpectedly insinuated himself into the party and dispensed the drinks. This method of living, which continued after August, 1961, was found to have so continued because both parties acquiesced in it. . . . On the facts found by the justices, I consider that the justices hearing the appeal were wholly justified in finding that the presumption existing in these circumstances [that a husband and wife living under the same roof are living together] was not rebutted, and that, therefore, the appellant was not a single woman within the meaning of the Affiliation Proceedings Act, 1957.

Question

What appear to have been the critical differences between this and the previous case which explain the different result arrived at? Were they sufficient in your view to justify the distinction drawn?

(c) What weight should be given to the precedent?

Having determined the status of the precedent as ratio or dictum and whether, and if so to what extent, it is in point, the lawyer will now wish to scrutinise the precedent minutely for its true worth. The process is similar to that of assaying precious metals. He will take into account a number of different considerations:

(1) *Which court decided the case?*

Other things being equal, the higher the court in the hierarchy the greater its authority.

(2) *Which judges were involved?*

All judges are equal but some are a little more equal than others. Not much can be made of this point, however, unless the judge(s) who decided the case were in the rare category regarded by the profession as being of special eminence – Lord Atkin, Lord Justice Scrutton, Lord Reid are three examples. Apart from the few luminaries, counsel is usually wise to avoid making invidious distinctions between the reputations of former judges.

(3) *Was there a dissent?*
The existence of any dissenting opinions would effect the weight of a decision, especially of course if the dissenting judge(s) were of particular eminence.

(4) *When was the case decided?*
If the precedent is old, one side no doubt will argue that it reflects well-settled law whilst the other will contend that it is no longer apt for modern conditions. Something may then turn on whether or not it has been challenged in previous cases. Every time that a precedent is put to the test of argument and emerges unscathed it develops new roots and accordingly to that extent becomes harder to dislodge. If, on the other hand, it has stood unchallenged, one side will suggest that this shows that its roots are shallow and flimsy whilst the other will argue that the fact of no challenge over a long period demonstrates the strength of the rule – it was so clear and so deeply rooted that no one even thought to contest the point.

(5) *How does the precedent fit with the surrounding law?*
Sometimes it can be argued that the precedent is based on faulty reasoning, or illogically drawn analogies, or that it is at odds with other, better established principles.

(6) *How has the decision been dealt with in later cases?*
There are various possibilities:

(a) It may have been overruled by the decision of a higher court that it was wrongly decided. Overruling can be explicit or implicit. The former is clear and has the effect of removing the precedent entirely from the field of play – subject only to the possibility of being brought back into the game if a still higher court decides that it was, after all, rightly decided. Implied overruling occurs where it is arguable that the decision cannot stand with a later decision of a higher court. But this contention often meets determined counter-argument.

(b) The precedent, whilst not being overruled, may nevertheless have been undermined either by direct aspersions cast upon it by judges in later cases or because it was not applied to factual situations that appeared to be well within the scope of the principle for which it stands (not following or restrictive distinguishing).

(*c*) On the other hand, it may have been approved and followed in later cases and expanded by being applied to new factual situations not apparently within the contemplation or the scope of the principle as first framed.

(7) *What reputation does the precedent enjoy generally?*

Any published comment on the case or the principle of law for which it stands could be significant in either strengthening or weakening its authority. The case may have been the subject of discussion in some scholarly writings. It may have given rise to problems in the community of which the courts could be made aware. Suggestions may have been made for the reform of the rule by law-reform bodies. Any such indications may create a climate of opinion about a precedent which can be turned to advantage by one or other side in litigation.

One of the peculiar features of English judicial method by comparison with that of most other countries is the high proportion of cases in which the judges deliver their judgments 'off-the-cuff' immediately after the case is over. This is so even in the Court of Appeal, though the House of Lords always reserves judgment. (When a court reserves judgment this is indicated in the law reports by the phrase *Cur. adv. vult.*) It is rare for counsel to make much of this point as a factor in evaluating the weight of the precedent, but a revealing lecture by Lord Justice Russell suggests that more attention might well be paid to this point:

Sir Charles Russell, 'Behind the Appellate Curtain', Holdsworth Club Lecture, 1969, pp. 3–8

It is important in considering appellate judgments to differentiate between reserved judgments and unreserved judgments. The quality of the former is, or should be, better than that of the latter. Many may think that in the Court of Appeal judgment should be more often reserved, since in I suppose 95% of cases it is in fact a judgment of the court of final decision. I would not dissent from that view. Some appellate judges have a great ability for stating the relevants facts without significant omission or error, and I think those with a background of summing up to juries in criminal cases have an advantage in this respect. Others – among whom I number myself – find some difficulty in giving judgment off the cuff, and would prefer reservation of judgments more frequently. But it must be recognised that the pressure of civil appellate business discourages the practice of reservation of judgments.

Accordingly I take, first, academic consideration by academic lawyers and others of reserved judgments of the Court of Appeal. The production of these may involve different combinations of events. Suppose that in general terms all three judges are at the end in agreement on the outcome. Away they go and write their judgments in draft and circulate them. Here sometimes is the crunch. Lord Justice Frog does not altogether approve of a particular ratiocination of Lord Justice Toad. What does he do? This is apt to depend upon the state of Frog, L.J.'s work. If he is busy – and he may now be sitting in a different division of the C.A. with its own problems – he may be content to leave his judgment to stand without arguing the toss or trying to persuade Toad L.J. to amend his judgment. Or he may add to his judgment words of doubt of the proposition of Toad, L.J. Now what happens? In the latter case lawyers – and not only academic lawyers – hasten to point out that Frog, L.J. took the opposite view. But in fact Frog, L.J. in his mind has done no more than *suspect* the proposition. He has not had the time to discuss the proposition with Toad, L.J. – one or other has had a committee meeting at 4.30 p.m. every evening for a fortnight, and Frog, L.J. lives in West Sussex. In effect the apparent dissent of Frog, L.J. should not be regarded as anything except an undigested reservation that has no persuasive value in the formation of legal principles. It should do no more than encourage a critical approach to the views of Toad, L.J. If he leaves it alone, this should not be taken as wholehearted agreement. Take another case of reserved judgments. There may be a full scale battle behind the scenes between Frog, L.J. and Toad, L.J. on some matter of principle, with Slug, L.J. a trifle out of his depth and relatively disinterested, but on the whole prepared to march with Toad, L.J. in the decision. Now in such a case Frog and Toad read each other's drafts. Frog observes in Toad what he considers to be gross heresy and amends his draft in a manner calculated to expose it as such, hoping that thus he will bring Toad to his senses. Undeterred, Toad fortifies his draft by analogy with other branches of the law. Frog is drawn unwillingly into this new field, and by postponing his first gin and catching the late train to West Sussex works hard at it for his third draft. Toad, L.J. – who lives in London and never touches gin – produces an amendment digging into ancient authorities including a resounding declaration about the turn of the century that has in fact (unknown to him because this tangential approach to the problem was never discussed by counsel) been later roundly disapproved. Frog, L.J. reads the amended judgment of Toad and is too busy to trouble further. What happens? Slug, L.J. agrees in general terms with Toad, L.J. Frog, L.J. has not objected to the reliance on the turn of the century declaration. And, lo and behold! it has apparently been reinstated as the law. This is an example that should warn us all that when in search of the law as authoritatively propounded by an appellate court (1) it is important to stick to what was necessarily said for the decision of the particular case, and (2) silence does not necessarily mean consent.

The latter point is even more relevant in the case of *unreserved judgments* in the Court of Appeal, and most particular caution is to be recommended in such cases. It must be realised that when the shorthand writer circulates transcripts of such judgments for correction he sends only the individual transcript to the individual Lord Justice. It is true that reported cases are entire: but speaking for myself I only check my own judgments in proof, being sufficiently hard put to remember what I had said.

Envisage, please, the production of unreserved judgments in the C.A. Ordinarily the first judgment is delivered by the presiding Lord Justice. Of course in many cases the way the minds are working on the bench has been to a greater or lesser extent displayed in the course of exchanges during the argument. If there has been an adjournment during the case no doubt the members of the Court have discussed the progress of the case and have exchanged tentative views on the points emerging. But in the end the moment arrives when judgment is to be given. Often a short huddle is to be observed in the face of the public. Sometimes – and I think with more dignity – the Court adjourns for a few minutes. But, whatever the discussion, in many cases Frog, L.J. is never quite sure how Toad, L.J. will express himself, and Slug, L.J. is unsure about both, however much they may all be agreed on dismissing or allowing the appeal. Toad, L.J. leads off. Slug, L.J. as the junior has decided to say nothing of his own. Frog, L.J. has decided to say a little piece of his own. Consider the situation of Frog, L.J. who prefers to jot down his thoughts. With his right hand and most of his brain he is doing this. With his left ear and the rest of his brain he is at the same time trying to follow what Toad, L.J. is saying – not really an easy exercise. All too often Frog, L.J. is rash enough to start his judgment with the words 'I agree'. Really he means by this that he agrees with the order proposed and that he has not been able to detect in what he has grasped of the judgment of Toad, L.J. any errors, or any error that he is able at such short notice to denounce as such or refute. But what happens? Other lawyers – and I do not confine them to the writers of text books or articles or the teachers of youth – pick upon those two introductory words and claim for some proposition the weighty authority of not only Toad, L.J. but also Frog, L.J. Whereas in truth Toad, L.J. had a brilliant notion half way through a sentence, a notion that he much later rather regretted, and Frog, L.J. never heard the notion, or having heard assumed that he had misheard or was unwilling to produce an undigested disclaimer. Moreover, even if Frog, L.J. follows the cautious practice – one that I approve myself – of never starting with 'I agree', but if anything at all with the phrase 'I agree that this appeal fails/succeeds', what happens? It is said by others that Frog, L.J. did not dissent from or disagree with what was said by Toad, L.J., therefore he must be taken to have agreed. And what of Slug, L.J. who had decided to say nothing original? He was as a result able to listen to everything that was said by the other two. But suppose that he heard from them or one of them something with which he was not altogether happy? Poor Slug is in rather a fix. Is he to recite his objections, which anyway he finds it difficult to formulate at short notice, and add 'otherwise I agree'? Or suppose he prefers the way in which Frog, L.J. has put it to that of Toad, L.J.? Does he say that for the reasons given by Frog, L.J. he agrees with the order proposed by Toad, L.J.? Even more delicate is his position if he happens to be Slug, J. standing in for Grub, L.J. who has been taken away from his proper task in order to conduct an enquiry on a subject on which he has no expertise, because the government is anxious not to carry the burden of decision? In the end Slug, L.J. or J. contents himself with saying tersely 'I agree' – though he may, frequently with every justification, continue 'and there is nothing I can usefully add', an addendum that denies its own function....

Now what is the moral of all this? For my address, so far, though based upon the principle that a light touch sometimes illuminates, is intended to seek a moral. As I see it it is one not only for the teacher and text book writer but also for the practitioner. In particular in the case of unreserved judgments weight should be attributed only to pronouncements that in express terms approve of other pronouncements, and with particularity rather than generality. All else should be suspect in point of value....

(d) Inconvenience and injustice

Counsel arguing a case is permitted to assert that a precedent has had unhappy consequences or, alternatively, that such consequences would ensue if the court adopted the rule proposed by his opponent. But counsel is not normally permitted to offer evidence as to the consequences of any existing or proposed formulation of law. He may not even cite official reports, statistics, or other economic or social data on the matter. The only exception is foreign law. Expert witnesses, normally practitioners in the foreign system, are permitted to testify on oath as to the prevailing state of the law on the matter in contention in the foreign country concerned. Foreign law, therefore, is treated as matter of fact to be proved by evidence. English law by contrast is something of which the court takes judicial notice.

The 'Brandeis brief'

In the United States, for most of this century, the courts have taken a more expansive attitude to the problem of providing information to courts about the present or likely future effects of rules of law. This technique of argument is called the 'Brandeis brief' – after the later Supreme Court Justice, Louis Brandeis, who first introduced it:

Alpheus Thomas Mason, *Brandeis* (1956), pp. 248–51

... in 1907, Mrs Florence Kelly and Miss Josephine Goldmark learned that the Oregon ten-hour law for women was to be contested before the United States Supreme Court. To defend the law, these women wanted the most competent legal talent in the land.... The next day they asked Brandeis, who accepted at once...

The invitation was gladly extended. Brandeis then outlined the material needed for his brief. The legal part he would himself cover in a few pages. For the economic and social data showing the evil of long hours and the possible benefits from legislative limitation, he would look to his sister-in-law. It was on these materials, not on the legal argument, that he would base his case.

This was a bold innovation.... Many years earlier he had recorded in his *Index Rerum*: 'A judge is presumed to know the elements of law, but there is no presumption that he knows the facts.' In this spirit he drew up his revolutionary social and economic brief....

Brandeis's brief-making enormously extended the bounds of common knowledge and compelled the court to 'take judicial notice' of this extension. In the Muller brief only two scant pages were given to conventional legal arguments. Over one hundred pages were devoted to the new kind of evidence drawn from hundreds of reports, both domestic and foreign, of committees, statistical bureaux, commissioners of hygiene, and factory inspectors – all proving that, long hours are *as a matter of fact* dangerous to women's health, safety and morals, that short hours result in social and economic benefits.

Brandeis appeared in oral argument in January 1908, before a court dominated by superannuated legalists, including Chief Justice Fuller, Justices Peckham, Brewer, and Day. The 'dry bones of legalism rattled' as opposing counsel argued that women were endowed, equally with men, with the fundamental right of free contract; that woman's 'freedom' to bargain with employers must not be impaired. This time, however, the court could not be screened from all knowledge of the living world....

The Oregon ten-hour law was upheld, and the court, speaking through Justice Brewer, approved Brandeis's technique and, most unusually, mentioned him by name. The court's spokesman, Justice Brewer, said:

'In the brief filed by Mr Louis D. Brandeis ... is a very copious collection of all these matters....

'The legislation and opinions referred to in the margin may not be, technically speaking, authorities, and in them is little or no discussion of the constitutional question presented to us for determination, yet they are significant of a widespread belief that woman's physical structure, and the functions she performs in consequence thereof, justify special legislation restricting or qualifying the conditions under which she should be permitted to toil.'

Here for the first time the Supreme Court was recognizing the need for facts to establish the reasonableness or unreasonableness of social legislation. For the time being the court had rejected its own freedom-of-contract fiction as regards working women. Brandeis followed up this advantage immediately. After the Muller case he appeared for oral argument in defence of other labour laws and sent briefs to some fourteen different courts.

The value of the Brandeis brief approach to legal argument can be seen in one of the rare English cases in which the court admitted, and appeared to have been decisively influenced by, evidence on a matter of law derived from statistics. In *Nowotnik* v. *Nowotnik* [1967] P. 83 the Court of Appeal had given an extremely narrow interpretation to a provision in the Legal Aid Act 1964 designed to compensate the successful defendant who had the misfortune to be sued by a legally aided plantiff. The section (now s. 13 of the Legal Aid Act 1974) provided that such a person could ask to have his costs paid out of the legal aid fund if he could show that he would otherwise suffer 'severe financial hardship'. N., the husband, was the successful respondent in divorce proceedings. He claimed under the Act. His costs had been £345. His capital was £5 17s 9d; he earned £24 a week as a manual labourer; he had a car and had had two holidays in Germany. The court (Lord Denning and four other lords justices) held that there was insufficient evidence of severe financial hardship. The husband's capital admittedly was low but he had not had to restrict his activities. They rejected his claim.

Three years later precisely the same issue came up in *Hanning* v. *Maitland* (*No. 2*) [1970] 1 Q.B. 580. The successful defendant had an earned income of £18 or £19 gross, and savings of between £2,500 and £3,000. The costs he was claiming from the fund were £325. Lord Denning, delivering judgment as he had in *Nowotnik*, said that the court had been given some figures by counsel for the Law Society who appeared as 'amicus curiae' (friend of the court – see p. 239 below). These showed the sums set aside each year in the legal aid accounts, for payments expected to be made out of the fund under the 1964 Act. In the first three years the Law Society had estimated the expected payments and the government had paid into the fund the sum of £40,000 a year against this liability. The payments out in the three years were £74, £838 and £243 respectively (*Nowotnik* was decided in the middle of the second year.) Lord Denning (at 587) said 'Those figures show one of two things: either that the Act itself was badly worded so that it did not give effect to the intention of the makers of it; or the courts have interpreted it wrongly so as to defeat the intention of Parliament. I am afraid that it is the second. We can and should learn by experience. In the light of it, I must confess that this court in *Nowotnik* v. *Nowotnik* interpreted the Act wrongly.' The court gave the defendant his costs, and so changed the interpretation of the phrase 'severe financial hardship' that in 1972 an insurance company was able to claim successfully under the Act – see *General Accident Fire and Life Assurance Ltd* v. *Foster* [1972] 3 All E.R. 877. (The case is also another example of the Court of

Appeal unanimously declining to follow one of its own previous decisions despite the clear indications of *Young* v. *Bristol Aeroplane Ltd.* Lord Denning referred specifically to the point by saying that the Court of Appeal was *not* bound by its own decisions; Lord Justice Salmon did not allude to the problem; Lord Justice Edmund Davies, somewhat disingenuously, said he was not 'conscious of departing substantially from the test of "severe financial hardship" laid down in *Nowotnik*'!)

Questions

Is there any valid reason for excluding evidence in the form of factual information about the background to disputed legal rules? If it were permitted, how could it be controlled so as to prevent the court being swamped? Should it be confined to written material or should it include oral evidence? (See further, p. 239 below for consideration of the American practice of having amicus briefs from non-parties to litigation, and p. 242 for the American practice of having written briefs to supplement oral argument.)

2. Are precedents law or only evidence of the law?

There is an important jurisprudential debate as to whether judges make law or whether they simply declare the law, and whether precedents are law or only evidence of the law. The two issues are closely related.

In the eighteenth century Blackstone said 'the decisions of courts of justice are the evidence of what is common law'.[1] In 1892 Lord Esher stated: 'There is in fact no such thing as judge-made law, for the judges do not make the law though they frequently have to apply existing law to circumstances as to which it has not previously been authoritatively laid down that such law is applicable.'[2] According to Professor Cross these views are mistaken. A rule stated in a precedent he argues 'is law properly so called and law because it was made by the judges, not because it originated in common usage, or the judge's idea of justice and public convenience'.[3] So far as Lord Esher's statement was concerned, the application of existing law to new circumstances could never clearly be distinguished from the creation of a

1. *Commentaries* (13th edn.) vol. i, pp. 88–9.
2. *Willis* v. *Baddeley* [1892] 2 Q.B. 324 at 326.
3. Cross, *Precedent in English Law* (3rd edn., 1977), p. 27.

new rule of law. If there were no such things as judge-made law, it would be impossible to account for the evolution of much legal doctrine which had been formulated by the judges and no one but the judges.[4] If a previous decision were only evidence of what the law is, no judge could ever be absolutely bound to follow it, and it could never be effectively overruled because a subsequent judge might always treat it as having some evidential value.[5]

But, with respect to Professor Cross, this is not entirely convincing. Of course there cannot be any cavil with his statement that 'the fact that our judges can and do make law is now universally recognised by writers on the British Constitution'.[6] As Lord Radcliffe said: '... there was never a more sterile controversy than that upon the question whether a judge makes law. Of course he does. How can he help it?'[7] But this leaves open the question whether there is not also merit in the declaratory theory of law and in the theory that precedents are evidence of law rather than law itself.

When a judge decides a point of law, he is declaring what he finds the law on that point to be. He is not saying what he thinks it ought to be but what he believes it is. In giving voice to his opinion as to what the law is, he may have added something new to the existing corpus of the law. In fact, unless he has simply restated an existing principle or applied it in a totally predictable way to new facts, he *will* have done so. Most decisions on points of law add something new in this sense and can therefore be said to be 'making law'. From the judge's point of view, his function is to declare the law; from the point of view of the observer, he may in declaring it have added something new or even changed the law. The 'declaratory theory' and the 'judges-do-make-law theory' therefore appear both to be right.

But there is a further dimension. It is possible that the judge, having stated what he thinks the law to be, proves to be in error. He may be reversed almost immediately on appeal or his ratio may be overruled in a later case by a higher court. This shows that inspection of a precedent at the time when it is handed down does not necessarily reveal whether the precedent reflects 'good law'. This will only emerge later when, with the advantage of hindsight, one will be able to say that the judge in 1976 stated what judges in the succeeding

4. Ibid.
5. Ibid., p. 28.
6. Ibid., p. 29.
7. Radcliffe, *Not in Feather Beds* (1968), p. 215 – see p. 199 below.

two or three decades agreed was the law on that point. Even then, fifty years later a different view may prevail.

The theory that precedents are no more than evidence of the law has the advantage that it seems to fit the facts. It explains one of the most fundamental and important aspects of the doctrine of precedent – that every principle that emerges from a judicial decision is capable of being changed. However well settled a principle of law may appear to be, it can be challenged and changed at any time. Even if the House of Lords itself has enunciated the rule, it can now be altered by the House of Lords. In other words, it is possible to look at the rule of law that seems to emerge from a precedent and say 'That cannot be right and to prove it I shall litigate the point up to a higher court to get the rule changed.'

Moreover, whenever a rule of law is enunciated by a court, its effect is retrospective. The rule is now the law and in theory always has been. Any different previous formulations of the rule were mistaken. The retrospective effect of the new rule is of course fiction – but it has the practical result that a person may bring an action based on an injury suffered before the new rule and claim the benefit of the new formulation. The only exceptions are where the case has already been litigated (in which case the doctrine of res judicata prevents the issue being reopened), and where the Statute of Limitations operates to bar the action through the lapse of time. (An action for personal injuries for instance cannot normally be brought more than three years after the injury has been suffered.) However, the theory that precedents are only evidence of the law is consistent with the reality that what is thought to be the law at one time may turn out to be wrong.

Professor Cross objects that if a previous decision were only evidence of what the law is, no judge could be bound to follow it and it could never be effectively overruled – because some other judge might always treat it as having some evidential value. But the doctrine of precedent can be said to operate something like the best-evidence rule in the law of evidence – that the court wishes always to have the best evidence on any issue. The doctrine of precedent lays down rules as to how the courts should approach precedents. A decision of the House of Lords, other things being equal, is better evidence than one of the Court of Appeal, etc. Moreover, so far as the Court of Appeal is concerned, a decision of the House of Lords is not only the best evidence of what the law is, but creates an irrebuttable presumption that it is correct. On the other hand, the House of Lords reviewing its own prior decision will treat the precedent as the best extant evidence of the rule, but the presumption that it is right is rebuttable since the House of Lords is free to depart from its own prior decisions. Equally there is no difficulty with the problem of overruling. Again, the doctrine of precedent acts, in effect, to prohibit a court from receiving as evidence a decision that has been overruled. The exclusion of otherwise admissible evidence is a familiar principle of the law of evidence.

The view that precedents are evidence of the law and not the law itself is not only consistent with the innate flexibility and fluidity of the common law system, but also reflects the actual practice of the courts. Argument in a court as to what the law is, is based on the marshalling of each side by its proofs – counsel comes armed with his precedents or his reinterpretation of his opponent's precedents and submits that his view of the law is the correct one. Having heard each side, the judge decides between them. To say that the precedents *are* the law is the equivalent of saying that the witnesses to a question of fact are the truth. Whether the precedents reflect the law cannot emerge authoritatively until after the judge has spoken and even then only in the partial and qualified sense that at most the decision reflects the best evidence available at that moment as to what the law is.

It is a nice question whether our doctrine of precedent promotes law-making in too rapid a way by overemphasising the importance of individual decisions. Whilst it is true that the ultimate shape of a rule cannot be fully discerned until it has had time to mature, there is nevertheless a tendency to dramatise the significance of the latest case. Lord Radcliffe has reflected on the dangers of this tendency:

Lord Radcliffe, *Not in Feather Beds*
(1968), pp. 216–17

I cannot help thinking that there is a tendency today to give too much importance to particular decisions, and by so doing to discover leading cases before they have proved that they have in them the quality to lead. There is too much forcing of unripe growth. Seen from the inside hardly any decision comes out ready made as of general authority; nor, I believe, do those who participate in it think of it in that way. One learns the vast difficulty of generalising on any matter of principle, just because, short of genius, there are very few minds that have the imaginative grasp to see the full implications of a generalisation and to pass in review its effect upon the interconnected strands of our body of law. It is not a question of playing safe: it is rather that a sensitive, not a blinkered, concentration upon the direct issue that has to be resolved makes for a sounder construction of that legal body. And, perhaps, only their successors who have to work upon them appreciate how flashy have been the gnomic utterances of some of our best known judicial sages.

I do not regret this counsel of reticence. It accords well with the methodology of our law-making. Just as under our system a court decision is formed out of the work of those who prepare a case, those who argue it before the court and those who ultimately explain and record their view, so a decision of even a final court, when pronounced, has only begun its life as a constituent of the full corpus of the law. It is a mistake, just because it is final, to think that the matter is then closed. On the contrary, it has been handed over to the care of the profession. It will be chewed over by barristers and solicitors, commented on in law journals, made the subject of moots and law lectures, reviewed by the writers of the legal text books. It will be read in the light of previous decisions, upon which it is itself a commentary: and it will be read in the light of later decisions, to which itself it forms a text. In the end, but only in the end, general legal opinion will come to assign to it a more or less determined place in the whole compendium of law, important or unimportant, formative or a dead end, malleable or rigid. Until a decision has been subjected to a process of this kind, in the course of which indeed it may come out wearing a very different air from that with which it entered and serving a purpose hardly intended by its authors, I should be reluctant to class it as a leading authority. We must not declare a vintage before it is made.

If you happen to share the rather sober view I am putting forward you may share too my strong feeling that contemporary comment tends to attach far too much weight to particular phrases or passages in the body of a decision. Analysis of this order is almost morbid in its intensity, and it can, so often, be only sterile skill and ingenuity. A man must work according to his material. The English language is peculiarly ill-adapted to such elaborate analysis, being, as we know, though copious and expressive, a pliable and shifting medium, in which even key words and phrases take shape and colour from their context and have no rigid internal structure of fixed meaning. The difficulty becomes that much the greater when the decision of a final court is conveyed not by a single pronouncement but in the separate deliveries of several judges. Then indeed a baffling task awaits the reader. Is one deliverance more leading than another, and, if so, how do you identify it? In course of time, no doubt, there will be selection through the operation of the kind of winnowing process that I have been describing. We all know how one particular speech or judgment comes to be regarded as the critical one, the one which is turned to as the core of the decision. But time is needed for that. Again, does a particular passage in one of the judgments represent the hinge of the author's conclusion, and, if it serves as such for him, ought one to think that it so serves for others just because they agree with his general conclusion?

3. The values promoted by the system of precedent

A catalogue of the values promoted by the common law system of precedent has been drawn up by Professors Hart and Sachs of the Harvard Law School in their widely known but unpublished set of materials on the legal process:

Henry Hart and Albert M. Sacks, *The Legal Process* (Tentative Edition, 1958, mimeographed), pp. 587–8

In furtherance of private ordering

(a) The desirability of enabling people to plan their affairs at the stage of primary private activity with the maximum attainable confidence that if they comply with the law as it has theretofore been announced, or can fairly be expected to be announced thereafter, they will not become entangled in litigation.

(b) The desirability of providing private counsel so far as possible with stable bases of reasoning. Think about this factor, in particular, from the point of view of efficient social engineering. The potential contribution of the legal profession in the avoidance of social friction is very large, is it not? A lawyer must have tools with which to work if he is to make this contribution.

(c) The desirability of encouraging the remedial processes of private settlement by minimizing the incentives of the parties to try to secure from a different judge a different decision than has been given by the same or other judges in the past.

In furtherance of fair and efficient adjudication

(a) The desirability, from the point of view of the litigants, of expediting litigation and minimizing its costs by sparing them the necessity of relitigating every relevant proposition in every case.

(b) The need, from the point of view of the judicial system, of facilitating the dispatch of business – indeed, the sheer impossibility of reexamining *de novo* every relevant proposition in every case.

(c) The need of discouraging a rush of litigation whenever there is a change of personnel on the bench.

(d) The desirability, from the point of view of fairness to the litigants, of securing a reasonable uniformity of decision throughout the judicial system, both at any given time and from one time to another.

(e) The desirability of promoting genuine impersonality of decision by minimizing the elements of personal discretion, and of facilitating the operation of the check of professional criticism.

(f) The propriety of according respect to the conclusions of predecessor judges.

(g) The injustice of disappointing expectations fairly generated at the stage of primary private activity.

In furtherance of public confidence in the judiciary

(a) The desirability of maximising the acceptability of decisions, and the importance to this end of popular and professional confidence in (1) the impersonality of decisions and (2) their reasoned foundation, as manifested both by the respect accorded to them by successor judges and by their staying power.

(b) The necessity, considering the amorphous nature of the limits upon judicial power and the usual absence of an effective political check at the ballot box, that judges be subject to the discipline and the restraint of an obligation to build upon the prior law in a fashion which can withstand the test of professional criticism.

There are however various problems associated with law-making by judges and the doctrine of precedent, which have to be set against the positive aspects of the system:

(1) It over-emphasizes the importance of individual decisions (see p. 179 above).

(2) It creates law which may upset expectations with no advance notice to those likely to be affected.

(3) The system depends on the accidents of litigation. A bad decision may stand for many years.

(4) It tends to be backward-looking and conservative, and therefore to be slow to respond to changing needs.

(5) Once a point has been decided at the level of the Court of Appeal or the House of Lords, it tends to remain the law whether or not it is apt for the situation.

(6) There are often technical problems associated with the fact that the judges give separate decisions so that it is difficult to ascertain what is the ratio. Or a judge may give several reasons for his decision so that again the ratio is obscure. Also the proliferation of precedents makes it difficult for lawyers to discover what the law is.

(7) The doctrine of precedent focusses attention on minute differences of fact between cases at the expense of consideration of principle and policy.

4. Flexibility and stability in the common law system

It is not the system but the judges that create the balance between flexibility and stability. Whether it is a good balance is for judgement in each country where the common law system operates. (More discussion of the problems posed by this question is presented in the next chapter.) But the system itself does permit both flexibility and stability. Inevitably with a system of precedent there is a strong tendency to follow the precedents whether they are binding or not and whether or not the precedent seems a wise one. A doctrine of precedent that progressed on the basis that precedents would only be followed when the court agreed with the decision reached in the earlier case, would be a weak doctrine. Equally it would dissipate much of the benefit of stability to which the system of precedent aspires. On the other hand, there is no doubt that the doctrine does sometimes lead to the perpetuation, sometimes for long periods, of bad decisions. Not infrequently they are even widely recognized to be bad decisions, and yet the courts somehow lack the energy to change them.

However the doctrine of precedent has many gaps to permit judges wishing to avail themselves of the opportunity to refuse to be crabbed by it:

(a) The House of Lords is not bound by its own decisions, nor is the High Court, and the Court of Appeal (Criminal Division) is only lightly bound.

(b) There appears to be a long list of exceptions to the rule that the Court of Appeal is bound by its own decisions (see p. 118 above).

(c) The Judicial Committee of the Privy Council is not bound by its own decisions and the English courts sometimes prefer to follow its decisions in preference to inconsistent decisions from within the system by which they are technically bound (see p. 127 above).

(d) An unwelcome precedent can in the last resort be distinguished and thus be avoided.

(e) The appeal system allows *any* principle of common law to be challenged and thus changed by a court high enough in the hierarchy.

Obviously, individual judges vary in their instincts – some are keener on stability, others prefer to emphasize the objective of keeping the law abreast of changing times. But each type of judge usually can find the means to achieve his purpose within the common law system. (See, further, Chapters 6 and 8 below.)

For further reading on precedent, see especially: R. Cross, *Precedent in English Law* (3rd edn., 1977); C.K. Allen, *Law in the Making* (7th edn., 1964); Benjamin Cardozo, *The Nature of the Judicial Process* (1925); Karl Llewellyn, *The Bramble Bush* (1930); Jerome Frank, *Law and the Modern Mind* (1930).

Appendix. The creation and elaboration of a new rule of law: the action for negligent misstatement

Until recently it was a well-established common law rule that no action lay in tort for a negligent misstatement causing pecuniary loss. Someone who suffered financial loss through an inaccurate or false statement might be able to recover damages for deceit or injurious falsehood, but the law required that he prove dishonesty and not merely carelessness.

Candler v. Crane, Christmas & Co.

The modern statement of the rule was in *Candler* v. *Crane, Christmas and Co.* [1951] 2 K.B. 164, in which a claim was based on negligent preparation of accounts by accountants as a result of which the plaintiff suffered loss. The majority of the Court of Appeal (Cohen and Asquith L.JJ.) held that a false statement carelessly but not fraudulently made by one person to another, though acted upon by that other to his detriment, was not actionable in the absence of any fiduciary or contractual relationship. This principle, the Court of Appeal said, had been established in *Derry* v. *Peek* (1889) 14 App. Cas. 337 and *Le Lievre* v. *Gould* [1893] 1 Q.B. 491 and it had not been qualified by the decision of the House of Lords in *Donoughue* v. *Stevenson* [1932] A.C. 562.

(In *Derry* v. *Peek* the House of Lords had held that no action lay in respect of a negligent misstatement made in good faith in a company prospectus which had resulted in the plaintiff buying the company's shares. Nothing short of fraud would suffice to give rise to such an action. In *Le Lievre* v. *Gould* mortgagees tried to sue on certificates prepared by a surveyor for the building owner. They had advanced money on the strength of the certificates and had sustained loss. The Court of Appeal ruled that all that the defendant had done was to give untrue certificates negligently and that this would not give rise to an action at law.)

In *Candler* Lord Justice Asquith asked whether *Le Lievre* v. *Gould* had been qualified or overruled either expressly or by necessary implication. He found that it had been qualified by *Nocton* v. *Ashburton* [1914] A.C. 932, which held that an action for negligent misstatement could lie where there was a fiduciary relationship between the plaintiff and defendant. (In that case the relationship was that of solicitor and client.) But that was all. It had not been overruled expressly. Nor had *Donoughue* v. *Stevenson* overruled it impliedly. In that case the House of Lords had held that an action lay against a manufacturer where the plaintiff had suffered shock and gastro-enteritis after a decomposed snail floated out of a ginger-beer bottle bought by her friend and from which she had drunk. Lord Atkin, who gave the leading judgment in *Donoughue* v. *Stevenson*, had referred to *Le Lievre* v. *Gould* without suggesting that it had been wrongly decided, or that his formulation of the law as to the liability for the consequences of negligence was inconsistent with it. Lord Atkin had formulated the principle of liability in classic words – 'You must take reasonable care to avoid acts or omissions which you can reasonably foresee would be likely to injure your neighbour. Who, then, in law is my neighbour? The answer seems to be – persons who are so closely and directly affected by my act that I ought reasonably to have them in contemplation as being so affected when I am directing my mind to the acts or omissions which are called in question.' This passage if read literally appeared to cover not only acts causing physical injury but statements causing pecuniary loss, but, Asquith L.J. said, if Lord Atkin had intended to cover such situations he would surely have said so. ('It seems to me incredible that if he thought his formula was inconsistent with *Gould's* case he would not have said so', at 189–90.) The inference was that Lord Atkin accepted the distinction between liability in tort for negligent misstatements and other forms of negligence.

Lord Justice Cohen agreed. *Le Lievre* v. *Gould* was binding on the Court of Appeal unless it had been impliedly overruled by *Donoughue* v. *Stevenson*. Lord Atkin in *Donoughue* v. *Stevenson* had actually cited with approval passages from the judgments of the majority in *Le Lievre*. 'I am unable to believe that if he had thought the ratio decidendi in that case was wrong he would have cited those passages without making it clear that he was not approving the decision' (at 200). Although Lord Atkin's words were in such general terms that they might cover misstatement, this was not intended.

Lord Justice Denning dissented. He posed the issue thus (at 176):

Now I come to the great question in the case: did the accountants owe a duty of care to the plaintiff? If the matter were free from authority, I should have said that they clearly did owe a duty of care to him. They were professional accountants who prepared and put before him these accounts, knowing that he was going to be guided by them in making an investment in the company. On the faith of those accounts he did make the investment, whereas if the accounts had been carefully prepared, he would not have made the investment at all. The result is that he has lost his money. In the circumstances, had he not every right to rely on the accounts being prepared with proper care; and is he not entitled to redress from the accountants on whom he relied? I say that he is.

He said that at the time of *Le Lievre* v. *Gould* current thought had been infected by two cardinal errors. One was that someone not a party to a contract could not sue on it, or on anything arising out of it. This had been exploded by *Donoughue* v. *Stevenson*. The second error was that *Derry* v. *Peek* meant that no action could lie for negligent misstatement. That had been exploded by *Nocton* v. *Ashburton*, which held that an action for negligent misstatement could lie where the circumstances disclosed a duty to be careful – in that case because of a fiduciary relationship. In his view the decisions of the House of Lords in *Donoughue* v. *Stevenson* and *Nocton* v. *Ashburton* entitled the Court of Appeal to re-examine the law regarding negligent misstatements.

Counsel for the accountants in *Candler* accepted that if a negligent misstatement gave rise to physical injury an action could lie, but he argued that if the injury was pecuniary this was not so. Lord Justice Denning did not accept the distinction. Once a duty to take care existed, liability could not depend on the nature of the damage.

The duty, he thought, affected persons such as accountants, surveyors, valuers and analysts 'whose profession and occupation it is to examine books, accounts and other things, and to make reports on which other people – other than their clients – rely in the ordinary course of business' (at 179). They owed a duty of care to use reasonable care in the preparation of accounts and the making of reports. They owed the duty to third persons to whom they showed the accounts or reports, or to whom they knew their client was going to show them. They would not, however, be liable for loss suffered by someone they could not foresee would be shown the report.

He did not wish to call in question *Le Lievre* v. *Gould*. In fact it illustrated the principle. The mortgagees there could not recover because the owner's surveyor owed no duty of care toward them. They should have employed their own surveyor. The surveyor for the owner could not have expected that the mortgagees would rely on his certificates. The relationship was too remote to raise a duty of care. But in *Candler* the accountants could foresee that the accounts would be used by the plaintiff in deciding whether to invest in the company. The duty did not however extend to further investments made at a later stage. The law would 'fail to serve the best interests of the community if it should hold that accountants and auditors owed a duty to none but their client' (at 184). In his opinion 'accountants owe a duty of care not only to their clients, but also to all those whom they know will rely on their accounts in the transaction for which those accounts are prepared' (at 185).

Hedley Byrne Co. Ltd v. Heller Bros.

In 1963 in *Hedley Byrne and Co. Ltd* v. *Heller and Partners Ltd* [1964] A.C. 465 the House of Lords held unanimously that there was no difference in principle between physical loss and financial loss, and that a duty to take care in making statements existed wherever there was a special relationship providing there had not been a disclaimer of responsibility. The appellants, an advertising agency, wanted to discover the credit-worthiness of a company that had instructed them to arrange substantial advertising contracts. They asked their bank to make inquiries. The bank made inquiries from Hellers, merchant bankers who were financing the company as well as being their bankers. The bank gave a satisfactory reference 'without responsibility'. The advertising agency relied on the reference and lost money as a result.

When the case reached the Court of Appeal it unanimously held itself bound by the decision in *Candler* v. *Crane, Christmas*. There was no fiduciary relationship nor any other relevant special relationship to take the case out of the general rule ([1962] 1 Q.B. 396). Lord Justice Pearson who gave the leading judgment said that even if the matter were free from authority he would not necessarily be inclined to hold a banker liable for a reference. ('Apart from authority I am not satisfied that it would be reasonable to impose upon a banker the obligation suggested, if that obligation really adds anything to the duty of giving an honest answer' (at 414). But in any event the Court of Appeal was 'clearly bound' by previous decisions of its own (at 415).

After hearing eight days of legal argument, the House of Lords agreed with the Court of Appeal that the plaintiff lost. But its reasons were wholly different. It based its decision on the fact that the bankers had given their reference 'without responsibility'. This was a valid disclaimer of liability. But all five Law Lords gave judgment to the effect that an action for negligent misstatement causing pecuniary loss could lie, and held that *Le Lievre* v. *Gould* and *Candler* v. *Crane, Christmas* were wrongly decided.

The duty to exercise care, according to the House of Lords, extended to all relationships where the inquirer was trusting the author of the statement to exercise a reasonable degree of care and when the other person knew or ought to have known that the inquirer was relying on him. (See [1964] A.C. 465 at 486, 502, 514, 529, 539 for the various ways in which the five law lords stated the principle.) Lord Justice Denning's dissenting judgment in *Candler* was specifically approved by Lords Hodson, Devlin and Pearce (at 509, 530, 538).

Technically it might be said that the speeches of the law lords were all obiter since the decision in the case was that no liability existed because of the disclaimer. But the judgments occupy more than forty pages in the law reports, and the bulk of this space was devoted to the statement by their lordships as to why the law as previously understood was wrong and to the formulation of the new principle. The reality was that *Hedley Byrne* changed the law. Cairns J. dealt with the point in a case that arose in 1967 – 'An academic lawyer might be prepared to contend that the opinions expressed by their lordships about liability for negligent misstatement were obiter, and that *Candler* v. *Crane, Christmas* is still a binding decision. In my judgment that would be an unrealistic view to take. When five members of the House of Lords have all said, after close examination of the authorities, that a certain type of tort exists, I think that a judge of first instance should proceed on the basis that it does exist without pausing to embark on an investigation of whether what was said was necessary to the ultimate decision' (*W.B. Anderson and Sons Ltd* v. *Rhodes Ltd* [1967] 2 All E.R. 850 at 857).

(At first sight this appears to be at variance with the view adopted by the House of Lords in *Miliangos* (p. 111 above) that the trial judge should follow the immediately superior court (the Court of Appeal) rather than the House of Lords where the two conflict. But it would appear that the *Miliangos* ruling applies where the Court of Appeal's decision is after that of the House of Lords, whereas Cairns J.'s view is correct when the decision of the House of Lords comes later.)

But although it was clear that *Hedley Byrne* had changed the law, it was less certain what was the extent of the new rule. From 1963 to 1979 there were no less than nine important decisions in the English reports in which *Hedley Byrne* was the subject of judicial examination.

The cases raised a variety of different problems including the following:

(1) *Must the defendant be in the business of making the kind of statements that led to the claim?*

In his dissenting judgment in *Candler*, Lord Justice Denning appeared to restrict liability to 'persons such as accountants, surveyors, valuers and analysts, whose profession and occupation it is to examine books, accounts and other things, and to make reports' ([1959] 2 K.B. 179, 180). As has been seen, Lord Justice Denning's judgment was specifically approved by Lords Hodson, Devlin and Pearce. In 1970 the Privy Council in an appeal from Australia considered whether advice could become the subject of legal action where it was given by someone who did not carry on the profession of giving that sort of advice (*Mutual Life & Citizens' Assurance Co. Ltd* v. *Evatt* [1971] A.C. 793). The plaintiff sued in respect of advice as to the financial stability of a company. The plaintiff was a policy-holder in the defendant insurance company. The advice was as to the safety of investments in another company in the same group as that of the defendant. The advice was that the company was sound, and in reliance on that advice the plaintiff invested money. In the event the advice proved to be wrong. It was not alleged by the plaintiff that the defendant company carried on the business of giving advice on investments or that it possessed any qualification, skill or competence to do so beyond that of the ordinary reasonable man.

The Privy Council, in the persons of Lords Hodson, Guest and Diplock, held that the defendants were not liable for their mistaken advice. Lord Diplock, delivering the judgment of the Board, said that according to Lord Reid in *Hedley Byrne* liability imposed on the author of the piece of advice the duty to take 'such care as the circumstances require'. This presupposed an ascertainable standard of skill, competence and diligence with which the adviser was acquainted or had represented that he possessed. 'Unless he carries on the business or profession of giving advice of that kind he cannot reasonably be expected to know whether any, and if so, what degree of skill, competence or diligence is called for, and a fortiori, in their Lordships' view he cannot be reasonably held to have accepted the responsibility of conforming to a standard of skill, competence and diligence of which he is unaware, simply because he answers the enquiry with knowledge that the advisee intends to rely on his answer' (at 807). In this particular case the company had been in a position to get reliable advice if it had chosen to do so, but there was no evidence that it had been asked to do so or that the inquiry had been addressed to an officer of the company who had the necessary skill or competence. In the absence of any allegation in the pleadings that the defendant company carried on the business of giving advice, or alternatively that they had let it be known that they claimed some skill or competence to provide this kind of advice, the defendant's duty was simply to give an honest answer to the question put by the plaintiff.

Two of their lordships, Lords Reid and Morris of Borth-y-Gest, dissented. (Both had been members of the House of Lords in *Hedley Byrne.*) They accepted that no liability could arise for advice given casually – say in a social context. But it might be going too far to suggest that only advice given in a business context could create liability. Here it was enough however to ask whether the advice was given on a business occasion. There was no doubt that this was the case. The service was a gratuitous one but that was quite normal in business affairs. If an adviser was invited in a business context to advise on a certain matter and he chose to accept the invitation and did so without qualification, was he to be allowed to turn round later and say that he was under no duty of care because in fact he had no sufficient skill or competence to give the advice? If liability were to be limited to experts, how expert did they have to be? 'Even a man with a professional qualification is seldom an expert on all matters dealt with by members of his profession. Must the adviser be an expert or specialist in the matter on which his advice is sought?' (at 163). In the judgment of Lords Reid and Morris it was enough that the plaintiff had consulted a businessman in the course of his business and made it plain that he was seeking considered advice and intended to act on it in a particular way. In such circumstances 'any reasonable businessman would realise that, if he chooses to give advice without any warning or qualification he is putting himself under a moral obligation to take some care' (at 163). This was well within the principle established by *Hedley Byrne.*

When the matter came up for further consideration, it was the view of the two dissenting judges that seemed to find support. In *Esso Petroleum Co. Ltd* v. *Mardon* the plaintiff-respondent sued on account of an inaccurate estimate he had been given of the likely sale of gallons of petrol at the filling station he was renting from the defendants-appellants. He had thought that 100,000 to 150,000 gallons per year was probable but he had been persuaded by an expert on the defendant's staff that 200,000 was more likely. In fact in the third year he was only selling 86,000 gallons. The company claimed for overdue rent and he counterclaimed for damages for negligence. It was contended for Esso that they had not been in the business of giving that kind of advice and that the majority view in *Mutual Life* should be followed. The trial judge Lawson J. said, however, that he preferred the view of Lords Reid and Morris ([1975] 1 All E.R. 203, 219), but in any event that even if the test proposed by the majority were applied the plaintiff would still win, since Esso had a direct financial interest in the advice they gave. The Court of Appeal unanimously dismissed Esso's appeal. Lord Justice Ormrod agreed with Lawson J. that he preferred the view of the minority in *Evatt* to that of the majority on this point. ('If the majority view were to be accepted the effect of *Hedley Byrne* would be so radically curtailed as to be virtually eliminated' ([1976] 2 All E.R. 5 at 22). But the decision of the majority is not binding on English courts since it was given was by the Judicial Committee of the Privy Council and it would be surprising if it prevailed. It seems much more probable that the English courts will prefer the broader approach of Lord Reid, Lord Morris, Lawson J. and Lord Justice Ormrod. (See however Lord Denning M.R. in *McInery* v. *Lloyds Bank* [1974] 1 Lloyds L.R. 246, 253–4 in which the Master of the Rolls appears to acquiesce in the majority's view in the *Evatt* case.)

(2) *How formal does a statement have to be to make it actionable if wrong?* There is general agreement that a professional man's statement given casually on a purely social occasion or, say, travelling to work would not make him liable for damages even if the person to whom it was made relied on it to his detriment. But what degree of formality is necessary to make the statement actionable? In his dissenting judgment in *Candler* Lord Justice Denning said that professional persons were 'not liable, of course, for casual remarks made in the course of conversation, nor for other statements made outside their work or not made in their capacity as [accountants]' ([1951] K.B. at 179, 180). This passage was approved in *Hedley Byrne* by Lord Devlin and Lord Pearce ([1964] A.C. 530 at 538, 539), and the other judges did not dissent from it.

In *W.B. Anderson and Sons Ltd* v. *Rhodes* (*Liverpool*) *Ltd* [1967] 2 All E.R. 850, action was brought on an oral statement to the plaintiffs by the defendant's employee of another company that 'they are all right'. The court found that this meant that the company was credit-worthy. The plaintiffs relied on this statement to their financial detriment and sued for damages. Cairns J. held the defendants were liable. The advice was asked in a business connection; it was not casual or perfunctory and there had been direct dealing between the parties. It was reasonable for the plaintiffs to rely on the skill and judgment of the defendant. The representation concerned a business transaction whose nature made clear the gravity of the inquiry and the importance and influence attached to the answer. The fact that the reply was informal, oral and made without research did not mean that it could not be sued on.

(3) *Does it make any difference that there is a contract between the parties?* In the *Esso* case it was argued for the defendants that the *Hedley Byrne* principle did not apply to statements made in pre-contract negotiations where these resulted in a contract. The rights and duties of the parties were then regulated by the contract and not by the law of tort (*Esso Petroleum* v. *Mardon* [1976] 2 All E.R. 5). The argument relied especially on the decision of Plowman J. in *Clark* v. *Kirby Smith* [1964] Ch. 506 that the liability of a solicitor for negligence was a liability in contract and not in tort, and that *Hedley Byrne* had not altered this rule which was based on cases going back 150 years. The same proposition was the basis of the decision by Diplock L.J. in *Bagot* v. *Stevens Scanlan and Co.* [1964] 3 W.L.R. 1162. Lord Justice Diplock, sitting as a High Court judge, held that the duty of an architect to exercise reasonable care and skill arose out of contract alone, and in case of professional relationships such a duty did not arise independently of the contract. The result was that the plaintiff's claim was statute barred whereas he could have brought his action if he had been able to sue in tort. Like Plowman J., he thought that *Hedley Byrne* had not altered the position.

But all three judges in the Court of Appeal in the *Esso* case rejected this view. Lord Denning ([1976] 2 All E.R. at 15) said that there were cases of high authority not cited to the judges in *Clark* v. *Kirby Smith* and *Bagot* v. *Stevens Scanlan and Co.*, which showed that the liability of professional persons to use reasonable care arose apart from contract. He cited an 1842 decision of the Court of Exchequer Chamber in which Chief Justice Tindal had said: '... there is a large class of cases in which the foundation of the action springs out of privity of contract between the parties, but in which, nevertheless, the remedy for the breach, or non-performance, is indifferently either assumpsit or case upon tort ... Such are actions against attorneys, surgeons and other professional men, for want of competent skill or proper care' (*Boorman* v. *Brown*, (1842) 3 Q.B. 511 at 525, 526). In affirming that decision in the House of Lords, Lord Campbell had said '... wherever there is a contract, and something to be done in the course of the employment which is the subject of that contract, if there is a breach of a duty in the course of that employment, the plaintiff may either recover in tort or in contract' ((1844) 11 Cl. Fin. 1 at 44). Moreover, Lord Haldane in *Nocton* v. *Ashburton* had said '... the solicitor contracts with his client to be skilful and careful. For failure to perform his obligation he may be made liable in contract or even in tort for negligence in breach of a duty imposed on him' ([1914] A.C. 932 at 956). Lord Denning thought that the existence of a contract made no difference to the liability of the professional person. Lord Justice Ormrod and Lord Justice Shaw agreed. Shaw L.J. said that there was no valid argument that a subsequent contract vitiated a cause of action in negligence which had previously arisen in the course of negotiations. There seems little doubt that this is now the law. Normally, where there is an action available both in contract and in tort it will make no difference which forms the basis of the proceedings. But if any difference exists – for instance, because of a different standard of damages or a different starting point for time running under the Statute of Limitations – the effect of the *Esso* ruling is to give the plaintiff the choice of the more favourable cause of action.

(4) *Must the plaintiff be able to show that the defendants voluntarily assumed responsibility?*

At least two of the judges in *Hedley Byrne* had appeared to make a voluntary assumption of responsibility by the defendant one of the essential ingredients of liability. Thus Lord Reid had said that if a reasonable man knowing that he was being trusted, or that his skill and judgment were being relied on, answered without making any disclaimer of liability he must be held to have accepted some responsibility for his answer being given carefully ([1964] A.C. at 487). Lord Devlin had spoken of a class of special relationships – 'that is where there is an assumption of responsibility in circumstances in which, but for the absence of consideration, there would be a contract'. The liability they were talking of, he said, was where there was 'a responsbility that is voluntarily accepted or undertaken either generally where a general relationship, such as that of solicitor and client or banker and customer is created, or specifically in relation to a particular transaction' ([1964] A.C. at 529).

In *Ministry of Housing* v. *Sharp* [1970] 1 All E.R. 1009 the point was taken that *Hedley Byrne* did not create liability where there was no such voluntary assumption of responsibility. An employee of a local council negligently failed to record a compensation notice and issued a clear land charges certificate. The ministry sued for damages against the council. It was argued that since the council did not voluntarily make the search or prepare the certificate for their clerk's signature, they did not voluntarily assume responsibility for the accuracy of the certificate and accordingly owed no duty to the minister. The Court of Appeal said it was true that the judgments in *Hedley Byrne* all referred in one way or another to voluntary assumption of responsibility. But that was because in *Hedley Byrne* the issue was whether the giving of the banker's reference had amounted to an assumption of responsibility. Here the council were under a duty to make the search and to issue the certificate. But all three judges had no difficulty in saying that this made no difference. (See Lord Denning M.R., at 1018–19; Salmon L.J., at 1027–8; Cross L.J., at 1038.)

(5) *Are there categories of persons exempt from the ambit of the Hedley Byrne principle?*

There was nothing in the speeches in *Hedley Byrne* to indicate that there might be any groups exempt from the general principle of liability. As has been seen, however, soon after the House of Lords' decision judges at first instance said that it did not create liability for solicitors (*Clark* v. *Kirby-Smith* [1964] Ch. 506) or architects (*Bagot* v. *Stevens Scanlan and Co.* [1964] 3 W.L.R. 1162). These two decisions were subsequently disapproved by the Court of Appeal in *Esso* v. *Mardon* [1976] 2 All E.R. 5. But at least two exceptions to the principle of *Hedley Byrne* do appear to have been accepted by the courts. One is the case of advocates in the course of litigation. The liability of barristers for negligence in advocacy was tested in *Rondel* v. *Worsley*. Both the trial judge Lawton J. and the Court of Appeal held that a barrister was wholly immune from such suit and that *Hedley Byrne* had made no difference. Lawton J. ([1966] 2 W.L.R. 300) ruled that immunity covered any advocate whether a barrister or solicitor on grounds of public policy. The Court of Appeal ([1967] 1 Q.B. 443) put the matter more narrowly as being an immunity for barristers based on both public policy and long usage. The House of Lords ([1969] 1 A.C. 191) returned to Lawton J.'s formula. Both solicitors and barristers had immunity from actions for negligence arising out of work done in the course of litigation or its preparation. Again the reason was public policy. Subsequently, the House of Lords refused to extend the immunity to advice given by a barrister as to what parties to sue – the advice was not immune unless it was 'intimately connected' with the conduct of the case in court and such advice was well outside the scope of the immunity (*Saif Ali* v. *Sydney Mitchell & Co.* [1978] 3 W.L.R. 849). The immunity, it seems therefore, is to be construed narrowly. (See generally Zander, *Modern Law Review*, 1979, p. 319.)

The second recognized exempt category appears to be someone who has acted in a quasi-judicial capacity as between two other parties in determining some question which requires him to hold the scales evenly between the two parties. This emerges from *Arenson* v. *Arenson* [1973] 2 All E.R. 235. A company's auditors were asked as experts rather than arbitrators to value shares in a private company. They knew that the valuation was needed for the purpose of deciding what price the uncle would pay for his nephew's shares in the company. The valuation was voluntary, i.e. without any fee, and the auditors were not under any contractual duty to prepare it. It was a gross undervalue and the nephew brought an action against the auditors for damages for negligence. Lord Denning dissenting, thought that the auditors were liable under the principle of *Hedley Byrne*. But his two brethren, Buckley L.J. and Sir Seymour Karminski, disagreed. The expert was acting in a quasi-judicial or arbitral capacity and public policy required that he be given an immunity for negligence, for without it the third party might be inhibited from performing his arbitral function in the free exercise of his judgment. The House of Lords by three to two allowed an appeal but the majority (Lords Simon of Glaisdale, Wheatley and Salmon) did not deny that the arbitrator could be immune. The appeal was allowed, since the House of Lords held that the statement of claim did disclose a cause of action the validity of which should be tested by a trial. A valuer could establish immunity by showing that there was an actual formulated dispute between two parties which he had been called in to resolve by acting in a judicial manner and that the parties had agreed to accept his decision. (See *Arenson* v. *Casson Beckman Rutley & Co*, [1975] 3 All E.R. 901). The two Law Lords in the minority (Lord Kilbrandon and Lord

Fraser of Tullybelton) did not agree that an arbitrator appointed to settle a dispute should have any immunity.

Conclusion

The scope and extent of the principle of the *Hedley Byrne* case are still being worked out by the courts. The actual words of the judgments of the five Law Lords are the beginning of this process but already within little over a decade they have been qualified, expanded and contracted in a variety of directions. As Lord Diplock said in the Privy Council:

As with any other important case in the development of the common law, *Hedley Byrne* should not be regarded as intended to lay down the metes and bounds of the new field of negligence of which the gate is now opened. Those will fall to be ascertained step by step as the facts of particular cases which come before the courts make it necessary to determine them' [*Mutual Life Assurance Co. Ltd* v. *Evatt* [1971] A.C. 793, 809].

6

The nature of the judicial role in law-making

A great deal has been written about the judicial role and no attempt can be made here to cover all aspects of this topic. The issues addressed are only some of those that affect the law-making process but they are perhaps some of the most important. The first is what role is played by the judge himself in the process.

1. The personal element in judicial law-making

The first extract is from the writings of one of Britain's most distinguished post-war judges.

Lord Radcliffe, *Not in Feather Beds* (1968), pp. 212–16

More and more I am impressed by the inescapable personal element in the judicial decision. We are fond of saying, approvingly, that a judge should be objective; but is it perhaps the wrong metaphor, an idea borrowed, like so much else that obscures our thinking on general topics, from an analogy between the physical sciences and things incommensurable with them? Say indeed that a judge must be fair, or that he must be impartial: that is essential. He must strip himself of all prejudices, certainly; except, I ought to add, those prejudices which on consideration he is prepared to stand by as his sincere convictions. You see how quickly, just because he is not a machine, one begins to tie oneself in words and qualifications of words. He has no right to be biased; but then no human mind is constructed with perfect balance. He must give an honest hearing to all points of view and to arguments that do not even introduce themselves to him as plausible: but it is unreal to think of a judge of experience as if he were a mere hearing aid. It was said of the late Lord Bryce that to him all facts were born free and equal. That may be all right for facts, before the work of evaluation begins, but a judge is a mature man, of long and professional experience, with prepared approaches and formed attitudes of mind, and it would be, I think, almost hypocritical to speak of him as if each case presented itself to his eye in the light of the first dawn of creation. To me fairness of mind cannot involve such innocence as that.

The truth is, I believe, that the law must not be mistaken for a scientific pursuit. Much contemporary analysis and criticism seem to be based on this false analogy. Let me put the contrasting points of view. At the back of your mind you may think of the law on some particular question as being a given fact, an absolute, which it is the judge's duty to discover. It is all there already, hidden in the ground and needing only excavation, or shrouded in a veil which requires no more than to be drawn apart. To excavate or to unveil, neatly and accurately, calls for the exercise of no minor talents, and to do the work well there should be a solid apparatus of equipment, a detailed knowledge of the formulae of law (statutes, authorities and commentaries) and an ability to use the reasoning power with strict regard to its own inherent rules. The legal answer, you may say, is written out in close print or even in archaic language on some distant tablet. To read it off, you should choose for your judge the man with unusual length of sight or one who has had the skill to construct a powerful telescope or, for that matter, one who has made a study of the ancient tongues. Then he will read it off and announce to you what is there.

I would not deny that, in a legal system such as that which we operate in this country, a great deal of a judge's work involves no more than the practice of this science or skill of 'reading off'. But the essence of that curious activity, the judicial decision, does not consist in that. The law has to be interpreted before it can be applied, and interpretation is a creative activity. The law was not there until that particular decision was given. Once it has been given, the whole enormous component, which is the body of the law, has changed its composition by the addition of a new element, significant or insignificant, which in some degree modifies the whole.

There are two things that have impressed themselves on me when I have thought in this way. One is that, if the judge is not a machine, however ingeniously constructed, that is to work a mechanical system, it does very much matter what personal quality he brings to his work, because it is not going to be only his command of the reasoning process or his knowledge and learning that will determine his interpretation, but, in the end, his experience of life and the structure of thought and belief that he has built upon it. Most questions are debatable, just as most arguments can be made plausible: but what will incline him to one side or the other is what I have called his whole structure of thought. I hope that you do not think that I am putting forward the judge as a sort of prophet or seer, making his pronouncements by some uncriticisable rite of divination. Perhaps a few of the great ones have been something of that order, and for better or worse, sometimes for the worse, we take them as such. I do not see him that way at all, but I do think that it is of some importance in the society of today that the judge's function should not be confused with that of a reading clerk and that it should be realized that judicial decisions, no matter who gives them, must always be related to certain basic beliefs about the nature and purpose of a human being which are held by another human being. In that sense he may not be 'objective'; but he can be honest and fair. Of the two it is much the more valuable achievement.

It has been a pity, I think, that so much of judicial opinion in this country has been conveyed by the method of logical deduction. It was natural enough that this should be the preferred route, since the deductive method based on the syllogism was the favoured weapon of Western European thinkers in the Middle Ages, and the judges probably inherited its use from them. But, as we know, syllogistic reasoning is only conclusive if you first import your chosen meaning into the words of the premise you start with. It is only a demonstration of a truth if you have already been converted to the truth. In our history of judgment-making too many decisions have begun by insisting that particular words have one particular meaning and then deducing that, if they have, certain consequences must necessarily follow. That is to put the icing on the cake, not to bake it. I am afraid that what I am saying is that the making of law is not a subject which is capable of anything like scientific demonstration, and there are some disadvantages in dressing it up to look as if it were. It is the unexpressed assumptions, which are nevertheless very much present, that are often the real hinges of decision. After all, what a judgment seeks to do is to persuade or convince, and there are sometimes cogent considerations that achieve this without having any resort to deductive reasoning. Arrangement, by which an illuminating spark is generated from the skilful combination of certain facts and considerations, is one of them. Anyone who makes a careful study of the judgments of a great master of exposition, such as was Lord Macnaghten, for instance, will see how much conviction he can bring from nothing more than his skill of arrangement.

In this contest there was never a more sterile controversy than that upon the question whether a judge makes law. Of course he does. How can he help it? The legislature and the judicial process respectively are two complementary sources of law-making, and in a well ordered state each has to understand its respective functions and limitations. Judicial law is always a reinterpretation of principles in the light of new combinations of facts, of which very relevant ones, unprovable by evidence, are the current beliefs of the society in which those facts occur. True, judges do not reverse principles, once well established, but they do modify them, extend them, restrict them or even deny their applicability to the combination in hand. But does Parliament do anything very different in its law making, except in some revolutionary context to which no ordinary rules can be referred? I doubt it. It is not that the well known phrase, 'That is not for us, it is for the legislature' does not carry plenty of significant meaning. What it means is, I think, that, while it is an illusion to suppose that the legislature is attending or can possibly attend all the time to all aspects of the law, there are certain areas of public interest which at any one time can be seen to be a matter of its current concern. It has recently legislated on that subject according to certain principles (if they can be detected) or it regularly legislates on the whole field covered by that subject (as, for instance, the law of taxation). In those areas I think that the judge needs to be particularly circumspect in the use of his power to declare the law, not because the principles adopted by Parliament are more satisfactory or more enlightened than those which would commend themselves to his mind, but because it is unacceptable constitutionally that there should be two independent sources of law-making at work at the same time.

The next extracts are from the pen of one of America's greatest judges:

Benjamin N. Cardozo, *The Nature of the Judicial Process* (1921) pp. 12–13, 111–15, 129, 141, 167–8.

There is in each of us a stream of tendency, whether you choose to call it philosophy or not, which gives coherence and direction to thought and action. Judges cannot escape that current any more than other mortals. All their lives, forces which they do not recognize and cannot name, have been tugging at them—inherited instincts, traditional beliefs, acquired convictions; and the resultant is an outlook on life, a conception of social needs, a sense in James's phrase of "the total push and pressure of the cosmos," which, when reasons are nicely balanced, must determine where choice shall fall. In this mental background every problem finds its setting. We may try to see things as objectively as we please. None the less, we can never see them with any eyes except our own. To that test they are all brought—a form of pleading or an act of parliament, the wrongs of paupers or the rights of princes, a village ordinance or a nation's charter....

I have spoken of the forces of which judges avowedly avail to shape the form and content of their judgments. Even these forces are seldom fully in consciousness. They lie so near the surface, however, that their existence and influence are not likely to be disclaimed. But the subject is not exhausted with the recognition of their power. Deep below consciousness are other forces, the likes and the dislikes, the predilections and the prejudices, the complex of instincts and emotions and habits and convictions, which make the man, whether he be litigant or judge. ... There has been a certain lack of candor in much of the discussion of the theme, or rather perhaps in the refusal to discuss it, as if judges must lose respect and confidence by the reminder that they are subject to human limitations. I do not doubt the grandeur of the conception which lifts them into the realm of pure reason, above and beyond the sweep of perturbing and deflecting forces. None the less, if there is anything of reality in my analysis of the judicial process, they do not stand aloof on these chill and distant heights; and we shall not help the cause of truth by acting and speaking as if they do. The great tides and currents which engulf the rest of men do not turn aside in their course and pass the judges by....

My analysis of the judicial process comes then to this, and little more: logic, and history, and custom, and utility, and the accepted standards of right conduct, are the forces which singly or in combination shape the progress of the law. Which of these forces shall dominate in any case must depend largely upon the comparative importance or value of the social interests that will be thereby promoted or impaired. One of the most fundamental social interests is that law shall be uniform and impartial. There must be nothing in its action that savors of prejudice or favor or even arbitrary whim or fitfulness. Therefore in the main there shall be adherence to precedent. There shall be symmetrical development, consistently with history or custom when history or custom has been the motive force, or the chief one, in giving shape to existing rules, and with logic or philosophy when the motive power has been theirs. But symmetrical development may be bought at too high a price. Uniformity ceases to be a good when it becomes uniformity of oppression. The social interest served by symmetry or certainty must then be balanced against the social interest served by equity and fairness or other elements of social welfare. These may enjoin upon the judge the duty of drawing the line at another angle, of staking the path along new courses, of marking a new point of departure from which others who come after him will set out upon their journey. If you ask how he is to know when one interest outweighs another, I can only answer that he must get his knowledge just as the legislator gets it, from experience and study and reflection; in brief, from life itself. Here, indeed, is the point of contact between the legislator's work and his. The choice of methods, the appraisement of values, must in the end be guided by like considerations for the one as for the other. Each indeed is legislating within the limits of his competence. No doubt the limits for the judge are narrower. He legislates only between gaps. He fills the open spaces in the law. How far he may go without travelling beyond the walls of the interstices cannot be staked out for him upon a chart. He must learn if for himself as he gains the sense of fitness and proportion that comes with years of habitude in the practice of an art. Even within the gaps, restrictions not easy to define, but felt, however impalpable they may be, by every judge and lawyer, hedge and circumscribe his action. They are established by the traditions of the centuries, by the example of other judges, his predecessors and his colleagues, by the collective judgment of the profession, and by the duty of adherence to the pervading spirit of the law. . . . Nonetheless, within the confines of these open spaces and those of precedent and tradition, choice moves with a freedom which stamps its action as creative. The law which is the resulting product is not found, but made. The process, being legislative, demands the legislator's wisdom.

For the view that the personal element in judicial decision-making is crucial, see further, in particular, Jerome Frank, *Law and the Modern Mind.*

The role of discretion available to the judge in deciding cases may vary according to the level of court. This is one of the points made in the extract that follows:

Brian Abel-Smith and Robert Stevens,
In Search of Justice (1968), pp. 167–73

Among the middle classes (and particularly among those members who have had little contact with the courts) the English judges are held in awe not only as the embodiment of 'all that is good and excellent', but also as the epitome of impartiality and objectivity. Politicians are not reticent about making use of this reputation. Embarrassing political situations may be resolved by setting up a tribunal chaired by a judge. . . . By importing a judge to head some Commission or Committee, the most embarrassing political matter can suddenly be taken out of politics. . . .

The non-political position of the judges has been enhanced by their withdrawal (or in some cases expulsion) from some of the more politically contentious areas of decision-making. During this century few new powers have been given to the courts. In exercising the powers which have remained in their hands, the judges have tended to stress that their task is merely to apply pre-existing doctrines of the common law to new fact situations and to apply the 'ordinary meaning' of words to the interpretation of statutes. They have thus assiduously cultivated the notion that the judicial process is a mechanical one which leaves virtually no room for discretion or the introduction of inarticulate premises or value judgements into their decisions.

In so far as the judicial role can be purely declaratory this has clear advantages for the lay public (and we do not for a moment deny that the very definition of law demands an element of predictability which in turn involves an element of the mechanical). In a way unknown in many other countries, the belief in 'the law' as something which has an existence and internal logic of its own enables counsel and judges to advise or hold on certain matters – that the law would or would not allow certain acts – with an assurance which lawyers abroad might well envy. Indeed counsel's opinion in some situations is accorded a quasi-judicial reverence.

Every legal system, of course, involves the existence of a body of principles which are thought of as binding, at least in some situations, but in England it sometimes seems to be assumed, even by leading lawyers, that the 'legal' answer to virtually any problem may be discovered by the appropriate use of legal logic and analogies. Moreover the predictability of most legal issues is thought to be so obvious that there is no need to resort to litigation. The English businessman expects to be given a clear answer about whether something is legal or whether an arrangement is binding or not. While from an academic point of view this may be intellectually unsatisfactory, the belief in such predictability often enables a decisive answer to be given. Thus the very reputation for predictability coupled with the analytic refinements of English legal thinking, if it leaves something to be desired because of its inflexibility and formality, does provide effectively for the settlement of a wide range of disputes outside the court room.

The coherence and predictability of the common law are made much easier to preserve not only because relatively few politically sensitive decisions are now left to the courts, but also because the number of judges at the higher levels is sufficiently small for them to have close contact with one another. . . . The appeal courts sit exclusively in London and the High Court is very much based on London. The extensive use of arbitration by businessmen and the establishment of administrative tribunals for certain purposes have all helped to limit the work and thus the size of the High Court bench. As the Permanent Secretary to the Lord Chancellor put it to the Franks Committee in 1957, the tribunal system has 'positively contributed to the preservation of our judicial system'. The facts that most administrative 'law' operates outside the courts of law, that most criminals are tried and sentenced by laymen, and that permanent civil courts of general jurisdiction for important cases are not available outside London are the price England pays for an élite corps of judges of the higher courts. In turn, the fact that there need be so few of them makes it easier to ensure that all those appointed will uphold the tradition of the judiciary for integrity and independence; and this in turn makes it possible to hand on the traditional beliefs in the certainty of legal doctrines and the predictability of legal reasoning. Predictability can, however, be sought at too high a price. In particular we would challenge the English assumption that certainty of doctrine and formality of approach necessarily produce predictability. If courts really operated like slot machines, it would rightly be asked why it was necessary to staff them with persons of such high intellectual calibre and pay such staff such large salaries, or why appeal courts were necessary. Moreover, the more predictable the law attempts to become the less it can be adjusted to changing circumstances....

The practical tasks of a judge trying either a civil or a criminal case are those of evaluating the credibility of witnesses and applying the relevant legal doctrine or doctrines. In most cases this consists of deciding, for instance, whether the defendant was negligent in his behaviour, or whether the activities of the accused amounted to larceny. In this sense, the judicial process is not a particularly creative one. It is true that the decision about whether some behaviour is negligent or dishonest, in so far as it is performed by the judge rather than the jury, may require some element of value judgement. But with the exception of those few cases where there is a disputed point of law or where some novel point of law has to be interpreted, this aspect of the trial judge's work is essentially a mechanical one – involving considerable skill in evaluating evidence, but not of necessity making the views of the judge of any major importance.

From the point of view of discretion, however, the power of trial judges comes into its own when, after the decision or verdict has been reached, the judge is required to assess damages, pass sentence or exercise any other form of discretion. In all these cases there will be some semblance of rules to guide him. There are principles for assessing damages, there has been growing agreement on sentencing policy, and even the exercise of discretion in favour of a petitioner in a divorce case has certain guidelines. But none of these principles or guidelines comes close to the apparently binding and objective nature of the rule of law as traditionally understood in England. In such areas as these, then, the judge is forced to exercise a genuine discretion and, as with other types of persons, the exercise of such discretion will, to some extent, reflect the social and political outlook of the judge. His legal training will instill a measure of rationality into such operation, but it can, by no means, obviate the personal value-judgment.

As a case proceeds farther up the judicial hierarchy, such social and political views are likely to become steadily more important. In the Court of Appeal the judges are primarily concerned to see that the judge of first instance applied the 'right' doctrine, or applied this doctrine correctly. They are also to some extent concerned with the proper interpretation of fact. But also to a greater extent than at the trial level, courts of appeal are concerned to develop doctrines, by deciding whether some particular principle should embrace the fact situation with which they are faced; or alternatively they are required to decide within which of two competing legal principles some fact situation falls. This creative role of the judges becomes more important still in the final court of appeal – the House of Lords. Here, although the judges work within the framework of legal principles, they are enabled to perform an essentially creative function by extending (or for that matter refusing to extend) some particular legal doctrine, or by interpreting some particular statute or section of a statute in a broad or a narrow way.

If the personal element in judicial decision-making is important, it may matter that most judges in most countries and certainly in England are drawn from a relatively narrow social class. It is hardly surprising that English judges are mainly from the class that sends their sons and daughters to public schools and to Oxbridge, for this is true of the Bar generally. (A study in 1977 by the College of Law showed that 84 per cent of its barrister students were from the professional, managerial, executive or administrative class – and the same was true of no less than 77 per cent of the solicitor students.*) It has often been said that the narrow social-class background of English judges influences them, and in particular explains the alleged fact that the judges have shown themselves to be biased against the trade unions. A study of judicial decisions affecting trade unions does not, however, quite bear out the claim that these decisions do show any clear bias. (Paul O'Higgins and Martin Partington, 'Industrial Conflict: Judicial Attitudes', 32 *Modern Law Review* (1969), p. 53.) The authors analysed every judicial decision arising out of disputes between groups of workers and employers or between groups of organized and unorganized workers. The cases in the study were those referred to in the three leading textbooks concerned with industrial conflict (*Citrine*,† *Grunfeld*‡ and *Wedderburn***). Between 1871 and 1966 there were seventy cases arising out of industrial conflict. Of these, fifty were civil and twenty were criminal. The article showed which side won in these seventy cases.

* Evidence to the Royal Commission on Legal Services of the College of Law, 1977, p. 5.

† N.A. Citrine, *Trade Union Law* (2nd edn, 1960).

‡ Cyril Grunfeld, *Modern Trade Union Law* (1966).

** K.W. Wedderburn, *The Worker and the Law* (1965).

On the basis of the information in the article, it is possible to present the data in tabular form:

	Determined in favour of workers	Determined against workers
Civil courts:		
House of Lords and Privy Council	5	8
Court of Appeal	17	12
High Court	16	29
Divisional Court	4	1
Total	42	50
Criminal courts:		
Court of Criminal Appeal	1	1
Divisional Court	2	11
First instance	3	17
Total	6	29
Grand total	48	79

(Based on 70 cases decided between 1871 and 1966. The numbers exceed 70 because the article traced the fate of appeals and many cases are therefore counted more than once.)

For an analysis of the male prejudices of English and American judges in cases involving sex-equality issues, see Albie Sachs and Joan Hoff Wilson, *Sexism and Judicial Bias* (1978); for the suggestion that judges' attitudes to landlord–tenant issues are influenced by conscious or unconscious pro-landlord attitudes, see J.I. Reynolds, 'Statutory Covenants of Fitness and Repair: Social Legislation and the Judges', 37 *Modern Law Review* (1974) p. 377. But by far the most substantial study of judicial attitudes and their influence on decision-making is Robert Stevens, *Law and Politics: the House of Lords as a Judicial Body, 1800–1976* (1979). The book is fascinating, for instance on the changing judicial attitudes to tax laws – see pp. 170–6, 204–8, 312, 392–6, 411–14, 600–13.

In a provocative book published in 1977 Professor John Griffith of the London School of Economics argued that judges generally (not just English judges) were biassed in their approach to certain issues not so much because of their social background as because of the nature of their function. According to this thesis the judge, by virtue of his office, is mainly concerned to uphold and maintain the status quo and therefore inevitably tends to find himself in conflict with any groups in society whose purpose is to seek change – the more so if they proceed by other than conventional methods:

J.A.G. Griffith, *The Politics of the Judiciary* (1977), pp. 204–15

The function performed by the judiciary in our society is not a peculiarly capitalist function. Some of its manifestations – such as its tenderness towards private property and its dislike of trade unions – may be traced to such a source. But its strong adherence to the maintenance of law and order, its distaste for minority opinions, demonstrations and protests, its indifference to the promotion of better race relations, its support of governmental secrecy, and its concern for the preservation of the moral and social behaviour to which it is accustomed, these attitudes seem to derive from a different ideology.

Moreover if the judicial function in the United Kingdom were wholly capitalist in origin, it would be surprising to find any similarities or even points of comparison with non-capitalist societies. Yet we find the judiciary in non-capitalist societies to be even more a part of their political and economic power groups. The Marxist analysis tells us a great deal about the differences between capitalist and non-capitalist societies but little about the differing roles played by the judges in the two societies. And this is for the excellent reason that the judges perform *similar* functions, reflecting their respective societies.

By this I do not mean that the influence exerted directly on the judiciary by the political arm of the State in the communist countries of Eastern Europe is paralleled by a similar direct influence in the capitalist countries of Western Europe. No doubt, in the great majority of cases before the courts, the judges in communist countries act independently of the Executive and are prepared to invalidate illegal actions by its members. But in the small number of crucial cases where the offences are political the political influence is more obviously direct. And here political offences means offences which may be drawn in broad terms to include conduct deemed detrimental to State interests. Further, I am speaking of the judiciary only and not of the activities of the political police, or of powers to detain without trial. If I were of a radical turn of mind with a leaning towards iconoclasm and a distrust of those in authority, I would (to put it mildly) find more scope and greater continuity for my activities in the capitalist west than in the communist east.

But the relative responsiveness of the judiciary to political pressure is not an attribute or a function specific to capitalism or to communism. It would be easy to name a score of countries which are undeniably capitalist and where the judges are as strongly under the influence of the political Executive as they are in any communist society. That relative responsiveness reflects the extent to which the judges share the aims and values of the political system, and the extent to which they are its enthusiastic supporters.

It is in this sense that I speak of judges in different countries performing similar functions, reflecting their respective societies, and the political power which operates in them....

Her Majesty's judges are unlikely to be under great illusions about the functioning of political power in the United Kingdom today. And I think we come close to their definition of the public interest and of the interests of the State if we identify their views with those who insist that in any society, but especially societies in the second half of the twentieth century, stability above all is necessary for the health of the people and is the supreme law.

It follows that Governments are normally to be supported but not in every case. Governments represent stability and have a very considerable interest in preserving it. The maintenance of authoritarian structures in all public institutions is wholly in the interest of Governments. This is true of all Governments of all political complexions, capitalist and communist alike. Whenever Governments or their agencies are acting to preserve that stability – call it the Queen's peace, or law and order, or the rule of law, or whatever – the judges will lend their support and will not be over-concerned if to do so requires the invasion of individual liberty....

My thesis, then, is that the judiciary in any modern industrial society, however composed, under whatever economic system, is an essential part of the system of government and that its function may be described as underpinning the stability of that system and as protecting that system from attack by resisting attempts to change it.

Many regard the values of the bench and bar as wholly admirable and the spirit of the common law (as presently expressed) to be a national adornment. The incorruptibility of the English bench and its independence of the Government are great virtues. All this is not in issue. When I argue that they regard the interests of the State or the public interest as pre-eminent and that they interpret those interests as meaning that, with very few exceptions, established authority must be upheld and that those exceptions are made only when a more conservative position can be adopted, this does not mean that the judges are acting with impropriety. It means that we live in a highly authoritarian society, fortunate only that we do not live in other societies which are even more authoritarian. We must expect judges, as part of that authority, to act in the interests, as they see them, of the social order....

Professor Griffith's thesis did not pass unchallenged however. It was critically examined by Lord Devlin in a review article:

Lord Devlin, 'Judges, Government and Politics', 41 *Modern Law Review*, 1978, pp. 505–11

The professor begins with a concise and interesting account of how judges work, what they are paid, their social origins and so on. This covers a good deal more ground than is necessary for his conclusion which is that the judicial political outlook, while not extreme, is right of centre. Judges are 'neither Tories, nor Socialists, nor Liberals' but 'protectors and conservators of what has been, of the relationships and interests on which, *in their view*, our society is founded.'[1] He is talking chiefly of the small group, less than 30, of the senior

1. J.A.G. Griffith, *The Politics of the Judiciary* (1977), p. 52.

judges in the House of Lords and the Court of Appeal whose views matter. '*These judges*,' he writes, '*have by their education and training and the pursuit of their profession as barristers, acquired a strikingly homogeneous collection of attitudes, beliefs and principles, which to them represents the public interest*.'[2] Since he is writing of men in their sixties and seventies whose working life has given them a common outlook on many questions, by no means all political, I have very little doubt that he is right. I have very little doubt either that the same might be written of most English institutions, certainly of all those which like the law are not of a nature to attract the crusading or rebellious spirit....

But the real question posed by the author is on other subjects. Do the judges allow their devotion to law and order to distort their application of the law when they apply it to those who do not think as they do? In exploring the cases to get the answer to this the author is faced with two difficulties. The first is the lack of discipline among the judges; they do not always toe what Professor Griffith declares to be their party line. The law lords are sometimes divided: more frequently they quarrel with the Court of Appeal. The second difficulty is that the scale of the work does not permit any analysis of the cases. Leaving Lord Halsbury to his own generation, it is difficult to get much from the modern cases without looking for the legal errors and examining them to see whether they disclose a pattern of thought. Without such an analysis the reader is left to go by the result: in the trade union cases, for example, the implication seems to be that a decision against the union cannot be in the public interest....

It is this section containing the cases which is the core of the book. What matters after all is not whether judges have the political prejudices of their age and upbringing, but whether or to what extent they allow the prejudice to get into their judgments. Most people, including judges, are prejudiced against crime, but judges have to learn to keep that prejudice out of a trial. Moreover, the author is dealing not with individual but with corporate prejudice. His purpose is to show that there are certain types of cases that the judges as a body do not decide fairly. I am not sure that in the end he proves much more than that there are cases which he, often in accord with dissenting judges, would have decided differently from the final court....

To my mind none of the evidence, general or specific adds much to the inherent probability that men and women of a certain age will be inclined by nature to favour the *status quo*. Is it displeasing to the public at large that the guardians of the law should share this common tendency? The editorial instructions to the author were to identify pressure groups. He does not name any; perhaps there is none. Perhaps no one is very dissatisfied with the situation except Professor Griffith and those who think like him. But they ought to be satisfied if it is possible to do so. So what ought to be done?

This is the question which the editors assigned to the third part of the book. Their instruction to the author for the first and second parts was to be objective. Professor Griffith has certainly tried to be objective and I think that in general he has been; he puts the other side of the case wherever he sees it and it is nothing to the point that a reviewer sees some of it differently.

2. *The Politics of the Judiciary* (1977).

Now, as he approaches the final question, he ought to be dropping objectivity and becoming polemical and stimulating. Professor Griffith cannot be unstimulating but he can be unpolemical and he is. In reaching his conclusion he is even more objective than before. He answers the question by saying in effect that there is nothing to be done. He thinks that the attitude of the judges is too repressive, too authoritarian, but he writes,

> 'We live in a highly authoritarian society, fortunate only that we do not live in other societies which are even more authoritarian. We must expect judges, as part of that authority, to act in the interests as they see them of the social order.'[3]

It is the same or worse in every country except for the Supreme Court of the United States which Professor Griffith twice praises.

What is wrong with this book is highlighted by this conclusion. It is its editorial setting. It is extravagant to talk of politics of the judiciary as one of the 'major issues of British politics today.' Their politics are hardly more significant than those of the army, the navy and the airforce; they are as predictable as those of any institution where maturity is in command. What the book presents is not a major issue but a problem, or rather one facet of the universal problem caused by the fact that in any peaceful and law-abiding democratic society in which the mortality rate is constantly declining government falls into the hands of the ageing. No doubt power rises upward from the people, who are of all ages, but it becomes effective only when it is channelled, and the controllers of the channels are, as Professor Griffith says, oligarchs. The oligarchs who rise to the top in a democratic society are usually mature, safe and orthodox men. Autocracy sometimes runs risks in selection, democracy hardly ever. So throughout the whole apparatus of the state, in every institution, whether it be the judiciary, the civil service or the political party, the men at the top, especially perhaps the senior judges because of their training, are seen by the young, among whom I count Professor Griffith because age has not wearied him nor the years condemned, as showing too much concern with stability and too little with movement. Of course the silent majority may see this as a very good thing: let the judges protect the laws and customs of the realm and the traditional values and leave movement to others. But assuming that the judges admire stability more than they should, what is the solution?

I half expected Professor Griffith to take the Supreme Court as an institution to be imitated and to revive the paeans of the early Warren days, the thumbs down for the 'look-it-up-in-the-library' types and the exaltation of the 'result-oriented' judgment. The solution would be to make the law lords much more like Supreme Court justices, give them a politician like Taft, Hughes or Warren as their leader, make the right attitude to social questions a more important qualification than learning in the law, open the door to professors, and by making direct appointments from the Bar get men at a far younger age than can be got if judicial experience is the prime quality desired. The really essential one of these qualifications is the right attitude to social questions; the others are ways of arriving at this desideratum.

3. Ibid., at p. 213.

But how do you ensure that they have the right attitude? If only law lords were all appointed by a socialist Prime Minister (not just any socialist, but one who like Professor Griffith is perhaps a little left of centre; Mr Callaghan would not be any good), all would be well. But it would be even more unwise to trust to that than to trust to the immutability of the Supreme Court. As Professor Berger's book reminds us there will come a day when the liquors for the 'empty vessels' are differently brewed and when 'due process' becomes once again, as it used to be, 'the symbol habitually evoked by private right, the barrier that guards the frontier of business against the interference of the state.'[1]

Is there then no solution except the pragmatic one of making the best of what we have got? I do not think that Professor Griffith exhausts the possibilities of this. For the social reformer the English judiciary should have three attractive features. First, it has not got its own source of power; there is no Constitution, no 'empty vessels' for it to fill. Second, if it has a bias, its bias is known and for a known bias allowance can be made. So regarded its homogeneity is a virtue; a gun that is wrongly sighted is less risky than one which is liable to go off in any direction. Third and most important, one of the advantages of even a mildly authoritarian state is that it does not put in command men and women who have not learnt to obey. A new minister with his ideas brought piping hot from the hustings may find his civil servants obstructive, but a positive command they will not disobey. Neither will the judges disobey an Act of Parliament. But where novel measures are imposed by a minister or by Parliament, they must be expressed in language which is emphatic enough and clear enough to penetrate the bias against them of those who are set in their ways: it is no use praying for the rejuvenation of the elderly. A strong minister can be as emphatic as he wants in his own ministry. But when the proposed measures have to be submitted to parliamentary and public criticism, under-emphasis is very seductive. A minister is unlikely, for example, to say bluntly in the House that the Race Relations Act was intended to restrict freedom of speech and should be so interpreted, still less to have the sentiment expressed as a preamble to the Act.

There is the other side of the coin. It must be part of any pragmatic deal that judges should watch out for the perils of maturity. It is as a warning to them that *The Politics of the Judiciary* is most valuable. It is not analytical but it is illustrative. When, for example, the courts are subjecting the proceedings of a domestic tribunal to the test of natural justice, is there a tendency to make the test stiffer for a tribunal that is disciplining an unco-operating trade unionist than for a university court that is disciplining a troublesome student? Surely this is a question which is worth asking. The judge who is confident that he has no prejudices at all is almost certain to be a bad judge. Prejudice cannot be exorcised, but like a weakness of the flesh it can be subdued. But it has first to be detected. This is the great value of the book. It presents the judiciary with its portrait as seen by some of its critics. It is a skilful presentation, moderate and friendly, and a pleasure to read. If only on the principle of *audi alteram partem* judges should read it.

1. *The Constitution Reconsidered*, ed. Conyers Reade (1938), p. 167.

Questions

1. Could it be argued that Professor Griffith and Lord Devlin are really saying much the same thing in different words. Professor Griffith argues that all judges, irrespective of their social class or the country in which they sit, are members of the Establishment who favour the status quo. Lord Devlin contends that judges tend to be 'mature, safe and orthodox men'.

2. Lord Devlin says that judges should 'watch out for the perils of maturity'. Is this is a practicable suggestion? What might be done to assist the process?

2. Should the judges be activist or passive?

If judges are human beings who have private opinions or even prejudices should their basic stance be activist or passive? Should they seek opportunities creatively to develop or even reform the law, or should they leave law reform to the legislature? Needless to say there are different schools of thought on this issue.

The traditional and dominant posture of the English judiciary on this question has been that the judge's role is broadly passive. The leading exponent of this approach in modern times has undoubtedly been Lord Simonds, who was Lord Chancellor from 1951 to 1954 but who sat in the House of Lords for nearly twenty years from 1944 to 1962. Robert Stevens has written of him that 'during the time that the House was dominated by Simonds, its purpose, intellectually and practically, remained the preservation of the status quo' (*Law and Politics* (1979) p. 342). In one case, for instance, he rejected Lord Denning's invitation to overrule the ancient rule that a third party cannot sue on a contract with a resounding affirmation of the principle of judicial conformity to what has previously been decided:

> To that invitation I readily respond. For to me heterodoxy, or as some might say, heresy, is not the more attractive because it is dignified by the name of reform. Nor will I easily be led by an undiscerning zeal for some abstract kind of justice to ignore our first duty, which is to administer justice according to law, the law which is established for us by an Act of Parliament or the binding authority of precedent. The law is developed by the application of old principles to new circumstances. Therein lies its genius. Its reform by the abrogation of these principles is the task not of the courts of law but of Parliament . . . I would cast no doubt upon the doctrine of stare decisis without which law is at hazard. [*Midland Silicones Ltd* v. *Scruttons Ltd* [1962] A.C. 446, 467–69.]

There are countless similar, if less vivid, statements in the law reports.

At the opposite end to the spectrum represented by Lord Simonds stands Lord Denning, who has been a judge since 1944 and Master of the Rolls since 1962. For him certainty in the law is an overrated virtue and judges not only do make law but should do so. On innumerable occasions, both on the bench and off, he has proclaimed the law-making potential of the judiciary:

The truth is that the law is uncertain. It does not cover all the situations that may arise. Time and again practitioners are faced with new situations, where the decision may go either way. No one can tell what the law is until the courts decide it. The judges do every day make law, though it is almost heresy to say so. If the truth is recognised then we may hope to escape from the dead hand of the past and consciously mould new principles to meet the needs of the present. ['The Reform of Equity' in C.J. Hamson (ed.) *Law Reform and Law-Making* (1953), p. 31.]

For him the function of the judge is to be active in reforming the law – 'If the law is to develop and not to stagnate, the House must, I think recapture this vital principle – the principle of growth. The House of Lords is more than another court of law. . . . It acts for the Queen as the fountain of justice in our land.' (*From Precedent to Precedent* (1959), p. 34. This statement was made whilst he was still in the House of Lords and before he returned to the Court of Appeal – the better, as he said, to make a mark on the law.) Lord Denning's recent stimulating book *The Discipline of Law* (1979) published to mark his eightieth birthday, is a celebration of his reforming zeal – with chapter and verse. Unfortunately, however, neither in his book nor elsewhere has Lord Denning expressed his passion for reform in any coherent philosophy. He has, for instance, never formulated principles to guide judges as to the kinds of cases in which they should intervene and when they should follow precedent and leave reform to the legislature. Over and over again he has chipped away at doctrines that seemed to him to be wrong – on third-party beneficiaries to a contract[1], sovereign immunity[2], the doctrine of frustration in contract[3], fundamental breach[4], the right of married women to remain in the matrimonial home,[5] the action for negligent misstatement[6], exclusion

1. *Midlands Silicones Ltd* v. *Scruttons Ltd* [1962] A.C. 446.
2. *Rahimtoola* v. *Nizam of Hyderabad* [1958] A.C. 379.
3. *British Movietonews Ltd* v. *London and District Cinemas Ltd* [1952] A.C. 166.
4. *Karsales* (*Harrow*) *Ltd* v. *Wallis* [1956] 1 W.L.R. 936.
5. *National Provincial Bank* v. *Ainsworth* [1964] 1 All E.R. 688.
6. *Candler* v. *Crane Christmas* [1951] 2 K.B. 164.

clauses in consumer contracts[7], equitable estoppel[8] and many others.[9] But there is no very clear articulation of the proper relationship between law and justice – beyond the repeated assertion that precedent must not stand in the way of justice. In the final words of his book Lord Denning says only that while precedent is the foundation of our system of case law it must not be applied too rigidly. 'You must cut out the dead wood and trim off the side branches, else you will find yourself lost in thickets and brambles. My plea is simply to keep the path to justice clear of obstructions which would impede it.'[10] But we are not told how the path may be recognized.

Between these two extremes of Lords Simonds and Denning there are a number of other significant voices. One certainly is Lord Devlin, who retired from the bench in 1964 at the early age of 59 after only three years in the House of Lords. His years on the bench coincided with the high-water mark of the Simonds era and in 1962 Lord Devlin was clearly despondent about the role of the judge. At that time he wrote: 'I doubt if judges will now of their own motion contribute much more to the development of the law'.[11] Even if the House of Lords changed the rule that it was bound by its own decisions 'it might do its own lopping and pruning . . . and perhaps even a little grafting, instead of leaving all that to the legislature. But it could not greatly alter the shape of the tree.'[12] But by 1975 he had formed a rather different view. Delivering the Chorley lecture at the London School of Economics, he expressed a conservative but by no means passive philosophy of the judicial role. He was against a judiciary that was dynamically activist, but on the other hand he saw a useful and quite considerable role for judges in shaping the common law:

Patrick Devlin, *The Judge*
(1979), pp. 3, 5, 9, 17

What is the function of the judge? Professor Jaffé has a phrase for it – 'the disinterested application of known law.'[13] He would put it perhaps as the

7. *Adler* v. *Dickson* [1955] 1 Q.B. 158.
8. *Central London Property Trust Ltd* v. *High Trees House Ltd* [1947] K.B. 130.
9. For an extended survey, see Robert Stevens, *Law and Politics* (1979), pp. 488–505.
10. Denning, *Discipline of Law*, p. 314.
11. *Samples of Lawmaking* (1962), p. 23.
12. Ibid., p. 116.
13. Jaffé, *English and American Judges as Lawmakers* (1969), p. 13.

minimal function. I should rank it as greater than that. It is at any rate what 90 per cent or more of English judges – and I daresay also of all judges of all nationalities – are engaged in for 90 per cent of their working lives. The social service which the judge renders to the community is the removal of a sense of injustice. To perform this service the essential quality which he needs is impartiality and next after that the appearance of impartiality. I put impartiality before the appearance of it simply because without the reality the appearance would not endure....

The disinterested application of the law calls for many virtues, such as balance, patience, courtesy and detachment, which leave little room for the ardour of the creative reformer. I do not mean that there should be a demarcation or that judges should down tools whenever they meet a defect in the law. I shall consider later to what extent in such a situation a judge should be activist. But I am quite convinced that there should be no judicial dynamics.

So much for the nature and function of the judge. I return to the lawmaker and consider what, if anything, judges and lawmakers have in common.

The lawmaker takes an idea or a policy and turns it into law. For this he needs the ability to formulate, and a judge in common with any other trained lawyer should have that. Is the judge any different in this respect from a professor or a parliamentary draftsman? Yes, because he has experience of the administration of the law. So has the barrister and the solicitor, but it is an advantage to see it working from the Bench. So there is no reason why, given the policy, a judge should not be a good activist lawmaker. The question, to which I shall return, is whether he should be the complete lawmaker or whether he would not do better work in committee, pooling his judicial experience with the social, commercial and administrative experience of others.

Let me repeat the distinction, since it may be one which I have freshly drawn, between activist and dynamic lawmaking. In activist lawmaking the idea is taken from the consensus and demands at most sympathy from the lawmaker. In dynamic lawmaking the idea is created outside the consensus and, before it is formulated, it has to be propagated. This needs more than sympathy: it needs enthusiasm. Enthusiasm is not and cannot be a judicial virtue. It means taking sides and, if a judge takes sides on such issues as homosexuality and capital punishment, he loses the appearance of impartiality and quite possibly impartiality itself. ... It is essential to the stability of society that those whom change hurts should be able to count on evenhanded justice calmly dispensed, not driven forward by the agents of change.

It is this evenhandedness which is the chief characteristic of the British judiciary and it is almost beyond price. If it has to be paid for in impersonality and remoteness, the bargain is still a good one. ... The reputation of the judiciary for independence and impartiality is a national asset of such richness that one government after another tries to plunder it. This is a danger about which the judiciary itself has been too easygoing. To break up the asset so as to ease the parturition of judicial creativity, an embryo with a doubtful future, would be a calamity. The asset which I would deny to governments I would deny also to social reformers.

I have now made it plain that I am firmly opposed to judicial creativity or dynamism as I have defined it, that is, of judicial operations in advance of the consensus. The limit of the consensus is not a line that is clearly marked, but I can make certain what would otherwise be uncertain by saying that a judge who is in any doubt about the support of the consensus should not advance at all. This however leaves open quite a large field for judicial activity. In determining its extent it is, I think, necessary to distinguish between common law and statute law. This is because the requirement of consensus affects differently the two types of law. The public is not interested in the common law as a whole. When it becomes interested in any particular section of it, it calls for a statute; the rest it leaves to the judges. The consensus is expressed in a general warrant for judicial lawmaking. This warrant is an informal and rather negative one, amounting to a willingness to let the judges get on with their traditional work on two conditions – first, that they do it in the traditional way, i.e. in accordance with precedent, and second, that parliamentary interference should be regarded as unobjectionable. In relation to statute law, by contrast, there can be no general warrant authorising the judges to do anything except interpret and apply.

But although there was scope for judicial activism, there were limits.

In every society there is a division between rulers and ruled. The first mark of a free and orderly society is that the boundaries between the two should be guarded and trespasses from one side or the other independently and impartially determined. The keepers of these boundaries cannot also be among the outriders. The judges are the keepers of the law and the qualities they need for that task are not those of the creative lawmaker. The creative lawmaker is the squire of the social reformer and the quality they both need is enthusiasm. But enthusiasm is rarely consistent with impartiality and never with the appearance of it.

Why is it, I ask in conclusion, that the denunciators of judicial inactivity so rarely pause to throw even a passing curse at the legislators who ought really to be doing the job. They seem so often to swallow without noticing it the quite preposterous excuse that Parliament has no time and to take only a perfunctory interest in an institution such as the Law Commission. Progressives of course are in a hurry to get things done and judges with their plenitude of power could apparently get them done so quickly; there seems to be no limit to what they could do if only they would unshackle themselves from their precedents. It is a great temptation to cast the judiciary as an elite which will bypass the traffic-laden ways of the democratic process. But it would only apparently be a bypass. In truth it would be a road that would never rejoin the highway but would lead inevitably, however long and winding the path, to the totalitarian state.

Question

If, as Lord Devlin suggests, judges are to restrict themselves to development of the common law within the consensus, how are they to know whether there is a consensus on the matter before the court? (For an account of Lord Devlin's own notable decisions developing the common law, see R. Stevens, *Law and Politics*, pp. 464–6.)

For Lord Radcliffe, 'The Law has to be interpreted before it can be applied and interpretation is a creative activity.'[1] But he preferred the judges to work creatively with caution and without alerting the populace to what they were about: '[I]f judges prefer to adopt the formula – for that is what it is – that they merely declare the law and do not make it, they do no more than show themselves wise men in practice. Their analysis may be weak, but their perception of the nature of law is sound. Men's respect for it will be the greater, the more imperceptible its development.'[2] If public opinion might lose respect for creative judges, parliament certainly would. 'I think that the judge needs to be particularly circumspect in the use of his power to declare the law, not because the principles adopted by parliament are more satisfactory or more enlightened than those which would commend themselves to his mind but because it is unacceptable constitutionally that there should be two independent sources of law-making at work at the same time.'[3] He saw (and exercised) a modest creative role for the judges but without advertising the fact.

Possibly the most influential judge of recent years has been Lord Reid, who was a Lord of Appeal from 1948 to 1974 and was senior judge in the House of Lords from 1962. Robert Stevens has admirably captured his views:

Robert Stevens, *Law and Politics*
(1979), pp. 468–88

In the period between 1948 and the end of 1974, and especially after he became the senior Lord of Appeal in 1962, Reid was the most influential judge in the House of Lords. Whether the issue was one of common law or statute, Reid's judgment was almost invariably the most sophisticated treatment and the one that commanded the most respect. As a Scottish lawyer he brought to the common law a sense of principle and breadth generally lacked by those who dominated the House when he arrived. Although he was comfortable putting the bulk of his effort into his judicial work rather than into extrajudicial public service, as a former politician he had an innate

1. *Not in Feather Beds* (1968), p. 213.
2. *Law and Its Compass* (1960), p. 39.
3. Ibid., p. 216.

sense of the relationship of the legislature and the courts – something often denied to more 'courageous or timorous' souls.... With respect to the common law his philosophy was simple:[1]

> I suppose that almost every doctrine of the common law was invented by some judge at some period in history, and when he invented it he thought it was plain common sense – and indeed it generally was originally. But, with the passage of time more technically minded judges have forgotten its origin and developed it in a way that can easily cause injustice. In so far as we appellate judges can get the thing back on the rails let us do so; if it has gone too far we must pin our hopes on Parliament.[2]

Reid was well aware that the relative functions of the courts and Parliament would have to vary in different areas. 'When we are dealing with property and contract it seems right that we should accept some degree of possible injustice in order to achieve a fairly high degree of certainty.'[3] But he saw no such underlying policy when it came to tort.[4] Criminal law, on the other hand, was not to be extended by the judges, although they might remain guardians of the requirement of mens rea. Yet, subject to these reservations, Reid had no doubt that lawyers' law – by which he meant the basic areas of common law delegated to the judiciary – was best developed by the final appeal court. 'If you think in months, want an instant solution for your problems and don't mind that it won't wear well, then go for legislation. If you think in decades, prefer orderly growth and believe in the old proverb more haste less speed, then stick to the common law. But do not seek a middle way by speeding up and streamlining the development of the common law.'[5]

Unlike many appeal judges, Reid, towards the end of his life, clarified his theory of the criteria for judicial development of the law. First, the direction in which the law should be developed was to be tested by the criterion of common sense, something that was 'not static', but that prevented 'technically minded judges [from pressing] precedents to their logical conclusions'.[6] Common sense appeared to serve Reid as a humanist substitute for the Christian base on which Radcliffe and Denning ultimately purported to rely.[7]

1. See, for instance, *Midland Silicones, Ltd.* v. *Scruttons, Ltd.*, [1962] A.C. 446, 475–77 (1961).
2. James S. C. Reid, 'The Law and the Reasonable Man', 1968, *Proceedings of British Academy*, 193, 194–95.
3. Reid, 'The Law and The Reasonable Man', 197.
4. 'A man knows quite well that what he intends to do may injure his neighbour; he may even intend such injury. Would the law be defective if his lawyer could not tell him with the same degree of certainty just how far he can go without having to pay damages?' Ibid.
5. 'Judge as Law Maker', *Journal of Society of Public Teachers of Law*, 1972, 28.
6. Ibid., 25–6.
7. See, for instance, his Holmesian position in one of his last decisions. 'I would not, however, decide the matter entirely on logical argument. The life blood of the law has not been logic but common sense.' He went on to reject an argument because '[t]he law may be an ass but it cannot be so asinine as that'; *R.* v. *Smith*, [1975] A.C. 476, 500.

Second, the new law had to take into account principle, although not narrow, notions of precedent.[8] 'Rigid adherence to precedent will not do. And paying lip service to precedent while admitting fine distinctions gives us the worst of both worlds. On the other hand, too much flexibility leads to intolerable uncertainty.'[9] Finally, judicial developments in the law had to be tested against public policy. While avoiding those cases where public opinion was sharply divided – to be left to Parliament[10] – judges should no longer be afraid of public policy. 'So long as the powers that be can see to it that the new race of judges are not mere technicians, but are men of the world as well, we can – indeed, we must – trust them to acquaint themselves with public policy and apply it in a reasonable way to such new problems as will arise from time to time.'[11] Indeed, by the end of his judicial career, Reid was a master of the art of balancing the conflicting policy goals involved in the decisions of the House.[12]

Yet, from the earliest part of his career he refused to be a slave to precedent.[13] He was committed to the idea that '[t]he common law ought never to produce a wholly unreasonable result, nor ought existing authorities to be read so literally as to produce such a result in circumstances never contemplated when they were decided.'[14] The same attitude characterized his approach when he found little authority. 'To my mind the best way of approaching this question is to consider the consequences of a decision in either sense. The circumstances are such that no decision can avoid creating some possible hard cases, but if a decision in one sense will on the whole lead to much more just and reasonable results, that appears to me to be a strong argument in its favour.'[15] ...

... Reid had no doubt that, at a certain point, either because of the strength of the earlier precedent or because of the subject matter of the appeal, radical change was the province of Parliament. Thus, in *Cartledge* v. *E. Jopling and Sons, Limited*, where the plaintiff did not discover he had pneumoconiosis until the limitation period had expired, so that Reid felt obliged to dismiss the appeal, he announced that 'some amendment of the law is urgently

8. 'Judge as Law Maker', note 8 above, 26.

9. Ibid.

10. Ibid., 23.

11. Ibid., 27.

12. See, for instance, *F. Hoffman-LaRoche & Co. A.G.* v. *Secretary of State for Trade & Indus.*, [1975] A.C. 295 (1973), where Reid articulated the conflicting goals of drug manufacturers and society and then attempted to balance the interests. He concluded that process by deciding that tradition and balancing required that an interim injunction be granted, but without the Crown's giving an undertaking on damages, adding, '[I]f I thought that the appellants had a strong case on the merits I would try to stretch a point in their favour to protect them from obvious injustice though I would find difficulty in doing so'; ibid., 342.

13. See, for instance, his dissent in *London Graving Dock C.* v. *Horton*, [1951] A.C. 737, 786: 'I have come to the conclusion that to hold there was such a duty would infringe no principle and would conflict with no binding or well-recognised authority.'

14. *Catledge* v. *E. Jopling & Sons*, [1963] A.C. 758, 772.

15. *Starkowski* v. *Attorney-General*, [1954] A.C. 155, 170.

necessary';[16] Parliament obliged almost at once.[17] So too, in holding that car manufacturers' records of cylinder block registration numbers were inadmissible under the hearsay rule in *Myers* v. *Director of Public Prosecutions* Reid announced, '[W]e cannot introduce arbitrary conditions or limitations; that must be left to legislation.'[18] In Reid's view judicial legislation should be limited to 'the development and application of fundamental priciples.'[19] While both of these cases were decided before the 1966 Practice Statement, the approach he exhibited in them probably continued to reflect his basic approach.[20]

Certainly Reid had a more developed sense than the other law lords about areas where it was inappropriate for the judiciary to legislate even interstitially. In the *Shaw* case, where Simonds led the attack to reactivate and extend the concept of criminal conspiracy, Reid countered:

> Even if there is still a vestigial power of this kind it ought not, in my view, to be used unless there appears to be general agreement that the offence to which it is applied ought to be criminal if committed by an indivudla. Notoriously, there are wide differences of opinion today as to how far the law ought to punish immoral acts which are not done in the face of the public. Some think the law already goes too far, some that it does not go far enough. Parliament is the proper place, and I am firmly of the opinion the only proper place, to settle that. When there is sufficient support from public opinion, Parliament does not hestiate to intervene. Where Parliament fears to tread it is not for the courts to rush in.[21]

One of the most sophisticated attempts to diagnose when courts should and should not legislate is that of Mr Michael Freeman in a major article in 1973 – 'Standards of Adjudication, Judicial Law Making and Prospective Overruling', 26 *Current Legal Problems* (1973), p. 166. He listed certain basic differences between courts and legislatures. First, judges were not democratically answerable to the electorate which made it inappropriate for them to enact their own social policies. Second, courts had to justify their decisions by articulating

16. [1963] A.C. 758, 773.
17. Limitation Act of 1963. On this incident, see Blom-Cooper and Drewry, *Final Appeal* (1972) 361.
18. [1965] A.C. 1001, 1021 (1964). See Blom-Cooper and Drewry, *Final Appeal* 362. Reid's position was attached by Jaffé, *English and American Judges as Lawmakers* 28–29. In fairness it should be noted that Parliament responded to Reid's plea by passing the Criminal Evidence Act of 1965.
19. *Myers* v. *DPP*, [1965] A.C. 1001, 1021–22 (1964).
20. The approach remained a 'balanced' one. See, for instance, his reactions in *Broome* v. *Cassell & Co.* on the issue of penal damages: '[F]ull argument ... has convinced me that I and my colleagues made a mistake in concurring with Lord Devlin's speech in *Rookes* v. *Barnard*'; [1972] A.C. 1027, 1084.
21. *Shaw* v. *DPP*, [1962] A.C. 220, 275 (1961).

reasons, whereas legislators were not under this constraint. Third, judges came from a narrow social background and represented only one profession. The information available to a court when it was considering law reform was very limited. Also the range of options available to the courts was much more limited:

When Parliament decides that something ought to be the law it can consider the different ways of achieving that goal. It might wish to stop policemen extracting confessions from suspects. It could do this in a number of ways. It could make such confessions inadmissible evidence. It could make the extraction of confessions a criminal offence and expose the offending police officer to a long term of imprisonment. It could set up a state board which paid compensation to victims of such police conduct. It could direct that offending police officers be dismissed or demoted. But the judge could only adopt the first of these steps. Or, to take a second example, the development of a 'deserted wife's equity'[1] by the Court of Appeal was an attempt (some would say of dubious propriety) to ground protection for the deserted wife in legal principle. With its collapse in *Ainsworth*,[2] the legislature intervened and passed the Matrimonial Homes Act in 1967. This set up machinery whereby a spouse could gain protection by registering a charge on the other spouse's property. The Court of Appeal had suggested this might be the solution, but with a court's limited powers they were unable to initiate such a scheme.

Judges then do not have available to them the very important instruments of administrative enforcement, licensing or positive rewards. They can use only damages and specific orders, injunctions, specific performance, *certiorari*, *mandamus*, declaratory judgments and so on. And without this institutional machinery the steps they can undertake are limited. [At p. 178.]

Another distinguishing feature had been seen by Lon Fuller in his *Anatomy of the Law* (Pelican, 1971). The rules applied by judges to individual cases must be 'brought into and maintained in, some systematic interrelationship; they must display some coherent internal structure' (p. 134). Parliament by contrast can take 'leaps into the dark'. If, as judicial decisions were to be predictable by practitioners and their clients, they must be grounded in principle. ('This means that judges develop the law incrementally' (Freeman, op. cit., p. 179). Society expected judges to decide disputes in a rational way. There was much room for creativity but the judge did not have a clean slate on which to write.

Freeman then illustrated what he regarded as good and bad examples of judicial activity and inactivity. He distinguished between

1. In *Bendall* v. *McWhirter* [1952] 2 Q.B. 466 and many other cases until 1965.
2. [1965] A.C. 1175.

judicial restraint, judicial cowardice, judicial boldness, and judicial creativity.

Judicial restraint was shown in *Morgans* v. *Launchbury* [1973] A.C. 127 which raised for decision the question whether injured persons could sue a wife whose husband had taken her car with permission and then loaned it to a third person who caused the accident. On accepted principles prevailing at that time there was no doubt that no such action lay, but the House of Lords was urged to introduce a new rule. It refused to do so (the Court of Appeal had held for the plaintiffs):

Lord Salmon recognised that

> 'it is an important function of this House to develop and adapt the common law to meet the changing needs of time'

but

> '[i]n the present case ... the proposed development constitutes such a radical and far-reaching departure from accepted principle that it seems to me to smack of naked legislation.[3]

There are similar sentiments in the judgments of Lord Cross and Lord Pearson,[4] but it is in Lord Wilberforce's judgment that we get the clearest exposition of the problem.

He was in no doubt that some adaptation of common law rules of agency could be made by the judges. He admitted that traditional concepts of vicarious liability might be proving inadequate. He saw some attractions in being creative. But he spurned any invitation to do so in this case. His reasons deserve careful examination. He said that the assumption was that it was desirable to fix liability in cases of negligent driving on the owner of the car. Such a policy was disputable, though his lordship saw no need to discuss such a question. He rather averted his attention to the different systems that could be introduced. He catalogued four: a system of liability based on the concept of the 'matrimonial' car; one based on the 'family' car; one stating that any owner who permits another to use his car should be liable by the fact of permission; and possibly even a system of strict liability. But as Lord Wilberforce rightly said,

> 'I do not know on what principle your Lordships acting judicially can prefer one of these systems to the others or on what basis any one can be formulated with sufficient precision or its exceptions defined. The choice is one of social policy; there are arguments for and against each of them.'[5]

... To summarise, *Morgans* v. *Launchbury* shows judicial restraint at its best. It was a polycentric dispute *par excellence*. It involved a policy choice upon

3. [1973] A.C. 127 at 151.
4. Ibid., at 146 and 142–3.
5. Ibid., at 136.

which the judges had no information or guidance. Law-making would have involved upturning the rightful expectations of thousands. The effect of a wider test on insurance, on premiums, on organisations like the Motor Insurers' Bureau could only be guessed at; and that is not an adequate basis for law-making [Freeman, pp. 187–9.]

To illustrate *judicial cowardice* Freeman used the case of *Myers* v. *D.P.P.* [1965] A.C. 1001. The question was whether the House of Lords would stretch the exceptions to the hearsay rule to include records kept in a mechanical way by a business. The prosecution wanted to introduce in evidence the numbers fixed onto cars to show that the defendants had stolen and altered parts of cars in order to conceal their origin. Three law lords (Lords Morris, Hodson and Reid) held the evidence was inadmissible.

Lord Morris stated that it had been decided eighty years earlier that hearsay is not admissible unless authority 'be found to justify its reception within some established ... rule.'[1] Lord Hodson took the position that to create a new exception 'would be judicial legislation with a vengeance in an attempt to introduce reform of the law of evidence which if needed can properly be dealt with only by the legislature.'[2] Lord Reid believed that the 'common law must be developed to meet changing economic conditions and habits of thought ... But there are limits ... If we are to extend the law it must be by the development and application of fundamental principles ... If an exception were created here, others should be created, and there would be a series of appeals ... If we are to give a wide interpretation to our judicial functions questions of policy cannot be wholly excluded, and it seems to me to be against public policy to produce uncertainty.'[3] He also advocated legislation.

Lord Pearce and Lord Donovan dissented. Lord Pearce's judgment is particularly persuasive. He showed that the admission of the evidence in question was fully in accordance with the shared principles and expectations of the legal profession. On a technical matter of 'lawyers' law' concerned with the machinery of justice this must be the appropriate audience. He demonstrated that they could admit the evidence in question without violating the substance of the rule purporting to exclude it. Indeed, that there were principles in the law which clamoured for its acceptance. Suppose, he argued, the anonymous workman could be identified. If he was dead, 'the records would be admissible as declarations in the course of duty.'[4]

Legislation was in due course passed,[5] but judicial legislation was feasible and apposite. The laws of evidence are better developed by those who operate them than by Parliament, though radical policy changes even in this area must be left to the legislature. If Lord Pearce's reasoning had been followed

1. [1973] at 1028.
2. Ibid. at 1034.
3. Ibid. at 1021–2.
4. [1965] A.C. 1001 at 1036.
5. Criminal Evidence Act 1965.

it is difficult to see whose reasonable expectations could have been thwarted. [Freeman, pp. 190–2.]

Judicial boldness Freeman said was exemplified by *Knuller* v. *D.P.P.* [1973] A.C. 435 which raised the question of extending the criminal law. *Shaw* v. *D.P.P.* [1962] A.C. 220, in which the House of Lords had in effect invented a new offence of conspiracy to corrupt public morals, had met with widespread opprobrium. But in *Knuller* the law lords went further and recognised another offence – of conspiracy to outrage public decency. The case was brought against the publisher of *International Times* in respect of small ads by homosexuals.

The Lords in *Knuller* created new law.... Lord Diplock's judgment is an exemplary exposure of the illogical, unhistorical and often hypocritical reasoning underlying the judgments in *Shaw's* case and those of his brethren in *Knuller*. But the other four Lords tied themselves into knots in their attempts to rationalise their judgments...

Knuller has injected uncertainty into criminal law and its administration. It flies in the face of legislative policy[6] and ministerial assurance.[7] If it endorses the values of certain sectional interests it flouts others. In a democratic society consensus demands compromise. Legislation embodies this: *Knuller* rejects it. It exemplifies judicial law-making at its worst. [Ibid., pp. 192–3, 194–5.]

The final category identified by Freeman, that of *judicial creativity*, he illustrated by *British Railways Board* v. *Herrington* [1972] A.C. 877 in which the House of Lords had to decide whether to overrule its own decision of *Addie* v. *Dumbreck* (1929) on the liability of occupiers towards trespassers. The most interesting judgment, Freeman thought, was that of Lord Wilberforce:

He made his ideology clear. A law of tort based on fault liability was 'outdated'. '[C]ases such as these could be more satisfactorily dealt with by a modern system of public enterprise liability devised by Parliament.'[8] But such wholesale institutional change could not be devised by judges, even if it were desirable for them to do so. Parliament had, of course, passed in 1957 the Occupiers' Liability Act, and this had preserved the common law ruling on trespassers. This did not mean that 'the House was bound hand and foot by *Addie*'s case at its narrowest.'[9]

The common law, his lordship argued, 'always leaves a residue to be

6. Obscene Publications Act 1959; Theatres Act 1968.
7. House of Commons, *Hansard*, vol. 695, col. 1212, 3 June 1964.
8. [1972] A.C. 877 at 922.
9. Ibid., at 921.

completed by common sense.'[1] Common sense dictated that the development of the law would best be served by concentrating on the particular type of case which worries the courts and on which the law has been tested by experience. Most twentieth-century litigation was brought against public utilities. A duty of care arises, he held, 'because of the existence, near to the public, of a dangerous situation.'[2] ...

Law-making such as that perpetrated by Lord Wilberforce is a legitimate activity. It does not create injustice (the argument of 'system') as public utilities and, for example, farmers are not 'alike'. In one sense what is being done is classification of legal concepts on to a more factual basis. It is right for a judge to take the minor step taken by Lord Wilberforce. He knows that other judges now have a framework, that as new problems arise there is something against which to test the formulation. *Herrington* clears a lot of dead wood, and enables judges to focus on unresolved problems. It may be that as they do this, as the *Herrington* ruling is tested and re-tested, that a new principle will emerge. But for the present the common law has been developed to accommodate a social problem: the pre-existing rules have hardly changed yet the seed of public enterprise liability has been sown. [pp. 198–200.]

Robert Stevens' massive study of the House of Lords' judges from 1800 to 1976 traces a succession of stages. He traces the gradual shift in the modern era from the period of rigid and narrow formalism under Lord Simonds to a more open and policy-oriented period under Lords Reid, Wilberforce, Diplock, Salmon and Simon: 'By the mid-seventies it [the House of Lords] was no longer regarded as the restater of accepted doctrines, but rather as the incremental developer of new doctrines.... [W]hile the belief in the predictability of 'clear rules' was no doubt still stronger than in any other common law jurisdiction, the belief in the anonymity and irrelevance of the judicial contribution had largely evaporated.'[3] The 1966 Practice Statement advising the world that the House of Lords might depart from its previous decisions added legitimacy to a process that had been going on since the late fifties and was accelerating in the early sixties.[4] 'The statement seemed to confirm that parliament had no objection to the judges' making law in those areas of society primarily entrusted to dispute settlement in the courts. Thus it is not surprising that, although rarely mentioned, the statement encouraged a greater flexibility of approach and, in particular, an emphasis on principle rather than rule and precedent and a noticeably greater inclination to talk about policy.'[5]

1. [1972] A.C. 877 at 921.
2. Ibid.
3. R. Stevens, *Law and Politics* (1979), p. 589.
4. Ibid., p. 621.
5. Ibid.

It was true that the traditional view of the role of the courts had by no means disappeared. A substantial element in the profession still preferred to emphasize the role of logic, certainty and predictability, and to play down discretion and creativity. Thus Sir Henry Fisher, formerly a High Court judge, attacked the 1966 Practice Statement arguing that judges 'should refrain from broad statements of principle and from obiter dicta. They should be scrupulous to apply the law as it exists even if they think it to be wrong or unfair or unjust and should resist the temptation to twist the law to conform with their sympathies or theories, as the proper instrument for the reform of the law is Parliament, aided where necessary by the Law Commission, a Law Reform Committee, or Royal or departmental commission.'[1] Professor L.C.B. Gower, a former Law Commissioner, urged the relative unsuitability of the House of Lords as a law-reform agency, and even the Law Commission had criticised the law lords' reform of the law on occupier's liability toward trespassers in *Herrington* v. *British Railways Board* [1972] A.C. 877 because it had not produced 'a clear principle applicable to the generality of cases'.[2]

Yet in spite of all these factors, by the mid-1970s forces were gathering and trends were developing that in the long run were likely to accentuate the creative force of the final appeal court.... By English standards the approach to precedent evidenced rapid changes. After 1966 even the more conventional law lords began to talk the language, if not the litany, of judicial creativity. When overruling, the House talked less about the errors of legal logic made in the prior case and more about the underlying policies that had changed since the earlier decision.

In 1955 ... lawmaking by judges had been seen in simplistic terms – it either competed with Parliament or it did not, and it was either good or bad. That had been largely abandoned. Various North American influences helped inject into English thinking the American concepts of judicial restraint and judicial activism[3] – that there are shades of desirability of law-making. Rather than the competition between the legislature and judiciary that had so concerned Radcliffe, it was increasingly argued that '[t]he organs of government are partners in the enterprise of lawmaking'. Out of this ... grew a much greater awareness of when judicial legislation was appropriate.[4]

Two examples of the courts dealing more openly with policy issues

Lord Denning has of course never been shy of looking at policy issues.

1. 119 *Solicitors' Journal* (1975), p. 854.
2. *Report of the Law Commission on Occupiers' Liability* (Cmnd. 6928, 1975).
3. Louis L. Jaffe, *English and American Judges as Lawmakers* (1969), pp. 28–9.
4. R. Stevens, op. cit., p. 624.

Yet he seems to approach such issues even more squarely of late. *Dutton* v. *Bognor Regis U.D.C.* is an example:

Dutton v. *Bognor Regis U.D.C.* [1972] 2 W.L.R. 299 at 313

LORD DENNING M.R.: This case is entirely novel. Never before has a claim been made against a council or its surveyor for negligence in passing a house. The case itself can be brought within the words of Lord Atkin in *Donoghue* v. *Stevenson*: but it is a question whether we should apply them here. In *Dorset Yacht Co. Ltd.* v. *Home Office* [1970] A.C. 1004, Lord Reid said, at p. 1023, that the words of Lord Atkin expressed a principle which ought to apply in general 'unless there is some justification or valid explanation for its exclusion.' So did Lord Pearson at p. 1054. But Lord Diplock spoke differently. He said it was a guide but not a principle of universal application (p. 1060). It seems to me that it is a question of policy which we, as judges, have to decide. The time has come when, in cases of new import, we should decide them according to the reason of the thing.

In previous times, when faced with a new problem, the judges have not openly asked themselves the question: what is the best policy for the law to adopt? But the question has always been there in the background. It has been concealed behind such questions as: Was the defendant under any duty to the plaintiff? Was the relationship between them sufficiently proximate? Was the injury direct or indirect? Was it foreseeable, or not? Was it too remote? And so forth.

Nowadays we direct ourselves to considerations of policy. In *Rondel* v. *Worsley* [1969] 1 A.C. 191, we thought that if advocates were liable to be sued for negligence they would be hampered in carrying out their duties. In *Dorset Yacht Co. Ltd.* v. *Home Office* [1970] A.C. 1004, we thought that the Home Office ought to pay for damage done by escaping Borstal boys, if the staff was negligent, but we confined it to damage done in the immediate vicinity. In *S.C.M.* (*United Kingdom*) *Ltd.* v. *W.H. Whittall & Son Ltd.* [1971] 1 Q.B. 337, some of us thought that economic loss ought not to be put on one pair of shoulders, but spread among all the sufferers. In *Launchbury* v. *Morgans* [1971] 2 Q.B. 245, we thought that as the owner of the family car was insured she should bear the loss. In short, we look at the relationship of the parties: and then say, as matter of policy, on whom the loss should fall.

What are the considerations of policy here? I will take them in order.

First, Mrs Dutton has suffered a grievous loss. The house fell down without any fault of hers. She is in no position herself to bear the loss. Who ought in justice to bear it? I should think those who were responsible. Who are they? In the first place, the builder was responsible. It was he who laid the foundations so badly that the house fell down. In the second place, the council's inspector was responsible. It was his job to examine the foundations to see if they would take the load of the house. He failed to do it properly. In the third place, the council should answer for his failure. They were entrusted by Parliament with the task of seeing that houses were properly built. They received public funds for the purpose. The very object was to protect purchasers and occupiers of houses. Yet they failed to protect them. Their shoulders are broad enough to bear the loss.

Next I ask: is there any reason in point of law why the council should not be held liable? Hitherto many lawyers have thought that a builder (who was also the owner) was not liable. If that were truly the law, I would not have thought it fair to make the council liable when the builder was not liable. But I hold that the builder who builds a house badly is liable, even though he is himself the owner. On this footing, there is nothing unfair in holding the council's surveyor also liable.

Then I ask: If liability were imposed on the council, would it have an adverse effect on the work? Would it mean that the council would not inspect at all, rather than risk liability for inspecting badly? Would it mean that inspectors would be harassed in their work or be subject to baseless charges? Would it mean that they would be extra cautious, and hold up work unnecessarily? Such considerations have influenced cases in the past, as in *Rondel* v. *Worsley* [1969] 1 A.C. 191. But here I see no danger. If liability is imposed on the council, it would tend, I think, to make them do their work better, rather than worse.

Next, I ask: Is there any economic reason why liability should not be imposed on the council? In some cases the law had drawn the line to prevent recovery of damages. It sets a limit to damages for economic loss, or for shock, or theft by escaping convicts. The reason is that if no limit were set there would be no end to the money payable. But I see no such reason here for limiting damages. In nearly every case the builder will be primarily liable. He will be insured and his insurance company will pay the damages. It will be very rarely that the council will be sued or found liable. If it is, much the greater responsibility will fall on the builder and little on the council.

Finally I ask myself: If we permit this new action, are we opening the door too much? Will it lead to a flood of cases which neither the council nor the courts will be able to handle? Such considerations have sometimes in the past led the courts to reject novel claims. But I see no need to reject this claim on this ground. The injured person will always have his claim against the builder. He will rarely allege – and still less be able to prove – a case against the council.

All these considerations lead me to the conclusion that the policy of the law should be, and is, that the council should be liable for the negligence of their surveyor in passing work as good when in truth it is bad.

For Lord Denning to speak so plainly is one thing; for the House of Lords to do so is something rather different. Yet, as Robert Stevens has shown, the House of Lords is increasingly willing to follow the Denning lead. Perhaps the clearest example is *Miliangos* v. *George Frank (Textiles) Ltd.* [1976] A.C. 443, in which, it will be recalled, the House of Lords had to decide whether to abolish the ancient rule that damages in an English court could only be awarded in sterling.

All the five judges who took part in the decision addressed themselves principally to the policy problems.

Four of the five law lords said that the rule should be changed, one thought it should not. The reasons advanced by the four who wanted to change the rule included:

(1) It was now possible procedurally to order payment of foreign currency debts in the foreign currency – this had not been possible before (Wilberforce at 462–3; Cross at 497; Edmund-Davies at 499).

(2) Sterling was no longer so stable a currency as before (Wilberforce at 463; Cross, at 497; Edmund-Davies at 500).

(3) There were two precedents in the field of arbitrations of awards in foreign currencies (Wilberforce at 463–4; Cross at 497; Edmund-Davies at 500).

(4) Changing the rule would 'enable the law to keep in step with commercial needs and with the majority of other countries facing similar problems' (Wilberforce at 467).

(5) It was possible to state a better rule (Wilberforce at 467–70).

(6) The fact that a rule was long established was not necessarily a reason to require that it be uprooted if at all only by legislation:

> LORD WILBERFORCE (at 469–70): My Lords, in conclusion I would say that, difficult as this whole matter undoubtedly is, if once a clear conclusion is reached as to what the law ought now to be, declaration of it by this House is appropriate. The law on this topic is judge-made: it has been built up over the years from case to case. It is entirely within this House's duty, in the course of administering justice, to give the law a new direction in a particular case where, on principle and in reason, it appears right to do so. I cannot accept the suggestion that because a rule is long established only legislation can change it – that may be so when the rule is so deeply entrenched that it has infected the whole legal system, or the choice of a new rule involves more far-reaching research than courts can carry out. A recent example of the House changing a very old established rule is *West Midland Baptist (Trust) Association (Inc.)* v. *Birmingham Corporation* [1970] A.C. 874. Lord Reid thought that it was proper to re-examine a judge-made rule of law based on an assumption of fact (as to the stability of money) when the rule was formulated but which was no longer true and which in many cases caused serious injustice. So in that case the House selected a new date and did not think it necessary or right to wait for legislation and I would not think it necessary or right here. Indeed, from some experience in the matter, I am led to doubt whether legislative reform, at least prompt and comprehensive reform, in this field of foreign currency obligation, is practicable. Questions as to the recovery of debts or of damages depend so much upon individual mixtures of facts and merits as to make them more suitable for progressive solutions in the courts. I think that we have an opportunity to reach such a solution here.

3. What the law is and what it ought to be

Is there a danger that through focussing more openly on policy issues the courts will come to decide cases on the basis of what the law ought to be rather than what the law is? This question lies at the heart of one of the most vital debates about the nature of the judicial process. It reflects the anxieties of the many judges and lawyers who have deprecated the efforts made in particular by Lord Denning to improve the quality of justice by looking beyond the form to the substance below.

Any young counsel unwise enough to argue in court that his submission represents what the law ought to be will immediately be interrupted by the court – 'Mr Smith,' he will be told, 'we are here to decide what the law is, not what it ought to be.' The statement, in one sense, is absolutely true. The court, in deciding the question of law before it, must decide on the basis of what it thinks the law is. (The only exception is if the court could say – we think the law in the past was *X* and that is the law we are applying to the present case, but in future we will decide that it is *Y*. This technique, known as prospective overruling, is discussed below.) But the statement that the court is only interested in what the law is, misrepresents the position. It is based on the false premise that, in determining the issue before it, the court is exercising no choice or discretion. This view is the classic formalistic position actually adopted by countless English judges. An example is the reply given in 1951 by Lord Jowitt, the Lord Chancellor, when he was asked at an Australian conference what the House of Lords would do if there was an appeal in the then recently decided case of *Candler* v. *Crane, Christmas*:

> We should regard it as our duty to expound what we believe the law to be and we should loyally follow the decisions of the House of Lords if we found there was some decision which we thought was in point. It is not really a question of being a bold or a timorous soul; it is a much simpler question than that. You know there was a time when the earth was void and without form, but after these hundreds of years the law of England, the common law, has at any rate got some measure of form to it. We are really no longer in the position of Lord Mansfield who used to consider a problem and expound it ex aequa et bona – what the law ought to be . . . I do most humbly suggest to some of the speakers today that the problem is not to consider what social and political conditions do today require; that is to confuse the task of the lawyer with the task of the legislator. It is quite possible that the law has produced a result which does not accord with the requirements of today. If so, put it right by legislation, but do not expect every lawyer, in addition to all his other problems, to act as Lord Mansfield did, and decide what the

law ought to be. He is far better employed if he puts himself to the much simpler task of deciding what the law is.*

Lord Jowitt's response would accurately reflect the view of generations of English lawyers and judges up to the present day. However, it would be difficult to find many American practitioners or judges who would today accept the proposition in that form. The difference in the two countries is that the American legal culture has in the past two or three decades absorbed the insights of the so-called Realist School, which flourished from the 1930s and whose leading exponents were writers such as Jerome Frank in *Law and the Modern Mind*. The chief contribution of the Realists was to expose the role of the judge himself in deciding the outcome of cases raising points of law. Some of the claims of the Realists no doubt go too far (a caricature of their view is that the decision is ultimately determined by, say, the state of the judge's digestion). But their central claim has now become fully accepted by virtually all American lawyers. By contrast, many and possibily even most English lawyers still live in an earlier (flat earth) age of innocence.

The validity of the Realist view seems readily demonstrable. The judge hears argument from two parties each of whom is normally represented by a professional lawyer. Each side advances argument as to why his position represents the law. The court must decide between them. Sometimes it may be that the question virtually decides itself. There are, let us say, six precedents each of which says that the law on the point is *X*. The proposition has been unchallenged for 150 years. Every textbook confirms it. *X* seems a reasonable rule – no one has criticized it. The party that seeks to show that the law on that point is *Y* obviously has an extremely up-hill task. Indeed few lawyers would undertake it. The great majority would advise the client that the prospects of success were nil and would urge him to spend his money on something more promising. This case is therefore most unlikely ever to reach the courts.

In any case before the courts where both parties are professionally represented (where one can therefore rule out the possibility of cranks and vexatious litigants), the court is almost always required to decide between two arguments that have some substance. One side may come with stronger precedents but the other side will perhaps have greater merits on the facts. Or the strength of the precedents may be

* Cited by W.K. Fullagar, 25 *Australian Law Journal* (1951) p. 278, and referred to by Robert Stevens in *Law and Politics*, p. 338.

fairly evenly matched and the real battle will be to capture the sympathy of the court for the client's position. Of course, in some cases the lawyers on both sides will accurately predict the outcome and to that extent it may be that there was little scope for the judge's individual discretion. He was 'forced' by the strength of the precedents and the lack of any solid argument to the contrary to decide in favour of one of the two litigants. But, again, those cases tend not to come to court and when they do the decision is often only predictable after the event – before it is handed down, there appears to be the possibility that it might go the other way. Moreover, after the decision there remains the chance of an appeal. The higher one goes in the appeal system, the greater the chance of getting free of the clutches of the precedents – one climbs above the clouds and can survey the mountain peaks. At the level of the House of Lords the judges are now absolutely free to decide either way.

The significance in this context of the House of Lords' Practice Statement has not yet been fully grasped by the English profession. If the House of Lords is free to depart from its own previous decisions, it means by definition that they do not necessarily reflect the law. When the House first enunciated the principle it thought the law was *X*; now it may conclude that the rule is *Y*. It is impossible for the precedents to reveal this – it must be the result of a conscious decision by the members of the House of Lords. But this is only a particularly clear demonstration of something that occurs each time a court reaches a view of the law which is contrary to the existing precedents – for instance through the ordinary process of overruling. The very possibility that the Court of Appeal can overrule the decisions of the High Court means, again by definition, that it need not follow even the clearest precedents established by the High Court. But precisely the same is true even of the High Court. Since the High Court is not bound by its own decisions, it too can look at the precedents and reject them – in the name of some other better argument. In other words, whenever a court is faced with precedents that are not binding on it, it has the choice of whether to follow them or not. Even if there are ten previous precedents all saying that the law is *X*, providing none is binding, the court is free to reject them and find the law to be *Y*. (Where the precedent is binding there is of course also a choice, since ultimately it is the court and not the precedent that decides that the precedent is apposite and not distinguishable.) Needless to say the court will be slow to reject a relevant precedent. It will need to have strong reasons for doing so. In some fields it will be most reluctant to upset settled rules. This is especially true in areas of the law where people can be assumed to have arranged their affairs in reliance on the existing state of the law, such as in commercial, tax or property matters. But in the final analysis, not being bound by a decision means that one can depart from it. Ten non-binding precedents still do not add up to a binding rule – ten times nothing remains nothing. Of course, ten non-binding precedents present more of an obstacle than one, but it remains an obstacle that a determined judge can surmount if he can be persuaded that it is worth the effort.

It has become respectable in recent years to recognise that judges make law – even conservative judges affirm as much. Thus Lord Edmund-Davies said in 1975: 'The simple and certain fact is that judges inevitably act as legislators. . . . The inevitable interim between the discovery of social needs and demands and the provision of legislative remedies to meet them presents judges with the opportunity (indeed, it imposes upon them the *duty*) of filling the need and meeting the demand in accordance with their notions of what is just. Nolens volens they thereby act as law-makers.' ('Judicial Activism' 28 *Current Legal Problems* (1975), p. 1.) Similarly, Lord Pearson, another judge who can hardly be described as a radical, said in *Herrington* v. *British Railways Board* [1972] 3 W.L.R. 537 of *Addie* v. *Dumbreck*, the House of Lords' decision that stood in the plaintiff's way: 'It seems to me that the rule of Addie's case has been rendered obsolete by changes in physical and social conditions and has become an incumbrance impeding the proper development of the law. . . . In my opinion the *Addie* v. *Dumbreck* formulation of the duty of occupiers to trespassers . . . has become an anomaly and should be discarded.'

But it has not yet become respectable to talk in courts of law of what the law ought to be. One is still constrained to talk there only of what the law is with no recognition of the fact that for the court the question what the law is necessarily *includes* the question what the law ought to be. To discuss what the law ought to be is only another way of defining the proposition that a court is inevitably and properly involved in law-making. As Lord Edmund-Davies put it – nolens volens they act as law-makers. But if they are law-makers, it would be preferable that the judges should not only recognise the fact but permit and indeed encourage debate before them of what law they should make.

(a) Prospective overruling as an aid to creative law-making

One sign of a new judicial attitude to law-making has been the reference in one or two recent cases to the American device of prospective overruling, whereby the court announces that it will change the relevant rule – but only for future cases. In *Jones* v. *Secretary of State for Social Services* [1972] A.C. 944 LORD SIMON OF GLAISDALE (at 1026) said:

I am left with the feeling that, theoretically, in some ways the most satisfactory outcome of these appeals would have been to have allowed them on the basis that they were governed by the decision in *Dowling*'s case, but to have overruled that decision prospectively. Such a power – to overrule prospectively a previous decision, but so as not necessarily to affect the parties before the court – is exercisable by the Supreme Court of the United States, which has held it to be based on the common law: see *Linkletter* v. *Walker* (1965) 381 U.S. 618.

In this country it was long considered that judges were not makers of law but merely its discoverers and expounders. The theory was that every case was governed by a relevant rule of law, existing somewhere and discoverable somehow, provided sufficient learning and intellectual rigour were brought to bear. But once such a rule had been discovered, frequently the pretence was tacitly dropped that the rule was pre-existing: for example, cases like *Shelley's Case* (1581) 1 Co.Rep. 93b, *Merryweather* v. *Nizan* (1799) 8 Term Rep. 186 or *Priestley* v. *Fowler* (1837) 3 M. & W. 1 were (rightly) regarded as new departures in the law. Nevertheless, the theory, however unreal, had its value – in limiting the sphere of lawmaking by the judiciary (inevitably at some disadvantage in assessing the potential repercussions of any decision, and increasingly so in a complex modern industrial society), and thus also in emphasising that central feature of our constitution, the sovereignty of Parliament. But the true, even if limited, nature of judicial lawmaking has been more widely acknowledged of recent years; and the declaration of July 20, 1966, may be partly regarded as of a piece with that process. It might be argued that a further step to invest your Lordships with the ampler and more flexible powers of the Supreme Court of the United States would be no more than a logical extension of present realities and of powers already claimed without evoking objection from other organs of the constitution. But my own view is that, though such extension should be seriously considered, it would preferably be the subject-matter of parliamentary enactment. In the first place, informed professional opinion is probably to the effect that your Lordships have no power to overrule decisions with prospective effect only; such opinion is itself a source of law; and your Lordships, sitting judicially, are bound by any rule of law arising extra-judicially. Secondly, to proceed by Act of Parliament would obviate any suspicion of endeavouring to upset one-sidedly the constitutional balance between executive, legislature and judiciary. Thirdly, concomitant problems could receive consideration – for example, whether other courts supreme within their own jurisdictions should have similar powers as regards the rule of precedent; whether machinery could and should be devised to apprise the courts of the potential repercussions of any particular decision; and whether any court (including an Appellate Committee in your Lordships' House) should sit in banc when invited to review a previous decision.

See, to the same effect, Lord Simon of Glaisdale's statement in *Miliangos* v. *George Frank (Textiles) Ltd* [1976] A.C. 443 at 490. Lord Diplock has also leant support to the idea. In a lecture several years earlier he referred to the fact that the retrospective impact of judicial decisions was one of the reasons that judges were reluctant to correct previous errors or to adapt an established rule to changed circumstances. Yet the retrospective effect of judicial decisions was simply a reflection of the legal fiction that the courts merely expounded the law as it always had been. The time had come, he thought, 'to reflect whether we should discard this fiction' and he thought that the development of prospective overruling in appellate courts in the United States deserved consideration. ('The Courts as Legislators', Holdsworth Club Lecture, 1965, pp. 17–18.)

The problems of prospective overruling are considered in the extract that follows:

Andrew Nicol, 'Prospective Overruling: A New Device for English Courts?' 39 *Modern Law Review*, 1976, p. 542

Prospective overruling is used by several [American] states and by the United States Supreme Court.... The justification most often advanced has been reliance. Several states, for instance, have been taking a fresh look at various immunities from tort suit.[1] A court may believe that the decision on which a particular immunity was based ought to be overruled, but it may also have to recognise that institutions which benefit from this immunity have not taken out insurance in reliance on it. Prospective overruling of the case granting the immunity has been used to break the *impasse*.... A somewhat different reliance has been claimed by prosecutors and police when faced with a court determined to tighten the procedures which must be followed in a

1. Units of government, *Molitor* v. *Kaneland Community School Dist.* No. 32, 163 N.E. 2d 89 (1959) Ill.; charities, *Kojis* v. *Doctor's Hospital*, 107 N.W. 2d 131 (1961) Wis.; intra-family, *Goller* v. *White*, 122 N.W. 2d 193 (1963) Wis.; religious institution, *Widell* v. *Holy Trinity Catholic Church*, 121 N.W. 2d 249 (1963) Wis. Plaintiff in this case had tripped over a negligently placed prayer kneeler.

criminal investigation. It is unfair, they say, to penalise the prosecution for failing to observe standards which were not set down until after the investigation has taken place.[2] The United States Supreme Court accepted this argument as one ground for limiting the effect of *Miranda* v. *Arizona*.[3]

Another justification for the use of prospective overruling has been that the desire which impels the court to overrule is the desire to implement a new policy, but a policy which need not be retroactive to be effective. In *Mapp* v. *Ohio*,[4] the United States Supreme Court held that evidence which was discovered in an unlawful search could not be used at trial. In *Linkletter* v. *Walker*,[5] the court held that the *Mapp* rule was to be prospective only. The new rule, the court said, was intended to discourage unlawful searches. It was too late to discourage those searches which had already taken place. Therefore nothing could be gained by giving *Mapp* retroactive effect....

Objections to prospective overruling

... (3) *It allows a court to make new law without applying it to the case before the court*: There are few lawyers now who would agree with Montesquieu that 'the judge are the mere mouthpieces of the law.'[6] The opportunity for creativity in choosing 'the' relevant statutes or precedents, in favouring one of a pair of antagonistic canons of construction,[7] in distinguishing a case on its facts or following it on principle, is apparent on both sides of the Atlantic.

However, a traditional restraint on this law-making power has been that courts are limited to expounding the law on the facts to dispose of the instant case and then add an unnecessary postscript as to how they will act in the future. Another version of the same argument is to say that the new rule is *obiter*, and therefore a waste of time.

Yet a similar practice is already used by the courts. In *Hedley Byrne* v. *Heller Partners*,[8] the House of Lords stated a new principle of liability for negligent misrepresentors, but the defendant, who came within the general description, was not held liable. The court added a rider, absolving from liability a representor who had expressly excluded his liability at the time he made his statement. An announcement by the court, as it prospectively overrules, that it will apply a new and different rule in other situations, is no more *obiter* than the House of Lords saying that in other cases it would hold negligent misrepresentors liable. In both situations, the court lays down a principle, argues that there is an exception, and finds that the parties to the suit come within the exception. While the principle is not conclusive, it is applied in the instant

2. *Johnston* v. *New Jersey*, 384 U.S. 719 (1966).

3. 384 U.S. 436 (1966). This case required the police to issue a caution before questioning a suspect, on pain of having the statement excluded from the trial. The caution is similar to the English one, except that the accused must also be told, if he is indigent, that he has the right to a free lawyer.

4. 367 U.S. 643 (1961).

5. 381 U.S. 618 (1965).

6. *Esprit de Lois*. XI 6.

7. See Llewellyn, 'Remarks on the Theory of Appellate Decision and the Rules or Canons of How Statutes are to be Construed', 3 Vand. L. Rev. 395, 401 (1950).

8. [1964] A.C. 465.

case, and it is difficult to see how it can be said to form no central part of the reasoning of the court.

(4) *The Hedley Byrne technique referred to in* (3) *is prospective overruling in disguise. A naked use of prospective overruling is therefore unnecessary*[9]: This is not so. In *Hedley Byrne*, the court was able to declare a new rule without applying it to the party in the instant case, but it achieved this result by qualifying substantively the new rule. If, the following day, a similar case had come up for judgment, but where the representor could not bring himself within the qualification, the representor would have been held liable, even though the representation may have been made many years previously. On the other hand, if *Candler* v. *Crane, Christmas*[10] had been prospectively overruled, the temporal qualification would have protected all persons (not liable under some other doctrine) who had made negligent misrepresentations before the date of the overruling. The *Hedley Byrne* technique goes some way, but not far enough, in protecting those who relied on a prior statement of the law.

(5) *A judge who uses prospective overruling has too much the appearance of a legislator*: It is argued[11] that however much judges are innovators in practice, in popular belief they are still the 'finders' of law, not its 'makers'. This belief, the argument runs, could not be sustained if judicial opinions read: 'this precedent is out-of-date and ought to be changed, but the change will only be effective from today.'

This writer has serious doubts as to whether the public would have greater respect for a court that slavishly followed precedent, than for one that tried to reconcile the competing claims of change and reliance. However, for the sake of appearances, there is another formula that the court might use: 'the rule that we announce today is and always was the correct view of the law. However, recognising the reliance which was placed on the old view, we will not apply the true view to events happening before today.'

This form was used in *Golak Nath* v. *State of Punjab*,[12] when the Supreme Court of India prospectively overruled the Land Reform Statutes. The court held that these statutes violated fundamental rights, guaranteed by the constitution, but because of the property interests which had been transferred and settled in reliance on them, they should be struck down with prospective effect only. . . .

(7) *If prospective overruling were available, it would make overruling more common and upset the certainty which results from a strict doctrine of* stare decisis: However, 'for the most part, certainty is an illusion.'[13] The discovery of old cases, the power to distinguish, the uncertainty of which facts will be believed in court[14]

9. Friedmann, 'Limits of Judicial Law-making and Prospective Overruling (1966) 29 M.L.R. 593, 605.

10. [1957] 2 K.B. 164, the Court of Appeal decision overruled in *Hedley Byrne*.

11. Devlin, 'Judges and Lawmakers' (1976) 39 M.L.R. 1.

12. [1967] 2 S.C.R. (India) 762 and see Pillai, 'Precedent in the House of Lords and the Doctrine of Prospective Overruling in the U.S.A. and India' (1967) 1 Sup. Ct.Jo. 79; Rajput, 'The Doctrine of *Stare Decisis* and Prospective Overruling' (1968) II Sup.Ct.Jo. 51.

13. Holmes, *The Path of the Law*, p. 465.

14. Jerome Frank, *Courts on Trial*, *passim*.

mean that the outcome of a particular dispute is not necessarily certain, even in a system where overruling is rarely used. It is appreciated that a sense of proportion is necessary. Many disputes are within the 'core application'[15] of a rule. Most rules would be affirmed on challenge, even by a court with the power to overrule prospectively. Nevertheless, one must ask, as Goodhart did,[16] whether, if the rule is unjust, certainty is not bought at too high a price. To add a gloss to Goodhart's comment; if through prospective overruling, we take away the element of individual reliance, then although stability and predictability are important, can it always be said that they will be more important than the removing of injustice or correcting the anomaly.

(8) *Prospective overruling is undesirable because it encourages judicial law reform. The principal thrust of law reform should come from a democratically elected Parliament, rather than an appointed judiciary:*

... In 1953, the Evershed Committee considered a proposal for financing litigation on points of law of general public interest. In its conclusion it stated:[17]

> We do not think this method of a law reform committee fully meets the public need. Legislation is slow and cumbersome. Parliamentary time is notoriously limited, and may in future become even more precious. Clarification of the law by judicial decision is a swifter and surer process which can go forward at all times, without regard to parliamentary time and quite independent of the political process.

Judicially developed law also has the advantage that it can be more cautious and developed according to experience. A judgment need not, indeed it is probably better if it does not, set out the whole ambit of the rule, complete with all qualifications. The courts are bound by the words of a statute, but only by the *ratio decidendi* of a decision. Statutory law has been scorned in the past for disturbing the growth of the common law. The scorn is often a reflection of the conservatism of the speaker, but it is true that the words of a statute have a rigidity which is not always desirable....

Thus, I conclude that judicial law-making is inevitable. Parliament and the courts, in the words of Jaffé, are in the law business together and should be continually at work on the legal fabric of our society.[18] The establishment of the Law Commission has reduced, but not abolished the part which the courts should play in law reform. They will always be the junior partner in the partnership, but even so their methods enjoy some advantages over statute. Prospective overruling gives the courts more scope for reforming judicially developed law, but does not deny the superior weight which must be given to the words of the senior partner.

15. H.L.A. Hart, *The Concept of Law*, Chap. VII and pp. 120 *et seq.*
16. 'Precedent in English and Continental Law' (1934) 50 L.Q.R. 934.
17. Final Report of the Committee on Supreme Court Practice and Procedure, H.M.S.O. Cmnd. 8878 (1953).
18. Jaffé, *English and American Judges as Lawmakers* (1969).

On the other hand, Lord Devlin has expressed himself unpersuaded by the arguments for prospective overruling:

Lord Devlin, 'Judges and Lawmakers'
39 *Modern Law Review*, 1976, p. 11

Courts in the United States have begun to circumvent retroactivity by the device of deciding the case before them according to the old law while declaring that in future the new law will prevail: or they may determine with what measure of retroactivity a new rule is to be enforced. This device has attracted the cautious attention of the House of Lords. I do not like it. It crosses the Rubicon that divides the judicial and the legislative powers. It turns judges into undisguised legislators. It is facile to think that it is always better to throw off disguises. The need for disguise hampers activity and so restricts the power. Paddling across the Rubicon by individuals in disguise who will be sent back if they proclaim themselves is very different from the bridging of the river by an army in uniform and with bands playing. If judges can make law otherwise than by a decision in the case at Bar, why do they wait for a case? Prevention is better than cure, so why should they not, when they see a troublesome point looming up, meet and decide how best to deal with it? Judicial lawmaking is at present, as Professor Jaffé phrases it,* 'a by-product of an *ad hoc* decision or process.' That this is so is of course in itself one of the objections to judicial lawmaking. Dependent as it is upon the willingness of individuals to litigate, it is casual and spasmodic. But to remove the tie with the *ad hoc* process would be to make a profound constitutional change with incalculable consequences. What is the business of a court of law? To make law or to do justice according to law? This question should be given a clean answer. If the law and justice of the case require the court to give a decision which its members think will not make good law for the future, I think that the court should give the just decision and refer the future to a lawmaking body.

See to same effect M.D.A. Freeman, 'Standards of Adjudication, Judicial Law-making and Prospective Overruling', 26 *Current Legal Problems*, 1973, pp. 166, 200–7. But see also Roger Traynor, 'Quo Vadis, Prospective Overruling: A Question of Judicial Responsibility', 1975, University of Birmingham, which supports the case for prospective overruling.

Question

Do you think that, on balance, prospective overruling has enough merit to justify the English judges experimenting with it?

(b) Better information for judges about the policy implications of law-making

If the judges are now supposed to engage increasingly in a more crea-

* L. Jaffé, *English and American Judges as Lawmakers*, p. 35.

tive role of judicial law-making, how can they inform themselves of the policy implications of alternatives offered to them? As has been seen above (p. 174), the English courts do not permit counsel to call evidence about the social and economic implications of existing or proposed future formulations of the law. Nor can counsel cite to the court written reports on such issues. In *Miliangos* Lord Simon suggested that if courts 'are to undertake legislative responsibilities, something might be done to equip them better for the type of decision-making which is involved. Official advice and a balanced executive view might be made available by a law officer or his counsel acting as amicus curiae' ([1975] 3 W.L.R. 792). Is this suggestion viable? Could one expect the law officers to provide such a service? If so, would the service be likely to be truly 'objective', or would it tend to put only or mainly the official view? Could there be a system for permitting others to come before the court (whether orally or through some form of written submission) to argue the policy issues? In the United States it is very common to have issues of law argued not simply by the parties but by other interested groups and bodies through *amicus curiae* written briefs. This institution is described in the piece that follows:

Ernest Angell, 'The Amicus Curiae: American Developments of English Institutions', 16 *International and Comparative Law Quarterly*, 1967, p. 1017

The amici whose names appear in the printed columns of reported decisions fall into three general categories. First, there are, as in the English practice, the legal representatives of the government, federal or state, counties, municipalities, government agencies and bodies. Secondly, there are private organizations of professional or other occupational membership: employers, business, commercial and industrial entities; labour unions; government and private industry employees by occupational class; bar associations and many others. In this category there should be included, though less common, a business unit which does not appear as part of an organized group and, rarely, an individual person. Thirdly, there are innumerable private associations, in general formally organized, which purport to speak for non-occupational, non-governmental, broad public interests; churches and religious bodies; minority groups such as Negroes (22 million in the United States) and Jews (5 million) civil libertarians, pacifists – the range is almost unlimited. . . .

Some reasons for the multiplicity of appearances amicus curiae *in American courts*
Avoiding dogmatic assertion of any single factor, one can state that several have disparately combined, without overall shaping by the courts. What does appear to be the most obvious is the American legal habit of presenting

printed or typed 'briefs'*, to marshal the facts and cite the pertinent authorities of cases, statutes and texts: (1) at the conclusion of a trial and often in support of a motion on evidence or for interlocutory remedy; and (2) universally on appeal to the reviewing court. In the absence of special leave granted to counsel for the *amicus* to make oral argument, the judges thus avoid the necessity of listening to expanded oratory of the intervenor, but do have the advantage of being able to study his written argument which may range beyond the industry and legal knowledge of counsel for the parties of record. Some judges give only perfunctory attention to oral pleading from any but the most persuasive advocates and rely much more heavily on the written word.

The universality of the written brief seems to have been born from the enormous sheer volume of American law – the decision of well over 100 federal courts and of several hundred courts of the 50 states; statutes, rules and regulations beyond the possibility of count; innumerable texts, the 'model' codes of the American Law Institute and 100 or so law 'journal' or law 'reviews' published by bar associations, learned societies and the many schools of law. No judge or lawyer can know or without immense labour pinpoint *ad hoc* anything more than a small fraction of the 'law' in America, compared with the wider familiarity of the English barrister with his own far more restricted volume of law. American counsel for a party of record may overlook what the court later finds to be the key point at issue and the available authorities. Our judges need more frequent and informed advice from the barristers before them; sometimes, perhaps frequently, this comes from the 'friend'....

Finally, the growth has been favoured by the proliferation in our society of the private non-profit organizations which exist to promote at the bar of courts, before legislatures and in public opinion, the interests of a class group and their convictions about the values of some social interest – the Red Indian, the conscientious objector, tighter control over excesses of the 'free press', the economic interest of railway clerks. Newspapers, magazines, television and radio abound with the highly vocal claims of conflicting legal interests put forward by organized groups alert for every occasion to speak publicly.

The courts cannot operate in an Olympian remoteness from the social scene; they must perforce listen to what class interest claims are laid upon the bench for judicial digestion. Moreover, the judges seek information and informed opinion by inviting such appearances by those believed to be able to render such assistance – by no means confined to law officers of government. It has become inevitable that the threads of argument spun by these intervening 'friends' are woven in to the fabric of formal decisions, sometimes visible to the inquiring eye outside the judicial chamber and, occasionally if more rarely, openly acknowledged in the formal opinion....

Procedure

... the court rules provide that *amicus* briefs may be filed merely with the consent of counsel for the formal parties to the case then pending; if consent is refused – as sometimes happens – then a motion may be made and the court passes upon this, generally granting it.

* See p. 242 below.

Question

The *amicus* plays an extremely limited role in English procedure, being mainly confined to representation of public interest issues by counsel for the Attorney-General or to representation of otherwise unrepresented interests or persons in civil proceedings. Do you think the *amicus* concept could be developed in England as in the USA? If not, why not?

Note

The concept of the *amicus* in English practice is mainly confined to the role of the Attorney-General. In *Adams* v. *Adams* [1970] 3 All E.R. 572 it was held that the Attorney-General has the right of intervention in a private suit whenever it may affect the prerogatives of the Crown. Certainly he had locus standi at the invitation of the court or with leave of the court. He also had a right of intervention at the invitation or with the permission of the court, where the suit raised any question of public policy on which the executive might have a view which it might desire to bring to the notice of the court (576–7, per Simon P.).

The concept is, however, also used in other circumstances. One example is the intervention of the Law Society. Sometimes it appears to protect its own interest in the legal aid fund – see, for instance, *Hanning* v. *Maitland* (*No. 2*) [1970] 1 All E.R. 812. But sometimes it appears in a more detached role – see, for instance, *Wallersteiner* v. *Moir* (*No. 2*) [1975] 1 All E.R. 849, in which it appeared as guardian of the rules of etiquette of solicitors in a case raising the propriety of contingency fee arrangements.

Another increasingly important development is the role of the Commission for Racial Equality and the Equal Opportunities Commission in promoting litigation and in arguing cases raising issues within their field of concern. In *Nassé* v. *Social Research Council*, for instance, counsel for both Commissions appeared in their own right in the Court of Appeal. In the House of Lords the law lords at first objected but then allowed it with the consent of the other parties. (Information supplied by counsel.)

See also Attorney General's Reference No. 2 of 1979 [1979] *Criminal Law Review*, 585, in which the Law Commission submitted a memorandum on the law of burglary to assist the court.

One problem with the role of amici is that procedure in English cases is almost entirely oral. If the concept of amici were to be developed, would there be value in permitting legal argument to be presented in written form in 'briefs', as in the United States? The difference between the two systems was discussed by Professor Delmar Karlen of New York University, rapporteur of an Anglo-American exchange of jurists to examine each other's system:

Delmar Karlen, 'Appeal in England and the United States', 78 *Law Quarterly Review*, 1962, p. 371

Papers on appeal

An outstanding difference between the two nations is the fact that 'briefs' are required in the United States, whereas in England they are not. The brief is a full-dress argument in writing often running to fifty or more printed or mimeographed pages in length. It states the facts, outlines the claimed errors in the proceedings below, and cites and discusses the authorities claimed to justify reversal or affirmance. The appellant serves his brief on the other side well in advance of the time for oral argument, and the respondent then serves his answering brief on the appellant, again well in advance of oral argument. Sometimes the appellant serves a reply brief.

In England such a document is virtually unknown. The closest approach to it is the 'case' normally required from both sides in the House of Lords and Privy Council. This, however, is a very abbreviated paper, seldom running more than six or seven pages in length, and is intended only as a preliminary outline of the extended oral argument to be made later. It does not discuss authorities in detail, or argue the propositions of law to be relied upon. Relatively few cases are cited (although this may be attributable more to the English theory of precedent than to the form which papers on appeal take). In the other appellate courts of England, no written arguments of any kind are used.

In both England and the United States, the judges are furnished with a record on appeal. It consists of the notice of appeal, pleadings and other formal documents, the judgment below, and so much of the evidence as may be relevant as to the questions raised on appeal. There is this difference, however. In England, there is almost always a reasoned (though often extemporaneous) opinion by the judge below, outlining the evidence, the authorities relied upon, the decision and the reasons therefore. In the United States, such a document is frequently lacking. If the case has been tried by jury, as many cases are, in place of a reasoned opinion, there will be simply the judge's instructions to the jury, without any citation of the authorities upon which his propositions of law are based. If the case has been tried without a jury, there ordinarily will be only formalized findings of fact and conclusions of law, again without the citation of authorities. Sometimes there is a reasoned opinion below, as where the case has gone through an intermediate stage of appeal, but this is the exception rather than the rule.

In England, the record on appeal is almost always mimeographed. In the United States, it often has to be printed at a great increase in cost. The practice, however, varies from one court to another, some courts permitting mimeographing or other relatively cheap forms of duplication.

The Evershed Committee considered but rejected the idea of introducing something akin to the American written brief:

(c) Should English appeal courts consider written argument?

Final Report of the (Evershed) Committee on Supreme Court Practice and Procedure, 1953, Cmnd. 8878

572. ... it seemed to some of us, at first sight, that the American system possesses certain marked advantages over the procedure for hearing appeals in this country, at any rate from the point of view of the saving of costs. These apparent advantages may be briefly summarized as follows:

(*a*) Since the grounds of appeal are precisely stated and the authorities relied on are cited in the written 'brief', there is no room for surprise. Not only are the members of the court apprised at once of the point that is to be decided, but the other side are fully aware, before the hearing, of what is going to be said against them.

(*b*) Formulation beforehand of the precise grounds of the appeal makes it possible in many cases to eliminate much of the evidence, both oral and documentary, which came before the trial Judge but which is not relevant to the particular question that forms the subject of appeal. This enables considerable economies to be made in the transcribing of evidence and duplication of documents.

(*c*) The 'brief' constitutes a permanent record of the argument on either side, which the judges can take away and consider at leisure. They are not so dependent therefore, on the notes which they are themselves able to make during the hearing or on their fleeting recollection of counsel's oral argument.

(*d*) Above all, at the cost of preparing the written argument, there is, at any rate in all but the smallest cases, an immediate economy in relation to the time occupied in the hearing of the appeal. As already pointed out, the consumption of time, involving as it does the payment of refresher fees to counsel, is the most expensive feature of our English appellate procedure.

573. Whatever may be thought to be the advantages of the American system of 'briefs', however, we found singularly little enthusiasm for it amongst the witnesses whose opinions we sought. The members of the Court of Appeal whom we consulted were emphatically opposed to the adoption of such a system in this country as also were the representatives of the Bar Council and Law Society. We also had the advantage of hearing evidence from Mr Justice Frankfurter, of the United States Supreme Court, as well as from Mr

John W. Davis, who was able to speak with a wealth of experience of appellate work in the United States Courts. We gained the impression from these witnesses that they were by no means whole-heartedly in favour of the American system of conducting appeals, but that they rather envied the system prevailing here of unrestricted oral argument. They appeared to regard the American 'brief' system, with its strict limitation of the time for oral argument, as a necessary evil forced upon them by the pressure of appellate work, the volume of which is so great that it would be simply impossible to get through it if unrestricted oral argument were permitted.

574. After giving the matter our careful consideration we have had little doubt in coming to the conclusion that the American system would provide in this country a less satisfactory system for conducting appeals than that now prevailing. Furthermore, we are satisfied that the American system would be quite unsuitable for adoption in this country in view of the different conditions prevailing here and would not be likely to lead to any marked reduction in the costs of appeals. Our reasons for arriving at these conclusions are briefly as follows:

(*a*) We are satisfied that there are real and substantial advantages in our system of unrestricted oral argument, whereby every point in a party's case is thoroughly sifted in the process of discussion between counsel and the members of the court. Furthermore, our system enables the members of the court to work together as a team, each member having the advantage of hearing the questions put by the other members and of weighing the answers of counsel thereto. Under this system, it is thought, there is a far greater chance of the court arriving at a common conclusion, so that in the majority of cases the parties have the advantage of a unanimous decision, and the court's decision on the question in issue carries all the greater authority.

(*b*) By contrast, the system prevailing in the United States leads to a higher proportion of dissenting judgments. It has seemed to us that the members of the appellate court, reading the 'briefs' and documents for themselves, and without the advantages of hearing unrestricted oral argument together, must tend to bring their individual minds to the case rather than work as a team.

(*c*) Under the American system there is likely to be much greater delay in reaching a decision. Having regard to the time which must be allowed for filing the 'briefs' – first that of the appellant, then that of the respondent, and possibly a 'brief' in reply by the appellant – a considerable time must elapse before the case can be brought on for hearing. What is perhaps more seious is the fact that the court can rarely deliver judgment at once, on the termination of the oral argument. The oral argument having been necessarily abbreviated, the members of the court must go away and digest the written argument and evidence, by reading it to themselves after the hearing, before they can form their opinions and are ready to give judgment. In the appellate courts of the United States almost every judgment must be reserved, and we were informed that it is not uncommon for a substantial time to elapse, often extending to many months, before the judgments are delivered.

(*d*) Perhaps the strongest objection to the introduction in this country of anything resembling the American system for conducting appeals arises from the fact that here the legal profession is divided into two branches. The system works in America largely because the profession is differently organized. The American lawyer is a member of a firm and has at his disposal an office staff of trained lawyers. The lawyer who is conducting the case can thus be relieved of the spadework of preparing the written 'brief' which a more junior member of the firm's staff can do. It is not difficult to fix a fair inclusive fee to cover the whole conduct of an appeal including both the preparation of the 'brief' in the office and the oral argument in court. If a similar system were adopted in this country, it is not to be thought that solicitors would find it possible, even if it were otherwise desirable, to prepare the 'briefs' in their offices. Few solicitors' offices in this country could have the staff to do so; and in any case it would be unfair to counsel who would be instructed to conduct the oral argument that he should have no hand in preparing the written 'brief'. In practice it would be inevitable that counsel would be employed to settle the 'brief'. The time which counsel would spend on doing so would not usually be less than, and might often far exceed, the time which under the present system would be occupied in conducting the oral argument. The fees charged by counsel for preparing a written 'brief' would necessarily be governed to a large extent by the time occupied, and it seems to follow inexorably that substantial fees would have to be charged. It is true that a somewhat smaller fee than that now paid would possibly be sufficient to cover the abbreviated oral argument, and there would be no refreshers. At the same time it is to be remembered that counsel would have to get up the case twice – once for the purpose of preparing the 'brief', and again for the oral argument, for which purpose he would have to be prepared for any point that might be raised against him in court. Bearing in mind this additional burden on counsel, we do not think that any marked reduction in counsel's fees could be expected. On the contrary, the overall total of counsel's fees for the preparation and hearing of an appeal might well be greater than it is at present.

575. For these reasons we do not think that the introduction of a system of written 'briefs' such as that prevailing in the United States would be likely to lead in the end to any material saving of costs, and bearing in mind the other objections to which we have referred we are not disposed to recommend the adoption of any such system in this country.

A written brief in an English case

Rondel v. *Worsley*
[1966] 3 W.L.R. 950
Court of Appeal

The plaintiff sued a barrister for negligence in the conduct of his defence at the Old Bailey. His statement of claim was struck out by Lawton J. as disclosing no cause of action. He applied to the Court of Appeal for leave to appeal. At that time he was acting in person. His application asked for permission to formulate another statement of claim and to get a solicitor to help him with it. In view of the importance of the matter, leave to appeal was given. After obtaining leave the plaintiff was assisted voluntarily by a solicitor who prepared for the consideration of the court a typewritten document of 116 pages setting out the arguments and authorities in support of the contention that barristers were liable for negligence. The members of the court agreed to receive the brief, and when the hearing began on 13 June 1966, Lord Denning MR referred to it as a very valuable document and said that the court had read it.

Commenting in the course of his judgment on the written brief, LORD JUSTICE DANCKWERTS, however, said:

> There are two other matters on which I want to comment and which I trust will not be allowed to occur in future cases.
>
> The solicitor acting for Rondel was allowed to present to us a typewritten document of 116 pages, in which he set out the legal arguments on behalf of the plaintiff's case, something in the style of the briefs which are allowed under the quite different procedure of the courts in the United States of America. Secondly, at the conclusion of the arguments by counsel on behalf of the defendant, Rondel was allowed to read nine typewritten pages, in the form of a reply which had obviously been prepared for him, notwithstanding that the arguments on his behalf had been presented by counsel instructed by the Official Solicitor, who were ready to make such arguments in reply as were proper. Both these matters were wholly irregular and contrary to the practice of the court and in my opinion should not be allowed as a precedent for future proceedings. It appears that counsel was in fact available to appear for Rondel without a fee, and the course mentioned above was deliberately adopted (p. 968).

[Neither of the other two judges referred to the matter.]

Question

The consideration by the Evershed Committee of the desirability of written argument seemed to proceed on the basis that it was a question of all or nothing – either we stay with our present procedure or we go over to the American system of written argument supplemented by extremely short oral argument. Can you see any way of combining the two procedures and, if so, would this be an improvement in our system of arguing cases and particularly of appeals?

Note

There have in fact been a few recent cases in which counsel have addressed written argument to the House of Lords. One example was *Nassé* v. *Social Research Council* [1979] 3 All E.R. 673 in which counsel for three of the parties submitted written summaries of their oral arguments which were accepted by the House of Lords.

7
Subsidiary sources of law

The two main sources of law – legislation and judicial decisions – dominate the field of law-making, but there are lesser sources that require to be mentioned. They are (1) textbooks; (2) custom; (3) European law; and (4) 'strings and mirrors'.

1. Textbooks

According to orthodox theory, textbooks fall into two categories – those that are authoritative and those that are not. Authoritative writers are those who are dead and in particular a select band of hallowed names such as Bracton, Glanvil, Littleton, Coke, Hale and Blackstone. Most practitioners go through their entire professional lives without ever having occasion to cite any of these giants. But if their views are brought to the attention of a court, they have an extra patina of respectability not available to lesser writers. On the other hand, it is questionable whether in practice their views are treated as any more persuasive – this depends on what they said and what other authorities counsel has been able to deploy. These names certainly evoke in English lawyers a Pavlovian respectful response. But this does not mean that their views are more likely to be followed.

The rule that an author must be dead before he could be cited as authority was said to be based on the somewhat feeble ground that until then it could not be known whether he might change his mind. (On that basis no living judge ought to have been cited either.) In practice lawyers circumvented the rule by the simple device of citing a living author and then saying they were adopting his views as part of their argument. But in recent years the courts have taken a more relaxed attitude and counsel would not today be reprimanded for boldly presenting the work of a living author in support of his proposition. There are a number of scholars whose books and articles are regularly honoured by being cited both by counsel and by the judges in their decisions. (Professor Rupert Cross' book on *Evidence*, Dicey on *Conflicts of Law*, Rayden on *Divorce*, Maxwell on *The Interpretation of Statutes*, Archbold on *Criminal Pleading, Evidence and Practice*, and Dymond on *Death Duties*, are familiar examples.)

But the contribution of scholars does not have the same role in the English law-making process that it has in many other countries. In the United States or on the continent of Europe, for instance, no self-respecting practitioner would present an argument to the court on a point of law without directing the court's attention to the views of the leading academic commentators. The decisions of the Supreme Court of the United States as well equally as those of lower courts cite a mass of academic authority as a matter of course.

The difference is probably due to the relatively low esteem in which academic lawyers have traditionally been held in the English legal profession. For centuries the only two English universities, Oxford and Cambridge, did not even teach English law. They taught only Roman and Canon law which were irrelevent to practitioners. Those who went into the profession as barristers learnt their law first at the Inns of Court and then in practice. Blackstone is said to have inaugurated the teaching of English law at the universities with his famous course on the Common Law from 1753, but in reality the teaching of the subject lapsed after his resignation. In 1800 the Downing Chair of the Laws of England was founded in Cambridge, but the subject did not flourish there either. When in 1846 a Select Committee inquired into the state of legal education in this country, it reported that 'no legal education worthy of the name is at this moment to be had'.* Whereas in Berlin, for instance, there were fourteen professors teaching some thirty branches of the law to hundreds of students, in Oxford and Cambridge there appeared to be neither lectures, nor examinations, nor for that matter any students.†

The Select Committee's Report led to changes. In 1852 Oxford established a B.C.L. degree and in 1855 Cambridge started an LL.B.

* *Report of the Select Committee on Legal Education*, 1846, Vol X, British Parliamentary Papers, p. lvi, para. 3.

† Ibid., para. 2.

degree. Law faculties were created at London University and in provincial universities as they were set up. By 1908 there were eight law faculties. But they had to struggle to establish their academic respectability. It was still a moot point whether law was a fit subject for university legal education. (That this particular canard dies hard may be judged from the fact that Lord Diplock told the annual meeting of the Society of Public Teachers of Law in 1966 that he had serious doubts on the question.‡ Lord Diplock was at the time not only chairman of the Council of Legal Education of the Inns of Court, but chairman of the Institute of Advanced Legal Education at London University!) The acid test of whether law was suitable for inclusion in university courses was whether it was 'liberal'. A distinction was drawn for this purpose between liberal education on the one hand and practical, technical or vocational training on the other. The essence of the difference between the two, it was thought, lay in the different content of each. Thus Roman law, jurisprudence and legal history were ideal subject-matter for liberal education, whilst company, tax or labour law manifestly were not. The closer the subject came to being concerned with the affairs of the ordinary man or, worse, the market place, the less it qualified as 'liberal'. Common law subjects such as contract and tort and even property law were somehow exempted, even though they plainly had practical importance.

The fallacy that liberality of pursuit is limited to certain subject-matter is not a new one. A hundred years after Newton's *Principia* Oxford and Cambridge were still making virtually no contribution to scientific thought because they refused to accept that science was a proper subject for study. In the medieval university the seven liberal arts were grammar, rhetoric, dialectic, geometry, music, arithmetic and astronomy. After the Renaissance the emphasis shifted to the language and literature of the Hebrews, the Romans and above all of the Greeks. More recently the classics have receded, as the concept of liberal education has expanded to embrace the imaginative and philosophical literature of modern Europe. Today none but the most sheltered humanist would deny that science has an honoured place in this great tradition.

The view that regards the content of liberal education as crucial ignores the fact that the most liberal subjects can be and often are taught in a narrow, pedantic and scholastic manner which is the very antithesis of the spirit of liberal education. It is not the content at

‡ *Journal of the Society of Public Teavhers of Law*, 1966, p. 193.

a particular place or time which is fundamental, but rather the way in which that content is imparted. As Samuel Alexander said: 'Liberality is a spirit of pursuit not a choice of subject'. If a subject is one in which principles can be discovered and reasons for facts can be related to the principles, then such a subject can be made the basis for liberal education. A practical subject, such as company law, can be taught in one of two ways – either as a means to achieving technical proficiency, or alternatively as a means of studying the problems of business organisation as a phase of human experience to be appreciated and understood as part of the economic and social problems of a wider society.

As a result of their worries about the liberality of the subject-matter the university law schools for decades failed to teach some of the most ordinary practical subjects which today we take for granted. The result was that even the minority of practitioners who had read law at the university, tended to regard their academic law studies as largely irrelevant to their professional work. They barely read the academic journals and, when they did, they found their prejudices amply confirmed. Worse, the teaching of the subjects that were supposed to be liberal was frequently arid, technical and dull. The legal academic world, with few exceptions, was detached from the concerns of the real world and was understandably ignored by both practitioners and judges.

In the past two decades this has all been changing. The law faculties are teaching subjects of importance to practitioners; books and articles in academic journals are of direct relevance to them; both teaching and textbooks are improved; practitioners have normally read law at university*; contact between the two worlds is more common and more on the basis of mutual respect instead of the old mutual disparagement. In this developing relationship it is probable that the courts will increasingly welcome the contributions of scholars as a useful additional source of guidance and support. But given the long tradition of distance between the profession and the academic community, it would be surprising if scholars came to exercise the same influence on the development of the law that they do in many other Western countries.

Even the judge who is also a scholar feels the difference between

* Between 1970 and 1978 the proportion of new solicitors who were law graduates rose from 40 per cent to 60 per cent – an astonishing rate of increase. (*Report of the Royal Commission on Legal Services*, 1979, Cmnd. 7648, para. 38.13, p. 609.)

the two forms of creativity. MR JUSTICE MEGARRY expressed this with his usual felicity when commenting on the authority of his own text-book which had been cited to him by counsel in a case:

I would add one comment, in amplification of certain observations that I made when during the argument counsel cited a passage from the 3rd edition of Megarry & Wade's Real Property. It seems to me that words in a book written or subscribed to by an author who is or becomes a judge have the same value as words written by any other reputable author, neither more nor less. The process of authorship is entirely different from that of judicial decision. The author, no doubt, has the benefit of a broad and comprehensive study of his chosen subject as a whole, together with a lengthy period of gestation, and intermittent opportunities for reconsideration. But he is exposed to the perils of yielding to preconceptions, and he lacks the advantage of that impact and sharpening of focus which the detailed facts of a particular case bring to the judge. Above all, he has to form his ideas without the aid of the purifying ordeal of skilled argument on the specific facts of a contested case. Argued law is tough law. . . . I would therefore give credit to the words of any reputable author in book or article as expressing tenable and arguable ideas, as fertilisers of thought, and as conveniently expressing the fruits of research in print, often in apt and persuasive language. But I would do no more than that; and in particular I would expose those views to the testing and refining process of argument. Today, as of old, by good disputing shall the law be well known. [*Cordell* v. *Second Clanfield Properties Ltd* [1968] 3 W.L.R. 864, 872.]

2. Custom

There are several separate meanings of the word 'custom' as a source of law. The first is *general custom* in the sense of common usage. It seems possible that after the Norman Conquest this was a real source of some law. As the country was gradually reduced to centralised order by the judges travelling around the country, they must have based at least some of their decisions on the common custom of the realm. According to Sir Frederick Pollock, 'The common law is a customary law if, in the course of about six centuries, the undoubting belief and uniform language of everybody who had occasion to consider the matter were able to make it so.' Coke described custom as 'one of the main triangles of the laws of England' and for Blackstone general customs were 'the universal rule of the whole kingdom and form the common law in its stricter and more usual signification'. But these claims are likely to be more poetic than historically accurate. In fact a high proportion of the so-called customs were almost certainly invented by the judges.

An article in the *Law Quarterly Review* in 1893 claimed, for instance, that there was 'a very strong presumption that the common law originated in the judicial adoption of the common customs of the realm'.* The kind of evidence cited for the proposition, however, hardly bears the weight of the argument. Thus the man who so negligently looked after his house that it caught fire and the fire spread to his neighbour's house was liable 'by the law and custom of the realm'. But what sort of custom was this? Is the plea that it was customary for every man to look after his own property so that fires did not arise and spread? Or is it rather that when such fires occurred the house owner was customarily held liable? The custom, in other words, was of the courts rather than of the people. Similarly, it is said that the law regarding the liability of carriers and innkeepers was founded on the custom of the realm. But what was the nature of the custom? Did the common carriers voluntarily pay their customers when goods entrusted to them were lost or damaged? It seems unlikely. Or did the populace demand that the rule be so? Even making the large and somewhat improbable assumption that the public did make such a demand, this hardly amounts to a popular custom but merely to popular pressure for a rule.† Although therefore, no doubt, general custom may have played some part in the early development of the law, it seems probable that even at that time the judges were the true originators of a good deal of the custom of the realm.

The second main meaning of custom as a source of law is in the sense of *local custom* in contrast to the common law. From early times the judges, for obvious reasons, established a series of rigorous tests or hurdles that had to be met by anyone claiming the benefit of some exception to the common law. The judges were trying to impose the Westminster brand of justice and did not look benevolently on too many local variations. There were seven main tests for a local custom:

(1) It must have existed from 'time whereof the memory of man runneth not to the contrary', or from time immemorial. This concept was arbitrarily defined by statute to mean from 1189. If proof could be brought that the custom did not exist in 1189, it was rejected. Thus in *Simpson* v. *Wells* (1872) it was shown that the appellant could not have a customary right to set up a refreshment stall on a public footway as he claimed from 'statute sessions' because these were first

* Greer, 'Custom in the Common Law', 9 *Law Quarterly Review*, 1893, pp. 157–60.

† I am indebted for these examples and the analysis presented to E.K. Braybrooke, 'Custom as a source of English law', 50 *Michigan Law Review*, 1951, pp. 71, 74.

authorised in the fourteenth century. More recently Mr Justice Lawton rejected a claim by a barrister that there was a customary rule that barristers could not be sued – on the ground that dicta in a case in 1435 suggested that at that time a barrister might be sued. (*Rondel* v. *Worsley* [1966] 2 W.L.R. 300, 307. However he was able to find other reasons to uphold the immunity.)

(2) The custom must have existed continuously since 1189 – any proved interruption defeated the claim.

(3) The custom must have been enjoyed peaceably without opposition.

(4) It must have been felt to be obligatory.

(5) It must be capable of being defined precisely – a requirement of certainty.

(6) Customs must be consistent one with another.

(7) Finally they must be reasonable – if it could be proved that it would have been unreasonable in 1189, again the claim would fail.

These formidable qualifying conditions gave the judges ample powers to reject any local custom they regarded as unsuitable for recognition.

Inevitably, claims to local custom in modern times are rare. They do occur however from time to time. In *Egerton* v. *Harding* [1974] 3 All E.R. 689, for instance, the courts upheld a customary duty on one of the parties to fence land against cattle straying from the common. Another case in the same year concerned the alleged right of the Mayor, Bailiff and Burgess and others to indulge in lawful sports including shooting on land in the centre of the borough of New Windsor:

New Windsor Corporation v. *Mellor*
[1974] 2 All E.R. 510 (Chancery Division)

The respondent caused certain land in the centre of the borough of New Windsor to be registered in the register of town or village greens maintained by the registration authority under s.3 of the Commons Registration Act 1965, claiming that the inhabitants of the borough had by custom acquired the right to indulge in lawful sports and pastimes on it. The borough objected to the registration and an inquiry was held by the Chief Commons Commissioner. The evidence before the Commissioner showed that in 1651 a lease of the land had been granted by the borough for 40 years, the lease containing a covenant by the lessee that it should be lawful for the 'Mayor Bailiffs and Burgesses and ... all and every other person and persons to have access' to the land 'as well as to exercise and use shooting or any other lawful pastime for their recreation at all convenient times'. The lessee also covenanted to set up a pair of butts 'for the inhabitants of the ... town to shoot at' and to repair and maintain them, and not to do anything which might be 'hurtful to the shooting or any other pastime then to be exercised for recreation of the people'. Further leases of the land for 40 year terms, containing similar covenants, were granted in 1704 and 1749. In 1819 the corporation granted a three year lease, the lease being made subject to the right 'of the Native Bachelors of Windsor of exercising all lawful sports games and pastimes' over the land, and, in 1822 a similar lease 'subject to the rights and privileges of the Bachelors of Windsor who are entitled to use the [land] for all lawful recreations and amusements'. After the Inclosure Act 1813 the borough held the land by virtue of their statutory title under that Act. Following an inclosure award in 1819, they held it free from any rights of common of pasture or turbary, but still subject to any rights to use it for lawful sports and pastimes to which it was formerly subject. The land was used annually for 'revels' until the 1840s. There were also in evidence extracts from newspaper reports and reports of meetings, a newspaper extract of October 1875 recording that the land had been used for sports by a large number of people and that the mayor had vetoed the holding of the sports, on wrong advice given to him by the town clerk on the legal effect of the inclosure award. From 1875 onwards the borough refused to recognise that the inhabitants had any right to use the land for recreation and accordingly it was no longer used for that purpose. At the time of the respondent's registration the land had for some years been used partly as a school sports ground and partly as a car park. It was listed in the development plan for the borough as the site for a multi-storey car park. On the evidence the Commissioner confirmed the registration, holding that a customary right to indulge in lawful sports and pastimes on the land had been acquired by the inhabitants of the locality from time immemorial and that the land was therefore a 'town or village green' within ss. 1 (1) and 22 (1) of the 1965 Act. The borough appealed, contending, inter alia, (i) that the evidence did not support the conclusion of long usage since there was no direct evidence of any user and the Commission had found that there had been no such user since 1875, and (ii) that the user was incapable of existing as a custom since, from the terms of the covenants in the 1651 lease, the user was not confined to the inhabitants of the borough, i.e. the 'Burgesses', but extended to 'all and every other person', i.e. persons residing outside the borough.

FOSTER J:

Long usage

There was, in my judgment, ample evidence on which the Commissioner could come to the conclusion that there had been long usage, and I, for my part, on that evidence would have come to the same conclusion.

That the claim had been made as of right

The Commissioner came to the conclusion that the user has been as of right, in view of the leases granted, subject to the right and to the events in 1819 and 1822, to which I have referred. In my judgment, his conclusion was right.

That the right claimed is capable of existing as a custom

It is well established that to create a custom the user must have been, by the inhabitants of an area, defined by reference to the limits of some recognised division of land such as a town. . . . This raises a question of construction of the words used in the lease of 1651. The Commissioner held that the words 'all and every other person or persons' and the words 'the people' must be read in their context and the covenant to set up a pair of butts 'for the inhabitants of the said town' to shoot at shows that those wide expressions should be limited to the inhabitants of the town. He therefore concluded that the custom was confined to the inhabitants of a particular locality.

Counsel for the borough submitted that the word 'burgesses' included all the inhabitants of the town, so that the expression 'all and every other person' must refer to persons residing outside the town, and reliance was placed on the definition of 'burgesses' in Wharton's Law Lexicon: 'Generally the inhabitants of a borough or walled town'. In Stroud's Judicial Dictionary, 'Burgesses' is defined as referring to men of trade. Earlier in the lease there are found the words 'Mayor Bailiffs Burgesses and their Successors', showing that the words 'Mayor Bailiffs and Burgesses' refer to the body corporate rather than to every person living in the town. It might well be ultra vires for the corporate body to provide benefits for persons not living within its boundaries, and it may be, but this is pure surmise, since there is only an extract from the lease, that after the words 'all and every other person or persons' there may have followed some words such as 'being inhabitants of the town', which occur later. I have, however, come to the conclusion that the Commissioner was correct in confining the expressions used to the inhabitants of the town.

Does the custom arise from time immemorial?

Counsel for the respondent submitted that once the first three points were established the court should be astute to find that the origin of the custom was from time immemorial, and he relied for his submission on three cases: *Cocksedge* v. *Fanshaw*[1], *Malcomson* v. *O'Dea*[2] and *Johnson* v. *Barnes*[3]. Counsel for the borough referred me to a statute of Henry VIII[4] which was not cited to the Commissioner, to show that the origin of the usage stemmed from that statute and not from time immemorial. If it could be shown that the right to use Bachelor's Acre stems from a statute passed after 1189, then the claim of a custom would be defeated (see *Simpson* v. *Wells*[5]).

Section 4 of that statute is in these terms:

'. . . (4) and also that Butts be made on this Side the Feast of St. *Michael* the Archangel next coming, in every City, Town and Place, by the Inhabitants of every such City, Town and Place, according to the Law of ancient Time used; (5) and that the Inhabitants and Dwellers in every of them be compelled to make and continue such Butts, upon Pain to forfeit for every three Months so lacking, xx.s. (6) and that the said Inhabitants shall

1. (1779) 1 Doug. KB 119.
2. (1863) 10 H.L. Cas. 593.
3. (1872) L.R. 7 C.P. 592.
4. 33 Hen. 8 c.9.
5. (1872) L.R. 7 Q.B. 214.

> exercise themselves with Long-Bows in shooting at the same, and elsewhere, in holy Days and other Times convenient.'

But from the terms of s. 4 (4) the words 'according to the Law of ancient Time used' show that the making of butts was not started by virtue of that Act. The provisions do not negative the right having existed from time immemorial.

The court should therefore be astute to find the origin from time immemorial and, in my judgment, the Commissioner was right to do so. For these reasons, in my judgment the appeal fails and I propose to dismiss it.

The question has been much canvassed as to whether a local custom is law regardless of the court's decision. If this is so the court recognises the custom because it is already law. This represents Professor Rupert Cross's view.* But there is an inevitable circularity about the argument. If the custom is not recognised, it was not law; if it is recognised, it was. It seems more accurate to posit that the custom is authenticated by the judicial decision which upholds it. Professor Cross objects that this is the equivalent of saying that a statute is not law until it has been interpreted by a judge. But the two cases are very different. A statute is undeniably law – every word is law and there is no possibility of argument about it. The document is tangible and certain and the contents are known even if the meaning is in dispute. There could never be litigation testing whether a statutory provision is law. By contrast, the fact that there is litigation over the existence of the custom indicates that there are serious doubts as to whether a court will uphold the claim. An alleged custom, the validity of which is as yet unrecognized by a court, may be more than half way to being a law; but it lacks the accolade of recognition without which it is merely a claim.

Much the same is true of *mercantile custom* which is often cited in the books as another instance of custom as a source of common law. The practices of merchants, it is said, were recognised by the courts and became rules of law because they were felt by the courts to be binding. But this is again to pay excessive regard to the rhetoric, and not to focus on the likely reality of the situation. The point has been made by a learned commentator, E.K. Braybrooke:

> If we take as typical of the custom of merchants the rule that if A draw upon B a bill payable to C, B (if he accept the bill) is bound thereby to pay C, we may readily see expressed in this rule the result of a long-continued course of practice among merchants; the crux of the matter is that acceptors of such bills have in the past acknowledged their liability to pay the payee, though

* R. Cross, *Precedent in English Law* (3rd edn, 1977), pp. 162–3.

there may be no privity of contract between them. All that remains to be done is for the courts to enforce this customary rule by allowing C to succeed in an action against B. But is the matter quite as simple as it looks? If acceptors of bills have customarily acknowledged their liability in the past, is it not because by all acknowledged *rules of contract* they are bound to A in any case. Certainly it may be the custom of merchants to *make* contracts of this kind; but how can the mere existence of this custom persuade a court to grant an action to the payee, in contradiction to its fundamental theories of the law of contract? This custom of merchants is a more complex affair than appears at first sight. The development of the bill of exchange in the form summarised above owes at least as much to the theories of lawyers as to the usages of merchants; and the notion of the direct liability of the acceptor to the payee is the end-product of a complex process of juristic reasoning on the part of ... lawyers'[1]... The adoption of mercantile customs by the common law courts was the product of a deliberate decision, motivated by a desire to extend the jurisdiction of those courts, not by any belief that the law-creating effect of popular custom compelled them to apply the rules of the law merchant professed to be based on such custom.[2]

When in 1657 Chief Justice Hobart said 'the custome of merchants is part of the common law of this kingdom, of which the judges ought to take notice'

the operative part of the statement was not the semi-fictional statement that the custom of merchants was part of the common law of the kingdom but the assertion that the judges would take notice ... of it.[3]

The same was true of the famous cases of the nineteenth and twentieth centuries concerning the attitude of the common law courts to mercantile custom:

We find this fact of deliberate adoption readily deducible from the decisions.... We may indeed see in the history of mercantile custom a reflection of the pattern which we may suppose the history of the general custom of the realm to have followed. No doubt at some early time the complex of popular and feudal practices and usages which was in fact, and not in name merely, the common custom of the realm, furnished a rich storehouse of rules and standards and principles from which the judges might draw the materials to lay down the foundation of fundamental rules and principles on which the common law was built. But once these fundamental rules and principles are established the same habit of mind which endows popular custom with what authority it possesses endows them with perpetual life; they become fixed, unalterable, fundamental. The general customs of the realm lose their

1. E.K. Braybrooke, 'Custom as a source of English law', 50 *Michigan Law Review*, 1951, pp. 84–5.
2. Ibid., p. 86.
3. Ibid., p. 87. There follows some discussion of the cases, which has been omitted here.

law-creating force; they can no longer prevail against the fundamental rules which were their own creation.... But the tradition that the common law is no other than the common custom of the realm survives as a fossilised doctrine long after it has ceased to correspond fully with the facts. Its survival may indeed become a source of embarrassment to those whose charge it is to lay down the common law; and so, we may conjecture, the doctrine becomes converted into a rule of pleading whose object is to prevent the judges, who are repositories of the common law, from possible coercion by evidence of a strong current of popular usage which they are unwilling to accept.[4]

What Braybrooke wrote of general, local and mercantile custom seems more convincing than the conventional theory that the courts were meekly following in the wake of the people in recognizing the existence of the custom. It is the court not the people that exercises the decisive voice. In this sense it is possible to acknowledge that custom is, and always has been, a vital source of law. In a multitude of ways the courts are constantly referring to the actions and practices of the community as a point of reference in order to determine either rules or the application of existing rules. Thus in the whole field of negligence, which forms the staple diet of most Queen's Bench Division judges, the court has to determine whether the conduct of the parties fell above or below the reasonable standard of performance required at any given time in the field in question. If the issue, for example, is whether a surgeon was negligent, the court hears expert evidence as to the practice of surgeons in regard to the procedure in question. It then decides that what was done by the defendant surgeon is acceptable and therefore free from liability, or not acceptable and therefore subject to liability. In making that judgment the court will bear in mind amongst other things the state of development of medical knowledge, the difficulty and cost of taking the precautions that were not taken in that case, the differences that may exist between the level of practice to be expected in a London teaching hospital as against a small provincial one and a host of similar considerations. The practice of the community will be fed into the process of decision-making as one of the factors to be taken into account. The court will not accept the particular procedure of surgeons as representing an acceptable standard unless it thinks it consistent with what can fairly be expected at that stage of development of medical practice. Custom in the sense of what the community does is therefore a potent living source of law in the sense that the courts draw upon it and rework it into the daily

4. 'Custom as a source of English Law', 50 *Michigan Review* 1951, pp. 87–8.

application of the common law. In this way the law is constantly renewed by contact with the life of the community and reflects back to the citizens the law's evaluation of what they do. Here again Benjamin Cardozo has expressed the reality:

Benjamin N. Cardozo, *The Nature of the Judicial Process* (1921), pp. 62–3

It is, however, not so much in the making of new rules as in the application of old ones that the creative energy of custom most often manifests itself today. General standards of right and duty are established. Custom must determine whether there has been adherence or departure. My partner has the powers that are usual in the trade. They may be so well known that the courts will notice them judicially. Such for illustration is the power of a member of a trading firm to make or indorse negotiable paper in the course of the firm's business. They may be such that the court will require evidence of their existence. The master in the discharge of his duty to protect the servant against harm must exercise the degree of care that is commonly exercised in like circumstance by men of ordinary prudence. The triers of the facts in determining whether that standard has been attained must consult the habits of life, the everyday beliefs and practices, of the men and women about them. Innumerable, also, are the cases where the course of dealing to be followed is defined by the customs, or, more properly speaking, the usages, of a particular trade or market or profession. The constant assumption runs throughout the law that the natural and spontaneous evolutions of habit fix the limits of right and wrong. A slight extension of custom identifies it with customary morality, the prevailing standard of right conduct, the *mores* of the time.

But it is the judge who decides – not the people nor the custom.

3. European law

On 1 January 1973 the United Kingdom became a member of the European Communities and Community law thereby became a source of the law of Britain. The law of the Communities is to be found in three different places – the treaties, the decisions of Community organs and in the decisions of the European Court.

The *treaties* are the Treaty of Paris 1951, establishing the European Coal and Steel Community, and the two Treaties of Rome 1957, establishing the European Economic Community and Euratom. It is the EEC treaty that is mainly in question. Its subject-matter is mainly agriculture, free trade, fair competition, transport regulation, social security, the free movement of persons, services and capital.

The *organs* of the community are (1) the *Council of Ministers*, which is the sovereign body of the Common Market. It is composed of one ministerial representative from each member state. The Council has the right to legislate but in most cases it can only act on proposals made by the Commission. Such proposals can become law by a majority vote – voting is on a weighted basis with the larger countries having more votes. (2) The *Commission*, which consists of one national from each of the member states, though they are supposed to act independently of their national origin as members of the Common Market's executive. The Commission is responsible for formulating policy on a day-to-day basis. By contrast, the Council of Ministers meets relatively infrequently. (3) The *Assembly*, which is a parliamentary body. Originally its members were chosen by national parliaments from amongst their own members but from 1979 onwards the members are elected directly by the national populations. The Assembly is primarily a forum for debating Community policies and problems. In theory it has ultimate control over the Commission, however, in as much as it can by a vote of censure force the members of the Commission to resign. In practice, however, this is not likely to happen. (4) The *European Court of Justice at* Luxemburg, which has one judge from each of the member states. The Court has two principal functions. One is to decide points of Community law which come up in the course of litigation in national courts. Under Article 177 of the Rome Treaty, any court may refer a point of law that arises before it to the European Court for decision. (In England this has even been done by a magistrates' court.) If the point comes up in a court that is the final court of appeal, then there is an obligation to refer it to the Luxemburg court. The litigation is then suspended while the European Court decides the issue. The case then continues in the national forum in the light of the European Court's ruling on the point of Community law. The Court's second chief function is to determine actions brought by Community organs, member states or individuals alleging breaches of obligations under Community law. If one state wishes to bring another before the Court, it must first approach the Commission. Only if the Commission does not succeed in resolving the issue can the state go to the Court. Individuals cannot take proceedings against states, but an individual affected by an act of a Community organ – say a Commission regulation – can apply to the Court to have it quashed. The Court does

* For a helpful and brief guide, see L. Neville Brown and Francis Jacobs, *The Court of Justice of the European Communities* (1977).

not enforce its own decisions. It is left to each state to provide machinery to enforce judgments against individuals or companies. There is no machinery for enforcing judgments against states. This is left instead to the pressure of membership of the Community, which seems so far to be sufficient to secure compliance with the small number of decisions concerning states.†

Membership of the Community creates a variety of situations where member states find themselves under an obligation under the Treaties to translate Community policies into effect – in many instances by passing national laws. But we are concerned here not with these indirect effects on English law but on the situations where membership of the Community has direct effect on the national law. There are several different ways in which national law is affected directly by membership of the EEC:

(1) Some of the provisions of the Treaties are directly applicable law in the UK, which means that they require no action by any UK authority to be fully effective as law. Not all the provisions of the Treaties are of this kind, but some are what the European Court has called 'complete and legally perfect'. They include for instance provisions prohibiting new (or preventing the extension of) discriminatory customs duties and internal taxes on other member states' products or prohibiting new (or the tightening of old) import quotas. Some are provisions that create direct rights for individuals. It is for the Court to determine which treaty articles are directly applicable. In doing this the Court looks at the clarity and conciseness of the article, the degree to which it envisages further acts by the Community or member states for its implementation, and the degree of discretion given to member states in deciding how to implement it. Generally the articles of the Treaties set out the broad framework of Community law and are therefore not directly applicable. The great bulk of Community law is contained in legislation made by the organs of the Community under powers conferred by the treaty.

† In February 1979, for instance, the Court held that the UK was obliged to comply with an order requiring tachographs (the 'spy in the cab') to be installed in over half a million lorries. Under EEC law tachographs were supposed to be installed by 1 January 1978. The British Government informed the Commission that it would 'neither be practical nor politic' to comply with the deadline. The Commission then brought the UK before the court which ruled that there was a breach of Community law and ordered the UK to comply. There were confident predictions in the press that the British Government would defy the order but on 5 March 1979, less than a month after the order, the Government announced that it would comply.

(2) Both the Council of Ministers and the Commission have power to legislate with immediate impact on UK law. In other words some of their acts are directly applicable law. There are five kinds of legislative act:

(a) *Regulations* – these are directly applicable. Article 189 of the EEC Treaty provides that regulations 'shall have a general application', and 'shall be binding in every respect and directly applicable in each Member State'.

(b) *Decisions* – these may be directly applicable depending on how they are framed. Under Article 189 'decisions shall be binding in every respect for the addressees named therein'. They can be directed at individuals or companies as well as member states.

(c) *Directives* – these impose obligations only on member states and do not create directly applicable law. They require some act by member states before they are fully in effect but they are binding on the states. Article 189 states 'Directives shall bind any Member State to which they are addressed as to the result to be achieved, while leaving to domestic agencies a competence as to form and means.'

(d) *Recommendations* – these have no binding force and are therefore not a source of law.

(e) *Opinions* – these likewise have no legal force. Article 189 states 'Recommendations and opinions shall have no binding force'.

The two kinds of legislative act that create directly applicable law are therefore regulations and decisions. Regulations are in practice the most common. Most of the Community law having direct internal effect in so far as it imposes obligations, does so in relation to industrial and commercial activities, and does not on the whole touch citizens in their private capacities.

Section 2 (1) of the European Communites Act 1972 provides in relation to directly applicable laws that all such Community rights, powers, liabilities and obligations that arise on entry or *in the future* are to be given effect within the United Kingdom without further enactment and shall be recognized and enforced accordingly. This includes not only regulations and directives but also treaty articles. It means that to this extent parliamentary sovereignty has been qualified. The section empowers the organs of the EEC over which parliament has no control and little significant influence to legislate with full internal effect over areas of economic and social importance.

(3) Decisions of the European Court interpreting Community law have direct effect in the United Kingdom, and take precedence over anything in UK law that may be contrary to such interpretation. It is an absolute principle of membership of the Community that in case of conflict Community law takes precedence over national law. This point was first established in the great case of *Van Gend en Loos* (Case 26/62 [1963] E.C.R. 1). The plaintiff had challenged a Dutch law as contravening an article of the Rome Treaty. The Dutch and Belgian governments argued that the European Court had no jurisdiction to decide whether the provisions of the EEC Treaty prevailed over Dutch legislation and that the solution to the problem was one exclusively for the national courts. The court rejected this argument and held that a provision of Community law 'produces direct effects and creates individual rights which national courts must protect' (at p. 16). The individual has no direct access to the European Court but if he takes action in the national courts these courts are required to follow the decisions of the European Court on a question of Community law. If the court is in doubt over the question it *can* refer the question to the Luxemburg court under Article 177 and if it is a hearing in a final court of appeal, it *must* do so.

The Court expressed its basic philosophy in the judgment in *Costa* v. *ENEL* (6/64 [1964] E.C.R. 575 at 593):

> By contrast with ordinary international treaties, the EEC Treaty has created its own legal system which, on the entry into force of the Treaty, became an integral part of the legal systems of the Member States and which their courts are bound to apply. By creating a Community of unlimited duration, having its own institutions, its own personality, its own legal capacity and capacity of representation on the international plane, and, more particularly, real powers stemming from a limitation of sovereignty or a transfer of powers from the States to the Community, the Member States have limited their sovereign rights, albeit within limited fields, and have created a body of law which binds both their nationals and themselves.

The issue came up squarely in the *Simmenthal* case ([1978] E.C.R. 629) in which the Court held unambiguously that it was the duty of national courts to apply directly applicable Community law *even in preference to subsequently enacted national law.* There could be no more dramatic illustration of the effect of joining the Community.

Of course, whether the English courts give effect to the principles of Community law is a matter for them but the indications are that they are following gamely the clear lead they have been given by the Luxemburg court. Lord Hailsham in *The Siskina* [1979] A.C. 243, said of Community law that was directly applicable, 'It is the duty of the courts here and in other member states to give effect to Community law as they interpret it in preference to the municipal law of their own country over which ex hypothesi Community law prevails. There is no question here of discretion' (at p. 262).

See also conflicting views in *Felixstowe Dock and Railway Co.* v. *British Transport Docks Board* [1976] C.M.L.R. 655 at 664–5, per Lord Denning; and *Re medical expenses incurred in France* (CS/2/77) [1977] 2 C.M.L.R. 317 at 332. For comment on the *Simmenthal* case and the English judicial dicta, see 3 *European Law Review*, 1978, p. 214. See, generally, L. Collins, *European Community Law in the United Kingdom* (1975); and Lord Mackenzie Stuart, *The European Communities and the Rule of Law* (1977).

4. Law-making by 'strings and mirrors'

'Law' is a magic word which conjures up a particular kind of response. The potency of the impact of the word explains why in all communities there are certain basic rules as to what is entitled to claim this response. So, for instance, a statement on a problem of law made by the Lord Chancellor in the course of a debate in the chamber of the House of Lords has no impact on the corpus of the law. It does not register at all. The same statement by the same Lord Chancellor in the same place delivered as part of his judgment in a case heard by the House of Lords in its judicial capacity may transform that branch of the law – at least if a majority of the Lords involved in hearing the appeal agree with the Lord Chancellor's pronouncement. In the one case the Lord Chancellor has used the accepted machinery for 'making law', in the other case, he has not.

There are, however, some examples of conduct on the part of official bodies which appear to be based on the appropriation of the word 'law' in circumstances where no law in fact exists. The official body acts as if it had some legal basis whereas in fact it has none. The two examples considered here are that of 'non-statutory concessions' administered on a regular basis by the Inland Revenue and, secondly, the pressures brought to bear on companies to comply with the non-statutory pay guidelines. It is not suggested that they are the only examples that could be cited.

(a) Extra-statutory concessions by the Inland Revenue

It is familiar constitutional law that the Crown's powers to dispense with or to suspend the laws were abolished by the Bill of Rights in 1688. The Bill of Rights declared that the 'pretended power of suspending of laws' by prerogative was unlawful. This fundamental principle is regularly flouted, however, by the Inland Revenue in an elaborate series of concessions (now numbering some eighty-six) offered to some taxpayers.

The concessions are listed in a booklet (Inland Revenue booklet IR 1(1976) as amended). So, for instance, the Revenue have agreed not to charge tax on cash payments to miners in lieu of free coal or on removal expenses borne by an employer where the employee has to change his residence to take up new employment. An allowance is given for an employee who has to bear the cost of upkeep of tools for his work.

From time to time the courts have expostulated about this practice. In *Absalom* v. *Talbot* [1943] 1 All E.R. 589 at 598, Scott L.J. said: 'No judicial countenance can or ought to be given in matters of taxation to any system of extra-legal concessions. Amongst other reasons, it exposes Revenue officials to temptation, which is wrong, even in the case of a service like the Inland Revenue, characterized by a wonderfully high sense of honour. The fact that such extra-legal concessions have to be made to avoid unjust hardships is conclusive that there is something wrong with the legislation.' (See, to like effect, *IRC* v. *Frere* [1965] A.C. 402 at 429, per Lord Radcliffe; *Gleaner Co. Ltd* v. *Assessment Committee* [1922] 2 A.C. 169 at 175, per Lord Buckmaster; and *Bates* v. *IRC* [1968] A.C. 483 at 516 per Lord Upjohn.)

In *Vestey* v. *IRC* Walton J. had to consider a variation on this theme in the form of a decision not to pursue tax made as a result of the circumstances of the individual case rather than on the basis of a general concession:

Vestey v. *Inland Revenue Cmnrs* [1979] 2 All E.R. 225 (Chancery Division)

WALTON J. (at 233):

There arises what counsel for the taxpayers has denominated as a serious constitutional question: namely what rights the Inland Revenue Commissioners have to pick and choose when recovering tax. The Solicitor-General says, and doubtless rightly says, that the commissioners are under no duty to recover every halfpenny of tax which may be due. One may say 'Amen' to that very readily, because the costs of recovery of extremely small amounts of tax would far outweigh the tax recovered. One expects the tax authorities to behave sensibly. ... What the Revenue authorities, through the Solicitor-General, are here claiming is a general dispensing power, no more and no less. He submitted that the system of extra-statutory concessions was well known and well recognised, and that what was happening in the present case was no more than the grant of an additional extra-statutory concession.

In the first place, I, in company with many other judges before me, am totally unable to understand on what basis the Inland Revenue Commissioners are entitled to make extra-statutory concessions. To take a very simple example (since example is clearly called for), on what basis have the commissioners taken it on themselves to provide that income tax is not to be charged on a miner's free coal and allowances in lieu thereof? That this should be the law is doubtless quite correct: I am not arguing the merits, or even suggesting that some other result, as a matter of equity, should be reached. But this, surely, ought to be a matter for Parliament, and not the commissioners. If this kind of concession can be made, where does it stop; and why are some groups favoured as against others?

... This is not a simple matter of tax law. What is happening is that, in effect, despite the words of Maitland[1] commenting on the Bill of Rights, 'This is the last of the dispensing power', the Crown is now claiming just such a power. If I may, I would respectfully adopt the words of Freedman CJ in the Court of Appeal in Manitoba in *R.* v. *Catagas*[2] a case which in terms decides that the Crown may not dispense with laws by executive action, where, after dealing with cases of prosecution for infraction of the criminal law in which in individual cases there was undoubtedly an element of discretion, he said:

> 'But in all these instances the prosecutorial discretion is exercised in relation to a specific case. It is the particular facts of a given case that call that discretion into play. But that is a far different thing from the granting of a blanket dispensation in favour of a particular group or race. Today the dispensing power may be exercised in favour of Indians, tomorrow it may be exercised in favour of Protestants and the next day in favour of Jews. Our laws cannot be so treated. The Crown may not, by executive action, dispense with laws. The matter is as simple as that, and nearly three centuries of legal and constitutional history stand as the foundation for that principle.'

But even if, contrary to my views, extra-statutory concessions are permissible and do form part of our tax code, nevertheless they do represent a published code, which applies indifferently to all those who fall, or who can bring themselves within, its scope. What is claimed by the Crown now is something radically different. There is no published code, and no necessity for the treatment of all those who are in consimili casu alike. In one case the Crown can remit one-third, in another one-half, and in yet another case the whole, of the tax properly payable, at its own sweet will and pleasure. If this

1. *The Constitutional History of England* (1908), p. 305.
2. [1978] 1 WWR 282 at 287–8.

is indeed so, we are back to the days of the Star Chamber. Again, I want to make it crystal clear that nobody is suggesting that the Crown has, or indeed ever would, so utilise the powers which it claims to bring about unjust results; or really, of course, which is not necessarily the same thing, results which it thought to be unjust. The root of the evil is that it claims that it has, in fact, the right to do so.

Presumably, if the concessions are reasonable, parliamentary approval would be available. If they are unreasonable, they should in any event not be allowed. Moreover the Inland Revenue has an opportunity to adjust tax laws on an annual basis in the Finance Act. It cannot therefore be said that requiring statutory authority for concessions would create any undue difficulties. There could even be statutory authority for the Inland Revenue to exercise some discretion in these matters, subject to whatever conditions parliament might impose. (For the suggestion that an ordinary taxpayer would have the *locus standi* to bring proceedings against the Inland Revenue to require them to fulfill their statutory duty to collect taxes, see G.W. Thomas, 'The Constitutionality of Extra-statutory Concessions', *Law Society's Gazette*, 27 June 1979, pp. 637–8.)

Note

The system of extra-statutory concessions used by the Inland Revenue may be compared with the practice of the police not to prosecute in certain kinds of situations. The police, for instance, commonly choose not to prosecute where the law in question is regarded as obsolete. They may refrain from prosecuting where they think the public interest is not served by charging someone – for example, in industrial relations disputes. (See especially A.F. Wilcox, *The Decision to Prosecute* (1972) – Mr Wilcox was formerly Chief Constable of Hampshire.)

In two cases before the Court of Appeal it was accepted by the court that the police had to have a discretion in the field of prosecutions. In the first of these Lord Denning, for instance, said 'It is for the Commissioner of Police of the Metropolis, or the chief constable, as the case may be, to decide in any particular case whether inquiries should be pursued, or whether an arrest should be made or a prosecution brought.... No court can or should give him directions on such a matter. He can also make policy decisions and give effect to them, as, for instance, was often done when prosecutions were not brought for attempted suicide' (*R.* v. *Metropolitan Police Commissioner ex parte Blackburn* [1968] 2 Q.B. 118 at 136; see to like effect *Blackburn* v. *Metropolitan Police Commissioner* [1973] 1 Q.B. 241, at 254. But there were some policy decisions that were beyond the proper power of the police. ('But there are some policy decisions with which, I think, the courts in a case can, if necessary, interfere. Suppose a chief constable were to issue a directive to his men that no person should be prosecuted for stealing any goods less than £100 in value. I should have thought that the court could countermand it. He would be failing in his duty to enforce the law.' [1968] 2 Q.B. 118 at 136, per Lord Denning).

Questions

1. Does it appear from the above that the courts view extra-statutory concessions by the Inland Revenue and prosecution decisions by the police in the same sort of way?
2. Are there any sound grounds for distinguishing between the two situations?
3. Would it be possible to operate a police force or a tax system without using discretionary decisions on the application and non-application of the rules? If the answer is no, how, if at all, can and should such discretion be controlled?
4. Is it less objectionable for public authorities to refrain from using existing legal powers or from complying with existing legal duties, than to act on the basis of non-existing legal powers? Is the non-use of powers preferable to the use of non-powers? (Refer also to the example that follows.)

(b) Enforcement of non-statutory guidelines on pay policy

In July 1975 the Labour Government published a White Paper (*The Attack on Inflation*, Cmnd. 6151) which stated (para. 22): 'From now on the Government in handling applications for assistance under the Industry Act 1972 will interpret the national interest as including observance of the pay limit. The Government will not give discretionary assistance under the Industry Act to companies which have broken the pay limit. The National Enterprise Board will also take these circumstances into account'. The following paragraph (23) stated: 'The Government will also take account of the firm's record of observance of the pay limit in its general purchasing policy and in awarding contracts.'

In 1976 a second White Paper (Cmnd. 6507, para. 21) reiterated the policy and the third White Paper in 1977 (Cmnd. 6882, para. 16) did so again. On each occasion the White Paper was specifically approved by the House of Commons.

The policy was in fact activated – a number of firms were denied discretionary assistance under the Industry Act 1975; a circular was issued to local authorities asking them not to invite tenders or to award new contracts to firms blacklisted for breaking the pay guidelines – in the event no list of names was circulated to local authorities but names were circulated later to health authorities, nationalized industries, universities and the Crown Agents. Altogether 35 firms were subjected to the blacklist (against a background of 32,000 pay settlements over two and a half years of which only 48 were said to be in breach.[1])

The legality of placing contracts by reference to compliance or otherwise with the pay policy seems undoubted. The government is free to contract or not to contract as it pleases. But can it use the threat of refusal of industrial assistance as a means to secure compliance with pay policy? In the view of one commentator, Gabrielle Ganz, it can.[2] Admittedly this is to use Acts of parliament for a different purpose than that intended, but the Industry Act makes reference to very vague phrases such as 'the national interest'. Even apart from such phrases, the promotion of the policy of counter-inflation would seem a legitimate matter for a government to have in mind when deciding whether or not to make discretionary grants to industry. (There must however presumably be some limits to the pressure that could lawfully be brought on a company. Could the government, for instance, deny a company industrial assistance on the ground that it was trading with South Africa?)[3]

Granted that the blacklist is legal, is it also fair? One problem seen by Miss Ganz was the randomness of the policy. There being no requirement to report pay settlements, the government got its information from a variety of sources including newspapers and informers. Sanctions were threatened in some cases that did not respond to informal pressure or discussions. The government insisted on maintaining a discretionary policy that could discriminate between different firms. It refused to hand the question of sanctions over to an independent tribunal or other independent body. A policy that has to be administered somewhat randomly will inevitably give rise to mistakes and is open to abuse.

1. G. Ganz, *Public Law*, Winter 1978, p. 333, on whose article this section is based.
2. Ibid. See, to like effect, R.B. Ferguson and A.C. Page, 'Pay Restraint: The Legal Constraints', 128 *New Law Journal*, 25 May 1978, p. 515.
3. The example was suggested by Miss Ganz.

Control over the policy by parliament was not very effective. MPs had difficulty in discovering which firms were on the blacklist until they were leaked in the press. Even then the minister told them that he would only reveal the name of a firm in respect of which action was being taken if the firm itself had already announced the fact.

Miss Ganz summarized her reaction to the blacklist controversy:

Gabrielle Ganz, *Public Law*, Winter 1978, pp. 345–6

The blacklist may be regarded as a sanction for a policy not legalised by statute, applied arbitrarily, without the safeguards of the rules of natural justice or appeal to an independent tribunal. On the other hand it can be justified as a valid consideration taken into account by the Government when exercising its discretionary power to award contracts or grant industrial assistance. The threat of withholding contracts and assistance is used as a bargaining counter to persuade companies to renegotiate settlements in line with the pay policy. The blacklist is, therefore, a list of failures rather than the successful tracking down of culprits.[1]

Thus it can be seen as an illustration of the trend of modern Governments to achieve their policies by persuasion and pressure rather than by law and force. The Conservative Government with the Industrial Relations Act 1971 and the Counter-Inflation Act 1973 tried to reverse this trend but its lack of success was used by its successors to justify their non-statutory incomes policy. The considerable degree of success of this policy would seem to show that consent is a more powerful force than law in this context.

To castigate the Government's policy as contrary to the rule of law is, therefore, tautologous as by definition it is non-statutory. But the charge has ideological overtones as in Dicey's definition the rule of law excludes the existence of arbitrary or even wide discretionary powers. Wide discretionary powers are a fait accompli but the line between their arbitrary and proper use depends on the criteria which are considered relevant to the object of the power. The distinction lies at the heart of the controversy about the blacklist. That the Government may use its power to award contracts to achieve social policies was established at least as far back as 1891 when the House of Commons passed the first Fair Wages Resolution. The United States has not hesitated to use its purchasing powers to discriminate in favour of minority groups. To what extent the Government in the United Kingdom should use its purchasing powers to achieve wider goals has been the subject of controversy but that the observance of incomes policy was a proper purpose for the use of such powers was accepted even by Mr. Enoch Powell.

This has not been universally accepted in the case of statutory powers. The issue may come up for decision before the courts but this is not the most suitable forum for settling the relationship between the Government's economic and industrial policies. This is a political issue which should be decided in the House of Commons. They did this when approving successive White

1. *The Observer*, 12 February, 1978–quoting a senior civil servant.

Papers. These cannot confer legal validity on the Government's policies but they do provide political legitimacy. They do not, however, provide controls over the exercise of the powers of the Government. These must be political and parliamentary since the Government has refused to sub-contract decisions to an independent body. Some of the existing mechanisms such as select committees and the Ombudsman have not so far been used. Questions have been deflected by the shield of confidentiality rather than secrecy though the Government cannot be entirely exonerated from the latter charge. Confidentiality rather than secrecy is also the hall-mark of the procedure by which decisions are reached but the line between them may be blurred when firms are not notified that they have been blacklisted, information is obtained from informers and criteria are not clearly spelt out in advance.[2]

The use of contract and general laws for purposes not explicit in the law itself to control the economy has been cited as characteristic of the corporate state[3] and the Government has been accused of fascism over the use of the blacklist. A similar charge could be made against the U.S.A. which has also used its contractual powers to achieve its policies. The existence of these powers are a by-product of the modern industrial state; they are not dangerous *per se.* What matters is the purpose for which they are exercised and the public accountability of those who administer them. The purpose for which the blacklist is used has been sanctioned by the House of Commons which also has the means to exercise eternal vigilance over its operation.

2. The government's detailed interpretation of the 1978 White Paper for use by civil servants was published in *The Times*, 29 September, 1978.

3. Winkler, 'Law, State and Economy: The Industry Act 1975 in Context', *British Journal of Law & Society* (1975), pp. 119 *et seq.*

8
The process of law reform

The problem of keeping the law abreast of changing times faces every system. Materials already presented earlier in this book have focussed on the role of the courts in reworking the common law and thereby removing its blemishes or simply adjusting it to new circumstances. But the courts cannot always succeed in this law-reform role. The problem of leaving law reform to the courts is addressed in the extract that follows:

Norman Marsh, 'Law Reform in the United Kingdom: A New Institutional Approach' 13 *William and Mary Law Review*, 1971, p. 263

Five considerations, some of which, if not entirely new, have at least intensified in recent years, and others, more or less inherent in a system of judge-made law, suggest that English law cannot, at least for the future, rely on that system as the main instrument of law reform.

First, it is no longer possible for the judge in modern English society to make those bold assumptions about family life and about relations between landlord and tenant, employer and employee, citizen and the State which underlie many reforms of a seemingly legal character. On the one hand, he lives in an era where many value assumptions are being challenged; on the other, he does not enjoy quite the unquestioned prestige, the charismatic authority, enjoyed by his Victorian forbears. As the House of Lords recognised, after a decade or more of attempted judicial innovations designed to provide protection in the matrimonial home for the deserted wife, and after an even longer period of judicial experiments aimed at protecting the economically weaker party to a contract from unfair exemption clauses, reform of the law may raise issues which in present conditions are more appropriately dealt with by the legislature.

Secondly, judge-made reforms are dependent on the issue coming before the courts, and more particularly on the issue reaching an instance which places the court in a position to overrule, ignore, or distinguish any awkward precedents which stand in the way of reform. This chance element is accentuated by another factor, namely, the respective means of the parties to the litigation in question. Between the litigant who qualifies for legal aid and the man, or more often the corporation or government body, for whom costs matter less than a satisfactory legal result, there is a large group of potential litigants deterred by lack of means from fighting a case through the courts and, if necessary, to the House of Lords. Sometimes it may profit a litigant with a business in which the same issue may reoccur, to settle a case in spite of a favourable ruling in, say, the Court of Appeal, in order to prevent a possible reversal in the House of Lords. Indeed, this is rather more likely since the House of Lords assumed power to overrule its own decisions. In such circumstances the average party to a case is likely to prefer the cash in hand to the doubtful distinction of running a large financial risk in the interests of a possible reform of the law.

A third and even more important consideration may be summed up by a slight modification of a well-known aphorism: hard cases make not so much bad as unsystematic, incoherent and therefore, from the point of view of the law as a whole, uncertain law. In other words, the hard case invites an equitable decision, which is not bad in itself, but requires a broader base of principle than the judge in that particular case is entitled to provide. If he does reach a decision, he only prepares the way for a further spate of litigation which may ultimately have to be stemmed by legislation....

Fourthly, it must be remembered that the reforming decision, which is welcomed by the critical academic lawyer, long familiar and impatient with some outdated but hitherto accepted piece of conventional legal wisdom, may be extremely unjust to the unsuccessful party. The latter is, in effect, the victim in a case of retrospective law-making. The danger of injustice by departing from the expected patterns of judicial behaviour was emphasised by the House of Lords when they announced in 1966 that they would no longer be necessarily bound by their own previous decisions. They would, they said, 'bear in mind the danger of disturbing retrospectively the basis on which contracts, settlements of property and fiscal arrangements have been entered into and also the especial need for certainty as to the criminal law.'

There is a fifth consideration which it would, in the context of English law, seem natural to bear in mind when assessing the potentialities of the judiciary as a source of law reform. It concerns, of course, the important part played by stare decisis in the Engish legal system. Clearly there is less scope, at least for rapid change, where that principle prevails than by the clean-sweeping enunciation by the legislature of some new general principle.

A sixth consideration, not referred to by Mr Marsh, is that the courts are likely to be relatively ill-informed as to the background to the problem that is said to require reform. The court relies normally on the arguments presented by counsel for the parties. It has no opportunity to consult with other persons, interested bodies, government departments or experts, as to what kind of reform would be most beneficial.

On the other hand, if the court abdicates responsibility for improving the law nothing may happen. Legislatures and government departments normally have more than enough to occupy their time and may not find time for a proposed project of reform. In particular they may lack both the time and the energy to conduct the necessary researches to formulate reform proposals that are well designed to meet the problem. It was this consideration that led to the call for some body to act as mediator between the courts and the legislature. As long ago as 1859 Lord Chancellor Westbury asked 'Why is there not a body of men in this country whose duty it is to collect a body of judicial statistics, or in more common parlance, make the necessary experiments to see how far the law is fitted to the exigencies of society. . . .' He argued that a body of men be appointed by a Minister of Justice to examine all law with a view to its improvement.*

In 1921 this call was taken up in New York by Benjamin N. Cardozo, the later Supreme Court Justice who was then a judge in New York. He proposed the establishment of a new agency to mediate between the courts and the legislature:

> The courts are not helped as they could and ought to be in the adaptation of law to justice. The reason they are not helped is because there is no one whose business it is to give warning that help is needed ... We must have a courier who will carry the tidings of distress ... Today courts and legislature work in separation and aloofness. The penalty is paid both in the wasted effort of production and in the lowered quality of the product. On the one hand, the judges, left to fight against anachronism and injustice by the methods of judge-made law, are distracted by the conflicting promptings of justice and logic, of consistency and mercy, and the output of their labours bears the tokens of the strain. On the other side, the legislature, informed only casually and intermittently of the needs and problems of the courts, without expert or responsible or disinterested or systematic advice as to the workings of one rule or another, patches the fabric here and there, and mars often when it would mend. Legislature and courts move on in proud and silent isolation. Some agency must be found to mediate between them. ['A Ministry of Justice', (1921) 35 *Harvard Law Review*, pp. 113–14.]

* (1859) 2 *Juridical Society Papers*, 129, 132.

1. The Law Commissions

Cardozo's call led in due course to an experiment in 1923 and to the setting up in 1934 of the New York Law Revision Commission.* Thirty years later Cardozo's plea was echoed in Britain by Gerald Gardiner QC in *Law Reform NOW*, a book published in 1963 which Gardiner co-edited with Professor Andrew Martin. In the next year Gerald Gardiner (by then Lord Gardiner) became Lord Chancellor in Harold Wilson's first Government. He took the post only on condition that his idea for a Law Commission was implemented and shortly after the Government came into office a White Paper was published:

(a) The White Paper

White Paper, 'Proposals for English and Scottish Law Commissions', 1965, Cmnd. 2573

One of the hallmarks of an advanced society is that its laws should not only be just but also that they be kept up-to-date and be readily accessible to all who are affected by them. The state of the law today cannot be said to satisfy these requirements. It is true that the administration of justice in our courts is highly regarded, and rightly so, in other countries beside our own; and it is also true that the spread of the ideas of personal liberty and respect for the rule of law which have been of such importance in the development of Western civilization has been profoundly influenced by the importance which our laws attaches to these concepts. But the very fact that English and Scottish law have a history stretching back for so many centuries is one of the reasons why the form of the law is now in such an unsatisfactory state.

England and Wales

English law today is contained in some 3,000 Acts of Parliament, the earliest of which dates from the year 1235, in many volumes of delegated legislation made under the authority of those Acts, and in over 300,000 reported cases. Although Parliament has been actively at work for so many years, much of the law is still to be found in the decisions of the courts operating in fields which Parliament has not entered. It is true that the law on certain subjects has from time to time been largely restated in codifying statutes, but these are few and far between and date mostly from the end of the nineteenth century. The result is that it is today extremely difficult for anyone without special training to discover what the law is on any given topic; and when the law is finally ascertained, it is found in many cases to be obsolete and in some cases to be unjust. This is plainly wrong. English law should be capable of being recast in a form which is accessible, intelligible and in accordance with modern needs....

* See John W. Macdonald, 'The New York Law Revision Commission', 28 *Modern Law Review*, 1965, p. 1.

There is at present no body charged with the duty of keeping the law as a whole under review and making recommendations for its systematic reform.* Each Government department is responsible for keeping under review the state of the law in its own field and from time to time Royal Commissions or independent committees are set up to examine and make recommendations on particular subjects. There are standing bodies such as the Lord Chancellor's Law Reform Committee, whose task is to review such small fields of the civil law as may from time to time be referred to it, while a similar task is performed in the case of the criminal law by the Home Secretary's Criminal Law Revision Committee. While valuable work has been done by these means and important changes in the law have been made as a result of the recommendations of these and other bodies, this work has been done piecemeal and it is evident that comprehensive reform can be achieved only by a body whose sole task it is and which is equipped with a professional staff on the scale required.

The Government therefore propose, subject to the approval of Parliament, to set up a Law Commission for England and Wales. This will consist of five lawyers of high standing appointed by the Lord Chancellor with an adequate legal staff to assist them. The Commissioners will be required to keep the whole of English law under review and to submit to the Lord Chancellor programmes for the examination of different branches of the law with a view to its reform. The programmes will include recommendations on the best means of carrying them out. When a programme has been approved by the Lord Chancellor after consulting other Ministers concerned it will be laid before Parliament. It may be appropriate for some of the detailed projects for reform contained in the programmes to be undertaken by the Commissioners, for others to be referred to the Law Reform Committee or the Criminal Law Revision Committee, and others again to be undertaken by the Government department concerned; or, particularly where important social questions may arise, for a topic to be referred to a Departmental Committee or a Royal Commission by, or at the instance of the appropriate Minister. The detailed proposals for reform prepared by the Commissioners or by those other bodies will be published, and if they are accepted by the Government the necessary legislation will be introduced.

The Commissioners will also be charged with the duty of pressing forward the task of consolidation and statute law revision. The object of the latter is to prune the statute book of dead and obsolete enactments, while consolidation consists of the bringing together in one Act of all the enactments on a particular branch of the law. It is true that some progress has been made with these tasks since the war, but much remains to be done.

It is generally agreed that in the field of law reform much valuable guidance can be obtained from the experience of other countries like the United States, the Commonwealth countries and the countries of Western Europe which

* For a review of the then-existing machinery of law reform, see E.C.S. Wade, 'The Machinery of Law Reform', 24 *Modern Law Review*, 1961, pp. 3–17; *Law Reform Now*, ed. Gardiner and Martin (1963), Chapter 1; J.H. Farrar, *Law Reform and the Law Commission* (1974), Chapters 1 and 2 and Appendices A, B, C, and D, setting out the achievements of the respective bodies (ed.).

have had to face problems similar to our own. While in some respects the insularity of English law has been one of the sources of its strength, there is no doubt that in other directions it is a source of weakness. There is much to be gained from comparative legal studies and this will be one of the tasks of the Law Commissioners. It is intended that the Commissioners should provide Government departments which are contemplating legislation with the research and advisory facilities which will be available to the Commissioners and this may well be of particular importance in enabling departments to take account of relevant Commonwealth and foreign experience. It is not, of course, proposed that the Commissioners should duplicate the work done by other bodies such as the British Institute of International and Comparative Law.

The Law Commissioners will be appointed by the Lord Chancellor for periods to be agreed upon at the time of their appointment. This will enable distinguished lawyers to be appointed to the Commission for a term of years before returning to work in their own field, whether on the Bench, in the practising legal profession or at the universities. It is likely that similar arrangements will be made in the case of some of the staff of the Commission so as to enable full advantage to be taken of the valuable work being done at the present time by academic lawyers in the field of law reform. The task of the Commission will be immense and will not be completed for many years.

The Commissioners will be required to make an annual report to the Lord Chancellor, which will be laid before Parliament.

The White Paper was published in January 1965 and the Law Commissions Bill was introduced the same month. It received the Royal Assent on June 15 and the names of the first Law Commissioners were announced the following day. (On the background and for an analysis of the Act, see Lord Chorley and G. Dworkin, 'The Law Commissions Act 1965', 28 *Modern Law Review*, 1965, p. 675). Each Commission consists of five lawyers, appointed in the case of the English Commission by the Lord Chancellor and, in the case of the Scottish, by the Secretary of State for Scotland and the Lord Advocate. The chairman has so far always been a judge.

The duties and functions of the Law Commissions are set out in s. 3:

(b) The 1965 statute

3. (1) It shall be the duty of each of the Commissions to take and keep under review all the law with which they are respectively concerned with a view to its systematic development and reform, including in particular the codification of such law, the elimination of anomalies, the repeal of obsolete and unnecessary enactments, the reduction of the number of separate enactments and generally the simplification and modernisation of the law, and for that purpose –

   (a) to receive and consider any proposals for the reform of the law which may be made or referred to them;

(b) to prepare and submit to the Minister from time to time programmes for the examination of different branches of the law with a view to reform, including recommendations as to the agency (whether the Commission or another body) by which any such examination should be carried out;

(c) to undertake, pursuant to any such recommendations approved by the Minister, the examination of particular branches of the law and the formulation, by means of draft Bills or otherwise, of proposals for reform therein;

(d) to prepare from time to time at the request of the Minister comprehensive programmes of consolidation and statute law revision, and to undertake the preparation of draft Bills pursuant to any such programme approved by the Minister;

(e) to provide advice and information to government departments and other authorities or bodies concerned at the instance of the Government with proposals for the reform or amendment of any branch of the law;

(f) to obtain such information as to the legal systems of other countries as appears to the Commissioners likely to facilitate the performance of any of their functions.

(2) The Minister shall lay before Parliament any programmes prepared by the Commission and approved by him and any proposals for reform formulated by the Commission pursuant to such programmes.

The nature of the new machinery was described by the first chairman of the English Law Commission, Mr Justice Scarman (now Lord Scarman):

Sir Leslie Scarman, *Law Reform – the New Pattern* (1968), pp. 11–16

The Commission is an advisory body; Parliament is to be the source of any new law that may arise from proposals of the Commission. The Commission has been called into being to advise the government and Parliament, first in the planning of law reform; secondly, in the formulation of detailed proposals for the reform of the law. The theory that underlies the Act is that law reform should be the province of the legislature; that the legislature requires specialist advice in the planning and formulation of law reform; and that this advice should be provided by a body independent of the executive and of Parliament....

It is clearly contemplated by the Act that, once the Lord Chancellor has approved a programme prepared by the Commission for the purpose of law reform, both the programme, and any proposals made by the Commission in the light of the programme, shall become public property. There is therefore a significant difference between government legislation and legislation based upon proposals by the Commission. It is the practice of governments to keep secret their detailed legislative proposals until the appropriate Bill is introduced. Law Reform Bills introduced pursuant to a Commission proposal are likely, however, to follow the draft of a Bill already published with the Commission's proposal.

A plain implication of these provisions of the Act is that proposals for the reform of the law, though made to the legislature, ought to be kept outside the field of political controversy. They are to be carefully considered by an expert body before the introduction of legislation. The public is to be given an opportunity of debating them – also before the introduction of legislation. And, finally, when Parliament itself has to consider them, it should have the benefit of expert advice and prior public discussion.

Two further features of the Commission should be mentioned. It holds an initiative in the reform process, and it is more than a mere committee, whose existence may be terminated by the stroke of a Minister's pen. It is an institution, having a statutory existence. Neither the anger of a Minister nor the rebellion and resignation of Commissioners can destroy it. It exists until Parliament by enactment delivers the coup de grâce. These two features merit a little reflection. Prior to the Act, law reform usually began with an investigation undertaken either by an ad hoc body, set up with clearly defined terms of reference, or by a standing committee, to whose attention specific topics would be referred from time to time. A good example of the ad hoc committee is the Goddard Committee, which in 1953 produced a report on Civil Liability for Animals. It could act only within its terms of reference and was dissolved upon submission of its report. The standing committee, in the field of law reform, has a long and honourable history. Modern examples of it are the Lord Chancellor's Law Reform Committee, established in 1952, and the Home Secretary's Criminal Law Revision Committee, established in 1959. Both these committees are active to-day. But neither of them has any power to propose topics for examination with a view to reform. They act only within specific terms of reference and are liable to dissolution at a stroke of their Minister's pen. I have already commented on the Law Commission's statutory existence. Equally important, however, is its right and duty to originate proposals in the field of reform. These proposals are embodied into a programme which, once it survives the veto of the Lord Chancellor, must be published, and confers upon the Commission independence of action within its limits.

(c) The method of working

The Law Commission published its First Programme of work on 19 July 1965, only a month after it was appointed. It covered an enormous range under seventeen subject heads, including codification of the law of contract, of the law of landlord and tenant, and of family law. The codification of criminal law was added in 1967. In addition to such vast projects it also proposed to tackle some minor matters. It has always maintained a balance between large-scale and small-scale issues. In November 1965 it outlined its proposals for a programme of statute law reform to improve the arrangement, accessibility and form of the statute book. This proposed chiefly consolidation (the bringing together into one statute of provisions that are scattered among many statutes) and statute law revision (the repeal of obsolete or unnecessary statutory provisions).

According to the Fourteenth Annual Report (for 1978–79), the staff of the English Law Commission was 47 (including 5 parliamentary draftsmen, 17 lawyers and 22 non-legal staff).

The Commission's method of working has been described by a former Law Commissioner:

Mr Norman Marsh, 'Law Reform in the United Kingdom: A New Institutional Approach', 13 *William and Mary Law Review*, 1971, p. 263

The process can best be illustrated by following the course of a project of the Law Commissions from the time that it appears as an item in an approved Programme until the stage when the completed report on the item is laid before Parliament with a draft Bill giving effect to the recommendations made in the report.

First, a detailed Working Paper with provisional recommendations, usually including information about the relevant legal position in other countries,[1] is prepared by a small team in the Law Commission, headed by one or two Commissioners. After the Working Paper has been discussed at length by the Commission as a whole and, as a result, often rewritten or amended, it is distributed in an edition of about 1500 copies, not only to the various interests in the legal sphere – the judiciary, practising, and academic lawyers (the latter two categories have set up special committees to deal with Law Commission papers) – but also to many lay organisations particularly interested in the subject-matter. Further, it is sent, as a matter of course, to the relevant government departments and to the national press, both general and legal.[2] It is worthy of note that the Commissions, although they welcome informal oral

1. The Law Commissions are required by s. 3 (1) (f) of the Act to obtain information on the relevant law of other countries.

2. The legal 'weeklys' generally print a summary of the Working Paper which the Commissions are careful to provide. Working Papers occasionally feature in the general press. Final reports, however, are given very considerable coverage in the national 'dailys', sometimes with 'leader' articles commenting on them. The Law Commissions take considerable pains to prepare appropriate press summaries which may bring out the salient issues of interest to lay readers. In general, it may be said that the Law Commissions have attached great importance to keeping their work before the general public and the individual Commissioners speak quite frequently on the subject at meetings, over the radio, and in the form of articles for the legal and general press. Their underlying thought has been that law reform is a cause which must be kept in the public eye if it is to achieve practical results.

consultations, do not hold anything in the nature of formal hearings. On the whole their experience is that the most satisfactory results are obtained from carefully prepared Working Papers which are not content to ask questions but which also set out in detail the basic material from which answers can be given, with some guidance as to the provisional thinking of the Commissioners, and a survey of other possible solutions with their accompanying advantages and drawbacks. It has been found that although this technique involves much work, in the long run it spares the Commission many irrelevant and time-wasting suggestions.

After an interval of perhaps six months to a year the comments received on the Working Paper are considered, first by a specialist team within the Commission who, with or without a general consultation with the Commission as a whole depending on the tenor of the comments received, proceed to prepare a draft Report. This Report, generally at this stage without an accompanying draft Bill, is debated by the whole Commission and sent back for any necessary amendments and the addition of the Bill, which is supplied by Parliamentary draftsmen attached to the Commission, in often prolonged consultation with the Commissioners and their staff. The Report as presented to the Lord Chancellor (in the case of the Law Commission for England and Wales) will not only outline the present law in the area covered by the Report and set forth the recommendations therewith, together with the implementing draft Bill, but it will also deal in detail with the process of consultation, including the names of those consulted and (unless there is some problem of confidentiality) the views they have expressed. The Law Commissions see the ultimate object of the elaborate process of consultation as assisting Parliament on matters of often great technical detail which can seldom be adequately investigated in the course of Parliamentary debate. This assistance is ineffective unless the scope and nature of the consultation is clearly set out on the face of the Report.

The English Commissioners are assisted by a total staff of about 50, of whom slightly over half are trained lawyers. The Scottish Law Commissioners have a relatively small staff. The resources which have been made available to the Law Commission, although not particularly striking by comparison with, for example, the departments concerned with law reform in some European Ministries of Justice, are considerable by earlier British standards. The Law Commission has thereby undoubtedly been helped to produce, within five years, a large number of Working Papers and final reports, a fact which, even apart from their content, is not without importance. A new institution, in a sense on trial, has been seen by Parliament and the public as capable of producing results.

The productivity and success rate in terms of reports implemented have both been remarkable. From 1966 to 1979 the Commission published no less than 72 Working Papers and 79 Reports (plus 14 annual reports and 4 programmes of work). Of 68 Reports published up to the end of 1977, the Fourteenth Annual Report in January 1980 stated that no less than 56 had been implemented by legislation.

Perhaps the most interesting and potentially important work of the Law Commission has been that of codification.

2. Codification

As has already been seen, codification was specifically referred to in s. 3 of the Law Commissions Act as one of the chief duties of the Law Commissions. The nature of the duty and of its implications was explored in a lecture in 1966 given by Mr Justice Scarman at Hull University.

Sir Leslie Scarman, 'A Code of English law?', Hull University, 1966

No one could suggest, without taking leave of his senses, that the present shape of English law is either simple or modern.... English law lacks coherent shape, is inaccessible save to those with the training, the stamina, and the time to explore the jungle of case and statute law, and is unmanageable save by the initiated. It retains the mystical, priestly quality of early law: it has survived into the modern world only because of the tremendous quality of its high-priests – the judges who, from their seats of judgment, have from time immemorial – often in prose of striking beauty and clarity – declared its principles and solutions....

But it may be that the quality of our judge-made law – its flexibility, its certainty, its capacity to develop in response to the stimuli of actual life conveyed through the channel of litigation to the minds of the judges – is such that its unmanageable bulk must be accepted. Can it be said that the refined gold of the common law is not to be had without the dust, darkness, and encumbrances of the mineworkings? I would not pretend in the time at my disposal to attempt an assessment of the value of our judge-made law, save to say that the achievements of the judges are immense. They have created one of the two great systems of jurisprudence existing today in the western world. Blessed as we have been with an unbroken legal development over a period of 600 years, we find in our judge-made law a wonderful consistency of legal thought and action, and a remarkable capacity for adjustment to changing social conditions. The risk exists that codification might well shatter it. Yet, if this is right, law reform by legislative process, even when it does not lead to codification, should in logic be abandoned as a danger to the unity of the common law. But no one suggests the need for so conservative an approach. And there are clear indications that under the strain of our times the courts, notwithstanding the quality of their work, can no longer be accepted as sufficient instruments for the reform or modernisation of the law...

The basic weakness of a system of law which relies upon judicial precedent for its development is that it is not the primary function of courts or judges to legislate. This criticism may be put somewhat differently: development by judicial precedent is development of the law by lawyers—a practice against which man has protested with more or less success since the dawn of civilisation. One is back in the priestly atmosphere which bemuses and bewilders the ordinary citizen, which outraged Bentham. Codification is, however, a true law-making process – not merely an incidental benefit thrown up by another process, that of adjudication. It provides for study, research, consultation, planning – all essential to orderly development: it looks forward to the shape of things to come as well as back to the achievements of the past. Further, in an English context, it is a process which enables the layman's voice to be heard in the process of law-making. The community and its experts are involved: and the final stage is critical discussion of the proposed code in and outside Parliament during its passage into law. Codification as a process is thus responsive to modern ideas, and can be so managed as to be deliberate, scientific and representative. And as a process it can be kept in continuous action. It is true that a code begins to grow old, to become obsolete as soon as it is enacted. But if there be machinery for its continuous review, a code becomes not the last but the first stage in codification. The coalition of enacted code, judicial interpretation, probing and application, and continuous review by a commission such as the Law Commissions Act creates, should ensure that codification continues, after as well as at the moment of the enactment of the code, to meet the endless challenge of simplification and modernisation....

Let us assume it can be done. What would its impact be on the common law? We must face it: the impact would be immense. First, in the use of precedent. It would be inconceivable, upon the view I have put forward of the nature and objects of a code, that precedent earlier in date than the enacted code could be used as a source of law. It would, I suppose, be permissible to refer to earlier case law if it should be relevant to discover what the earlier law was: otherwise, with the enactment of the code, the curtain would drop for all save legal historians upon the earlier case law. Secondly, in the function of the judges. They would be interpreters of the law as found in the code. No doubt, as in France, a considerable judge-made jurisprudence carrying great authority would arise: for, as Aristotle once remarked, 'no piece of legislation can deal with every possible problem'.

The MacMillan Committee on Income Tax Codification (Cmnd. 5131, 1936) described the relationship of code and judges in these words (p. 17):

> Nothing short of omniscience would suffice to enable the draftsman to conceive and provide for every possible contingency.... It is not practicable to pursue any given topic to its last details. There must always remain a margin within which the process of judicial interpretation and application is left to operate.

Thus the judges would retain a vital legislative function when confronted with situations with which the code had failed to deal. Both as legislators, therefore, and as interpreters, their part in developing as well as applying the law would continue to be of immense importance. They would also fulfil a vital function as critics in continuous session.

... [I]t will be the judges who will find the weaknesses, the ambiguities, the gaps, and so provide the opportunities and the incentive for keeping the code in 'efficient working order'.

They would, however, have to be freed of the rigidities of our present 'stare decisis' rule; for through precedent would have a persuasive role to play of great importance, it could not be allowed to become sovereign. Code and persuasive precedent can co-exist to the advantage of law. Further, a code will require a 'fair, large and liberal' interpretation: the priorities now obtaining among the many rules of statutory interpretation, that at present our law offers, according to context, to the judge, would call for re-assessment. Further, it will be necessary to consider whether new aids to interpretation should not be made available: for example, a Law Commission memorandum or commentary on the code.

All this may at first sight appear to portend legal revolution. But it is not so very drastic if viewed against the background of the legal development of the past 100 years. Much of our criminal law, our company law, our laws as to competition and consumer protection, our planning and property law, our tax law is already embodied in statute: our judges already spend a great part of their time upon the interpretation of statute law. Even before the Law Commissions Act, our law was on the move towards codification: a universal codification would not be such a strange new world as some lawyers fear.

The observations that I have made do not enable a decisive answer to be given to the question – will English law become a codified system? I have endeavoured only to suggest grounds for believing that codification of our law – in part, if not in whole – is both desirable and possible. A final answer can be given only when its problem and implications have been subjected to more scientific study than has yet been thought necessary.

In an article contributed to the Symposium on the Code Napoleon and the Common Law World, Roscoe Pound listed a number of conditions which he suggested experience had shown led to codes. It may be helpful to conclude by a glance at the extent to which those conditions are to be found in English law today. I enumerate his conditions with my comments:

First, when case law is not rising to new situations: I venture to suggest that this is true of English law today.

Secondly, when there are such defects of form as – want of certainty, unwieldy bulk ('the difficulty is not so much to know the law as to know where to find it'): I suggest these defects are also to be found in our law today.

Thirdly, when the growing point of a legal system has shifted to legislation, and there is an efficient organ of legislation on matters of law: the Law Commissions Act shows clearly enough the shift. The question-mark remains, however: will Parliament by the proper organisation of its time make itself an efficient organ of legislation on matters of law?

Fourthly, the need for one law: such a need certainly exists in the Kingdom – United save in its legal systems.

Finally, Roscoe Pound made the comment 'Attempt to reshape the law by judicial over-ruling of leading cases is no substitute for well-drawn, comprehensive legislation'. I suggest experience shows this to be fair comment when applied to English law.

On a different occasion in 1966 Sir Leslie Scarman also considered the form or style of the proposed codes:

Mr Justice Scarman, 'Codification and Judge-made Law', Birmingham University, 1966

... I come now to the question – what sort of code is likely to come – one replete with detailed provisions or one confined to general declarations? The history books provide few examples in modern times of the short general code. The German civil code is more typical – 2,385 sections – than the Swiss, which is a short generalized code. What should we choose?

It is pertinent to remember we are codifying piecemeal – preparing codes, not one Digest of all the law. It is likely that the character of each code will be determined not so much by theoretical considerations as to the nature of codified law but by the subject-matter of the particular branch of law being codified. Nevertheless, any codification may find itself impaled upon the horns of a dilemma. If it is to be simple and easily understood, it will in eschewing detail attract so much subsequent case law that it will rapidly lose any practical importance as a source of law: the history of Articles 1382-86 of the French civil code is an object lesson. It was such a fate that Bentham had in mind when he called for codification in great detail: for it was his view that:

'the code having been prepared, the introduction of all unwritten [i.e. not enacted] law should be forbidden.'

But, if the code be detailed, will it not lose the qualities of brevity, intelligibility, and accessibility to which the advocates of codified law attach importance?

The escape from the dilemma is to be found, I suggest, by concentrating attention on subject-matter. Complex social conditions, of course, necessitate complex laws. It is disingenuous to ask of law that it should be simple, when its subject-matter is not. The problem becomes one of degree. In certain branches of the law, e.g. contract, property, the criminal law, the ordinary citizen requires guidance. He enters into business agreements: he buys and sells; he owns property; he has to determine his personal conduct in society. In these fields it is not merely the judge who wants to know how to decide his case; it is the ordinary citizen who, without recourse to litigation, has to regulate his dealings and his conduct. In such branches of the law the code must condescend to detail, thus ensuring that its provisions are not overlaid by judicial decision which, by and large, will be accessible only to the legal profession. But where the law is concerned more to provide a remedy than to chart a course, e.g. in the law of negligence or, I would suggest, in a properly developed administrative law, less detail is needed, and a wider discretion may be left to judicial decision. But, whatever the degree of detail, the code must be such that in its field of application it is in practice as well as in theory the authoritative and exclusive source of law.

If one of the alleged virtues of codified systems is that they are easier to use than the common law system, the experience of practitioners is relevant. One who practised both in Germany and in England was the late Dr Ernst Cohn who compared the two systems:

Dr Ernst Cohn, 'The German Attorney', *International and Comparative Law Quarterly*, 1960, pp. 586–7

Codification renders the task of the practising lawyer very much easier than it is in an uncodified system. No code solves more than some problems. Freedom of interpretation and casuistry must remain and do remain. But only a very bad code would fail to deal clearly and succinctly with the vast majority of the day-to-day problems that are the bread and butter of the routine lawyer's life. These codes have been ably commented upon by numerous authors during the last sixty years. Commentaries vary in size from a little one-volume pocket edition to huge standard works approximating in size our 'Halsbury'. But it is believed that a good selection of pocket commentaries together with a more elaborate edition of one or two codes, plus the last fifteen years of the leading legal periodical, *Neue Juristische Wochenschrift*, and the current official Statute Book will do for the needs of a large percentage of attorneys in all but a fairly small number of cases, in particular if this "library" is supplemented by some of the better-class students' textbooks from his university days.

By the term 'codification' I mean, of course, what may well be styled the "radical codification" which is the only form of codification known to the Continent of Europe. This type of codification differs from what is designated by the same term in this country by the fact that it will make recourse to all the accumulated mass of earlier material – whether statutes or decisions or other works of authority – completely unnecessary except perhaps in a case of the most extraordinary character. This radical codification furthermore differs from the common law type of codification by its attempt at laying down principles of a sweepingly wide and general character, rather than deciding in a binding manner typical cases as do so many common law statutes. This seemingly abstract type of code has the beneficial effect of drawing into its net a far larger number of actual cases. A practitioner who has grasped the rules of the first book of the German Civil Code and those of the first part of the second book is thereby alone well equipped to deal satisfactorily with an astonishingly large number of everyday problems. A question which would require a common law practitioner to search in books of reference for one or several quarters of an hour could be solved by his Continental colleague completely satisfactorily in as many minutes.

Dr Cohn's view has, however, been challenged.

H.R. Hahlo, 'Here Lies the Common Law', 30 *Modern Law Review*, 1967, p. 241

Whether codification renders the routine work of legal practice and adjudication easier is a question on which opinions differ. Dr E.J. Cohn, who has practised in Germany and England, asserts ... that

> 'There can be no doubt at all ... that codification renders the task of the practising lawyer very much easier than it is in an uncodified system,'

and that

> 'A question which would require a common law practitioner to search in books of reference for one or several quarters of an hour could be solved by his Continental colleague completely satisfactorily in as many minutes,'

referring in support to an article by Mr E. Moses on 'International Legal Practice'.[1]

Other lawyers with experience of practice, both on the Continent and under an uncodified system, have been heard to assert, with equal assurance, that the task of a French, Dutch or German lawyer in arguing a legal point is not substantially easier than that of his English, American or Scottish colleague, and that there are as many points of controversy in modern Continental systems of law as there are in the common law.

Ex cathedra statements of this sort, even if supported by an 'of course' or 'no doubt', are in the nature of things capable of neither proof nor disproof. Since a code wipes out the past, it generally obviates the need for historical research going back in time beyond the date of the code and, to this extent, it makes legal work easier, but how many cases arise, after all, in any stystem of law, in which deep historical research is required? In an uncodified as well as a codified system, it is rarely necessary to go beyond the last thirty years of law reports.

Dr Cohn, after having told us that codification 'renders the task of the practising attorney very much easier ...,' goes on to say that the German codes 'have been ably commented upon by numerous authors during the last sixty years. Commentaries vary in size from a little one-volume pocket edition to huge standard works approximating in size our *Halsbury*.' He then informs us that a library consisting of 'a good selection of pocket commentaries together with a more elaborate edition of one or two codes [one of the "huge" standard works?], plus the last fifteen years of the leading legal periodical, *Neue Juristische Wochenschrift* [which contains, apart from articles, extensive case notes], and the current official Statute Book ... supplemented by some of the better-class students' textbooks ...' will 'do for the needs of a large percentage of attorneys in all but a fairly small number of cases.'

Reading this, one cannot help wondering whether practice on the Continent can really be so very much easier than in England. How much more by way of materials does an English lawyer require in all 'but a fairly small number of cases'?

[1] (1935) 4 *Fordham Law Review*, p. 244.

Professor Hahlo listed a variety of reasons for the belief that codification was unlikely to be a remedy for the alleged ills of the common law system:

The immediate effect of the introduction of a code, so far from making the law more certain, is to create a lengthy period of increased legal uncertainty. True, many hitherto doubtful issues will have been settled, but the re-formulation of the old rules and the adoption of new rules, added to the systematisation of the law, are bound to open up new disputes. For each head of controversy that has been cut off, there will arise, hydra-like, one or more new ones. And it will only be decades later, after the code has become overlain with a thick encrustation of case law, that the old measure of legal certainty (or uncertainty) will be restored.... But it is not only the growing body of case law which will soon provide the nakedness of the infant code with a wardrobe rivalling in its variety and complexity that of the common law prior to codification. Almost as soon as the ink is dry the need for legislative amendments will become manifest.

... In addition to the growing body of case law, there will soon be an ever growing body of amending legislation, followed in due course by judgments explaining the amending legislation, and amendments upon the amendments.

How long this process can continue before the need for wholesale code revision arises, depends upon the tempo of social and economic change and the readiness of the legislature and the profession to undertake the enormous task of redrafting the code. That, sooner or later, wholesale revision will be required, is certain – and sooner rather than later in a time such as ours, when the rate of social change is far quicker than it was when the Continental codes were drafted, and is accelerating at a rate undreamt of by our forbears. There is no turning back once the law is codified, you have to go on codifying. Like the sourcerer's apprentice, the codifier is forever pursued by the spirits he evoked from the deep....

It is of the nature of law that the bulk of it should be certain, but that there will always be a fuzzy zone of uncertainty around the edges. It is also of the nature of law that it stands perpetually in need of revision if it is to remain in keeping with changing conditions. To think that law could be rendered either more certain or more stable by codification, is to blame a certain form of law for attributes which are in fact inherent in the nature of law, whatever form it may take.... Codification of a country's law must be paid for, and the price is heavy.

First of all, there is the work of preparing the code which, if Continental experience is any guide, will keep the best legal brains in England and Scotland busy for the next twenty or thirty years.

Secondly, there is the need for re-learning the law. Only one who has never worked with a code can believe that codification is nothing but a formal change, requiring no fundamental adjustments in approach and method. A code is not just a large statute, it is a different species of law, demanding different techniques, and these techniques have to be learnt by the legal profession. Even where a rule of the common law is merely restated, the fact that it is now laid down in writing and forms part of a system of interrelated rules, affects its meaning and scope. Legal textbooks have to be rewritten. Judges, practitioners and academic lawyers have to learn an entirely new system, a task likely to tax the capacity of some of the older members of the profession to the limit....

Another portion of the price to be paid, to which reference has been made earlier, is the increased legal uncertainty which follows in the train of any new major piece of legislation, and ends only when its meaning and effect have been clarified by the courts. How long this period is going to last in England it is, of course, impossible to foretell. Much will depend on the method of codification and the type of code chosen.

Each one of the great Continental codes, from Napoleon's *Code Civil*, came into life complete and fully-formed. The Law Commission has chosen to proceed on the instalment system of codification. Starting with the general part of the law of contract, it proposes to proceed, step by step, to the codification of other branches of the law – special contracts, the law of obligations, a family code....

The choice between codification in one piece and codification on the instalment system is somewhat like choosing between having all one's teeth out in one go or one by one. For better or worse this particular choice has been made. A choice which has still to be made by the Law Commission is what type of codification to adopt.

On the one side, there is the pattern of the *Code Civil*, which eschews definitions and favours broad principles, leaving it to the courts to fill in the gaps. On the other, there is the pattern of the far more detailed and definitive German civil code.[1] Broad general principles leave the law flexible and permit the courts considerable latitude in doing justice within the framework of the code, but they leave the law uncertain until the courts have had time to build up a body of case law. Detailed rules provide a greater measure of certainty and, hence, predictability, but leave the courts less space in which to manoeuvre....

The English civil code will have no resemblance in form to the common law. Modelled on Continental codes, it will consist of definitions and principles, systematically arranged. The Law Commission, no doubt, hopes to preserve the substance of the common law, whilst changing its form, but in law, more than in any other field, substance and form go together. Once the common law is codified, it will, of necessity, cease to be the common law, not only (rather obviously) in form, but also in substance.

The effect on the role of English law in the world may turn out to be profound. It is of the essence of a codified system than any legal inquiry takes its starting point from one or more specific provisions in the code. The result is that no country which does not have identical code provisions can derive much benefit from its case law. Once English law is codified, the legal-cultural tie between England and other countries governed by the common law will become attenuated. The courts of the various American states, of the common

[1] On the various types of codes, see also F.H. Lawson (1960) 2 *Inter-American Law Review*, at pp. 2–3.

law provinces of Canada, of Australia and of New Zealand, unless they decide to take over the new English civil code *en bloc*, will discover that they no longer derive the same assistance from English cases as before....

If this be true, it does not appear unlikely that as a result of codification, the influence of English law outside the United Kingdom will decrease, and that, so far from becoming entrenched in its position as a world system, it will suffer a *capitis deminutio*, being reduced in status from that of the senior member of the Anglo-American common law family to that of a purely national system, governed by just one more code among many.

Considerable scepticism about the alleged advantages of codification was also expressed by Professor Aubrey Diamond in a lecture published three years before he himself became a Law Commissioner.

Professor Aubrey Diamond,
'Codification of the Law of Contract',
31 *Modern Law Review*, 1968, p. 361

Various reasons have been given over the years why codification is desirable. The case for codification in England at this time rests on the following arguments.

1. *Accessibility of the law to the legal profession*

On several occasions Lord Gardiner has stressed the inaccessibility of the law: over 3,000 separate Acts of Parliament, dating from about 1235, contained in 359 different volumes, ninety-nine volumes of subordinate legislation; and well over 350,000 reported cases.

The Lord Chancellor may be right in believing that this is the real case for codification, though it is important not to get carried away by the practical difficulties of the common law. One must not think that the mass of reports and statutes is all that daunting to the practitioner, whatever the effect it may have on the student.

The truth is that there are many practitioners who rarely open a law report more than two years old. Apart from keeping up to date with the latest *Weekly Law Reports* or *All England Law Reports* they will rely for their law on Halsbury's *Laws of England* (forty-two volumes, including index volumes, and a two-volume cumulative supplement), specialist textbooks and books of precedent forms and Halsbury's *Statutes* (forty-seven volumes up to and including the loose-leaf volume for 1967, and two volumes of supplement). Probably they will also take *Current Law* and one or more journals.

Even for those lawyers who do refer to case reports in their daily practice, the figure of 350,000 cases given a false impression. It is difficult to know how much cases really are used. In an attempt to find out, we may analyse the 434 cases reported in the three volumes of the *All England Law Reports* for 1965. In those 434 cases 3,865 cases were cited in judgments or referred to in argument. This gives an average of 8·9 authorities to a case, but like most averages this does not give a true picture. In thirty-six cases no authorities were cited, and in 108 cases – one-quarter of the total – two or less authorities were referred to. At the other extreme, there were forty-eight cases in which twenty or more authorities were referred to, the highest number being ninety-two (in *National Provincial Bank* v. *Ainsworth*,[1] the case of the deserted wife's equity). In 130 reported cases (30 per cent.), ten or more authorities were referred to.... More than three-quarters of them (2,959 cases, 76·6 per cent.) were reported in this century and nearly a half (1,766 cases, 45·7 per cent.) were reported since 1945. Only 12·9 per cent. (502) date from before the Judicature Acts (1875 or earlier), and only 1·7 per cent. (sixty-seven cases) from before 1800. There was one Year Book case (in 1470). This scarcely gives the appearance of an antique law (remember that the Civil Code of France dates from 1804).

It is of interest, incidentally, to see that included in the 3,865 cases are thirty unreported cases, sixty-five Scottish cases, thirty-seven Australian, twelve Irish, twelve Canadian, ten American, four New Zealand, three Northern Irish and two South African cases, and one Indian case.[2]

A similar survey of the ten years from 1957 to 1966 enables us to compare the cases on the law of contract with those on codified branches of the law. During this period I found thirty cases that seemed to me to be based fairly and squarely on provisions in the Sale of Goods Act, the Bills of Exchange Act or the Marine Insurance Act. In those thirty cases some 388 authorities were referred to, giving an average of 12·9 authorities per case, appreciably greater than the overall average for 1965 (which of course included cases on recent statutes). (The authorities cited in individual cases ranged from two to forty-nine.) In the same period there were fifty-six cases on points of contract law that would probably be incorporated into a code: here a total of 968 authorities were referred to, an average of 17·3 authorities per case. ... the statistics suggest, and common sense tells us, that a code does make the law more accessible than the uncodified common law.

2. *Accessibility of the law to the public*

If a code makes the law more easily accessible to the legal profession, it thereby makes the law accessible to the public.... English lawyers have never laid much stress on lay knowledge of the law. They have preferred the esoteric nature of our legal system.

... Nevertheless, some recent social surveys have been undertaken to discover how far the English are acquainted with particular legal rules. One survey, sponsored by the Latey Committee on the Age of Majority, investigated the familiarity of people aged between 16 and 24 with the incapacities of youth; the other, conducted under the auspices of the Consumer Council, sought to evaluate public knowledge of consumer rights under the law of sale of goods, codified for over seventy years.... [W]hereas 94 per cent knew the minimum age for being served in a public-house, only 22 per cent knew that under the Sale of Goods Act the retailer can be made liable for faulty goods. The results demonstrate that the subject-matter of a rule contributes more

[1] [1965] 2 All E.R. 472, H.L.

[2] This breakdown does not include cases cited in Privy Council Appeals.

to its becoming widely known than the form of the law or, perhaps, that we are more interested in pubs than in shops.

3. *Improvement of the law*

The real case for codification, I believe, is that it facilitates law reform. We can improve the content of the law when we create the new code; and we can improve it later by revising the code.

There are two kinds of codes. One merely seeks to reproduce the existing law, to translate case-law into statute-law without radical change; the other aims to produce a new set of principles, as the Uniform Commercial Code does. The Law Commission intend the new contract code to be of this second kind: 'The intention is to reform as well as to codify.'[3]

Difficulties of Codification

Commendable as these objectives are, it would be foolish to ignore the difficulties that lie in the way of successful codification. These centre on the problems of statutory interpretation and the limitations of draftsmanship.

(a) *Judicial conservatism*

A code is intended to replace the earlier common law. How can one ensure that the judges, brought up on the common law and familiar with it, will wipe out their knowledge of the cases from their memories and concentrate on the statutory words? This has been a very real problem that has not always been successfully dealt with.

The Civil Code of California, passed in 1872, declared in section 4 that:

> '4. The rule of the common law, that statutes in derogation thereof are to be strictly construed, has no application to this code....'

But the very next section, section 5, was not wholly in harmony with that sensible rule of interpretation:

> '5. The provisions of this code, so far as they are substantially the same as existing statutes or the common law, must be construed as continuations thereof, and not as new enactments.'

Exactly what was the purpose of this section is far from clear. The Californian courts were understandably uncertain whether they ought to have regard to prior common law authorities until 1884, when Professor J.N. Pomeroy published a series of articles on the method of interpreting the Code. He pointed out that many provisions in the Code were meaningless except to a person educated in the common law, and argued that the Code provisions 'are to be regarded as simply declaratory of the previous common law and equitable doctrines and rules, except where the intent to depart from those doctrines and rules clearly appears from the unequivocal language of the text.' This approach was soon adopted by the Californian courts, and consequently the prior common law remained a living source of the law.

3. The Law Commission, First Annual Report, 1965–66 (Law Com. No. 4), para. 31.

Exactly the same question arose at the same time in England, where the Bills of Exchange Act had been passed in 1882. Chalmers had included in section 97 (2) the following provision:

> 'The rules of the common law, including the law merchant, save in so far as they are inconsistent with the express provisions of this Act ..., shall continue to apply to bills of exchange.'

In 1885 the case of *Re Gillespie, ex p. Robarts*[4] came before Cave J. In ignorance, no doubt, of Pomeroy's articles in California, he followed the same method: 'The first question is, whether previous to the Bills of Exchange Act 1882, damages of this kind could be recovered.... Then comes the Bills of Exchange Act 1882, and the first provision to which it is important to call attention is section 97 (2).... It therefore follows, unless there is something in the Act expressly inconsistent with the ancient law, that the right to prove for damages of the kind which I have spoken of still exists.'[5]

All six members of the Court of Appeal applied the same technique in *Vagliano Brothers* v. *Bank of England*[6] four years later. Lord Esher M.R., dissenting in his conclusions, said: 'In order to arrive at the true interpretation of [the Bills of Exchange Act], I think it is necessary to consider not merely what was the law at the time of the passing of the Act, but what were the principles on which the different cases which declared the law were founded.'[7] The majority, as distinguished a Bench as one could hope to find, agreed that one must start with the prior law. In the House of Lords[8] Lord Bramwell (and perhaps Lord Field) adopted the same approach. Fortunately the majority thought differently – fortunately because otherwise a code would in no way have served to make the law more accessible, but instead would merely have added an additional stage in a consideration of the authorities.

It was in this case that Lord Herschell gave us the classic statement of how to interpret a codifying statute:

> 'I think the proper course is in the first instance to examine the language of the statute and to ask what is its natural meaning, uninfluenced by any considerations derived from the previous state of the law, and not to start with inquiring how the law previously stood, and then, assuming that it was probably intended to leave it unaltered, to see if the words of the enactment will bear an interpretation in conformity with this view.'[9]

But he went on to open the door to previous decisions 'if, for example, a provision be of doubtful import,'[10] and it is an unusually well-drafted statute that admits of no doubts. In practice, judges often look at the pre-code cases: this is particularly noticeable in cases on the Marine Insurance Act 1906,[11]

4. (1885) 16 Q.B.D. 702.
5. *Ibid.* at p. 704.
6. (1889) 23 Q.B.D. 243, C.A.
7. *Ibid.* at p. 247.
8. *Bank of England* v. *Vagliano Brothers* [1891] A.C. 107, H.L.
9. Ibid., at p. 144.
10. Ibid., at p. 145.
11. See, e.g., *British & Foreign Marine Insurance Co. Ltd.* v. *Sanday & Co.* [1916] 1 A.C. 650, H.L., per Lord Loreburn at p. 656, Lord Atkinson at p. 660, Lord Parmoor at p. 667 and Lord Wrenbury at pp. 672–3; and *Yorkshire Insurance Co. Ltd.* v. *Nisbet Shipping Co. Ltd* [1961] 2 All E.R. 487, per Diplock J. at p. 492.

while there are several cases on the law of sale of goods where the Act is not even mentioned.[12]

The truth is that it is very difficult to prevent judges from applying the law they know, and have learnt to love, instead of the new and strange statute.

The real difficulty is in envisaging a completely self-contained code. According to the Law Commission: 'The object of a code is, in our understanding, to set out the essential principles which are to govern a given branch of the law.' A court, they go on, 'is expected to discover in the code the principles from which the answer to a particular problem can be worked out.'[13]

This is certainly the theory of continental codes,[14] but it would be a radical departure for a common law code.[15]

As we have seen, one thing is certain. The existing English 'codes' have not wiped out the old law. In Chalmers' *Sale of Goods Act* nearly half of the cases cited still date from before the Act, and even in the more modern narrative works as many as 20 per cent. of the cases are from before the Act.

(b) *Professional prejudice*

It is not necessary to dwell on the undoubted prejudice against legislation felt by common lawyers. A leading legal periodical will discuss the implications of a decision by a puisne judge but has no regular feature giving similar attention to new statutes. There are still people who distrust a code because it is impossible to foresee everything: but one seldom hears the common law criticised because only things that have already happened come before the courts. The notion of the completeness of the common law is today universally acknowledged to be a legal fiction, but its habits of thought remain.

(c) *The problem of drafting*

David Dudley Field saw clearly the problem: 'There should be neither a generalisation too vague nor a particularity too minute, in the Code....'[16]

The trouble is that there is a difference between case-law and statute-law. In case-law we are concerned with ideas, in statutes we are concerned with words. The Statute Book is littered with phrases that have become battle-grounds – 'arising out of and in the course of the employment', 'absolutely void', 'debt, default or miscarriage of another person'. This problem of fixing the right level of abstraction is really: how much discretion should be left to the judge? Some of the difficulties arising from existing codes such as the Sale of Goods Act are due to excessive detail caused by Chalmers' attempt to codify the existing, but still developing, law. What started as the germ of a judicial idea, which might have been distinguished or overruled, became statute-law, binding on all courts including the House of Lords.

12. See, e.g., *McDougall* v. *Aeromarine of Emsworth Ltd.* [1958] 3 All E.R. 431; *Victoria Laundry (Windsor) Ltd.* v. *Newman Industries Ltd.* [1949] 2 K.B. 528. C.A.

13. The Law Commission and the Scottish Law Commission: Published Working Paper on The Interpretaion of Statutes, 1967, p. 45.

14. See, e.g., A. T. Von Mehren, *The Civil Law System*, pp. 60, 64 and generally.

15. Cf. A. P. Sereni, 'The Code and the Case Law', in *The Code Napoleon and the Common-Law World*, pp. 58–59.

16. *First Report of the Commissioners of the Code to the New York Legislature*, 1858, cited Honnold, *The Life of the Law*, at p. 109.

(d) *Restriction on legal development*

The most telling objection to a code in a common law jurisdiction is that it limits the development of the law. The common law grows and changes. Statute-law is static until it is changed by the legislature. 'It is the function of courts,' says a modern master of the common law, 'to mould the common law and to adapt it to the changing society for which it provides the rules of each man's duty to his neighbour.'[1] But courts do not see it as their function to mould statute-law or to adapt it to our changing society.

Part of the problem lies in the lawyer's approach to an Act of Parliament. He does not see it as a creative force in the formation of new law, but rather as an interference with the 'natural' development of the law by the judges. Hence the notion that Acts of Parliament must be strictly construed and the extraordinary presumption that a statute leaves the common law unchanged. Lawyers do not argue by analogy from statutes as they do from judgments, and many would think it wrong to do so. The late James Landis, Dean of the Harvard Law School, expressed this in a paragraph that cannot be bettered:

> 'When the highest tribunal of England in 1868 decided that the land-owner who artificially accumulates water upon his premises is absolutely liable for damages caused by its escape[2] that judgment had an enormous influence throughout Anglo-American law.... Had Parliament in 1868 adopted a similar rule, no such permeating results to the general body of Anglo-American law would have ensued. And this would be true, though the Act had been preceded by a thorough and patient inquiry by a Royal Commission into the business of storing large volumes of water and its concomitant risks, and even though the same Lords who approved Mr. Fletcher's claim had in voting "aye" upon the measure given reasons identical with those contained in their judgments. Such a statute would have caused no ripple in the process of adjudication either in England or on the other side of the Atlantic....'[3]

If we could devise a way to stimulate the judicial mind, to distinguish between statutes laying down limited solutions to limited problems and those containing in them more widely applicable truths, progress might be made.

(e) *Accretion of case-law*

It may be that on the day the code is passed one can look at the Queen's Printer copy of the statute and say: 'That, and that alone, is the English law of contract.' But there is no reason to think that lawyers will stop regarding judicial decisions as binding authorities, whether on a common law rule, an ordinary statute, or a codifying statute, and once the judges start to interpret the code it will no longer be possible to rely on the statutory words alone. Thus recent books on the law of sale of goods, though based substantially on the Sale of Goods Act 1893, refer to between 400 and 850 cases decided since the Act was passed. In this way the accessibility of the law, to the profession and to the public, is inevitably marred.

1. Diplock L.J. in *Indyka* v. *Indyka* [1966] 3 All E.R. 583, 591.
2. *Rylands* v. *Fletcher* (1868) L.R. 3 H.L. 330. (Footnote in original.)
3. 'Statutes and the Sources of Law,' in *Harvard Legal Essays*, 1934, p. 213 at p. 221. The whole of this valuable essay repays careful study.

This is unavoidable. Neither judicial nor academic commentary on the code can be prevented. Attractive though the idea may seem, it would not be possible to emulate the *c. Deo auctore* which forbade commentaries on Justinian's *Digest* (and which was not long observed).[4] The approach of Cardozo J. is more realistic: '... code is followed by commentary and commentary by revision, and thus the task is never done.'[5]

CONCLUSION

If the new code is well done lawyers will be in the Lord Chancellor's debt for generations, and like the first Lord Chancellor Gardiner he will be in office a hundred years after his death. If it is not well done, Sir Frederick Pollock's sane and balanced comment will offer a crumb of comfort to the Chancellor and his Law Commission: 'It is strange how little harm bad codes do.'

Note

So far, at least, the process of codification is moving ahead very slowly. In its Eighth Annual Report (for 1972–73) the English Law Commission said that it had reviewed its plan to produce a contract code. Instead of trying to produce a complete code, the Commission would instead publish Working Papers on specific problems in order to determine whether, and if so what, reforms were needed. The work on the code would be suspended pending such more particular inquiries. In its Thirteenth Annual Report (for 1977–78) the Commission said it had reconsidered the proposed codification of the law of landlord and tenant. This had started with work on three interim projects (relating to obligations of landlords and tenants, termination of tenancies, and covenants against disposition, alteration and use). The first of these interim projects was published in 1975; the others were still in preparation. But it was clear that a complete code on the law of landlord and tenant would involve an immense amount of work. It was therefore intended to proceed on a piecemeal basis. ('In this way we would hope to build up the code section by section over what we emphasise would be a long period of years.') In the field of criminal law, the Report said that the work already published and in preparation on the criminal law was designed as 'steps towards the eventual production of a criminal code'. Most progress has been made toward the code of family law

4. Carolina once 'absolutely prohibited' any form of 'comments and expositions on any part' of the law (though I am not clear whether this applied to judges): 'The Fundamental Constitutions of Carolina', art. 80, in 5 *The Federal and State Constitutions, Colonial Charters, and Other Organic Laws* (ed. F. Thorpe) 2782 (1909), cited Mellinkoff, *The Language of the Law*, p. 209.

5. Cardozo, 'A Ministry of Justice' (1921) 35 Harv.L.Rev. 113.

– but again through the medium of isolated pieces of work on different problems in the field.

Questions

1. Lord Scarman predicted that the codes would descend like a curtain and that reference to pre-code case law would not be permitted. Professor Diamond thinks this improbable. Which view is the more likely to be right, and which would give the best results?

2. Lord Scarman suggested that a code would require that the judges be released from the rigidities of our present rules of precedent. Do you agree?

3. Lord Scarman also considered that a code would require different principles of interpretation from those applied to ordinary statutes. Why is this so?

4. Would codes make the law more accessible to ordinary people or to lawyers?

5. How would codes themselves be kept up to date?

6. Compare a code with the common law as a source of developing law to meet changing times.

7. In its Seventh Annual Report (for 1971–72), the English Law Commission said:

> Codification, as we see it, is not confined to the restatement in statutory form of existing law. It includes law reform where needed and calls for the embodiment of the law in one or more statutes of a type different from the British pattern. The code must not be so general in terms that it affords little or no guidance to the legal adviser or judge concerned with the facts of a particular case, or so detailed that its complexities are comprehensible only to the expert.

Do you believe that the codes when they emerge will in fact usher in a new era of statutory drafting?

3. The Law Commission and some problems of law reform

Delivering the Third Nehru Lecture in India in 1979, Lord Scarman (chairman of the Law Commission from 1965 to 1972) said that although the institution had achieved much there were several identifiable problems.

(1) *The Law Commission as an adviser to government*

Too much of the time of the Law Commission was taken up in responding to requests for advice and assistance from official agencies.

The Commission had prepared its first programme in 1965, its second programme in 1968 and its third programme in 1973. But it had issued no programme since 1973, which was 'a dangerous omission'. The Commission had the right to put anything it wanted into its programme. The Lord Chancellor could exercise a veto* but he could not tell the Commission what to put into its programme. ('The programme is part and parcel of the Commission's independence.')

But there were other ways in which the Commission could become involved in work. It was under a duty to 'receive and consider any proposals for the reform of the law which may be made or referred to it' (s. 3 (1) (a)). It was also bound to provide advice and information to government departments and other official bodies concerned with the reform or amendment of any branch of the law' (s. 3 (1) (e)). In its Thirteenth Annual Report the Commission had said 'a much greater proportion of our work now comes from special references'. In other words, Lord Scarman told his Indian audience, 'the government is largely determining what work the Commission will undertake'. Again, the Thirteenth Report gave details of such references – five draft EEC conventions or directives, four draft conventions of the Council of Europe, two Hague conventions on Private International Law topics, one Commonwealth topic and one United Nations draft convention. All of this no doubt was important work. 'But it is departmental stuff, not law reform.' If such references multiplied, 'the Law Commission will cease to be the watchdog of all the law and run the risk of becoming something resembling a law research division of a Ministry of Justice'. Departmental encroachment – though flattering – was 'a bear's hug'. 'It could squeeze the breath out of the Commission, leaving it neither the time nor the energy for the work of law reform conceived in the comprehensive terms of s. 3 of its statute.'

Questions

1. Should the Law Commission be given a power to decline ministerial requests for assistance?

2. If not, is there any other way in which the Law Commission

* The Lord Chancellor for instance vetoed the Law Commission's proposal that a Royal Commission examine administrative law – see 'Administrative Law,' Law. Com. No. 20, Cmnd. 4059, 1969. In May 1979 JUSTICE, the British Section of the International Commission of Jurists, announced that it had established a review body to carry out the comprehensive inquiry into administrative law that ten years previously the Law Commission had advocated.

could preserve itself from time-consuming work of little general consequence?

(2) *Law Commission confined to lawyers' or technical law reform*

Departments of state, Lord Scarman said, were 'only too relieved to turn to the Law Commission to lighten the darkness of common market conventions or private international law'. But they 'resist strongly intrusion by the Commission into fields where they believe they have a commanding expertise'. Company law, labour law, constitutional and administrative law 'are kept firmly away from the Commission'. Apart from its paper on divorce reform,* the Commission had on the whole 'been steered away from socially or politically controversial questions'. The future of the law was bleak 'if the institution established to keep under review all the law may not examine some branches of the law merely because they lie in an area of political or social controversy'. Not that all law reform should be channelled through the Law Commission. The Lord Chancellor's Law Reform Committee, the Home Secretary's Criminal Law Revision Committee, Royal Commissions and departmental committees all had a role to play. The Commission's greatest successes had been in family law, criminal law and consumer protection, and in the statute law revision programme. There was no reason why it could not tackle socially sensitive areas. The Scottish Law Commission had been asked to advise on the constitutional implications of devolution. Lord Scarman suggested that 'By using carefully its working paper and consultative technique, [the Law Commission] can tackle controversial issues, and take the heat out of them.'

Questions

1. Is there any real distinction between lawyers' law reform suitable for the Law Commission and political or general law reform that requires a broader approach?

2. Should the Law Commission be used for controversial law-reform projects?

3. Should there be a law-reform supremo to decide who inquires

* In 1966 the Lord Chancellor asked the Law Commission to advise on the various alternatives in divorce law reform. The Commission's Report ('Field of Choice') offered no proposals, but implicitly the logic of the analysis strongly supported the concept of divorce based on marital breakdown without proof of fault. This became the method adopted in the Divorce Reform Act 1969.

into what? If so, should the power to decide this be given to a minister or to the Law Commission?

(3) *Judicial law-making in the light of the existence of the Law Commission*
When the Law Commission was set up, some took the view that this spelled the end for judicial law-making. One distinguished observer who expressed this opinion at an early stage was Lord Devlin:

Lord Devlin, 'The Process of Law Reform', 63 *Law Society's Gazette*, 1966, pp. 453–62

There can be no doubt that the institution of the Law Commission marks a great step forward in the process of law reform. It has immediately and easily assumed command of the first stage of the process and its institution, taken in conjunction with other measures, holds out hope of widening the bottleneck in the second stage so that there is a much needed flow of beneficial reform. Its command on the first stage will mean that the importance of judicial law-making, which has been dwindling now for a century or more, will probably almost entirely vanish but without, I hope, dimming the name and reputation of Lord Denning, who will stand for future generations as the last great judicial innovator.

The trouble about judicial law reform was never, as it is with parliament, lack of time but lack of opportunity – that and the multiplication of courts of appeal. When Lord Mansfield laid down the law, new law was created more or less from the moment he said it. But since his time the delay before a point of principle reaches the House of Lords may be so long as to outdistance by ten times or more the parliamentary process. With the Law Commission speeding the work of statutory reform and codifying the law, the day of the judicial law-maker is brought quite to an end.

Realization of the concept of codification as conceived by Lord Scarman is still in the future. In the meantime there is not much evidence that the existence of the Law Commission has significantly altered the judges' attitude to law reform. They appear to be no less (though equally hardly more) ready to undertake a role in the improvement of the law than before the Law Commissions were set up.

For further reading, see generally J.H. Farrar, *Law Reform and the Law Commission* (1974).

4. Can more be done to involve the community in the process of law reform?

The Law Commission pioneered the use of Working Papers which are widely circulated to experts and interested bodies as a means of stimulating response to draft law-reform proposals. But although the recommendations are often mentioned briefly in the lay press, this method of consultation has not made much impact on the general public. In a paper delivered in September 1979 at Warwick University, at the annual meeting of the UK National Committee on Comparative Law, the chairman of the Australian Law Reform Commission, Mr Justice Kirby, outlined efforts made by his commission to broaden the process of consultation.

(1) *Consultative documents*

One method used was to employ a range of lay consultants. On every project a team of such consultants was set up – mainly on a voluntary basis. The willingness of experts to come forward without remuneration was 'a heartening reflection of the interest in the community in law improvement'. The choice of consultants was broad and so far as possible reflected very different interests. So in a project on the introduction of class actions in Australia, the President of the Consumers Association sat down with representatives of business and industry. In the project on the recovery of debt the Director of the Finance Conference took part with persons experienced in helping and counselling the poor. In the project on laws governing transplants, medical experts were balanced by a Professor of Philosophy and two theologians. For the reform of defamation laws no fewer than thirty consultants had been appointed including journalists, newspaper editors and managers, and academics. The end result was 'a remarkable collection of disciplinary talent which has greatly enriched the thinking of the law commissioners'.

Another technique still well within the accepted traditions of law-reform bodies was the use of discussion papers in briefer form than the full Working Papers, designed to be read by lawyers and laymen who did not have time to read the fuller document. Such discussion papers were normally limited to 20–30 pages, were written in somewhat less technical form and concentrated on the issues of general policy.

Attempts were also being made to translate this document into even briefer and simpler form suitable for disadvantaged, migrant and less well-educated groups 'whose legitimate interest in law reform may be as great as that of the educated middle class'.

The practice had also been developed of circulating large numbers of copies of regular four-page summaries of discussion papers.

The Australian Commission was continuing to experiment with 'a number of consultative documents of varying length, technicality and sophistication to ensure that communication with different groups is achieved'.

(2) *Public hearings*

A bolder approach had been that of the public hearing at which experts, lobby groups, interested bodies and institutions as well as the ordinary citizen could come forward to express their views on the Commission's tentative proposals for reform of the law. Such hearings had now become a regular feature of the work of the Commission. They were widely advertised in the press and on the radio and television. Specific invitations were addressed to bodies and individuals who had already submitted written evidence. The dates were usually fixed four to five months ahead of time.

The public hearings were conducted informally. There was no need for the person making a submission to have produced a written document – though some did. The procedure was inquisitorial, with the chairman of the hearing taking the witness through his statement. Commissioners would then put questions. Legal representation was not permitted. Sometimes when a particular federal authority was closely concerned, it was allowed to ask questions of some witnesses, and subsequently to comment on individual submissions. There were no rules of evidence. Hearings were normally in daytime but trials were being made of evening hearings in addition.

Public hearings were arduous and time-consuming but they had proved more useful than many had supposed was likely. Normally they were well attended and they served a variety of ends. It was useful to have the different parties and interests involved to come together to express their viewpoints and to hear the viewpoints of others. The ordinary citizen could personalize his own problems and thereby often throw new light on the issues under consideration. The various interest groups could to some extent orchestrate their participation by bringing forward witnesses to different arguments.

Mr Justice Kirby said that considering the time and effort already devoted to the problem 'surprisingly enough, public hearings often identify aspects of a problem which have simply not been considered by the Commissioners'. But apart from the argument of utility there was also a point of principle:

> The business of reform is not just a technical exercise. It is the business of improving society by improving its laws, practices and procedures. This involves a consideration of competing values. Lawyers inevitably tend to see social problems in a special way, often blinkered by the comfortable and familiar approaches of the past, designed in times less sensitive to the poor, deprived and minority groups in the community. There is a greater chance of avoiding lawyers' myopia if a window is opened to the lay community and the myriad of interests, lobbies and groups that make it up.... Increasingly there is an awareness that a theoretical say through elected representatives is not always adequate because of the pressures of party politics and heady political debates. What is needed is new machinery which realistically acknowledges the impossibility of hearing everybody but affords those who wish to voice their grievances and share their knowledge the opportunity to do so.

It was appropriate to note that cases of abuse of the process were rare. 'The fears of irrelevant and long-winded submissions or of hordes of unbalanced or nuisance witnesses has not been born out.'

(3) *Use of the media*

Mr Justice Kirby said that newspapers, radio and television had all come to play an important part in the process of better consultation. The reality was that 'the printed word is no longer the means of mass communication for the ordinary citizen'. The caravan had moved on. The electronic media were the means by which most people received news and information and considered topics of public interest and concern. Law-reform bodies had to become skilled in using these techniques. Commissioners took part in television debates, radio talk shows, and national programmes with audiences in millions. The Prime Minister and the Governor-General of Australia had both acknowledged the effectiveness of this departure. Brief but accurate and well-presented news releases helped the media to report the activities of the Commission.

(4) *Surveys and questionnaires*

The Commission had used surveys and questionnaires in a variety of projects. In the study of federal offenders it had administered a survey to federal prosecutors to elicit information about prosecution practice. For the project on child welfare laws, a survey was being conducted in which the police were being asked for facts and views about prosecution decisions. Children coming before the courts would also be interviewed. In the project on sentencing, the Commission had asked all judges and magistrates to fill out a questionnaire that took about an hour and a half to complete. The response rate was nearly eighty per cent. The Commission was also seeking prisoners' views and experiences in a questionnaire that was being sent sealed and uncensored direct to the Commission from prisoners in all federal prisons. Commissioners were currently engaged in visiting the remotest parts of Australia in order to try to discover the views of aboriginals on the laws that affected them. The difficulties of communication were daunting but if the procedures of consultation meant anything, 'they require an effort that goes far beyond tokenism and that reaches out to those who will be affected by a reform proposal'. Statistics and social surveys provided a means by which the inarticulate and disadvantaged could speak to law-makers.

Conclusion

All these varying methods were ways of assisting the clearer public articulation of issues and arguments for and against law-reform proposals. The whole process raised the quality of the public debate about law reform. It also mirrored the growing openness of government, law-making and public administration in Western societies. Another benefit was the possibility that the social education involved in explaining the defects in the law might help to generate a perception of injustices that would otherwise be shrugged off, overlooked, or worst of all, not even perceived. Finally, Mr Justice Kirby argued:

> A lasting value of law reform commissions may be that by involving the community and the legal profession together in the improvement and modernisation of the law, they contribute to the stability of society. The rule of law, that unique feature of the Western communities is, after all, only worth boasting of if the rules which the law enforces are just and in tune with today's society.

Index